I0813418

LOW-MAINTENANCE ECO GARDENS

DEDICATION

For my grandmother and mother, who always encouraged me to play outside.

—Fred Meyer

For my parents, who nurtured my love of plants, and for my beloved children, whom I absolutely delight in watching grow and flourish.

—Jen Kardos

Low-Maintenance Eco Gardens
Editor: Christa Oestreich
Designer: Leslie Hall
Proofreader: Jeremy Hauck

ISBN 978-1-58011-616-9

Library of Congress Control Number: 2025944930

To learn more about the other great books from Fox Chapel Publishing, or to find a retailer near you, call toll-free at 800-457-9112
or visit us at www.FoxChapelPublishing.com.
We are always looking for talented authors.
To submit an idea, please send a brief inquiry to acquisitions@foxchapelpublishing.com.
Or write to:
Fox Chapel Publishing
903 Square Street
Mount Joy, PA 17552

Printed in China
First Printing

LOW-MAINTENANCE
ECO GARDENS

A Practical Guide to Creating an Easy & Sustainable Garden that Nourishes You

Fred Meyer & Jen Kardos

PUBLISHER'S LETTER

Gardening should be all about ***connection, not perfection.***

It's not often that a book comes to us with such a powerful message, and so brilliantly conveyed, that everyone is raving about it. But *Low-Maintenance Eco Gardens* and authors Fred Meyer and Jen Kardos are a true gem. We are so excited to bring this to you.

What we love about this book is the focus on keeping our personal needs in mind. This might mean letting go of perfection. But it also means trying to find the joy in working in the garden! Nature is something we can, and should, enjoy. It can steady our minds and help settle the stress of the day in ways that other outlets might not. A garden doesn't need to be the best on the block—if you are happy, then that's all that matters!

Your average garden book will present a reader with images of expansive lawns of vegetables and flowers, then describe all the work that goes into maintaining them. Endless hours spent tilling and weeding; high standards must be maintained when cultivating perfect plants and planning for colors and textures; arduous work is involved in building up compost, creating soil mixtures, and removing pests. For some, the results may be worth the effort. But for so many gardeners, this is not realistic. There isn't enough time in the day to maintain a picture-perfect yard, which turns our big plans into a constant reminder of regret.

We are inspired by Fred and Jen's approachable method to gardening. They help you nail down exactly what you want from your outdoor space no matter what that means or looks like. Do you only have a small balcony? *Sounds like the perfect spot to add a happy place!* Do you only want to spend a couple hours a week for maintenance? *Same here! No problem!* Is your garden overgrown? *Sometimes it's fun to let things get wild! But if you want to start over, that's also covered!*

Once you have that mantra in mind, it's easy to incorporate these lessons into your everyday life. This book has plenty of information that will support you through every step of planning and working in your garden, providing detailed breakdowns on plants and projects. But what will stay with you is the joy of doing that work. What a special gift!

We hope you like *Low-Maintenance Eco Gardens* as much as we do. Happy gardening!

—THE CREATIVE HOMEOWNER TEAM

Christa Oestreich and Sherry Vitolo, Editors
Leslie Hall and David Fisk, Designers
Alan Giagnocavo, Publisher

FOREWORDS

If someone offered you a passport to paradise right on your doorstep, would you take it?

Eco-, Greek for household, wedded to *Gardens,* from the Persian word denoting paradise, does just that. Rich with crisp illustrations, clear writing, and a handsome layout, this pleasing package unrolls an easy on-ramp to the sophisticated design science of permaculture.

Centering "People Care," one of permaculture's three ethics, Meyer and Kardos aim to help beginners, offering choices in every chapter to achieve the Holy Grail of *Low Maintenance.* More experienced gardeners will also find much to appreciate, especially in the plant profiles, small bed designs, and efficient methods meant to seduce the uncertain and woo back the overworked.

The shining inner light of the book, however, is that it radiates an appeal to our higher nature. Yes, gardening feeds the body, the soil, and the wild beings all around: yet its most critical gift is the soul nourishment it affords if we embrace its subtle rhythms, avoid excess ambition, and adopt a menu of simple techniques to cut labor and cost. With a small-scale focus throughout, and meticulously detailed step-by-step instructions on every page, the authors invite their readers to cultivate joy and serenity, along with culinary and nutritional abundance.

—PETER BANE

Peter Bane is the author of *The Permaculture Handbook* and the President of the Permaculture Future Foundation.

Gardens nurture our soul. They provide fulfillment few other things can.

I did not make my living from gardening or horticulture. I was a farmer. I farmed 6,000 acres near Bismarck, North Dakota. In the mid-1990s, I was "blessed" with three consecutive years of hail and then a year of drought. I say "blessed" because, with little income, I had to learn how to farm without fertilizers, pesticides, or other costly inputs. I simply did not have the money. What I learned was how to work with nature instead of against it. I focused on promoting life—all life. By growing cover crops, I not only attracted bees and other beneficial insects but also fed billions of soil microorganisms. Those microorganisms, through their living and dying, provided nutrients to plants.

Many of those plants also formed associations with mycorrhizal fungi. These fungi transfer nutrients to plants and secrete glomalin, which binds sand, silt, and clay into aggregates. Soil aggregates allow water and air into the ground, building resilience. The longer I worked with nature, the more productive my land became. The food I produced grew more nutritious. My farm became, in its own way, a low-maintenance farm.

How I wish I had known, during those hard years, the principles that Fred and Jen so aptly describe in *Low-Maintenance Eco Gardens*. Contained within these chapters is a wealth of information.

From designing to planning, from seeding to care and maintenance, this book offers guidance not only on vegetables but also on fruits, herbs, flowers, and companion crops. It is a library in and of itself.

I am always amazed by the sight of a bee moving from colorful flower to flower, searching for the sweet nectar contained within. From the tantalizing aroma of the blossoms to the hum of wings beating more than two hundred times per second, the experience overwhelms the senses.

To appreciate those sights, sounds, and fragrances is to enjoy the simplicity—and the complexity—of nature. That simple act does not require our oversight or planning. Yet it offers us immense joy, if we allow it. The same can be true of a garden. It does not require as much time and attention as one might believe, and yet the rewards are both gratifying and delicious.

I remember my parents' garden. Each spring, it was roto-tilled because the soil was hard as rock. It was constantly under siege from pests, weeds, drought, and disease. What a contrast to the garden I have today. I have not tilled it in more than thirty years; I add no fertilizer, and it produces abundantly—enough to feed four families. Just as important to me, it is a place of peace and enjoyment. It is truly, as Fred and Jen describe, a low-maintenance eco garden.

I would like to call attention to one other especially important aspect: this book's attention to personal health. Gardens nurture our soul. They provide fulfillment few other things can. I encourage you not only to read this book but also to take it to heart—and act on it. You will be glad you did.

—GABE BROWN

Gabe Brown is one of the pioneers of the current soil health movement. He is a regenerative farmer and author of *Dirt to Soil: One Family's Journey into Regenerative Agriculture.*

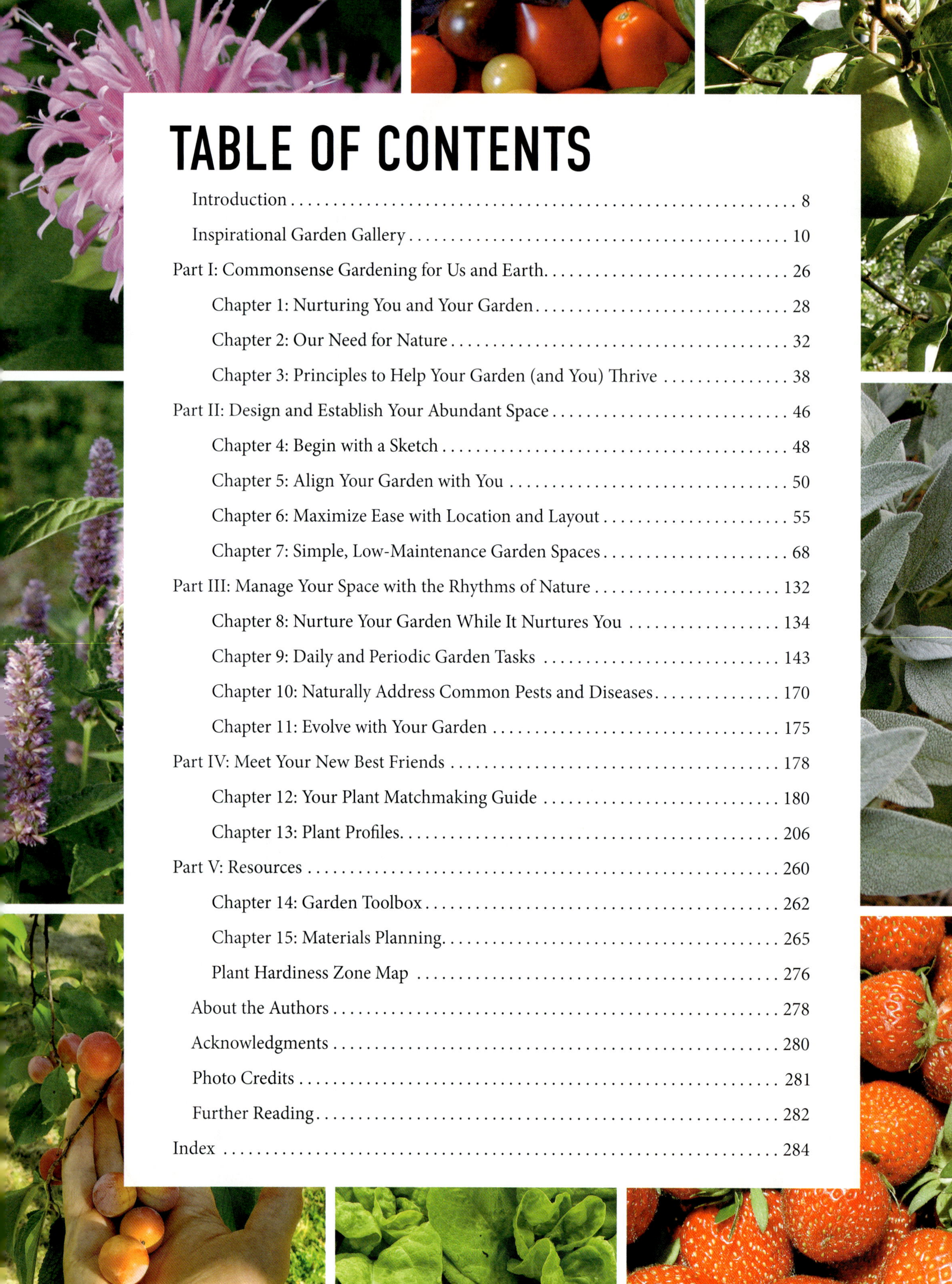

TABLE OF CONTENTS

28

32

38

48

50

55

68

134

143

170

175

180

INTRODUCTION

Something deep in you is tugging, nudging you to look up from your screen and sink your hands into what is truly important. As the world shifts in big, uncertain ways, many of us are yearning for steady ground—something we can grow, touch, and trust.

With more responsibilities and devices pulling at us than ever before, it's natural to wonder how we can return to simpler times—those we're reminded of when a cat lounges in the yard, when we wander through a farmers market, or when birdsong drifts in through an open window. Some quiet part inside still knows: it's time to get back in the garden, to feel more connected to the earth and its generous abundance.

How is it that every other creature on Earth gets all food directly from nature, while we sit at desks trying to earn enough to buy it in plastic from a store?

This book isn't about growing all your own food—though you will learn to grow food in ways that are enjoyable, satisfying, and nourishing. No high-maintenance crops here. It's also not solely about creating the perfect wildlife habitat for pollinators or birds—though you'll delight in the visitors you attract.

This book is about building a relationship with your yard, your balcony, or whatever patch of green you call your own, without stressing yourself out. It's about learning to garden in ways that rejuvenate you, while also making your space better for all who share it—human and nonhuman alike. This is a guide to growing connection, not perfection.

We (Fred and Jen) have spent years weaving together the practices of vegetable gardening, fruit orchards, wild edibles, and wildlife habitats, sharing what we've learned along the way. We've helped individuals and community spaces—like the Edible Classroom and GuideLink Center featured in this book—transform blank slates and weedy messes into interactive, abundant spaces that nourish both people and the planet.

Most of this work has unfolded over the past two decades through EarthMind Practice (formerly Backyard Abundance), a nonprofit connecting people with nature through engaging, hands-on experiences that build practical skills in ecological gardening, wilderness living, and everyday resilience while offering moments of calm, confidence, and reconnection. Fred teaches these principles as adjunct faculty at the University of Iowa, while Jen integrates her love of nature-based therapy into her work as a licensed mental health therapist.

We've worked in hundreds of spaces with thousands of clients and students, helping them build relationships with their eco gardens, grow food and habitats, and dramatically reduce the time it takes to maintain their landscapes. This book is the culmination of all that work. And with our background in education, we've done our best to make it as complete, accessible, and enjoyable as possible.

As our work has evolved—and as the pace of life continues to speed up—we've found that the calming, grounding power of time in nature is just as important as the food and flowers we grow. More than ever, people are feeling anxious, scattered, and overwhelmed. As certified Health and Wellness Coaches (NBC-HWC), we recognize the growing need for stress relief and meaningful reconnection with the natural world.

This is a unique perspective our book offers: an invitation to approach eco-garden tending as a way to cultivate peace, presence, and personal resilience alongside beauty and bounty.

DISCOVER HOW TO . . .

- **Adapt to Any Space:** Implement practical projects and flexible methods that cater to all garden sizes—from compact balconies to expansive yards—so you can cultivate abundance anywhere.
- **Simplify Maintenance:** Use proven strategies and easy-care plants to transform existing gardens or establish new ones, ensuring long-term success with minimal effort.
- **Blend Diverse Gardening Techniques:** Seamlessly integrate annual vegetable gardening, container planting, perennial orchards, and foraging to maximize yields and ease.
- **Embrace Realistic Practices:** Avoid the pitfalls of overambitious gardening promises. This guide provides honest advice, steering clear of high-maintenance plants and labor-intensive methods, focusing instead on enjoyment and practicality.
- **Cultivate Well-Being:** Experience the therapeutic benefits of gardening as a pathway to self-care and self-reliance, offering nourishment for the body, tranquility for the mind, and hope for the spirit.
- **Use Eco-Friendly, Organic Techniques:** Adopt simple, sustainable gardening practices that conserve resources, support beneficial wildlife, and create thriving ecosystems.
- **Enhance Aesthetic Appeal:** Create a productive, visually appealing garden that blends with your surroundings, whether you're aiming for neighborhood-friendly curb appeal or a private sanctuary.
- **Grow with Confidence:** All plant recommendations and techniques are tailored for USDA Plant Hardiness Zones 4–8, ensuring success in temperate climates with distinct seasons. Whether you're dealing with short growing seasons, unpredictable weather, or poor soil, you'll find practical solutions to help your garden thrive with ease.

We wish you joy and success in all your gardening endeavors. And if we can support you in transforming a container garden, a backyard, a community space, or even your inner landscape into a more living, connected place, please don't hesitate to reach out through the EarthMind Practice website: www.EarthMindPractice.org. We'd love to hear from you.

Inspirational Garden Gallery

These real gardens show that beauty, habitat, and food can flourish without taking over your life. Each one began with small steps: a pot of herbs by the door, a pair of raised beds, a fruit tree, a patch of prairie. Over time, those choices became places that feed people, welcome birds and pollinators, soothe the nervous system, and spark curiosity. Use these stories to inspire ideas you can adapt to your space, budget, and energy. Start where you are, enjoy the process, and let nature meet you halfway.

REAL-WORLD GARDEN BUDGETING

Each of the landscapes in this gallery was shaped by different needs, timelines, and budgets. Some were created all at once with the help of contractors. Others unfolded slowly over months or years, with a few new plants added each season and most of the work done by hand. Some cost thousands, others grew on a shoestring.

This book was written with your real life in mind. Whether you're aiming to spend $50 this season or saving up for a bigger project next year, your garden can grow in phases with your budget. Here's a glimpse at some of the ranges and approaches:

- **Low-Budget and DIY:** Jen built her garden gradually over three years, spending just a few hundred dollars annually on plants and materials.
- **Quick and Contractor-Built:** Sara transformed her yard in one season with professional help, investing a few thousand dollars for a full install.
- **DIY and Contractor Help:** At Aurora, large-scale soil improvement was done by contractors, while the rest was established by the owners themselves.
- **Slow and Evolving Over Time:** Mary and Blair as well as Shannon and Bob transformed their yards slowly over a decade, entirely by their own hands, with no set timeline or defined budget.

Grow at your own pace: there's no rush.

What began as bare mulch and a few stakes now flourishes with fruit trees, rhubarb, currants, and herbs—all planted to nourish both people and pollinators, while keeping care low and harvests high.

MCPHERSON EDIBLE FOREST

This city park became an edible forest, which blends food, habitat, and education.

In a sunny corner of James Alan McPherson Park, a free-for-all public resource invites passersby to taste what an Iowa City neighborhood can grow. Guided by community visioning sessions hosted by EarthMind Practice, the mini-orchard design blends fruit trees and berry shrubs with stepping-stone paths and an understory of herbs and ground covers that knit the soil. A low native prairie at the entry bridges food and habitat, making it easy to see how public edibles and ecological care can share the same ground. All food is free to harvest, and no synthetic pesticides are used.

Managed by EarthMind educators, city staff, and dedicated volunteers, the grove is tended once a week for one to two hours—mostly for weeding—with more work in spring. Each year, new beds and herbs are tucked into gaps. A living pantry and outdoor classroom, visitors learn as they wander: how orchard crops might fit into a home garden, how clover feeds the soil and reduces weeding, and how layered planting cools the ground and welcomes wildlife.

With just a few hands and a shared vision, this once-empty entryway became a buzzing native prairie, where purple coneflower, anise hyssop, butterfly weed, and bee balm now greet every visitor.

AFTER

JEN KARDOS

Co-author of this book and busy mother, Jen wanted a sensory-rich, productive space to relax, grow food, and deepen her connection to nature. Her low-maintenance backyard evolved slowly over time and now offers a peaceful retreat filled with vibrant life.

"When I bought my home, I placed a few containers on my back patio for easy-to-reach greens, basil, and strawberries. Raised beds followed, then a pair of dwarf fruit trees. Growth happens as time and budget allow; nothing is hurried. Now my backyard hums with life: bees lift from anise hyssop and sunflowers, birds nestle into serviceberries, and swallowtail caterpillars claim the dill. The design favors low-maintenance habits—dense ground covers, layered plantings, and reach-in beds with simple paths—so the space stays generous without feeling demanding.

"I spend about 10–20 minutes a day watering, harvesting, or just enjoying the garden, with one longer session each week (30–90 minutes) for deeper tending. It feels more like self-care than labor. After a full day of work and parenting teens, I step outside to tuck in a few seeds, water my plant companions, and gather herbs for supper. Bit by bit, the yard has become a restorative, sensory sanctuary: somewhere to exhale, learn the names of winged neighbors, and feel part of something steady and larger than myself."

What began with one small raised bed built during a class has blossomed into a vibrant backyard garden now packed with herbs, veggies, and pollinator plants that delight the senses just steps from the door.

Each new season brought new beds and more abundance. Slowly, the space became a growing haven for food, fragrance, color, and connection.

Expanding slowly and planting with intention, Jen turned grassy patches and existing beds into a thriving mini-orchard where fruit trees, herbs, and pollinator-friendly flowers mingle in a lush, low-maintenance tapestry of scent, color, and flavor.

SARA

Homeowner Sara quickly turned her landscape into a hands-off oasis with help from EarthMind Practice.

"I began with a couple of in-ground beds, but upkeep tugged at my limited time. I asked EarthMind Practice to design a backyard space that reduced mowing, simplified food growing, and welcomed the wildlife I love. The layout is straightforward: tuck protected edibles near the back door and let a low-growing native prairie carry most of the work across the rest of the yard. Establishment unfolds in comfortable phases as budget and know-how grow. Rabbits test the boundaries, so produce sits in raised beds ringed by rabbit-resistant herbs, with a few currants and two young peach trees for seasonal harvests. A broad sweep of prairie already fills one-third of the yard, with plans to expand.

"I spend around 15 minutes, two to four times a week, checking in on the garden, watering raised beds, and harvesting. Springtime is a bit busier, but most weeks are easy. The place is lively: monarchs drift over butterfly weed, goldfinches bob on coneflowers, rabbits shelter in tall grasses, and my indoor cats stay glued to the windows. The result feels like a private nature preserve with a tidy corner for supper. Less maintenance, more life, and a front-row seat to the seasons."

Tired of mowing grass that gave nothing in return, Sara transformed the space just outside her door into a productive mini-orchard that combined fruit trees, berry bushes, raised beds, veggies, and herbs.

Replacing much of her lawn with native prairie brought Sara the beauty, pollinators, and movement she craved, while reducing unwelcome mowing maintenance and creating a safe haven for wildlife.

This full design, done by EarthMind Practice, helped Sara reimagine her backyard into a blend of edible abundance and wild habitat.

AFTER

SHANNON AND BOB

Parents Shannon and Bob transformed their standard yard into a living classroom—part pantry, part playground—where kids help grow dinner and learn by doing.

"What started as lawn and two raised beds has become a series of kid-friendly 'rooms': a playscape for climbing and make-believe; berry lanes; herb borders that perfume pathways; and productive beds of greens, tomatoes, squash, and peas. We started small and kept learning. The entire corner landscape slowly blossomed into a pantry that feeds and educates our family through play and shared establishment.

"Our maintenance changes seasonally. In spring and early summer, we spend about a couple hours each week planting, watering, and weeding with our children, with short daily check-ins to harvest or tidy up. Chickens peck in a side run, fruit trees anchor corners, and native flowers keep beneficial insects close. It's productive, playful, and welcoming—a place where we can pick dinner, stage creative play, count butterflies, or relax in a small grassy patch. Our secret isn't speed; it's steady, joyful expansion."

Once a plain corner lot with a few shrubs, this yard now overflows with fruit trees, berries, and herbs, offering an abundance of food, beauty, and habitat.

BEFORE

AFTER

An uninspired lawn now bursts with life, where berry bushes, fruit trees, and fragrant herbs wrap the home in seasonal color and function.

BEFORE

AFTER

See how the once-empty backyard transforms into a dynamic space with a natural playscape, a thriving veggie garden outside the backdoor, and plenty of room to gather and enjoy everyday life.

MARY AND BLAIR

Homeowners Mary and Blair, now in their later years, transformed their lawn into a deeply spiritual and medicinal garden that practically tends itself.

"Years ago, we traded our mower for mulch. Bit by bit, turf gave way to fruit trees, berry hedges, hardy herbs, and swaths of low-care native perennials. Today, meandering paths cross a mosaic where birds shelter in trees, bees enjoy coneflower and creeping thyme, and we gather mint, chamomile, and basil for tea and supper. Our motto is 'food is our medicine,' and the garden makes that real with nutritious harvests a few steps from the kitchen and soothing herbs through the seasons.

"We tend the garden in short, joyful visits: 10–30 minutes most days, plus three or four seasonal sessions of 60–90 minutes for deeper weeding. It rarely feels like work. Because we planned for ecological function—layered canopies, living mulches, and habitat edges—the landscape largely tends itself. It's beautiful, generous, and spiritually grounding: a place to greet the morning, offer thanks for rain, and feel held by the rhythms of a healthy yard."

What started with a deep layer of leaf mulch to smother grass became a lush, pollinator-filled front yard where native plants bloom with color, movement, and meaning.

A whimsical raised bed, made from rainbow-painted cinder blocks, grows herbs and veggies right outside the front door.

A once-ordinary sidewalk now winds through a living tunnel of native prairie plants, Dutch white clover, and creeping thyme, delighting passersby with color, scent, and the buzz of life.

Around a backyard firepit surrounded by violets, Blair shares stories and skills with students during a class, turning the garden into a place of learning, community, and deep-rooted connection.

SUCCESSFUL LIVING

As a private group home and therapeutic nonprofit, Successful Living offering a peaceful and restorative place for visitors to unwind, reflect, and connect in this backyard garden.

This fenced therapeutic garden, created in collaboration with EarthMind Practice, supports calm, connection, and everyday use. It complements Successful Living's person-centered mission to provide safe avenues for growth and recovery for adults living with chronic mental illness. Wide, predictable routes lead to comfortable seating for private conversations or quiet reflection. Raised beds of herbs and vegetables offer gentle, grounding tasks: snipping mint for tea, watering strawberries, and noticing bees lingering on anise hyssop.

Care is shared among staff and clients living there, with 10–30 minutes of light tending most days, and seasonal weeding sessions a few times a year. Sensory plantings are easy to reach, with soft textures, earthy scents, and enlivening color. The clear layout reduces cognitive load and invites self-regulation throughout the day—an outdoor extension of compassionate care.

What was once just grass is now a soothing, sensory-rich space with raised beds and comfortable seating, designed to support mental health through calm, connection, and daily engagement.

A simple patch of lawn was transformed into a nurturing backyard retreat, where a hammock swings in a protected corner and shaded seating invites rest, reflection, and therapeutic care.

This EarthMind Practice design shows how a small backyard can become a healing landscape—thoughtfully laid out to support privacy, ease of engagement, and emotional regulation.

PREUCIL PRESCHOOL PLAYSCAPE

This private preschool playscape was designed to support imagination, learning, and nature engagement for young children through sensory plants and playful design.

Designed in collaboration with EarthMind Practice, this compact playscape turns curiosity into daily practice. Children balance across a path of half-buried stumps, dig deep in the sandbox, and compose breezy concerts on chimes and a xylophone. A stage hosts dramatic retellings from the fairy garden. Beds brim with sensory plants—soft lamb's ear, fragrant mint, cheerful coneflowers—and a pocket prairie invites up-close encounters with bees and butterflies. Cozy "sit spots" offer space for drawing or quiet observation.

In this newly established landscape, staff anticipate visiting the garden two to three times a day with the children, using 30- to 45-minute sessions for weeding, watering, and harvesting as part of the outdoor experiential play. The space mirrors the school's philosophy: a nurturing, arts-rich, play-based approach that encourages the development of the whole child.

AFTER

BEFORE

An ordinary patch of lawn with the strong beginnings of a natural playscape was reimagined as a vibrant space filled with an entryway garden, music, fairy gardens, and magical corners that spark creative play.

A path winds through red currants and sensory plants, encouraging little hands to touch, observe, smell, and taste.

Near the outdoor stage, a musical chime invites children to create breezy concerts of movement, sound, and storytelling.

DAWN KEITH: AURORA HEALING GARDENS AND EVENT CENTER

This semi-public healing space supports therapeutic practices, movement classes, and quiet moments through ecological landscaping and abundant habitat.

"As the owner of Aurora Counseling, I wanted to create a space that supported healing both inside and outside the therapy room. I hired EarthMind Practice to help design a landscape next to our counseling office that could nurture well-being in gentle, natural ways. Together, we envisioned a space that felt welcoming, restorative, and alive with possibility.

"My husband, Tharren, established much the garden with the help of a few contractors. EarthMind's design included accessible paths that wind through therapeutic nooks, an orchard for seasonal harvests, and open areas for movement classes and celebrations. Shaded seating offers space for quiet reflection, while wide sweeps of native plantings invite in birds, soften sound, and help manage rainwater.

"Though the landscape is newly installed, we anticipate tending it about once or twice a week for 30–90 minutes, with springtime requiring more attention. The garden beautifully extends the work we do at Aurora. Clients often stay after their sessions to walk the paths, gather herbs, or simply watch birds arc over the prairie. It's become clear: this place is more than a backdrop—it's part of the healing itself."

A once-empty stretch of soil now bursts with colorful prairie plants and annual flowers, wrapping around a grassy gathering space designed for celebration, movement, and exploration.

Surrounded by young plants that will one day form a living outdoor room, this group-therapy space already invites openness, reflection, and connection to the natural world.

This EarthMind Practice design shows how thoughtful planning can turn open ground into a layered landscape that supports therapy, celebration, and deep restoration.

A welcoming arbor leads into a cozy fire circle—a gathering place where stories are shared, healing unfolds, and nature gently supports conversation.

PART I:

COMMONSENSE GARDENING FOR US AND EARTH

Before any seeds are sown or containers are filled, it helps to pause and reimagine what gardening can be. This section invites you to shift your perspective—from gardening as a list of tasks to gardening as a relationship. By blending ancestral wisdom, modern insights, and nature's own rhythms, you'll create a space that nurtures the land alongside your body, mind, and spirit.

CHAPTER 01: NURTURING YOU AND YOUR GARDEN

Just steps from the back door, this patio of containers overflows with thriving herbs and greens—proof that a beautiful, productive garden doesn't require perfection, extra time, or a big yard. Everything you see here is within easy reach, and this book will show you exactly how to create it.

If you have a garden—whether it's for flowers, food, or both—it probably feels like it constantly demands attention. "Weed me. Water me. Prune me. Mulch me." The excitement of spring planting has long faded, and now gardening feels like another task on your to-do list. So, you reluctantly don your hat and gloves, gather your tools, and haul the hose to that distant weedy, needy patch. Another long afternoon of work passes, and instead of feeling rejuvenated, you feel like you're fighting with your garden rather than enjoying it.

Autumn brings slower growth and a sigh of relief. As unharvested tomatoes rot on browning vines, you wonder: "Was all that effort really worth it?" You harvested a few flowers, some cucumbers, and maybe a handful of beans, but nothing close to what you'd hoped. Where was the joy promised in books and online posts?

Maybe you've thought:

"I just don't have a green thumb."

"I don't have enough time to keep up with it."

"Gardening is supposed to be relaxing, but this feels like work."

If any of this sounds familiar, you're not alone—and this book is for you.

Gardening can be a source of nourishment, beauty, and peace, rather than being tiresome. Imagine stepping outside and being greeted by a flourishing garden that practically takes care of itself. You harvest fresh food with ease, watch butterflies dance among the flowers, and feel a deep sense of connection with the earth—without being overwhelmed by upkeep.

With this book, you'll learn to design, establish, and enjoy a garden that gives back more than it takes—one that brings lasting satisfaction, feeds both body and soul, and invites you into ease rather than burdening you with work. Whether you have a small balcony, a suburban yard, or a larger homestead, you'll find practical, time-saving solutions to create a beautiful space that rejuvenates you.

An Approach to Abundance and Ease

Gardening is meant to be a source of nourishment and joy—but too often, it becomes a struggle. We've been taught that successful gardens require constant watering, weeding, fertilizing, and pest control. These high-maintenance methods dominate many farms, public spaces, and even backyard gardens, making it easy to assume that only effort will equal success.

But nature doesn't garden that way. In the wild, forests flourish, meadows bloom, and wildlife helps create balance, all without human intervention. This book will show you how to borrow from nature's wisdom to create thriving, low-maintenance gardens.

This nature-inspired approach—often called permaculture—isn't complicated; it's simply common sense that's rarely put into practice. Small shifts in how you design, plant, and care for your space will lead to a garden that grows to be more abundant and enjoyable every year.

WHAT YOU WILL GAIN

Whether you're starting fresh or refining an existing space, this book will help you:

- **Make Gardening Easier:** Use proven, low-maintenance techniques to reduce weeding, watering, and pest issues.
- **Grow More with Less Effort:** Increase yields of food, fun, and beauty, creating a garden that nourishes you without exhausting you.
- **Improve Your Local Ecosystems:** Create a haven for pollinators, beneficial insects, and birds using organic, nature-based practices that improve soil health and biodiversity.
- **Turn Your Garden into a Retreat:** Create a space that reduces anxiety and brings stability, offering a place of calm and renewal during uncertain times.
- **Fit Gardening into Your Life:** Implement scalable, flexible strategies that work with your time, budget, and energy levels—whether you have a balcony, patio, backyard, or homestead.

A single raised bed, thoughtfully planted, yields an abundant harvest of Swiss chard—no tilling, no perfectionism, and no overwhelming feeling. With nature as your partner and a few simple shifts in approach, this kind of abundance becomes your new normal.

WHY THIS BOOK IS FOR YOU

No matter your experience level, this book will help you grow with confidence.

For New Gardeners: No experience? No problem. You will get up to speed quickly with easy, low-maintenance methods that don't require special skills or expensive tools. Each project includes clear, step-by-step instructions to guide you from planning to harvest, even if you've never grown anything before. Everything is broken down into manageable, rewarding tasks to ensure success from the start.

For Experienced Gardeners: Already love gardening but tired of labor-intensive upkeep? You'll learn smart, time-saving techniques by adopting nature's principles and rhythms. Your garden will become more self-sustaining, resilient, and abundant so you can spend less time maintaining and more time enjoying.

HOW TO USE THIS BOOK

You don't need to read this book cover to cover. Think of it as a handy gardening companion that you can turn to at any time—whether you're planning a new area, tweaking a garden that isn't working, or looking for ways to reconnect with nature. You'll find creative ideas, practical projects, and flexible guidance that fits your time, space, and energy. Your needs will shift over time, and this book is here to grow with you.

- **Low-Maintenance, High-Reward Projects:** Discover tried-and-true garden setups that countless gardeners have needed, requested, and loved. These simple, effective designs make it easy to grow food, create beauty, and establish a thriving garden.
- **Practical and Clear:** Every project includes simple, step-by-step instructions, along with materials lists, troubleshooting tips, and shortcuts to ensure success.
- **Hands-On and Actionable:** No abstract theory—just real-world examples and time-tested techniques you can apply right away.
- **Designed for Real Life:** Quick-reference sections make it easy to find what you need, when you need it, without reading cover to cover.
- **Flexible and Customizable:** No rigid schedules or one-size-fits-all methods. Adaptable techniques fit your space, time, and budget, so your garden works for you—not the other way around.

This is more than just a gardening book—it's a guide to a simpler, more abundant way of living. By using proven, low-maintenance strategies, you'll create a space that feeds your body, nurtures your mind, and supports the environment, without exhausting yourself in the process. By adopting these practices, you'll find fulfillment in watching your garden—and yourself—flourish.

Harvesting fruit like these sparkling goumi berries is part of a more flexible, nourishing approach to gardening—one that blends veggies, berries, herbs, and even wild edibles into a space shaped by your needs and lifestyle. This book helps you design a garden that works for your time, your space, and the way you live.

Planting becomes a fun, shared moment when the garden is designed for connection, not perfection. This book invites the whole family into a simpler way of growing that supports well-being, learning, and togetherness.

CHOOSE YOUR STARTING POINT

Start wherever makes the most sense for your current goals, energy level, or season of life.

CHAPTER 02: OUR NEED FOR NATURE

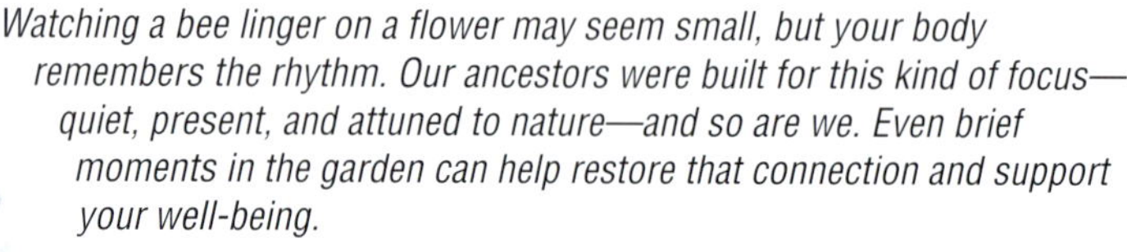

Watching a bee linger on a flower may seem small, but your body remembers the rhythm. Our ancestors were built for this kind of focus—quiet, present, and attuned to nature—and so are we. Even brief moments in the garden can help restore that connection and support your well-being.

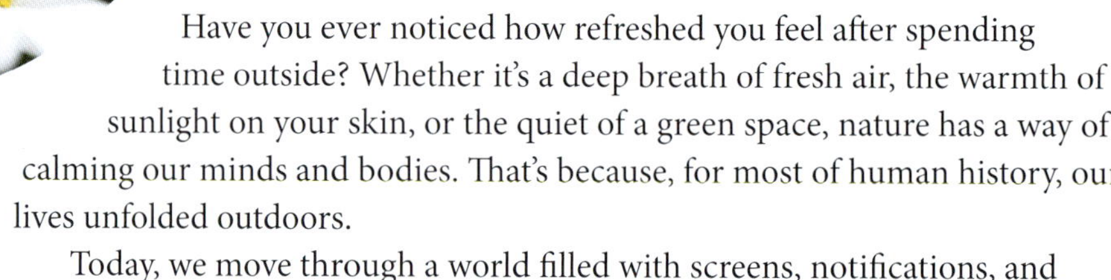

Have you ever noticed how refreshed you feel after spending time outside? Whether it's a deep breath of fresh air, the warmth of sunlight on your skin, or the quiet of a green space, nature has a way of calming our minds and bodies. That's because, for most of human history, our lives unfolded outdoors.

Planting an herb may seem like a small task, but it echoes an ancient rhythm—one our bodies still recognize. In the quiet focus of hands in soil, distractions fall away, and something deeper awakens: presence, peace, and a sense of grounding.

Today, we move through a world filled with screens, notifications, and endless to-do lists. While modern life offers incredible convenience, it also keeps us mentally overloaded and physically disconnected from nature, stimuli our bodies and minds were never designed for. The good news? You don't have to live off the grid to restore that balance. Even small interactions with the natural world—tending a garden, feeling soil between your fingers, or watching a bee visit a flower—can have profound effects on your well-being.

Gardening is one of the simplest, most rewarding ways to reconnect. It gently shifts your attention away from digital distractions and into the present moment. Our ancestors focused on one task at a time—gathering food, tending a fire, or crafting tools—and our minds and bodies evolved to thrive in that rhythm. Gardening allows you to follow that same ingrained ancestral rhythm through planting, watering, or simply watching things grow. In return, the garden rewards this familiarity by lowering your stress, lifting your mood, and offering you a sense of peace that's hard to find elsewhere.

Stress, Environment, Outdated Models

Reflect for a moment on your most cherished memories, whether from childhood or treasured moments as an adult. Think of times when you felt awe, joy, happiness, or pure, carefree delight. How many of those moments happened indoors? And how many unfolded outside—in a park, at the beach, swimming in a lake, or even in your own backyard? There's a unique magic in nature that reconnects us with what truly matters, draws us into the present, and slows time, leaving us wishing those moments could last forever.

Add a touch of magic to your garden; whimsical elements like fairy houses, stepping stones, or playful sculptures can spark joy and help you reconnect with the wonder you felt in your favorite outdoor memories.

WE ALL NEED A WAY TO RECHARGE

Ever wonder why spending time in the garden feels so refreshing? Researchers studying how nature affects the brain have found that green spaces help us recover from mental fatigue. Psychologists Rachel and Stephen Kaplan call this Attention Restoration Theory—the idea that natural environments captivate us with effortless fascination, giving our overworked minds a break from the constant demands of daily life.

Attention Restoration Theory outlines four key principles:

1. **Being Away:** Experiencing mental or physical distance from routine stressors that tug at you.
2. **Fascination:** Immersion in environments that effortlessly capture and hold your attention.
3. **Sense of Wholeness:** Being in a space that feels rich, harmonious, and naturally cohesive.
4. **Compatibility:** Finding an environment that feels safe and aligns with your natural inclinations; it's a "good fit" for you.

That's why this book encourages you to make your garden feel more like a beloved forest path instead of a perfect weed-free plot. Uniform plots of grass and neat rows of vegetables are modeled after commercial agriculture and rarely align with these principles that bring deep peace. After all, when was the last time you yearned to picnic in a cornfield or slowly hike through a commercial farm? Yet, we often lay out our gardens in similar grids, spending most of our time fighting with weeds and feeling guilty for not enjoying the process. Did your favorite hiking trail become magical because someone weeded it endlessly and ensured specific plants grew in just the right locations? Your garden can feel like a refuge—a place where you exhale and let the natural world take some of the burden off your shoulders.

Planting a garden invites focus without fatigue. Nature's quiet details, like the feel of soil or the scent of mint, offer what researchers call "effortless fascination." In moments like these, the mind gets a much-needed chance to rest and reset.

Your garden doesn't need to be controlled. It can be shaped for feelings and experiences. A garden can offer peace without demanding perfection, inviting you to slow down, breathe deeply, and release the pressure to get everything "just right."

LET NATURE DO SOME OF THE WORK

How can you apply these principles to create a space that restores you, rather than drains you? The secret is shifting your mindset away from control and toward partnership with nature. Instead of feeling like a taskmaster overseeing every detail, you become an observer and participant in a space that supports both you and the ecosystem around you.

Let's take those four principles from the Attention Restoration Theory and come up with some garden ideas inspired by them:

- **Being Away:** Create a sense of escape from daily pressures. When you step outside, let yourself be greeted by plants that delight you—ones that draw you out of your indoor routine.
- **Fascination:** Design for sensory engagement. Watch bees, butterflies, and birds enjoying your space. Peer into a semi-wild patch to discover what's budding or pluck a fresh edible treat straight from the vine.
- **Sense of Wholeness:** Prioritize the natural over the orderly. Keep herbs and favorite edibles close to your door for easy harvesting, while letting other spaces flourish as naturalized havens for both you and the local wildlife.
- **Compatibility:** Grow what you love. Fill your garden with plants and edibles that bring you joy and attract critters that make you smile every time you see them.

Perhaps you've participated in a guided meditation where you were invited to imagine a safe, beautiful space—often a garden or a quiet forest. Why not bring that vision to life in your own yard, patio, or balcony? Your garden doesn't have to be a place of endless tasks and perfectionism. Instead, it can be the sanctuary where you release stress rather than accumulate it. When you sit quietly to observe the world waking up in the morning, stroll barefoot while nibbling fresh herbs, or take a few minutes to mindfully water plants, like meditation, you're practicing restoration rather than obligation.

Simply drifting through your garden and noticing what's around you can be deeply restorative. Quiet moments of observation shift your garden from a list of tasks to a place of calm, beauty, and ease.

Why Healing Happens in the Garden

Unlike the constant demands of modern life, plants don't rush us or expect perfection. They offer something gentler: a chance to step away from digital noise and into a slower, more grounded rhythm. For millions of years, plants have generously nourished people and wildlife alike, offering food, medicine, materials, beauty, and emotional comfort. When you step into their world, you reconnect with that deep, ancient relationship—one built on presence, not pressure.

COMMUNITY AND RECIPROCAL RELATIONSHIPS

We often think of gardening or yard work as "work," but what if we approached it more like a partnership, one where we receive just as much as we give? Think about how we interact with our pets. Caring for them can seem like work, especially when they're young or adjusting to a new home. Yet, their companionship enriches our lives in countless ways. They remind us to be present, to play, to seek comfort. A pet's joyful greeting or quiet companionship during difficult moments is a simple and powerful reminder that relationships—whether with animals, people, or even plants—are reciprocal.

Humans are social creatures, wired for connection, and gardening is a powerful way to build community with people and all living beings. When you garden with family, neighbors, or even a pet, you reinforce bonds of cooperation, patience, and generosity. A simple act, such as planting seeds with a child or trading homegrown herbs with a friend, reminds us that we thrive when we care for and support one another.

Rather than viewing gardening as another task on your to-do list, you can reframe it as an opportunity to step into a reciprocal relationship, one where you care for your plants, and in turn, they nourish, heal, and support you. This partnership is for everyone who interacts with the garden, be it children marveling at a sprouting seed; a pet finding shade under a fruit tree; or the birds, bees, and butterflies that come to visit. In this way, your garden becomes a community where every living thing plays a role in supporting one another. And just like in any strong community, the more you engage, the more you receive.

Like our pets, plants respond to care and return it in quiet, meaningful ways. Presence, comfort, and joy flow both ways when we tend with love.

Harvesting together turns a simple task into something richer: connection, laughter, and shared abundance. In the garden, community can grow just as naturally as fruit.

PLANTS TEND AND HEAL US (EVEN WITHOUT EATING THEM)

Caring for plants provides remarkable, science-backed benefits to human health. Interacting with plants has been shown to significantly lower cortisol levels—the body's primary stress hormone—which in turn reduces blood pressure, heart rate, and overall feelings of anxiety. Even just 30 minutes of gardening can ease stress more effectively than indoor leisure activities like reading. And because gardening also engages the body through simple, steady movement, regular gardeners often show lower percentages of heart disease and stroke.

In addition to cardiovascular support, gardening strengthens the immune system and enhances overall resilience. Soil contains beneficial microbes that stimulate serotonin production, acting as a natural antidepressant. This connection to the earth can improve immune responses, helping the body fight infections and reduce inflammation.

Tending to plants also cultivates mindfulness, easing symptoms of anxiety and depression. Bloodwork studies have documented increased levels of endorphins and dopamine—the "feel-good" hormones—after gardening. Even the rhythmic motions of weeding and watering activate parasympathetic nervous system pathways, shifting you into a calming "rest and digest" state.

As mentioned previously, the relationship between humans and plants is deeply reciprocal. As you nurture your garden, it nurtures you in return, supporting your physical and mental well-being. Reflect on your own experiences; compare the sense of rejuvenation you feel after a day spent in nature versus a day at the shopping mall.

Microbes in healthy soil can boost serotonin levels, support immunity, and lift your mood.

As we tend the garden, the garden tends to us—lifting our mood, soothing the nervous system, and strengthening the immune response. Plants have a way of reminding us to slow down, breathe deeply, and just be.

Growth doesn't need to be perfect to be beautiful. In the garden, like in life, patience, presence, and compassion help everything bloom in its own time.

GARDENING CULTIVATES SELF-COMPASSION AND ACCEPTANCE

Gardening offers a gentle path to nurture self-compassion and adaptability. It challenges perfectionist tendencies, encouraging you to surrender to life's natural rhythms. Plants grow on their own schedule, often in ways that may surprise you. A seed may sprout late, a flower may bloom unevenly, or a vegetable may come out misshapen—yet these imperfections still hold their own beauty and charm. Witnessing this in the garden can help cultivate greater acceptance of your own and others' imperfections.

The act of gardening invites surrender. Weather shifts unexpectedly, pests may appear, and plants will thrive or falter regardless of our meticulous plans. Some plants might wildly exceed expectations, while others may only contribute to the compost pile. These experiences teach resilience and acceptance, reminding you that not everything is within your control. Growth and impermanence are part of life's natural processes. Over time, gardening helps embrace these truths, encouraging you to try again next season and appreciate the unique outcomes that arise from the partnership between you and nature.

If you find traditional seated meditation challenging, gardening provides an alternative way to stay present and grounded. Weeding, planting, and watering require focus but aren't mentally taxing. These simple tasks quiet self-critical thoughts and create space to appreciate your efforts without judgment. Unlike the taxing demands of responding to online messages, gardening lets you see tangible results of your care and attention. As you nurture plants, you may discover a growing tenderness toward yourself—a recognition that growth, like gardening, is messy and nonlinear.

Ultimately, gardening becomes a mirror for radical acceptance. Seasons change, setbacks happen, and yet beauty persists. Just as a garden flourishes when allowed to adapt and grow naturally, so do you when you embrace yourself as you are—even when things don't go as planned.

CHAPTER 03: PRINCIPLES TO HELP YOUR GARDEN (AND YOU) THRIVE

There's something deeply satisfying about being part of a system where soil, plants, and people support one another. As the garden matures, nature takes on more of the work—yielding food, beauty, and a wildlife habitat.

When we nurture life with intention and humility, we become part of a system where every act of kindness ripples outward.

Permaculture, short for "permanent culture" or "permanent agriculture," was coined by a pair of ecological visionaries in the 1970s who recognized the environmental harm caused by modern farming methods. Seeking a more regenerative path, they studied traditional societies that had cultivated thriving, productive gardens for thousands of years—gardens that enriched local ecosystems rather than depleting them. What emerged was a toolkit of ethics, principles, and practices that work with nature's processes, making it easier for people to grow food, nourish the land, and restore balance in both their landscapes and lives.

Whether you're working with a balcony, backyard, or a sprawling homestead, these tools make gardening easier over time by shifting the workload into nature's capable hands—allowing plants, soil, beneficial insects, and seasonal cycles to do much of the heavy lifting. As you practice these methods, you'll likely experience a shift in thinking that helps you connect with nature's rhythms and find a sense of balance in an often-chaotic world.

ETHICS FOR A THRIVING GARDEN (AND PLANET)

At the heart of permaculture are three core ethics:

- **Care for People:** We all have unique struggles, and we all need support. A thriving community starts with looking out for one another, sharing knowledge, and building resilience together.
- **Care for the Earth:** This planet is our home and it's been sustaining life for billions of years. When you nurture soil, protect pollinators, and make choices that support biodiversity, you contribute to its continued health as well as your own.
- **Create and Return a Surplus:** Nature is abundant; plants produce more seeds than necessary, trees drop leaves that enrich the soil, and one thriving tree can feed an entire community of insects, birds, and people. You can emulate this natural generosity by sharing extra harvests, creating wildlife habitat, and composting.

Nature's Restorative Principles

Each of the following permaculture principles forms the foundation of a garden that works with you, rather than against you. By following nature's lead, you'll create spaces that nourish both the land and your well-being.

SLOW DOWN AND PAY ATTENTION (OBSERVE AND INTERACT)

Your garden will yield more when you listen closely to nature's deep wisdom. Instead of diving in with big plans and heavy labor, start by patiently observing—watch how sunlight moves through the space, notice where rain collects or runs off, and pay attention to what plants (and weeds) already grow well. Every yard, balcony, or community plot has its own rhythms, and working with them will save you time, effort, and frustration down the road.

Traditional gardening often skips this step, leading to struggling plants in the wrong location, wasted water, or constant battles with pests. Instead, spend an entire growing season to observe and interact, making small changes, and learning from what happens. A shady corner might not be great for tomatoes, but it could be perfect for tender greens. A windy balcony might seem difficult, but a sturdy trellis of climbing beans could create a sheltered microclimate for a container garden. When you let the garden and nature guide you, everything falls into place more easily.

Read More: This approach is built into the design process found in "Maximize Ease with Location and Layout" (page 55). By starting with observation, you'll make choices that lead to less work and better results, creating a garden that supports both your well-being and the earth's natural flow.

Let the garden guide you. Observing light, water, and plant patterns helps you work with nature, not against it, creating a space that thrives with less effort.

Pulling crisp red rhubarb from the garden is the start of something delicious, such as a tangy compote or a just-sweet-enough crumble. When you grow what you love to eat, the garden becomes a place that feeds both your body and your joy.

GROW WHAT FEEDS YOU (OBTAIN A YIELD)

Gardening is nourishing when it gives back. This could mean fresh greens for the kitchen, beautiful cutting flowers that also attract pollinators, or a peaceful nook where you can unwind after a long day. A well-designed space feeds your body and soul, offering something meaningful in return for your care.

Many traditional landscapes focus on plants and spaces that require endless upkeep without offering much in return: lawns that demand mowing and weeding, ornamentals that need constant pruning, or rows of vegetables that overwhelm in peak season. Instead, design spaces that enhance your life: a compact container garden outside your kitchen, a sitting garden filled with chamomile and other fragrant herbs, or a compact orchard of peaches, rhubarb, and alpine strawberries.

Read More: This principle is highlighted in "Align Your Garden with You" (page 50) and explored in "Your Plant Matchmaking Guide" (page 180), where you'll find plants suited for your lifestyle and your space.

EVERYTHING IS CONNECTED (FUNCTIONAL INTERCONNECTION)

Yarrow draws in beneficial insects like ladybugs that help keep pests in check. When your garden is designed with connection in mind, nature does more of the work for you.

Nature doesn't work in isolation—every plant, insect, and element in a garden plays a role in the larger system. The healthiest gardens emulate these natural connections by ensuring that everything supports something else. Dutch white clover naturally fertilizes the soil by working with beneficial bacteria to capture nitrogen from the air and convert it into a form that helps nearby plants grow. A fire pit attracts people to a gardening space, serves as a practical way to dispose of seed-laden weeds, and turns those weeds into nutrient-rich ash that can be used as a natural potassium fertilizer. Yarrow draws ladybugs that help keep pesky aphids managed. The more connections you create, the less effort your garden requires to stay healthy and balanced.

Conventional gardening often ignores this, treating plants and spaces as individual units rather than part of a living system. This means more work for the gardener: manually fertilizing depleted soil, visiting multiple areas in the landscape, harvesting from inconvenient locations, or constantly fighting pests.

Read More: The "High-Yield Mini-Orchard" section (page 94) exemplifies this principle by creating a small ecosystem of interconnected parts.

ONE THING, MANY BENEFITS (MULTIPLE FUNCTIONS)

When every element in your garden does more than one job, it means less work for you. A pear tree that produces fruit, offers shade, creates a border for an outdoor room, supports beneficial wildlife, and improves soil health is far more valuable than a standalone ornamental pear that only looks nice. As another example, a trellis can support climbing plants, provide privacy, and act as a windbreak.

Traditional gardens often rely on single-purpose elements, like a lawn that only acts as a decorative green carpet but requires constant mowing, weeding, fertilizing, and watering. By contrast, multifunction designs ensure that every element earns its place in several ways.

Diversity plays a key role in this approach. Instead of a monoculture that depletes the soil and invites pests, a polyculture of plants with different functions—such as fruiting shrubs, deep-rooted vegetables, pollinator-friendly flowers, and soil-building ground covers—creates a resilient, self-supporting system. A mix of species ensures that plants complement and protect each other, reducing the need for fertilizers and pesticides while increasing yields.

A garden filled with diverse veggies and herbs does more than just feed you—it builds soil, invites pollinators, reduces pests, and fills your space with color and scent. When every plant serves multiple purposes, your garden works smarter and feels more alive.

Read More: This idea is woven throughout "Relaxing Sensory Garden" (page 110), where the space provides relaxation, herbs, and pollinator habitat. The principle is also expressed in "Layer to Maximize Growth" (page 60), where plants and structures create a dynamic, stacked ecosystem—vines climb trellises, ground covers suppress weeds, shrubs shelter beneficial insects, and deep-rooted trees anchor the landscape—ensuring every layer works together for abundance and ease. Use the Plant Matchmaker (page 187) to fill your garden with a rich variety of plants that bolster resilience and help your space thrive through challenges and change.

BUILD BACKUPS (REDUNDANCY)

A patchwork ground cover of creeping thyme, oregano, and wild strawberry protects the soil, retains moisture, supports pollinators, provides food, and looks beautiful. If one plant falters, another steps in. Redundancy like this helps your garden thrive through uncertainty.

In nature, no system relies on a single point of failure; if one plant or pollinator struggles, another takes its place. A resilient garden ensures that important functions—like soil fertility, pest control, or food production—are supported in multiple ways.

Traditional gardening often leans on one solution at a time: a single row of tomatoes, a single fertilizer, a single watering system. If that tomato row gets hit by blight, if the store runs out of nitrogen, or if the hose breaks, everything struggles. By building in redundancy, such as growing multiple types of crops, planting a mix of soil-building ground covers, and using mulch to retain moisture, you create a system that adapts and thrives under pressure.

Read More: In "Materials Planning" (page 265), you'll see several soil mixes and mulches that can be interchanged based on what is readily available.

MAKE IT EASY ON YOURSELF (MINIMIZE EFFORT)

When your garden is just steps from the kitchen and close to a water source, harvesting fresh herbs and greens weave naturally into your daily rhythm.

A well-designed garden becomes less work over time. When your garden is just steps from the kitchen and close to a water source, harvesting fresh herbs and greens weaves naturally into your daily rhythm. If you find yourself constantly weeding, watering, and troubleshooting, it's a sign the design needs tweaking. Mulching, thoughtfully selecting durable plants, inviting beneficial insects, and placing elements in convenient locations lets you enjoy the many rewards of gardening.

Conventional gardening often assumes maintenance is a necessary and endless chore. But by designing for efficiency and ease, you create a garden that cares for itself.

Read More: This concept is central to "Maximize Ease with Location and Layout" (page 55) and is demonstrated in the sheet-mulching technique (page 145), which minimizes constant tilling, weeding, watering, and fertilizing.

Placing containers and raised beds where you already walk makes gardening easier, more successful, and a lot more joyful.

TURN WASTE INTO ABUNDANCE (PRODUCE NO WASTE)

In nature, nothing is wasted—everything cycles back into the system to fuel new life. Leaves decompose into rich soil, fallen fruit feeds wildlife, and even the smallest creatures have a role in breaking down organic matter. A garden designed with this principle in mind ensures that every resource—water, nutrients, plant material—is used to its fullest potential rather than being discarded.

Traditional gardening often generates a surprising amount of waste: piles of pulled weeds, yard clippings, discarded plant pots, and uneaten produce thrown into the trash. Synthetic fertilizers are purchased instead of building soil with compost. Rather than letting cucumbers yellow and spoil on the vine, share the abundance with friends, family, or neighbors. Autumn leaves could be raked around trees and shrubs instead of purchasing and transporting woodchip mulch in single-use plastic bags. By shifting your mindset, you can turn these so-called "waste" materials into assets.

Read More: This concept is woven into "Compost for Free Fertilizer" (page 125), where kitchen scraps and yard waste are transformed into nutrient-rich soil. If an area becomes overwhelmed with weeds, the "When Weeds Won't Quit" (page 153) section describes how to transform this problem into a soil-building opportunity.

Compost is a reminder that nature already knows how to transform leftovers into life. Kitchen scraps, clippings, and fallen leaves all return to the soil, closing the loop.

LET NATURE TAKE THE LEAD (SELF-REGULATION)

A truly sustainable garden places much of the micromanagement into Mother Nature's hands. Instead of treating every problem as something to "fix," self-regulating gardens find their own balance over time. The more you encourage beneficial insects, soil microbes, and natural cycles, the less you'll need to intervene.

Traditional gardening often works against nature, relying on pesticides to kill pests, synthetic fertilizers to force plant growth, and heavy tilling that disrupts soil life. But these quick fixes often create more problems than they solve, leading to imbalances that require even more work to correct in the long run. Instead, by trusting nature's time-tested ability to self-correct, you'll find that problems often resolve themselves. Aphids might appear in early spring, but if you've planted flowers that attract hungry ladybugs, nature will restore balance without your help. When soil is left undisturbed and covered with mulch, it will naturally suppress weeds and retain fertility without needing constant inputs.

Read More: This idea is highlighted in "Naturally Address Common Pests and Diseases" (page 170), which emphasizes working with, rather than against, nature's helpers and cycles.

A ladybug quietly managing aphids is nature's way of saying, "I've got this." When you design with balance in mind, your garden begins to regulate itself—reducing pests, supporting plant health, and saving you from constant intervention.

WORK WITH NATURE'S TIMETABLE (SUCCESSION)

A garden isn't a static thing—it evolves, just like any natural landscape (or person). Plants grow, mature, and die, but in a well-designed space, each stage of growth sets the stage for what comes next. This concept of succession ensures that the garden remains productive and self-sustaining over time.

Traditional gardening often follows a start-stop cycle, where beds are cleared at the end of the season, leaving bare soil that must be rejuvenated and replanted the following year. But in nature, there are no empty spaces—one plant's end is another's beginning. Fast-growing lettuce can be planted in the cool early spring before heat-loving tomatoes take over in summer. In a newly established orchard, the succession of ecosystems can be imitated by planting beans, peas, and squash to build soil, but over the years these annuals will eventually give way to the shade of perennial fruit trees and shrubs.

Read More: This idea is embedded in "Adapt with Life's Changes" (page 175), which encourages working with natural changes in the garden and your life rather than fighting them.

Creating a new bed in an established garden reflects both the garden's evolution and yours. When following nature's rhythm, nothing stays static—not the soil, not the plants, and not the gardener.

START SMALL, GROW SLOWLY (SMALL-SCALE SOLUTIONS)

If a new gardening project feels small, consider making it even smaller. Success builds confidence, and it's far easier to expand on a thriving, manageable garden than to recover from an overwhelming one. Learning happens naturally as you go, and starting small ensures that your time, energy, and resources stay in balance with your growing knowledge. A few well-tended containers on a patio can yield just as much satisfaction (and food) as a large raised bed, and a single raised bed can teach you as much about creating soil health as an entire acre. By beginning with a scale that fits your life, you gain confidence, enjoy the process, and set yourself up for long-term success.

Traditional gardening often promotes the idea that bigger is better, encouraging a leap into large-scale projects that demand heavy investments in money, materials, and maintenance. But small-scale solutions are often more efficient, easier to sustain, and better suited to real life. A self-watering container can eliminate the challenge of watering on a busy schedule, a compact herb garden can provide fresh ingredients within arm's reach, and a few carefully chosen berry bushes can yield large harvests without the need for annual replanting.

Read More: This principle is at the heart of "Compact Container Garden" (page 70), where you'll see how even the smallest spaces can be highly productive. You may even discover that a small garden is all you need to bring well-being into your life.

Start small and grow with your confidence. Even a tiny garden bed can teach you everything you need to know while keeping the joy, time, and effort in balance.

Just a few small pots can be the perfect place to begin. Start with something manageable and let your garden grow at your own pace.

RECONNECTING WITH NATURE'S WISDOM

You may be thinking that these principles are simply common sense. And they are—they're just not common practice. For much of human history, we lived in close relationship with nature, observing its rhythms, working with its cycles, and understanding that our well-being was intertwined with the health of the land. But somewhere along the way, we began to see ourselves as separate from nature, believing we could control it, improve upon it, and bend it to our will. Conventional gardening reflects this mindset: landscapes designed for aesthetics alone, soil treated as lifeless dirt that needs constant inputs, and backyard gardens that require backbreaking work just to maintain.

Following nature's principles offers a different way forward, one that trusts in the vast intelligence of nature, refined through millions of years of evolution. When these principles are applied together, they create spaces that are productive, deeply rewarding, easier to maintain, and more in tune with Earth's rhythms. Instead of seeing gardening as a chore, these principles can help you approach it as a collaboration.

A nature-based garden nourishes your body, calms your mind, gives you a sense of belonging, and reminds you that you are part of something larger.

Harvesting together reminds us that gardening isn't just about growing food—it's about growing connection. When we return to nature's rhythms, we remember that we're not separate from the land, we're part of it.

PART II:

DESIGN AND ESTABLISH YOUR ABUNDANT SPACE

A thriving garden begins with you. This section helps you design a space that reflects your daily rhythms, values, and dreams. By honoring what brings you joy and what truly fits your life, you'll lay a strong foundation for a garden that feels abundant, beautiful, and sustaining.

CHAPTER 04: BEGIN WITH A SKETCH

Gather your mapping supplies and head outside. Creating a base map sets the stage for thoughtful garden design.

While it may be tempting to grab your shovel and start digging, beginning with a sketch will lead to more success. Whether you're working with a backyard or a balcony, a simple concept jotted down on paper can make a world of difference. This initial step will help you record important notes, visualize your future oasis, and avoid common pitfalls like overcrowding plants or forgetting essential pathways. By taking the time to plan, you'll ensure a smoother and more enjoyable gardening experience.

Creating Your Base Map

A base map is a scaled drawing that serves as the foundation for your garden plan. It will include your future garden area along with any existing features that are unlikely to be moved or changed. It doesn't need to be a work of art—just enough to guide your planning.

Aerial imagery from your county's GIS system or an online map tool makes a great starting point for your base map, especially when paired with tracing paper. It helps you capture key features and scale with ease.

1. CHOOSE YOUR APPROACH

There are several ways to create a base map, so choose what feels easiest and most practical for you:

- **Hand-Drawn on Graph Paper:** Great for small, detailed spaces.
- **Printed from Online Aerial Imagery:** Ideal for larger areas or quick mapping. Check your county's Geographic Information System (GIS) or a free online map tool for up-to-date satellite imagery.
- **Combination:** Print an aerial image then refine it with hand-drawn measurements.

2. GATHER SUPPLIES

- Tape measure (or pace out the measurements if you're short on time)
- Graph paper or printed aerial image
- Clipboard
- Pencil and eraser
- Tracing paper (optional, but useful for experimenting)

3. OUTLINE YOUR SPACE

Start by marking the boundaries of your garden area. If measuring by hand, use a tape measure and jot down dimensions. If using a printed aerial image, check the scale (often listed at the bottom) and adjust accordingly.

For small gardens, a 1 square = 1 foot (30.5cm) scale works well. Larger spaces, like a mini-orchard, might be easier to map using 1 square = 5 feet (1.5m) or another ratio that fits comfortably on your paper.

4. DRAW EXISTING FEATURES

Measure and add anything that's likely to stay put, such as:

- Buildings, fences, patios, pathways, or walls.
- Trees, shrubs, or other significant plants.
- Raised beds, trellises, or other structures.

If precision isn't your strong suit, don't worry—an approximate layout is enough to make informed decisions.

5. MAKE IT YOUR OWN

Pat yourself on the back; your base map is complete!

Use it to record important notes and sketch your future garden. For simple projects like small container gardens, you can write directly on the base map. For more complex designs, using one or more pieces of tracing paper on top of your base map will keep the drawing tidy while you experiment with ideas.

Remember, your garden plan is a living document. As you and your garden grow, you may need to adjust the design. Embrace this natural process of evolution, and don't be afraid to make many changes.

CHAPTER 05: ALIGN YOUR GARDEN WITH YOU

Grow food, create a habitat, or carve out a peaceful corner; there are many ways your garden can quietly reflect your values.

Before we dive into your garden space, let's take a moment to focus on *you*. Your garden will become a part of the land where it grows, but how might it elegantly become a part of you?

BE REALISTIC ABOUT YOUR TIME

First, let's talk about reality. How much time do you genuinely have to create and maintain a garden—not just in bursts of excitement but throughout the seasons? Consider when you typically take vacations, when life gets busiest, and the amount of time you'd like to spend simply enjoying your garden rather than working in it. A good rule of thumb: estimate your available gardening time each week throughout the season, then subtract 25 percent. This buffer will help prevent feeling overwhelmed and ensure your space remains a source of joy, not stress.

LEVERAGE YOUR STRENGTHS

What unique skills, knowledge, and resources do you naturally bring to your garden? Leveraging your natural gifts in the garden will breathe beautiful life into it and make a space that is an extension of you.

- **Generous Sharer:** If you find joy in giving, then grow fresh vegetables, herbs, and flowers to share with friends and neighbors.
- **Artist or Crafter:** Add personality by painting containers or incorporating artistic elements into your space.
- **Culinary Connoisseur:** Grow ingredients that enhance home-cooked meals, bringing fresh flavors to your kitchen.
- **DIY Enthusiast:** If you love hands-on projects, repurpose materials into creative garden structures.

A box of free zucchini along the sidewalk reflects a surplus of both food and generosity. Whether your strength is creativity, cooking, sharing, or building, there's a meaningful way to let it shine, shaping a space that truly feels like you.

REFLECT YOUR VALUES

Your garden can also be a mirror for what matters most to you.

- **Resilience and Self-Sufficiency:** Consider perennial vegetables, fruit trees, and medicinal herbs for long-term nourishment and security.
- **Sustainability:** A pollinator-friendly garden with native plants, composting systems, and water-wise techniques aligns with an eco-conscious mindset.
- **Relaxation Sanctuary:** A sensory garden filled with fragrant chamomile, soft textures, and calming colors can offer a restorative retreat.
- **Family-Friendly:** A child-friendly, educational garden with raised beds and easy-access pathways fosters family bonding while keeping maintenance simple.
- **Creativity:** A garden bursting with vibrant flowers, unique trellises, and artistic arrangements can become your living masterpiece.
- **Budget-Conscious:** Maximize space and resources with repurposed containers, vertical gardens, and other resourceful design solutions.

When your garden reflects your values, rhythms, and joys, it becomes a space that supports you just as much as you tend to it.

NATIVE AND NON-NATIVE PLANTS: A THOUGHTFUL MIX

Native plants evolved right where you live. Over thousands of years, they've adapted to your region's soil, seasons, and wildlife. Because of that, they thrive with less maintenance while naturally supporting pollinators, birds, and other vital species that keep ecosystems in balance. Including natives is a powerful way to restore habitat and give back to the place you call home.

At the same time, many beloved edibles—like tomatoes, peaches, basil, and cucumbers—aren't native but still grow beautifully in temperate gardens. These non-native fruits, vegetables, and herbs feed your body, engage your senses, and help reduce pressure on wild lands that may otherwise be cleared for agriculture.

We recommend a blend: native plants for habitat and resilience, non-native edibles for nourishment and joy. Together, they create a garden that's beautiful, bountiful, and aligned with the kind of future you want to help grow.

Not sure what's native to your area? Start with your state's native plant society, university extension service, or regional botanical gardens. They often offer beginner-friendly plant lists and guides tailored to your zip code or growing zone.

CONSIDER ACCESSIBILITY AND EASE

The goal isn't to create the "perfect" garden but to design one that fits your lifestyle, brings you happiness, and makes tending it feel like a natural extension of your daily rhythm and abilities.

- **Reduce Strain:** Use raised beds, tall pots, or vertical structures if bending and kneeling are challenging.
- **Low-Maintenance Plants:** Choose perennials and self-seeding annuals for minimal effort.
- **Inclusive Design:** Consider the needs of friends or children who may join in the gardening experience.
- **Climate Considerations:** Plan for extreme weather, such as opting for drought-tolerant plants if summer heat makes watering unpleasant.
- **Set It and Forget It:** Design a garden that can largely care for itself when life gets busy.

Color, texture, and playful design turn this garden into more than a growing space—it becomes an expression of the gardener's personality and spirit.

CREATE A GARDEN THAT FITS YOUR LIFE

Taking time to consider your unique gifts and important needs helps establish a healthy partnership between you and the land. The more you align it with who you are, the more both you and it will flourish.

Your Garden, Your Rules

You want a garden that brings joy and ease, so forget outdated rules of how a garden "should" appear. This is your space, your sanctuary, and you get to decide how it takes shape.

This bed is divided into tidy squares, which offers a clear, satisfying sense of structure.

LOVE ORDER?

If you thrive on neatness and efficiency, embrace the "square-foot gardening" method. Picture a perfectly organized grid where every plant has its designated space, maximizing productivity while keeping maintenance low. Each 1' (30.5cm) square is carefully planned—radishes and beans nestled side by side, trellised cucumbers reaching upward, and leafy greens filling the gaps—all working together in a compact, harmonious system.

This method is ideal for precision lovers who want a low-weed, high-yield garden that practically plans and runs itself. With just a glance, you'll know exactly where to plant, when to harvest, and what needs tending. No wasted space, no guesswork—a perfect blend of order and abundance.

If you prefer order, square-foot gardening might be your perfect match. With every lettuce leaf tucked neatly into place, this method creates a garden that's just as satisfying to admire as it is to harvest.

NEED IT SIMPLE?

If low maintenance and a limited budget are top priorities, embrace small and practical solutions. A compact raised bed or a few well-placed containers can bring the joy of gardening into your life without the worry of getting overwhelmed. Remember, small is beautiful, and bigger isn't always better; a well-tended 4' x 4' (1.2 x 1.2m) raised bed can produce just as much as a sprawling, neglected garden.

Think outside the traditional garden box and repurpose everyday items into thriving planting spaces. A wooden crate lined with burlap, a reclaimed recycling bin, or an old wheelbarrow with drainage holes drilled in the bottom can all become charming, functional gardens without ever digging into the ground or visiting the store.

This petite, elevated bed turns a front porch into a cheerful greeting zone, bursting with blooms that lift your spirits each time you arrive home. Simple bed, big joy.

WANT TO ESCAPE?

Maybe your garden is less about production and more about peace and presence. A sensory garden filled with fragrant herbs, soft pathways, and cozy seating can become your personal sanctuary. Imagine a quiet meditation nook nestled among lavender, anise hyssop, and mint, where you pluck fresh leaves for a soothing cup of tea while listening to birdsong and soaking in the warmth of the sun. Weave in edible delights to snack on as you unwind—a pot of strawberries, a small container of bush beans, or a tiny raised bed brimming with lettuce, Swiss chard, and kale. This is more than a garden; it's a space designed to nourish your body, calm your mind, and restore your spirit.

A bee sipping from blooms of anise hyssop is a reminder that peace lives in the present moment. A sensory garden invites you to slow down and breathe while surrounded by color, fragrance, and quiet companionship.

DRAWN TO NATURE'S MAGIC?

If you dream of a garden that feels vibrant, enchanting, and teeming with surprises, let nature's effortless design be your guide. Leave patches of lawn unmowed to invite the magic of wildflowers, the hum of pollinators, and the observation of life unfolding. Wildlife will love you for these untamed spaces, where diversity offers shelter for creatures to scamper, flutter, crawl, and hide.

Nature rarely favors straight lines, so trade rigid rows for flowing, organic curves that emulate its beauty. Try a keyhole bed where a short, central path leads to a lush, edible oasis. Consider a half-circle garden that evokes the intimacy of a woodland glade, or an herb spiral (a tiered mound of soil that twists upward like a living sculpture) bursting with fragrance and flavor. Let your paths meander and soften, where plants spill over edges and ground covers weave freely.

And when a wayward squash vine stretches across your garden without yielding much fruit, or bush beans get tangled in a sea of ground ivy, embrace it as part of the journey. Your harvest isn't just food—it's wisdom. You're learning nature's ancient rhythms, observing the quiet, wildly intelligent ways Mother Earth tends herself. Celebrate the imperfections and surprises, and you'll find yourself growing in harmony with your garden.

A pumpkin growing in the street is a reminder that neither you nor nature are meant to stay inside the lines. Let your garden sprawl, spiral, or surprise. This is your space, and it's most powerful when it reflects your authentic self.

GROW YOUR OWN WAY

No matter your style, the only rule is that it works for you. Don't let society's obsession with tidy perfection limit your creativity. Nature isn't neat, and neither is real resilience. The world needs rebels to rewild our spaces, nourish ourselves, and redefine what a garden can be. This garden is yours—make it a space that reflects your unique style and personal values.

Neat or Natural?

Expressing your values through your garden is liberating—weaving together beauty, nature, and function creates a space that's both pleasing to the eye and practical. This thoughtful balance keeps neighbors content, sparing you from dealing with complaints when you'd rather be in the garden. Balancing neatness with natural beauty allows you to express creativity while maintaining a functional, welcoming space. Combining thoughtful design and creative wild elements helps you create a garden that invites connection with nature, neighbors, and yourself. On the next page are tips to help you achieve this harmony.

DESIGNATE WILD AND ORDERLY ZONES

You'll likely want to keep the front yard a bit neater and more polished while hiding creative chaos in the backyard. Projecting a tended appearance in the front yard—structured beds of veggies and herbs, tidy mulched pathways, an abundance of colorful flowers—will help you enjoy time gardening rather than responding to inquiries and raised eyebrows. Reserve wilder experiments—unmowed pollinator havens, rambling winter squash vines, or native plant clusters—for the backyard or less-visible areas.

Framed by a strip of mowed greenery, even the exuberance of a summer prairie feels intentional. Simple edges, such as a path, border, or trellis, offer just enough structure to let your garden's wild beauty shine while signaling care and intention.

FRAME WITH PURPOSE

Even wild gardens benefit from a clean, defined frame. A mowed grass border, stone edging, or gravel pathway creates a visual boundary that says, "This space is intentional." For example:

- Use a 2'–3' (61–91.4cm) strip of mowed grass around natural wildflower patches to contain their exuberance.
- Add large stepping stones or a wide, mulched path through unruly areas for accessibility and aesthetic appeal.
- Consider trellises or arbors to frame entryways and create a sense of structure amid natural abundance.

Stiff-stemmed coneflowers and black-eyed Susans sway behind a crisp line of bullet edging. The strong "bones" created by this border add a quiet sense of order, ease, and intention.

STRONG "BONES" ADD ORDER TO WILDNESS

Clear structural elements, such as raised beds, stone borders, or permanent pathways, help ground the potential visual chaos of a productive garden. In-ground beds and mini-orchards will look more purposeful with edging or simple fencing. If plants get unruly late in the season, these "bones" still signal intention and care.

COMMUNICATE THE GARDEN'S PURPOSE WITH SIGNS

A small, thoughtful sign can transform a seemingly wild garden into a purposeful space. These signs help neighbors and visitors understand that your space isn't neglected—it's designed with intention. Examples include:

- "Pollinator-Friendly Garden"
- "Welcome to Our Garden"
- "Sharing Garden: Take What You Need"

Consider pursuing certifications like:

- Monarch Watch's "Monarch Waystation" program (www.monarchwatch.org)
- National Wildlife Federation's "Certified Wildlife Habitat®" program (www.nwf.org)
- Wild Ones' "Certified Native Habitat" program (www.wildones.org)
- Xerces Society's "Pollinator Protection Pledge" (www.xerces.org)

A simple sign, such as this "monarch waystation," turns a wilder garden into a statement of purpose. It invites curiosity, fosters understanding, and lets neighbors know your space is intentional, beneficial, and part of something bigger.

CHAPTER 06: MAXIMIZE EASE WITH LOCATION AND LAYOUT

A cluster of pots just steps from the door makes it easy to snip herbs for dinner or check in with your plants each morning. When your garden lives where you already roam, it weaves itself effortlessly into your daily life.

Design your garden so it's something you naturally want to engage with every day. Place it near areas you already frequent; use trellises or arbors to bring plants within easy reach; build narrow beds you can access without strain; and create clear, firm pathways that invite movement. Think of your garden as an extension of your daily life—not a separate destination, but a space that flows with how you already live and move.

Put Your Garden Where You Roam

"The gardener's shadow is the best fertilizer." This timeless gardening proverb reminds us that proximity and attention often outshine even the best soil amendments. Imagine your garden as a cherished companion—a source of comfort during tough times and joy during good ones. You want your garden close enough to visit often and effortlessly—like a nearby friend—rather than an out-of-the-way obligation.

When planning where to place your garden, ask yourself: How close can I get it to where I already spend time and frequently travel? A conveniently located garden naturally becomes part of your daily rhythm, inviting it to nurture you while you to nurture it.

CONVENIENCE CONSIDERATIONS

To ensure your garden fits seamlessly into your life, look for overlaps of the following elements when choosing a location:

- **Easy Access to Daily Life:** Place your garden near spots you frequently visit—like your driveway, back patio, kitchen door, or outdoor seating area. The more visible and accessible it is, the more likely you'll interact with it regularly.

This cozy, horseshoe-shaped garden sits right off the back patio—easy to water, tend, and harvest with a short stroll and a cup of coffee in hand.

- **Access to Water:** Plants thrive when watered consistently, especially those in pots or raised beds. Proximity to a water source, such as a spigot or rain barrel, makes a big difference.
- **Ample Sunlight:** At least six hours of sunlight daily is ideal for most edible plants. More sun often means more abundant yields.
- **Tool Storage Nearby:** A shed, toolbox, or even a simple bucket of essentials kept near the garden ensures you'll always have your rake, pruners, or trusty hori hori knife (see page 262) within arm's reach.

While the aim is to create a relaxing space where you can enjoy and maintain your garden effortlessly, it's okay if your chosen location doesn't meet every criterion perfectly. Proximity to your daily routine outweighs ideal conditions. A container garden in partial shade outside your door will yield more food, fragrances, and fun than a perfect sunlit plot you rarely visit.

AVOID PROBLEMATIC LOCATIONS

While convenience is key, a poorly chosen location can leave plants struggling. Here's how to spot and steer clear of potential problem areas.

- **Too Close to Trees and Shrubs:** These tall neighbors might offer shade, but their branches and roots can be tough competitors. They can block vital sunlight and lap up water and nutrients from the soil. This can leave your garden struggling to thrive, especially in-ground gardens. A good rule of thumb: Keep your garden at least as far from trees or shrubs as the reach of their outermost branches (known as the "drip line").
- **Low-Lying Areas:** Does water linger after a rainfall? If so, roots may suffocate, and soggy soil can invite rot and disease. Wooden raised beds will also degrade faster in perpetually damp conditions. To avoid these issues, aim for flat or slightly elevated ground with good drainage. If a low spot is your only option, use plastic raised beds or containers to keep plants out of the wet.
- **Contaminated Soil:** If you're growing edibles, pay close attention to soil history. For structures built before 1978, lead from old paint might exist in nearby soil, making it unsafe for growing food. Similarly, areas near old driveways or garages may harbor heavy metals or chemicals. If contamination is suspected, keep gardens at least 5' (1.5m) from potentially risky spots, or grow in containers or raised beds lined on the bottom with durable weed-barrier fabric.
- **Herbicide Drift Zones:** Herbicides sprayed on nearby lawns or fields can drift into your garden and harm your plants. To protect your garden, establish it at least 10'–15' (3–4.6m) away from treated areas, and consider adding windbreaks like a sturdy fence or a hedge to block any drifting chemicals.
- **Bare or Struggling Soil:** Look closely at the plant life already in your desired spot. If the area is mostly bare or supports only scraggly, unhealthy plants, the soil might lack the nutrients or structure that your garden needs. If this is the only area available, consult "Build Healthy Soil: Testing and Improvement" (page 143) to rehabilitate the soil before planting or consider a container garden.

If grasses or plants are already struggling, your garden likely will too. Bare or brown patches may point to compacted, nutrient-poor, or even contaminated soil. While these spots could be rehabilitated over time, you can bypass the trouble by using containers or deep raised beds.

CREATIVE LOCATION IDEAS

Here are a few potential places to integrate your garden into your daily flow.

- **Patio Planters:** Containers filled with herbs, lettuces, or cherry tomatoes on your deck or patio keep fresh ingredients within arm's reach of your kitchen while helping protect them from hungry critters.
- **Driveway Edge:** A sunny patch a few feet from the edge of your driveway is perfect for easy-to-maintain raised beds or rows of currant bushes, strawberries, or dwarf fruit trees.
- **Outdoor Sitting Area:** Surround a favorite seating area with fragrant and edible plants like chamomile, thyme, or nasturtiums.
- **Sunny Porch Steps:** If you have steps leading into your home, arrange pots of leafy greens, herbs, or strawberries along them. This setup is both charming and convenient.
- **Pathside Plantings:** Line a frequently walked path with edible and sensory plants like alpine strawberry, French sorrel, yarrow, or chives. These look beautiful and are easy to enjoy as you pass by.
- **Playscape Escape:** Integrate plants into a play area with sunflower forts, bean teepees, and pumpkin archways. Add a narrow raised bed or containers for hands-on planting with fragrant herbs and easy edibles.

While raised beds make gardening easier and keep maintenance lower, placing them far from your home can add extra steps and make daily care less inviting. The best garden is one that fits naturally into your daily rhythm—close enough to enjoy, tend, and harvest with ease.

YOUR GARDEN AS YOUR COMPANION

When you make your garden part of your daily journey, it rewards you in kind. By cultivating a connection to areas you already frequent, your garden becomes an integral part of your life—close enough to nurture and be nurtured in return. Wherever you choose, think of your garden as your companion on the path to well-being and abundance.

This back patio garden—featuring containers and an elevated bed—stays within easy reach, making it simple to tend, harvest, and enjoy in small moments throughout the day.

THE BACK-CORNER GARDEN

Have you ever wondered why gardens often end up tucked into the furthest corners of the yard? While it might seem logical to keep these "messy" plants out of sight, this often leads to a space that's also "out of mind." A distant garden requires extra effort for watering, weeding, and harvesting, which can lead to neglect. When this happens, the garden can't help you thrive, and you can't help it flourish. Over time, it can feel more like a chore than a joy, losing both its beauty and purpose.

Historically, this positioning might stem from cultural biases. In the past, home gardens were closely tied to subsistence farming, a practice associated with lower economic status. Wealthier households favored ornamental landscapes as status symbols, relegating vegetable gardens to less visible, less prestigious corners of the property. Over time, this practice became habitual, even though it often defies practical logic.

By placing your garden where it intersects with your daily routine, you ensure it stays within reach of your attention and care. A visible, vibrant garden integrates into your life, becoming a source of joy and convenience rather than a forgotten corner.

When your garden is tucked too far from daily life, it's "out of sight, out of mind," and harder to maintain. Bringing it closer makes tending easier and reconnects you with the joy it was meant to bring.

Many gardens begin far from the home. But convenience matters. Choosing a spot closer to where you walk and unwind makes it easier to maintain and enjoy.

Place Plants for Comfort

Imagine tending a garden where every plant is within easy reach—no awkward stretching or strain, just a fun flow of movement among beautiful, edible, and fragrant companions. A thoughtfully designed garden ensures planting, weeding, watering, and harvesting become enjoyable acts rather than aching tasks.

ACCESSIBLE BED WIDTH

The width of your garden beds is key to how comfortably you can reach each plant. Use these steps to find the ideal size.

Use a tape measure to test how far you can comfortably reach. This becomes your personal guideline for bed width.

1. **Consider How You'll Access the Bed:** Will you bend forward, squat, kneel, or sit? Each position affects how far you can comfortably reach.
2. **Test Your Reach:** Place a ruler or tape measure in front of you and stretch forward as far as is comfortable. If the bed is against a wall, this measurement is your maximum bed width. For beds accessible from both sides, double your reach measurement, but subtract a bit to ensure you can easily reach the center.
3. **Account for Garden Helpers:** Are kids, family members, or friends joining you? Adjust bed widths to accommodate shorter reaches or varying abilities, ensuring the garden is accessible to everyone.

In this newly established backyard garden, two pathway solutions set the stage for long-term ease: wide stepping stones offer stable access along the edge, while straw-mulched paths between in-ground beds simplify maintenance. Together, they protect soil and make caring for the garden more pleasurable.

PERMANENT PATHWAYS FOR EASY MOVEMENT

Imagine a garden where pathways are as reliable and enduring as the plants themselves—designed to reduce the effort of every task. Permanent pathways eliminate the need for seasonal re-creation, reducing maintenance and costs while enhancing flow and ease of movement. These paths never need watering or fertilizing, keep weeds at bay with the help of your footsteps, and prevent soil compaction in your planting beds. They can also be used to store mulch before spreading it into beds.

Here's how to design and establish pathways that bring lasting ease and efficiency to your garden.

A wide central path runs the length of this in-ground bed, with shorter side paths dividing the space into easily accessible 4' (1.2m) wide planting areas. Deep straw mulch suppresses weeds and provides a comfortable walking surface. Applied in early spring, the straw will be gradually moved into the beds around plants as the season unfolds.

- **Width for Comfort:** Establish paths that are wide enough to accommodate easy movement. A minimum width of 2' (61cm) is fine for foot traffic, but if you'll be using a wheelbarrow or garden cart, aim for at least 3'–4' (0.9–1.2m). This ensures hassle-free navigation while hauling soil, compost, or harvests. When in doubt, aim for wider pathways as they tend to shrink as seasons progress.
- **Eco-Friendly and Budget-Wise:** Use old cotton sheets or flattened cardboard covered with straw or woodchip mulch to quickly construct pathways that are cost-effective and environmentally friendly.
- **Accessibility for All:** While mulched paths are quick and budget-friendly to set up, paved or gravel options provide a clean, mud-free surface that stands up to wear and tear. These options can be smoother and more even, making them safer and more accessible for kids, older adults, and anyone with mobility challenges.

PRIORITIZE PLANT PLACEMENT

Each plant has different needs, and you'll visit them with varying frequency.

- **Frequent Visits Go Up Front:** Make daily-use plants—such as lettuce, basil, or mint—easiest to access by placing them at the front of beds, by pathways, or in accessible containers.
- **Weekly Visitors Are in the Middle:** Plants harvested once or twice a week—such as peppers, beans, or kale—can sit slightly farther back in the bed.
- **Infrequent Visitors Live in Back:** Low-maintenance or infrequently harvested plants—such as winter squash, potatoes, or flowers for bouquets—can be placed in the middle or back of beds or can live in beds farther from main circulation areas.

This arrangement ensures every plant is as close as it needs to be, making your garden efficient and enjoyable.

Placing a potted plant on a tall stand is a simple way to bring your garden within easy reach.

ELEVATE FOR COMFORT

Elevating plants to reduce bending and stretching creates a more comfortable gardening experience.

- **Raised Beds:** Bring plants closer to your natural reach and reduce strain on your back and knees. Check out "Basic Raised Bed" (page 76) for practical ideas.
- **Vertical Growing:** Use trellises and arbors for vining plants like peas, pole beans, and cucumbers. This saves space and keeps plants easy to reach. Refer to "Layer to Maximize Growth" (page 60) for more techniques.
- **Elevated Containers:** Raise pots off the ground by placing them on tables, stands, retaining walls, or stairs. Hanging planters might also be an option. For additional ideas and inspiration, check out "Compact Container Garden" (page 70).

An elevated bed paired with a nearby chair makes gardening more comfortable and invites you to linger with your plants.

ADDITIONAL ACCESSIBILITY TIPS

Make gardening more comfortable with these thoughtful touches.

- **Seating Options:** Bring a kneeling pad or portable chair into the garden, or place a cozy bench near areas you visit most. Prioritizing rest and comfort encourages you to pause, unwind, and fully appreciate the beauty you've nurtured.
- **Ergonomic Tools:** Invest in tools with padded grips, adjustable handles, or long reaches to reduce strain on your hands, back, and wrists.

A lightweight garden chair makes it easier to tend, rest, and linger a little longer. Portable seating invites you to slow down and savor the garden you've lovingly grown.

YOUR COMFORTABLE SANCTUARY

A well-planned garden becomes a personal haven—an accessible space where you can easily care for plants that nourish your senses, provide beauty, and yield delicious harvests. By arranging plants thoughtfully and prioritizing comfort, you can transform a space into a source of joy and relaxation.

Layer to Maximize Growth

When space is limited but the desire for a high-yield garden is strong, layering techniques provide a way to maximize productivity while increasing beauty, ease, and plant health. Just like a natural forest grows in multiple layers—trees, shrubs, vines, herbs, and ground covers—you can design your garden to make the most of sunlight and soil nutrients through vertical spacing.

VERTICAL GROWTH BENEFITS

Growing upward with trellises, stacked containers, and hanging baskets enables you to harvest more while using less ground space. Cucumbers, peas, pole beans, winter squash, and other climbers thrive when given vertical support. Benefits include:

- **Better Airflow:** Reduced risk of fungal diseases.
- **Fewer Pests:** Reduced access to slugs, insects, and soil-borne diseases.
- **Sunlight Exposure:** Increased growth and fruit production.
- **Less Ground Space:** More room for lower-growing crops.
- **Simpler Harvesting:** Easier to see when crops are ripe and less bending to pick the abundance.

TRELLISES: SIMPLE VERTICAL SUPPORT

Trellises are the easiest way to elevate plants. A wide variety are available for purchase, or they can be easily built from common materials.

- **Traditional Flat:** A versatile choice for all vining plants, vertical flat trellises can be built from lightweight wood or bamboo for peas and pole beans or sturdier metal cattle panels to support cucumbers and heavy winter squash.
- **Teepee:** Made from bamboo or poles tied at the top, teepee trellises are perfect for pole beans and peas. Kids also love the "secret garden" feel of a large, empty space in the center that is covered in greenery.
- **A-Frame:** A triangular structure that supports heavy climbers like winter squash while providing space underneath for shade-loving plants like lettuce or cilantro.
- **Tomato Cage:** Insert a wire tomato cage in a container or bed, then encourage short vining plants to grow up it.

A sturdy cattle panel trellis stands in this spring garden, ready to elevate vining plants and support the weight of abundant harvests.

This bent cattle panel in the Iowa City Edible Classroom creates a tunnel-like arch, providing sturdy support for climbing squash and pumpkins while adding a playful, functional feature to the garden.

BUILDING A TEEPEE TRELLIS

Building a teepee trellis from cedar wooden posts is a simple and sturdy method for supporting vining plants. This design draws inspiration from a wilderness-lashing technique that uses cord to securely bind posts together.

MATERIALS & TOOLS

- **3 Cedar or Bamboo Posts:** 5'–8' (1.5–2.4m) long, sturdy, and straight.
- **Natural Jute or Sisal Twine:** Approximately 3'–4' (0.9–1.2m) for tying the posts together and an additional 6'–8' (1.8–2.4m) (or more, depending on the height and spacing) for wrapping the tiers.
- **Scissors or Knife.**

INSTRUCTIONS

1

Lay Out the Posts: Place the three posts flat on the ground, parallel to each other. Align them at one end so the tops are even.

2

Start Tying the Cord: Tie the twine securely around one post, about 6"–10" (15.2–25.4cm) from the top. Ensure the knot is tight so the cord won't slip.

3

Begin the First Weave: Lightly weave the twine over and under the other two posts in a figure eight pattern.

4

Weave Back to the Starting Post: Continue the figure eight pattern by weaving the twine back toward the first post. Pull it snug to secure the posts.

5

Add Stability by Reinforcing the Weave: Repeat the figure eight weaving pattern three to five more times, going back and forth and moving upward along the posts. Tighten the twine with each pass to bundle the posts firmly together.

6

Begin the Wrap: After weaving, bring the twine through the middle of the posts. Make sure the posts remain aligned at the top.

7

Wrap Between Posts: Tightly wrap the twine three to four times around the center of the weave between two of the posts. This locks the posts together.

8

Finish the Wrap: Move the cord between the other posts and secure everything by repeating the tight-wrapping process.

TIPS FOR LONGEVITY AND STABILITY

For added stability, consider using a fourth post in your teepee design, spacing it evenly with the others.

While the trellis can be left in place over the winter, keep in mind that natural twine, such as jute or sisal, will likely degrade due to weather exposure. To save time during the next growing season, you can fold up the structure and store it in a shed or garage, protecting it from the elements. However, even with careful storage, the cord may only last one additional season before needing replacement.

9

Tie Off: Complete the process by tying a secure knot on the starting post. Trim any excess twine.

10

Set Up the Teepee Shape: Stand the bundled posts upright. Gently spread the legs outward to form a balanced teepee shape, ensuring even spacing between the posts. Push or gently pound the bottom ends 4"–8" (10.2–20.3cm) into the soil for stability. Adjust as needed to keep the structure symmetrical.

11

Start the Base Wrap: Tie twine securely to one post about 1" (2.5cm) above the soil. Pull the twine across to the next post, keeping it 1" (2.5cm) from the ground, and wrap it around the post once.

12

Complete the Lower Wraps: Continue wrapping the twine around the third post at the same height. Return to the first post, wrapping it 4"–5" (10.2–12.7cm) above the initial base layer. This lower section ensures that plant tendrils can easily reach the twine without your guidance.

13

Wrap Up the Teepee: Spiral the twine upward around the posts, leaving 6"–10" (15.2–25.4cm) of vertical space between each wrap.

14

Secure the Top and Finish: When you reach the top of the trellis, tie the twine securely to one of the posts. Cut off any excess twine.

ARBORS: FUNCTIONAL AND BEAUTIFUL

Arbors add structure and charm while serving as an inviting entryway to your garden. They create shady tunnels of greenery that enhance both aesthetics and productivity.

- **Store-Bought:** Available in decorative metal or wood designs, store-bought arbors provide instant structure. They may need secure anchoring to prevent tipping once covered in lush vines.
- **DIY Tunnel:** Arch a sturdy cattle panel between two beds and anchor it with posts. Vining crops like grapes, cucumbers, pole beans, or winter squash form a beautiful, edible tunnel.
- **Kid-Friendly:** Turn an arbor into a playful garden hideaway with runner beans, Wee-B-Little pumpkins, or winter squash, creating a magical, interactive space for children.

LAYERED PLANTS

Maximize space, soil, and sunlight by thoughtfully combining plants of different heights and growth habits.

- **Tall Plants as Trellises:** Sturdy sunflowers can serve as living supports for pole beans. To prevent vines from overwhelming them, wait until sunflowers reach 12"–18" (30.5–45.7cm) before planting climbers at their base. Early on, vines may need gentle guidance up the stalks.
- **Intercropping:** Pairing deep- and shallow-rooted plants optimizes soil use and minimizes competition. Beets thrive near lettuce, and radishes grow well alongside beans without interfering with their roots.
- **Shading Techniques:** In hot climates, position taller plants like tomatoes so they cast dappled shade on heat-sensitive greens, such as lettuce and cilantro, helping them stay productive longer into the season.

A custom cedar arbor at the Iowa City Edible Classroom supports climbing cherry tomatoes while serving as a stunning structural element. Premade arbors, available in wood or metal, offer an easy way to bring beauty, shade, and vertical growing space into your garden.

LAYERED CONTAINERS

By stacking, hanging, and mounting planters, you can turn just about any space into a lush, beautiful garden.

- **Tiered Containers:** Arrange pots on tables, boxes, stands, shelves, retaining walls, or stairs to create a multilevel growing system. Place shorter plants like basil, cilantro, and strawberries in small containers in the front, with taller crops like tomatoes in larger containers behind them to ensure each one gets adequate sunlight.
- **Hanging Baskets:** Make the most of overhead space by growing plants in hanging baskets. Because these containers dry out quickly, drought-tolerant options like chamomile, cosmos, thyme, and oregano are ideal. However, if you're able to water daily, consider strawberries, cherry tomatoes, or cascading nasturtiums for a vibrant, tasty display.
- **Wall Planters:** Maximize vertical surfaces by mounting shelves, pots, or repurposed gutters to grow small herbs, salad greens, or strawberries. Like hanging baskets, these planters have limited soil volume and will require frequent watering, especially in hot weather.

Herbs in a vertical wooden planter are an efficient and space-saving solution that brings tasty greenery to eye level. These types of containers dry out quickly, so keep an eye on moisture, especially during hot or windy days.

This tiered bed with a back trellis makes the most of limited space by growing in layers. Tall climbers can reach for the sun while lower plants thrive beneath, creating a compact, accessible setup.

LAYERS OF AN EDIBLE FOREST GARDEN

A thriving, self-sustaining garden emulates nature's efficient layering system, maximizing sunlight, soil nutrients, and water retention. Edible forest gardening, which aligns with the "High-Yield Mini-Orchard" design (page 94), provides a structured way to stack plants vertically, creating a productive and low-maintenance food system.

1. **Canopy:** Dwarf fruit trees and serviceberries form the uppermost layer, offering shade, wind protection, and a steady fruit harvest.
2. **Vine:** Vertical growers like grapes can be trained onto trellises and arbors at the orchard's edge. (Avoid establishing grapes on fruit trees, as they can quickly overwhelm and reduce fruit production.)
3. **Understory:** Shrubs—such as gooseberry, currant, and raspberry—thrive in the dappled light beneath the trees, producing berries while providing wildlife habitat.
4. **Herbaceous:** A mix of edible and beneficial perennials—including rhubarb, yarrow, French sorrel, and Egyptian walking onion—fills the lower level, adding diversity and deterring pests.
5. **Ground Cover:** Low-growing plants—such as wild strawberry, self-heal, Dutch white clover, and creeping thyme—spread across the soil, suppressing weeds, retaining moisture, and improving soil health.
6. **Root:** Before the orchard matures and tree roots dominate, underground crops like beet, radish, and garlic utilize available space efficiently, providing food while aerating the soil.

This mature edible forest at the Iowa City Edible Classroom showcases its layered design—from the sweet cherry tree and climbing grapevine above, to red currant shrubs, rhubarb, mint, and blooming bulbs below. Together, these layers transform a compact urban space into a vibrant, multilevel garden inspired by nature.

A repurposed recycling bin, perched on a sunny retaining wall, becomes a simple raised planter, bringing fresh basil up to an easy-to-reach height that encourages daily harvests.

CHAPTER 07: SIMPLE, LOW-MAINTENANCE GARDEN SPACES

Starting your garden is about finding the right option for your unique budget, time, goals, and interests. The key is to choose something that resonates with you.

Common Problems	Garden Spaces That Can Help
Limited Space	**Compact Container Garden:** Transform any small space into a thriving garden with just a few containers.
Time Constraints	**Wild Edibles:** You may already have plants thriving in your yard or a natural area that you can begin harvesting with no cultivation effort. **Compact Container Garden:** With just a few pots and your favorite herbs, you can tend to your garden without it feeling like a time-consuming task. Adjust the number of containers as needed through the seasons.
Budget Constraints	**Compact Container Garden:** Use containers you already have or find free ones. Seedlings and seeds can often be found for free or at low prices. **Compost for Free Fertilizer:** Turn your kitchen scraps into rich, free fertilizer for containers or garden beds.
Physical Limitations	**Compact Container Garden:** Placing the right container in the right location can eliminate most bending and kneeling. **Basic Raised Bed:** A raised bed makes tending your plants easier on your back and joints.
Inexperienced with Gardening	**Wild Edibles:** Let thriving edibles in your yard or a public natural area teach you the basics of food cultivation before committing to a dedicated garden bed. **Compact Container Garden:** Planting in pots is a great way to learn the basics of gardening on a small scale. **Relaxing Sensory Garden:** Dive into gardening without the pressure of large food yields by creating a sensory space that allows you to choose from a wide variety of plants.
Harsh Climate Conditions	**Nutrient-Dense In-Ground Garden:** One focus of an in-ground bed is building healthy soil to buffer plants from drought and other extreme weather. **High-Yield Mini-Orchard:** Once established, the hardy, perennial plants of an orchard can endure conditions that cause annual plants to struggle.
Soil Issues	**Compact Container Garden:** Avoid soil challenges altogether by using a potting mix in containers. **Basic Raised Bed:** Elevate your garden with a raised bed of fertile, loose soil mix that sits atop poor soil. **Compost for Free Fertilizer:** Create a compost pile on the future site of a garden bed to improve the soil structure, moisture retention, and nutrient content.
Sunlight Issues	**Compact Container Garden:** Select small pots and move them to follow the sun throughout the growing season. **High-Yield Mini-Orchard:** Use strategic plant selection and placement to work with limited sunlight.
Water Conservation	**Nutrient-Dense In-Ground Garden:** In-ground gardens are naturally more water-efficient than containers or raised beds. **High-Yield Mini-Orchard**: Once established, your orchard's deep, expansive roots will naturally tap into groundwater.
Pest Management	**Basic Raised Bed:** A raised bed is easier to protect from curious critters and hungry insects due to its elevation and help from fencing, row covers, or netting. **High-Yield Mini-Orchard:** A diverse mix of durable perennial plants and beneficial insects helps create a resilient ecosystem that naturally reduces pest problems.

Compact Container Garden

A container garden is a space-saving invitation to grow beauty and nourishment within arm's reach. Whether you're working with a small patio, a balcony, or simply looking for an easier way to tend plants, container gardening brings nature closer.

WHY CHOOSE CONTAINER GARDENS?

Container gardens meet you where you are, adapting to your space, schedule, and needs. They provide an accessible way to grow food and flowers without the commitment of a full in-ground garden. They are perfect for beginners wanting to dip their toes into gardening, busy individuals seeking a manageable way to grow fresh produce, or those who need a garden that adjusts to their mobility.

- **Garden Anywhere:** Even the smallest spaces can support a thriving garden. Whether you have a balcony, a small patio, or just a sunny doorstep, container gardens make it possible to grow fresh food, herbs, and flowers wherever you live. Watering, pruning, and harvesting become a ritual that offers a moment of calm.
- **Convenience:** Placing containers near your kitchen means harvesting basil, cilantro, or Swiss chard is as easy as stepping outside. The proximity also makes it simpler to care for your plants and enjoy their growth.
- **Accessible and Low Maintenance:** Elevated and tall containers reduce the need for bending or kneeling, making them a flexible choice for those with mobility concerns. Containers also have fewer weeds, are easier to protect from hungry pests, and can be moved for better light, temperature, or aesthetics.

POTENTIAL CHALLENGES

While container gardens are adaptable and rewarding, they do come with a few unique considerations.

- **Watering Needs:** Because containers hold less soil, they dry out faster than in-ground gardens, especially in warm weather. To keep your plants thriving, position containers near a water source, use self-watering containers, add a layer of mulch to slow evaporation, and check moisture levels daily.
- **Heat Management:** Unlike garden beds, container soil heats up quickly, which can stress plant roots. To help plants stay comfortable, use light-colored pots to reflect heat, cluster pots together to create a cooler microclimate, and grow heat-tolerant plants like tomatoes, broadleaf sage, thyme, and oregano.
- **Nutrient Replenishment:** With a limited amount of soil, plants in containers use up nutrients quickly. To keep your plants healthy and productive, add organic compost or fertilizer in spring, refresh the soil yearly to replenish nutrients, and avoid overcrowding.

With tall containers in back and smaller pots up front, this vibrant lineup of herbs, greens, and flowers shows just how much beauty and abundance can fit into a small space.

Containers dry out quickly—especially in warm weather—so they'll need to be watered often to keep your plants thriving.

CHOOSING CONTAINERS

The foundation of your container garden is, of course, the containers. You don't need to spend a fortune—almost anything can become a planter as long as it holds enough soil, allows water to drain, and fits the needs of your plants. Here are some general considerations to keep in mind:

- **Size:** Larger containers allow for more root growth, better moisture retention, and less-frequent watering. If space is a concern, consider stacking containers, hanging pots, or using rectangular planters to maximize growing room.
- **Budget-Friendly Options:** If cost is a factor, you can often acquire 2–5 gallon (7.5–19L), food-grade plastic buckets for free from grocery stores, bakeries, or restaurants. They may not be the most aesthetically pleasing, but a coat of paint or some creative placement can help them blend into your space. Just be sure to drill drainage holes in the bottom before planting. Old tubs, milk jugs, and wooden crates can also be repurposed for a rustic or whimsical touch.
- **Drainage is Key:** Waterlogged roots are a fast track to plant failure. Always check for drainage holes—if a container doesn't have them, ensure you can drill or punch holes yourself. For larger planters, consider raising them on small bricks, a stepping stone paver, or a wheeled stand to ensure the weight of the container does not restrict drainage.
- **Material Choices:** Each container material has its own advantages and challenges. Consider durability, weight, moisture retention, and aesthetics to find the best fit for your space and climate.
    - **Plastic and Fiberglass:** Lightweight and durable, making them easy to move and less likely to break in freezing temperatures.
    - **Composite or Resin:** A modern, lightweight option that often emulates the look of natural materials while being resistant to cracking in freezing weather.
    - **Terracotta and Unglazed Clay:** Classic and affordable, but dries out quickly, requiring frequent watering.
    - **Glazed Ceramic:** Beautiful but heavy; best for more permanent placements.

Here are some specific container options to consider for your space:

- **Self-Watering Containers:** If you have a busy schedule or don't want to water daily, self-watering containers are a game-changer. These include a built-in reservoir that gradually hydrates your plants from below, providing consistent moisture and reducing stress on thirsty vegetables like tomatoes, cucumbers, and Swiss chard. On the other hand, many herbs tend to tolerate drying out between waterings, so they may not require this feature.
- **Elevated Beds:** Think of these as oversized containers lifted to a comfortable working height, perfect if you'd rather not bend or kneel. They offer ample space for growing a variety of crops while keeping your garden tidy and accessible. Some models even include built-in water reservoirs, combining the benefits of self-watering containers with the convenience of raised gardening.
- **Rolling Containers:** Placing pots on a wheeled caddy or dolly makes it easy to move them to follow the sun, protect them from harsh weather, or adjust for space.
- **Hanging Pots and Vertical Planters:** Short on space? Hanging baskets or wall-mounted containers are perfect for growing cascading plants like strawberries, nasturtiums, and oregano. These dry out very quickly, so position them near a convenient water source.

With a pepper seedling nestled beside cilantro and marjoram, this repurposed 5 gallon (19L) bucket proves that functional gardens don't require fancy containers. Upcycled planters like this offer a practical, creative start to your container garden—just add drainage and a little love.

If a large container will sit on soil, place a paver or bricks underneath to prevent its weight from restricting drainage.

Plant	Minimum Container Size	Number of Plants per Container
Basil	1 gallon (3.75L)	1–2 plants
Beans	2 gallon (7.5L)	2–3 plants
Bee Balm	2 gallon (7.5L)	1 plant
Beet	2 gallon (7.5L)	Thin to 2"–3" (5.1–7.6cm) apart.
Butterfly Weed	2 gallon (7.5L)	1 plant
Chamomile	1 gallon (3.75L)	1 plant
Chives	1 gallon (3.75L)	5–6 clumps
Cilantro	1 gallon (3.75L)	4–5 plants
Collard Greens	2 gallon (7.5L)	1 plant
Cucumber	2 gallon (7.5L)	2 plants
Dill	1 gallon (3.75L)	2–3 plants
Garlic	2 gallon (7.5L)	5–6 bulbs
Kale	2 gallon (7.5L)	1 plant
Lettuce	1 gallon (3.75L)	4–6 plants
Mint	1 gallon (3.75L)	1 plant
Nasturtium	1 gallon (3.75L)	1 plant
Onion, Egyptian Walking	1 gallon (3.75L)	5–6 bulbs
Oregano	1 gallon (3.75L)	1 plant
Parsley	1 gallon (3.75L)	1 plant
Peas	2 gallon (7.5L)	2–3 plants
Potato	5 gallon (19L)	1 plant
Radish	1 gallon (3.75L)	Thin to 1"–2" (2.5–5.1cm) apart.
Sage, Broadleaf	1 gallon (3.75L)	1 plant
Spinach	1 gallon (3.75L)	Thin to 3" (7.6cm) apart.
Strawberry	1 gallon (3.75L)	1 plant
Sunflower (Dwarf)	2 gallon (7.5L)	1 plant
Sweet Potato, Ornamental	5 gallon (19L)	1 plant
Swiss Chard	1 gallon (3.75L)	1 plant
Tatsoi	1 gallon (3.75L)	4–5 plants
Thyme	1 gallon (3.75L)	1 plant
Tomato	5 gallon (19L)	1 plant
Violet	1 gallon (3.75L)	1 plant
Yarrow	2 gallon (7.5L)	1 plant

Elevated beds are like oversized containers raised to a comfortable height. This one features a built-in reservoir for easier, more consistent watering.

A wheeled caddy or dolly makes it easy to move heavy pots to chase the sun, shield plants from harsh weather, or simply rearrange your space.

MATCH PLANTS WITH POTS

When it comes to container gardening, bigger is almost always better. The sizes listed in the table on the opposite page are minimums—going up a size (or two) will give your plants more room to stretch their roots, retain moisture longer, and reduce the need for frequent watering. For plants with taproots, such as beets and radishes, a deep pot is especially important, as shallow containers can lead to stunted growth.

Look for dwarf or compact versions of your favorite plants. Many tomatoes, cucumbers, and other plants come in smaller, container-friendly sizes that thrive in limited space while still producing abundant harvests.

STEP-BY-STEP DESIGN

Setting up a container garden might seem as simple as picking out pots and filling them with soil, but a little thoughtful planning will help you create a space that thrives with ease. Without planning, challenges like overcrowding, mismatched plant needs, or inconvenient placement can quickly turn excitement into frustration. By designing with intention, you'll create a garden that provides nourishment, beauty, and a sense of calm—a space that cares for you as much as you care for it.

1. **Choose the Perfect Spot:** The first step is selecting a location that works for both you and your plants. Consider where you spend time naturally—a kitchen-adjacent patio, a quiet balcony, or a backyard corner that could become a retreat. Think about sun exposure and protection from harsh winds. Sun-loving plants like tomatoes, radishes, and chamomile will need a bright spot, while shade-tolerant options like mint or violets will thrive with less direct sunlight. Keep containers near a water source to make watering easy.
2. **Discover and Dream:** Small spaces can deliver big joy. What role will your container garden play in your daily life? Will it be a flavorful extension of your kitchen, bursting with basil and cherry tomatoes? A peaceful nook with soft textures and calming scents like lavender and thyme? Or a vibrant welcome for bees and butterflies with nasturtiums and calendula? Jot down a few plants that spark excitement or bring you comfort, then explore "Your Plant Matchmaking Guide" (page 180) to choose varieties that thrive in containers and in your particular conditions. When your garden reflects what you love, tending it becomes a delight, not a chore.
3. **Arrange Your Containers:** Set up your containers in a way that makes watering, harvesting, and daily maintenance simple. Grouping plants with similar sun and water needs streamlines care. Clustering pots in odd-numbered groupings creates a lush, natural feel; vary the height of containers for added visual interest, and think about how your arrangement will look from inside your home. If you'd like, sketch a rough layout or use empty pots to test different setups.

Before filling containers with soil mix, arrange them while they're still empty—this lets you easily experiment with the layout to find the perfect fit for you and your space.

4. **Plan Plant Placement:** With your containers roughly in place, begin thinking about where each plant will be located. Place herbs like oregano and chives within easy reach for a quick snip while cooking. Tuck fragrant flowers near seating areas so you can enjoy their scent, and use trellises for climbers like peas or cucumbers, making sure they don't shade neighbors too much. To help visualize your design, place seed packets, notes, or seedlings in the pots. As you place plants, you'll likely adjust your container layout.
5. **Live with Your Layout:** Once you've arranged your containers, take a few days to observe how the space feels. Does the sun hit plants as expected? Is watering convenient? Do you find yourself naturally drawn to spend time there? Adjust as needed before planting to ensure the setup works both for your plants and for your daily rhythm.

STEP-BY-STEP ESTABLISHMENT

MATERIALS

- **Containers.**
- **Container Mix:** Lightweight, well-draining mix designed for containers.
- **Compost.**
- **Fertilizer.**
- **Straw Mulch.**
- **Tongue Depressors and Permanent Marker:** Label plants and seeds.
- **Seeds and Seedlings.**

See "Materials Planning" (page 265) for details about quantities.

ESSENTIAL TOOLS

- **Trowel or Hori Hori Knife:** Digging and transplanting.
- **Utility Knife:** Open bags of soil mix.
- **Pruning Snips or Scissors:** Pruning, harvesting, deadheading.
- **Watering Can or Hose:** Keep plants hydrated. If using a hose, consider a gentle spray attachment to avoid disturbing soil.

OPTIONAL TOOLS

- **Garden Gloves:** Protect your hands.
- **Hand Rake:** Smooth soil and incorporate compost.
- **Soil Moisture Meter:** Monitor water levels to prevent under- or overwatering.
- **Wheeled Plant Dolly:** Reposition large containers to follow the sun or move them to a protected location during winter.

See "Garden Toolbox" (page 262) for details about each tool.

Before adding soil to large containers, be sure they're in their final spot. Once filled, they're heavy and hard to move.

Seedlings sit atop freshly filled containers, ready to settle into their new homes. Don't forget to label your new leafy companions.

Freshly planted and full of promise, these patio containers are more than functional—they're the beginning of a daily ritual. As your plants grow, so will your connection to this little oasis.

Strawberries, mint, parsley, basil, and Swiss chard burst from their containers in a vibrant celebration of summer abundance. A compact container garden like this transforms any patio or balcony into a lush, nourishing retreat, woven effortlessly into the flow of your life.

Establishing your container garden is an exciting process that transforms your vision into a lush and productive space. Follow these steps to set up your containers for success.

1. **Acquire Your Containers:** Choose containers that match your needs and budget.
2. **Prepare for Drainage:** Good drainage is crucial to prevent root rot. If your chosen container doesn't have holes, drill several in the bottom. To improve drainage and stability, place a layer of clay balls, broken pottery, or small stones at the bottom before adding soil.
3. **Purchase the Right Soil Mix:** Use a high-quality container mix, not garden soil, which compacts too easily. If the mix doesn't already have nutrients in it, mix in compost or a slow-release organic fertilizer to provide long-lasting nourishment.
4. **Finalize Placement Before Filling:** Large containers are difficult to move once filled, so double-check your layout and sunlight conditions before adding soil, or set them on a wheeled caddy for easy repositioning.
5. **Fill the Containers:** Fill each container with container mix, leaving about 1" (2.5cm) below the rim to prevent overflow when watering. If handling heavy bags is difficult, place the bag inside the container, cut it open, and distribute the soil from there.
6. **Water and Settle the Soil:** Before planting, give the soil a thorough watering to settle it and eliminate air pockets. This ensures roots will make immediate, healthy contact with the soil.

7. **Plant with Care:** Now for the fun part! Transplant seedlings or sow seeds according to spacing recommendations—see "Plant a Plant" (page 160) and "Sow a Seed" (page 154) for tips. The loose, rich soil makes planting easy and encourages quick root establishment. Poke in markers or labels to identify plants.
8. **Water Consistently:** Container plants rely on regular, deep watering since their soil dries out faster than garden beds. Check moisture daily—especially in hot weather—by inserting a finger 1" (2.5cm) into the soil. If it's dry at that depth, water until it drains from the bottom.
9. **Add Mulch:** Add a thin layer of straw or shredded bark to reduce evaporation and moderate soil temperature. This helps cut down watering frequency and keeps roots cool. Avoid mulching directly over newly sown seeds—wait until they sprout and are growing well before adding mulch around them.
10. **Enjoy the Journey:** Your container garden is more than just a collection of plants; it's a daily retreat, a living part of your space that invites you to slow down. Visit often, whether to harvest a sprig of oregano, admire nasturtiums tumbling over edges, or simply breathe in the scent of chamomile on a warm day. With each small act of care—watering, pruning, or just pausing to appreciate its beauty—your garden will care for you in return.

Basic Raised Bed

Raised beds combine aesthetic charm with practicality and can significantly reduce the effort needed to maintain a thriving garden. In this section, we'll guide you step-by-step to create your own small, budget-friendly raised garden bed.

Overflowing with Swiss chard, potatoes, lettuce, and herbs, this raised bed is both beautiful and bountiful. With a bit of planning, raised beds offer a simple, low-maintenance way to grow a vibrant garden.

WHY CHOOSE RAISED BEDS?

Raised beds offer numerous benefits that make gardening more accessible, efficient, and enjoyable.

- **Healthier Soil:** You can craft the ideal soil blend for your plants, free from the limitations of poor ground soil. This is especially beneficial in areas with rocky or compacted soil.
- **Improved Drainage:** The elevated design ensures water flows freely, reducing risks of waterlogging and root rot.
- **Easier on Your Body:** Raised beds reduce bending and kneeling, which makes planting, weeding, and harvesting more comfortable, especially for those with mobility concerns.
- **Natural Pest Defense:** A raised bed structure can naturally help deter some ground pests, such as slugs and snails. The edges can be more easily surrounded with a low fence or covered with lightweight netting or fabric to protect plants from animals and insects.
- **Fewer Weeds:** The raised edges create a natural barrier against encroaching weeds.
- **Extended Growing Season:** Raised beds warm up faster in spring, extending their enjoyment and yields.
- **Aesthetic Appeal:** Beyond functionality, raised beds provide structure and style, transforming your yard into an organized and inviting space.

This custom raised bed features simple hoops that support netting to protect plants from hungry insects and curious critters.

With better drainage, enriched soil, and comfortable access, raised beds offer a practical and attractive way to grow food, such as these freshly planted strawberries settling into their new home.

Raised beds bring planting, weeding, and harvesting within easy reach, reducing the need to bend or kneel—an ideal solution for gardeners who prefer or require accessible, comfortable gardening spaces.

POTENTIAL CHALLENGES

Like all garden features, raised beds come with a few considerations:

- **Initial Setup Effort:** Building or assembling a raised bed, and filling it with soil mix, requires time and energy. But with the right plan, this can be an enjoyable weekend project.
- **Upfront Costs:** Raised beds often require an investment in materials and soil mix.
- **Watering Needs:** Raised beds dry out more quickly than in-ground soil, meaning plants need more frequent watering, especially in warm weather.
- **Root Depth:** For crops with deep roots, be sure to plan for adequate soil depth or place your bed over enriched ground.
- **Maintenance Over Time:** Wooden raised beds deteriorate over time and will eventually require replacement or repair.
- **Nutrient Replenishment:** Unlike in-ground beds that often have much more soil life, additional organic compost or fertilizers will need to be added annually to keep plants thriving. See "Compost for Free Fertilizer" (page 125) for ideas.

Topped with straw and ready for spring planting, this cedar elevated bed offers a rabbit-proof, easily accessible growing space, ideal for tending plants without bending or kneeling. The trade-off for that convenience, however, is frequent watering, especially as temperatures rise.

Filling large raised beds with bulk compost takes effort upfront, especially before topping them off with container mix. But that layered investment sets the stage for healthier plants, easier care, and abundant harvests.

This old raised bed, built from thick pine lumber, shows how sturdy materials and thoughtful repairs can extend a bed's life. Corner brackets reinforce the corners, and posts support the sides, helping the structure remain stable over time. As expected, the lowest boards are beginning to rot; additional repairs, or full replacement, will eventually be needed.

CHOOSING RAISED BED KITS

We recommend purchasing a raised bed kit. Kits are a convenient, beautiful, and cost-effective option that will get you gardening sooner than building a bed from scratch. With an array of sizes, shapes, and designs available online or locally, these kits are easy to assemble with just a few basic tools.

If you enjoy woodworking, however, building your own raised bed can be a fun and creative process. Sourcing the lumber, measuring, cutting, and assembling a bed allows you to fully customize the dimensions to suit your space. Whether you buy or build, the key is creating a raised bed that suits your needs and makes gardening a joy.

OUR TOP MATERIAL PICK: CEDAR

Cedar is an excellent choice for raised beds. Naturally rot-resistant and visually appealing, it's also resistant to insects and fungal damage without the need for chemical treatments. A cedar bed will typically last 10–15 years, making it a solid investment for long-term gardening. Additionally:

- **Eco-Friendly:** Cedar is a renewable resource that is often harvested sustainably.
- **Aromatic:** Its natural oils give off a pleasant scent while repelling some pests.
- **Beautiful:** Cedar weathers gracefully, developing a silvery patina over time.

These two cedar raised beds—one 4' x 8' (1.2 x 2.4m), the other 2' x 8' (0.6 x 2.4m)—provide flexibility to suit different gardeners. Narrow beds are ideal for kids or anyone with a shorter reach, while wider beds offer more growing space for those who can easily tend from both sides.

These custom raised beds are laid out with generous room between them, creating a defined, accessible garden space that's simple and lower maintenance.

OTHER MATERIAL CHOICES

- **Pine Lumber:** Pine is a more affordable alternative to cedar, making it a popular choice for gardeners on a budget. However, it is significantly less durable, lasting only three to five years in most climates before succumbing to rot. If you choose pine, consider applying a nontoxic wood preservative to extend its lifespan. For those who don't mind replacing their beds sooner, pine can still serve as a functional and cost-effective option.
- **Logs:** Logs can be a rustic and eco-friendly choice for raised beds, especially if you have access to fallen trees and the tools to cut them to size. While this option is free and visually striking, logs naturally decompose over time and may need replacement every few years.
- **Corrugated Metal:** Corrugated metal is an appealing option for its durability and sleek, modern look. However, it can heat up quickly in the sun, which may harm soil organisms and plants while increasing watering needs. Newer galvanized metal is safe for gardening. **Caution:** If you're using reclaimed or older sheets, ensure they don't have harmful coatings that could leach into the soil. Adding an interior liner of heavy landscaping fabric can help insulate the metal and protect the soil.

This corrugated metal raised bed creates a striking, modern welcome at the front door. Durable and stylish, metal beds are a great choice, though they may heat up quickly in full sun.

This small raised bed, built from cinder blocks and topped with bricks for added charm, offers a durable and long-lasting alternative to wood.

- **Concrete Blocks:** Concrete blocks, or cinder blocks, are highly durable and widely available. They create a sturdy raised bed that does not rot while adding a clean, geometric look to your garden. Blocks can retain heat, which may benefit plants in cooler climates but could overheat soil in hot regions. **Caution:** Be wary with older cinder blocks, as some may contain coal ash, which can leach heavy metals into the soil.
- **Bricks or Stones:** Bricks and stones create a beautiful raised bed that requires almost no maintenance. They are ideal for gardeners looking to add a permanent and aesthetic feature to their space. While installation can be labor-intensive, the result is a long-lasting structure. Stone can be expensive to source, but its beauty and longevity might justify the investment.
- **Recycled Plastic Lumber:** Made from postconsumer recycled materials, plastic lumber offers a rotproof and long-lasting solution for raised beds. While it eliminates decay concerns, it is more expensive than wood and may lack the natural charm of traditional materials. Extreme temperatures can also cause some plastic lumber to warp over time, so ensure the material is rated for long-term outdoor use.
- **Treated Lumber:** Pressure-treated lumber is designed to resist rot and insects through the infusion of chemical preservatives. However, this resistance doesn't last forever—treated wood will still decay over time, and the chemicals it contains can leach into the soil. These substances may affect the health of your plants and, ultimately, your own well-being if consumed. While modern treatments are marketed as "safer," they can still introduce undesirable compounds into your garden over time. To ensure a healthy growing environment, it's best to avoid treated lumber for raised beds, especially for edibles.

STEP-BY-STEP DESIGN

Designing a raised bed might seem straightforward, and it's tempting to immediately order a kit, assemble it, and move it around until you find a spot that works. However, skipping the planning phase can lead to frustration if the bed turns out to be the wrong size or shape for your needs and space. Investing a little time upfront to measure, assess, and dream ensures the raised bed you choose will save you time, effort, and money.

1. **Choose the Perfect Spot:** Start by identifying a location that's both convenient and enjoyable. The placement of your raised bed depends on what you plan to grow. Keep culinary herbs and leafy greens close to the kitchen for easy access. Flowers for cutting might enhance a seating area or draw you to a quiet corner of the yard. A "sharing garden" brimming with produce could welcome neighbors near your front sidewalk. Vegetables like tomatoes and peppers thrive in sunny, open spaces, while shade-tolerant greens can nestle under taller plants or near buildings. For more ideas, refer to "Put Your Garden Where You Roam" (page 55).
2. **Discover and Dream:** Think of your raised bed as a blank canvas, ready to reflect your values, creativity, and cravings. What would make this space meaningful to you? Maybe it's homegrown produce that cuts your grocery bill, a spot to teach your kids where food comes from, or a pollinator playground filled with blooms and buzzing bees. Visit "Maximize Ease with Location and Layout" (page 55) and "Superstar Vegetables and Herbs" (page 190) to assess what your site can support. Then let your imagination wander: Which crops make your meals more memorable? Which bring you peace just by looking at them? Use the Plant Matchmaker sheet (page 187) to make a list of plants you love, then prioritize them based on what will thrive in your chosen spot.
3. **Research the Right Kit:** Take time to research raised bed kits and consider their materials and dimensions. Narrow beds—4' (1.2m) or less—are ideal for lower maintenance, putting everything within reach. Taller beds are easier on your back and knees but require more soil mix and a slightly higher budget. Strike a balance between your comfort, budget, and maintenance preferences. Once you've shortlisted a few kits, keep their dimensions handy for the next steps. See "Raised Bed Kit" (page 266) for a few more tips.

4. **Sketch Your Plants:** With graph paper and pencil, sketch a rough layout of where each plant will go in the raised beds you're considering. This helps visualize your garden, ensuring you can fit in your favorites while allowing room for expansion. Tracing paper can be invaluable for experimenting with different layouts.
5. **Lay Out and Visualize Your Bed:** Whether you like to plan things out on paper or prefer to get hands on right away, both approaches work; choose what feels natural for you. If you're exploring several different bed sizes or orientations, measuring the space and sketching on graph paper first might help compare ideas and save time. Be sure to include pathways that are 2'–4' (0.6–1.2m) wide, and consider how lawn mowers, wheelbarrows, or carts will go between them. When you're ready, head outside and use tape measures, garden hoses, ropes, sticks, or stakes to outline your bed and pathways. Seeing the layout in real space will reveal what looks and feels right, so adjustments can be made. Refer to "Begin with a Sketch" (page 48) and "Place Plants for Comfort" (page 58) for extra ideas and inspiration.
6. **Live with Your Layout:** Spend some time with your marked layout before committing to it. Observe how sunlight moves through the area during the day. Imagine watering, weeding, and harvesting. Does the space feel right? Are you able to navigate comfortably? This is your chance to fine-tune the design and ensure it meets your needs for the long term.
7. **Set the Stage:** Once you're confident in your design, mark the edges of your raised beds with stakes or sticks. These markers serve as a guide for assembly, locking in your thoughtfully crafted layout.

This U-shaped cedar bed was quickly assembled from a kit. Raised bed kits come in all shapes and sizes, so choose one that fits your space, gardening goals, and personal style.

STEP-BY-STEP ESTABLISHMENT

MATERIALS

- **Raised Bed Kit.**
- **Raised Bed Soil Mix:** Nutrient-rich, well-draining blend that holds moisture better than garden soil.
- **Compost.**
- **Straw Mulch.**
- **Tongue Depressors and Permanent Marker:** Label plants and seeds.
- **Seeds and Seedlings.**

See "Materials Planning" (page 265) for details about quantities.

ESSENTIAL TOOLS

- **Garden Gloves:** Protect your hands.
- **Level:** Ensure beds are level with the ground.
- **Spade or Mattock:** Raise or lower the beds in the soil to ensure they are level.
- **Utility Knife:** Open bags of soil mix and compost.
- **Steel Rake:** Smooth soil, compost, and mulch.
- **Trowel or Hori Hori Knife:** Digging and transplanting.
- **Pruning Snips or Scissors:** Pruning, harvesting, deadheading.
- **Watering Can or Hose:** Keep plants hydrated. If using a hose, consider a wand with a gentle spray attachment to avoid disturbing soil.

OPTIONAL TOOLS

- **Measuring Tape:** Lay out beds and planting rows.
- **Long Straight Board:** Use with the level to place across the bed to ensure it is level.
- **Rubber Mallet:** Helps level beds.
- **Hand Rake:** Smooth small areas of soil and incorporate compost.
- **Pitchfork:** Loosen and aerate soil.
- **Drill with Screwdriver Bit:** May be needed to assemble some beds.

See "Garden Toolbox" (page 262) for details about each tool.

Establishing your raised bed is an exciting process that turns your vision into reality. Follow these simple steps to set up your bed for success.

1. **Procure the Bed:** Purchase your raised bed kit from a reputable source, ensuring it's made from high-quality, durable materials like cedar.
2. **Determine the Soil Mix:** Refer to "Raised Bed Mix" (page 266) to calculate how much soil mix you'll need for your bed's dimensions. Purchase premixed raised bed soil, as garden soil or topsoil is too heavy and doesn't drain well in raised beds.
3. **Consider a Bottom Lining:** If burrowing critters like moles or gophers are a concern in your area, adding a layer of metal hardware cloth to the bottom of your raised bed can provide an effective barrier, protecting your plants from unwanted visitors. Similarly, if your garden site is plagued by persistent weeds, such as bindweed or ground ivy, heavyweight weed fabric can prevent these plants from sneaking into your carefully prepared soil.

Freshly filled and ready to grow, this elevated raised bed marks the start of a simple, joyful gardening journey. With the thoughtful preparation, your garden begins working with you from day one.

4. **Assemble the First Level:** Now for the fun part—putting your raised bed together! Start by positioning the first level in your chosen spot, shifting it slightly if needed to ensure the placement feels right. Use a level to check that the frame sits evenly, and adjust by adding or removing soil beneath the boards.

Staking out the raised bed with string ahead of time helps you visualize the layout and saves time on adjustments later.

If the area is sloped, use a mattock or flat-bladed spade to dig a shallow trench along the higher side. This gives your boards a level, stable surface to rest on and helps your bed sit evenly.

Assemble the first level of your bed, adjusting soil under the boards as needed to keep everything solid and straight. Use a long level, or a short one paired with a straight board, to make sure your bed sits evenly. No need for perfection; just keep the boards from looking lopsided.

5. **Line the Bottom:** If you're installing a barrier, now's the time. Use metal hardware cloth for protection from burrowing critters or durable weed fabric for aggressive weeds. If your bed is shallow and placed over grass or annual weeds, a single layer of cardboard or contractor's paper will smother growth.
6. **Assemble Remaining Levels:** Stack and secure the remaining levels according to the kit's instructions. This step is highly visual, so take your time and enjoy the transformation unfolding before you.

Lining the bottom of a shallow bed with cardboard or contractor's paper helps block grass and weeds from pushing up through your soil mix, saving you time and hassle later.

Stack and secure the remaining levels, ensuring everything is stable and aligned as you build upward.

With the frame complete, your raised bed is ready to be filled.

7. **Fill the Bed:** Filling your raised bed with soil is a satisfying step, and there's an easy way to save your back in the process. Place the bag of soil mix directly in the bed, then use scissors or a utility knife to slice it open from top to bottom. Simply pull the bag away to release the soil to avoid awkward lifting and dumping. Use a steel rake to smooth and level the soil after each bag or two is emptied.

To save your back, place the soil bag in the bed before opening. Slice it from top to bottom, then peel the bag away to let the soil spill out—no heavy lifting required.

Use a steel rake to spread and level the soil after every bag or two. This keeps the mix even and helps prevent air pockets as you fill the bed.

The bed is filled. With the hard part completed, step back, admire your work, and celebrate.

8. **Settle the Soil:** Before planting, settle the soil to eliminate air pockets and help it compact slightly. Thoroughly water the bed or let a heavy rainstorm do the work for you. This step ensures the soil is properly hydrated and ready to grow your plants.
9. **Mulch:** Optionally cover the bed with straw mulch to protect the soil until it's time to plant.
10. **Plant with Care:** With your raised bed filled and ready, it's time to plant! Take a moment to admire the fresh soil mix—the foundation of your garden's success. Begin by carefully sowing seeds or setting seedlings into their new home. Use tips in "Plant a Plant" (page 160) and "Sow a Seed" (page 154) for guidance. Planting in a raised bed is a joy, as the rich, loose soil makes this process easy and satisfying.
11. **Water Regularly:** Raised beds dry out faster than in-ground gardens, so consistent watering is critical, especially during the early stages of growth. Check your bed daily, as young plants and seeds need steady moisture to thrive. Water deeply, ensuring the soil stays evenly moist but not waterlogged. This daily ritual is an enjoyable opportunity to connect with your garden and observe the progress of your sprouting and growing friends.
12. **Mulch for Moisture and Health:** Once your plants are well established and sturdy, apply a layer of straw mulch around them. Mulch helps retain moisture, suppress weeds, and regulate soil temperature—all essential for a thriving raised bed garden. This simple step reduces ongoing maintenance and keeps your plants healthy and happy.
13. **Monitor and Harvest:** Regular visits to your raised bed allow you to catch any issues early and enjoy the beauty of your growing garden. Look out for pests, diseases, and signs of stress, and take proactive steps to address them. Refer to "Naturally Address Common Pests and Diseases" (page 170). Harvest crops as they ripen to enjoy peak flavors and encourage continued yields.

Covering the bed with a layer of straw mulch helps protect the soil from erosion, weeds, and drying out—especially if you're not planting right away.

Lush greens and vibrant veggies are your reward for working with nature and starting small.

STORY OF THE EDIBLE CLASSROOM

Nestled on the southside of downtown Iowa City's recreation center lies a vibrant oasis buzzing with life: the Edible Classroom. For over 50 years, this small patch of grass was diligently manicured for sunbathers from the adjacent indoor pool, but it was seldom used. The expenditure of fossil fuel, water, and time mirrored the low-reward upkeep of many American front yards.

In 2016, the Iowa City Parks & Recreation Department reached out to EarthMind Practice for guidance on reinvigorating this underused space. Through a series of visioning sessions, community members expressed their desire for an educational outdoor room brimming with organic fruits, vegetables, and herbs that were all free to harvest.

This dream swiftly took root, thanks to the hardworking hands of industrial technology students from the nearby Clear Creek Amana School District in Oxford, Iowa. Their dedication, coupled with generous donations from local businesses, transformed uninteresting grass into a picturesque landscape of elegant raised beds, tall arbors, and attractive limestone edging.

At its heart is a compact edible forest garden where fruit-bearing shrubs and herbal ground covers flourish under a canopy of two sweet cherry trees. Each year, the raised beds burst into life with an array of annual vegetables and herbs, carefully planted by University of Iowa students and volunteers.

Vibrant flowers weave between vegetables and herbs in cedar raised beds designed with wide board tops, inviting visitors to sit, linger, and garden in comfort.

The Edible Classroom is more than just a garden; it's a living classroom where the community gathers to learn, harvest, and celebrate the joys of low-maintenance, organic gardening. Through public classes and hands-on harvesting experiences, residents discover the simplicity and benefits of permaculture gardening. Whether it's a busy mother relaxing while her kids safely explore nature's curiosities, a budget-strapped college student harvesting nutrient-rich food, or a retiree taking a class to discover the joy of nurturing plants, this garden offers a serene escape from the pressures of daily life.

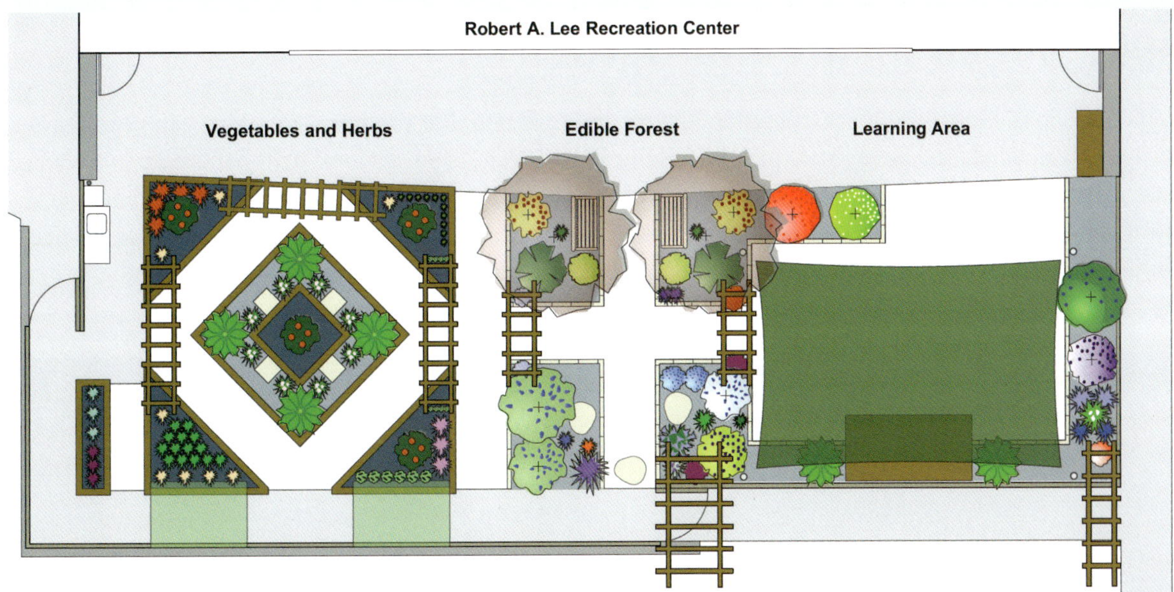

A thoughtfully designed plan laid the foundation for a vibrant, multifunctional garden—blending beauty, accessibility, and community-driven purpose into every element.

Before the Edible Classroom took root in 2016, this south-facing lawn near the Robert A. Lee Recreation Center was carefully maintained but rarely used. Like so many front yards, it demanded time and resources without giving much back.

The raised beds and arbors were built and installed by the skilled hands of local students. Chosen over in-ground beds, the raised beds significantly reduce maintenance while creating a more accessible and organized growing space.

A central feature of the Edible Classroom is its lush forest garden, where fruiting shrubs and herbal ground covers grow in harmony. This currant bush is one of many plants that the community is welcome to harvest and enjoy.

During a hands-on class, participants explore the garden together, learning to identify, harvest, and enjoy fresh, foraged foods right from the landscape.

Nutrient-Dense In-Ground Garden

An in-ground garden is a timeless choice, rooted in history and tradition. For thousands of years, gardeners have used these beds to cultivate food, and when most people imagine a garden, it's an in-ground bed that comes to mind.

A nutrient-rich garden provides fresh, flavorful produce that supports your body's ability to thrive and recover from illness. The in-ground garden we present here can become a foundation of health and well-being, but any garden—whether in-ground, raised bed, container, or orchard—can be designed to maximize nutrients. If your goal is to grow a garden that nourishes both you and the earth, prioritizing nutrient density is a great way to start.

A fresh in-ground bed, prepped and ready for spring planting, sets the stage for a garden rooted in tradition and health. With the right care and soil-building techniques, this space will soon yield nutrient-rich food that nourishes both body and soil.

WHY CHOOSE AN IN-GROUND GARDEN?

In-ground gardens offers a simple, cost-effective way to grow a wide variety of plants.

- **Quick Setup and Flexible:** Easily established with flexible shapes and sizes to fit any yard.
- **Great for Larger Plants:** Ideal for crops like squash and tomatoes that need space to spread.
- **Budget-Friendly:** More affordable than raised beds or containers, as they utilize existing soil and have fewer materials.
- **Natural Soil Ecosystem:** Relies on existing soil-building organisms, reducing the need for added fertilizers.
- **Better Moisture Retention:** Holds water more effectively than containers and raised beds, making it more forgiving when watering is inconsistent.

WHY GROW NUTRIENT-DENSE FOODS?

Eating healthy often comes with higher grocery bills, especially for fresh, organic produce. In addition to nutritious food, it's important to remember that a truly health-supporting lifestyle benefits from activities that reconnect us with nature, reduce stress, and expose us to beneficial bacteria—all of which gardening offers naturally. We will help you choose plants for nutrient density, ease of growth, and reliability, so you can grow a beautiful garden that supports both your body and your budget.

This vibrant in-ground bed showcases the beauty and abundance possible with a simple, budget-friendly setup. Swiss chard, kale, zucchini, and cucumbers climbing a trellis grow side by side—proof that in-ground gardens offer space, flexibility, and rich rewards without the high cost.

In this in-ground bed, curly kale—lush with nutritious blue-green leaves—is supported by sturdy stakes and string. This simple staking method lifts the plants toward the sun while keeping pathways clear for easy tending and harvest.

POTENTIAL CHALLENGES

While in-ground gardens offer many benefits, they come with a few challenges to consider.

- **Pest Protection:** Without tall edges, these gardens are more accessible to rabbits, deer, and other hungry critters.
- **More Weeding:** Weeds can get in easier without a barrier provided by a raised bed or container.
- **Soil Quality Variability:** Existing soil may need improvement through compost or amendments.
- **Physical Effort:** Requires more bending, kneeling, and digging compared to raised beds and containers, which can be challenging for those with mobility concerns.

A low mesh fence helps keep curious rabbits at bay, while piles of leaves along the edges suppress weeds and creeping grass. Simple solutions like these make in-ground gardens easier to maintain.

CATEGORIES OF NUTRIENT-DENSE PLANTS

A nutrient-dense diet rooted in well-being includes a wide array of plants. Those listed here are especially easy to grow and harvest, making them perfect companions for a busy lifestyle. But your journey toward nourishment doesn't need to stop here. Many nutrient-dense plants thrive with just a little extra attention, and you're warmly invited to explore beyond this list. Even if growing certain plants isn't feasible right now, you can still enjoy their benefits through teas, dried herbs, culinary spices, and indoor microgreens. A sprinkle of cinnamon, incorporated ground ginger root, or a steaming cup of nettle tea can carry a world of nourishment in a tiny package.

For a deeper understanding of the healing power of plants, Dr. Terry Wahls offers a compelling framework in her book *The Wahls Protocol: A Radical New Way to Treat All Chronic Autoimmune Conditions Using Paleo Principles*. Her work illustrates how diverse, plant-rich diets can play a profound role in supporting long-term health.

A well-rounded, nutrient-rich diet includes foods from three key categories: colors, greens, and sulfurs.

- **Colors:** Vibrant vegetables, such as tomatoes, beets, and squash, provide essential antioxidants that support cellular health. These plants may require more space, but their health benefits make them a worthwhile addition.
- **Greens:** These thrive in temperate climates and are inexpensive to grow at home. Kale, lettuce, and spinach provide an excellent return on investment, as greens are often pricey at the store.
- **Sulfurs:** Cruciferous vegetables like chives and garlic add robust flavors and sulfur-containing compounds that aid in detoxification, cell repair, and brain function. These plants are also less appetizing to deer and rabbits. Many sulfurs—collard greens, kale, radish, Swiss chard, tatsoi—also overlap with greens, so including these in the garden provide sources of both greens and sulfurs.

This raised bed demonstrates how nutrient-dense plants can thrive together in harmony. Collard greens, lettuce, and Swiss chard surround a cheerful cluster of sunflowers, creating a vibrant blend of colors, greens, and sulfur-rich crops. Just like our bodies, a thriving garden benefits from diversity and balance.

LEAFY GREENS

- Basil
- Cilantro
- Collard Greens
- Dandelion
- Dill
- Kale
- Lambsquarters
- Lettuce
- Mint
- Nasturtium
- Oregano
- Radish
- Sorrel, French
- Spinach
- Swiss Chard
- Tatsoi
- Thyme

COLORS

- Beans
- Beet
- Cucumber
- Parsley
- Peas
- Squash, Winter and Summer
- Strawberry
- Tomato

SULFURS

- Chives
- Collard Greens
- Garlic
- Kale
- Onion, Egyptian Walking
- Radish
- Swiss Chard
- Tatsoi

STEP-BY-STEP DESIGN

Creating an in-ground garden isn't just about finding a place to grow food—it's a journey of transforming a humble patch of yard into a vibrant, life-supporting oasis. This process blends practicality with mindfulness, allowing you to design a space that nurtures your body and the (wild) life you desire. Each step invites you to connect more deeply with your garden, your goals, and the natural rhythms of your environment.

1. **Choose the Perfect Spot:** Begin by selecting a location that's convenient and enjoyable. Keep your future garden close to where you spend time, whether that's near the kitchen for easy harvesting or visible from a favorite window so you can admire your handiwork. For helpful tips, see "Put Your Garden Where You Roam" (page 55).
2. **Discover and Dream:** This garden can be your foundation for nourishment and resilience. As you explore "Maximize Ease with Location and Layout" (page 55) and "Superstar Vegetables and Herbs" (page 190), ask yourself: What would it mean to step outside and gather the ingredients for an entire meal? Which crops will offer the most nutrition with the least effort? Which ones bring joy, connection, or a sense of self-reliance? Let your vision blend practicality with possibility—leafy greens tucked between rows of garlic or nasturtiums at the edges that add beauty and edibility. Use the Plant Matchmaker sheet (page 187) to jot down what excites you, and prioritize the plants that match both your dreams and your site.

As winter melts away, sunny patches reveal themselves as a promising spot for a future garden. Easy to access and bathed in light, it's the kind of place where food, beauty, and daily connection can take root.

A wide perimeter path of stepping stones offers easy access around the garden, while narrow, mulched paths provide comfortable entry between beds. Along the edge, edible nasturtiums create a confetti-like border of color and charm.

3. **Draw Your Bed:** Head outside with a pencil, graph paper, and measuring tape to create a scale drawing of your garden area. Keep beds narrow (4' [1.2m] or less) to ease maintenance and make paths that are 2'–4' (0.6–1.2m) wide to ensure you'll have plenty of space to move between them. If your area is on an incline, try to align beds and pathways along the contour of the slope, which will help reduce runoff of water, soil, and nutrients. Refer to "Begin with a Sketch" (page 48) and "Place Plants for Comfort" (page 58) for detailed guidance.
4. **Sketch Your Plants:** Now it's time to imagine how your garden will look. On graph paper, roughly draw where each plant will be located based upon its mature size. Make sure all your favorites fit while leaving some room for future plants. Tracing paper is great for lots of experiments.
5. **Bring the Sketch to Life:** Take your design and translate it onto the ground using everyday items like hoses, ropes, tape measures, sticks, or stakes. This step turns your vision into a tangible layout, helping you visualize your garden as it will appear in real life.
6. **Live with Your Layout:** Once your layout is marked, take time to sit with it. Visit the space during different times of the day, pretend to water and harvest, and imagine how you'll interact with it. Does the design feel right? Is it aligned with the sun's path and your practical needs? Use this opportunity to make adjustments before finalizing your layout.
7. **Set the Stage:** When you're satisfied with the design, mark the bed edges using stakes or sticks. This step locks in your plan, giving you a clear starting point for turning your garden dreams into reality. From here, you can proceed with establishment at your own pace, knowing you've created a thoughtful and functional design.

STEP-BY-STEP ESTABLISHMENT

ESSENTIAL MATERIALS

- **Contractor's Paper or Cardboard:** Smother existing vegetation.
- **Compost.**
- **Straw Mulch.**
- **Tongue Depressors and Permanent Marker:** Label plants and seeds.
- **Seeds and Seedlings.**

OPTIONAL MATERIALS

- **Garden Stakes:** Lay out beds and mark plant locations.
- **Arbors or Trellises:** Support vining plants.
- **Steel Fence Posts:** Support arbors, trellises, or fencing.
- **Wire Mesh:** Fencing to protect from deer and rabbits.

See "Materials Planning" (page 265) for details about quantities.

ESSENTIAL TOOLS

- **Garden Gloves:** Protect your hands.
- **Shovel, Trowel, or Hori Hori Knife:** Digging and transplanting.
- **Steel Rake:** Smooth soil, compost, and mulch.
- **Measuring Tape:** Lay out beds and planting rows.
- **Utility Knife:** Open bags of compost. Cut cardboard when sheet mulching.
- **Pruning Snips or Scissors:** Pruning, harvesting, deadheading.
- **Watering Can or Hose:** Keep plants hydrated. If using a hose, consider a wand with a gentle spray attachment to avoid disturbing soil.

OPTIONAL TOOLS

- **Rubber Mallet or Hammer:** Drive in stakes for laying out beds.
- **Flat-Bladed Spade:** Create clean bed edges.
- **Hand Rake:** Smooth small areas of soil and incorporate compost.
- **Wheelbarrow:** Haul materials.
- **Stirrup Hoe:** Remove weeds.
- **Post Pounder:** Drive in fence posts.
- **Pitchfork:** Loosen and aerate soil.

See "Garden Toolbox" (page 262) for details about each tool.

Now that your garden design is ready, it's time to roll up your sleeves and bring it to life. Follow these steps to create a thriving in-ground garden that's as low-maintenance as it is productive.

1. **Outline and Edge:** Start by outlining your garden bed according to your layout. Establish the edges using a method that suits your style and budget—options like plastic, stone, or a simple trench work well. These borders help define your space and keep everything neatly contained. See "Edging" (page 272) to help make your edging choice.
2. **Prepare the Soil:** Healthy soil is the foundation of a successful garden. If your soil isn't that rich, crumbly loam gardeners dream of, don't worry; follow the tips in "Build Healthy Soil: Testing and Improvement" (page 143) to improve its quality. Take a moment to dig your hands into the earth, observe the life within, and know you're creating a welcoming environment for both plants and beneficial soil creatures.
3. **Sheet Mulch:** If you're starting with a patch of grass or weeds, summer or early fall is the perfect time to sheet mulch. This simple layering technique smothers existing vegetation and transforms it into nutrient-rich soil over time. Check out "Sheet Mulching: Prepare and Revive Garden Beds" (page 145) for step-by-step instructions.
4. **Establish Protection:** If rabbits or other critters may be frequent visitors to your yard, setting up a protective meta mesh fence around your garden is a smart move. Purchase galvanized wire mesh that's 2'–3' (61–91.4cm) tall with openings no larger than 1" (2.5cm). Make sure to include an entryway that opens and closes easily—constantly stepping over a fence can turn into a frustrating barrier that keeps you out as much as the critters. For extra security, bury the bottom of the fence 2"–6" (5.1–15.2cm) deep to prevent animals from digging underneath. Anchor the fence firmly using sturdy stakes placed every 6'–8' (1.8–2.4m) for stability.
5. **Procure Seeds and Seedlings:** While your sheet mulch is working its magic, use fall and winter to research and purchase seeds that excite you. When spring arrives, visit local nurseries or farmers markets to find healthy seedlings.
6. **Strategically Group Plants:** As the final snow melts away, create a plan that places your plants in ways that simplify their care and your convenience. For example, place frequently harvested lettuce and other greens near pathways for easy access; give sprawling plants like squash plenty of room farther away. For more tips on optimizing your layout, refer to "Maximize Ease with Location and Layout" (page 55).
7. **Savor Spring Planting:** Spring is finally here and it's time to plant! Gently pull back the straw from your sheet-mulched bed to reveal the rich, dark soil beneath. Pause for a moment to savor the earthy aroma and marvel at the loam you've cultivated with help from nature's soil-building team. Spread the straw across your garden pathways or tuck it neatly at the end of the bed to keep it out of the way until it's needed again. With your bed prepped, take plenty of time to sow seeds or set seedlings into their new home, following the tips in "Plant a Plant" (page 160) and "Sow a Seed" (page 154).

A sunny spot behind a garage becomes a future garden as stakes, boards, and string bring the design to life. Taking time to visualize and adjust the layout ensures the space will be both functional and inviting.

Now sheet-mulched with cardboard, compost, and straw, the bed is tucked in and preparing for spring. This simple, low-effort method transforms grass into fertile ground ready to grow when the time is right.

8. **Water Regularly:** Watering is critical during these early stages of growth. Use this time to connect with your garden as your seedlings grow strong and steady. Aim to check in daily or every other day to provide water when the soil feels dry.
9. **Mulch for Moisture and Health:** When your plants are sturdy enough to resist the munching of soil-building bugs, add a layer of straw mulch around them. This reduces weeding, conserves moisture, and keeps your plants thriving with less effort.
10. **Monitor and Harvest:** When possible, regularly inspect your garden for pests, diseases, and signs of stress. Frequent visits ensure you can intervene early while you enjoy the benefits of hands-on care. Harvest promptly for the best flavors and to encourage continuous growth.

This freshly sheet-mulched bed was established in early spring—not ideal, but still full of promise. With layers of cardboard, deep compost, and straw, it will support some growth this season and set the stage for even greater abundance in years ahead.

High-Yield Mini-Orchard

Imagine stepping outside into your own bountiful slice of abundance, where fruit trees sway gently above berry bushes and herbs. This is the essence of your high-yield mini-orchard, designed as an edible forest garden. This space-efficient orchard is 4'–5' (1.2–1.5m) wide and can stretch as long as your area permits.

WHY CHOOSE AN EDIBLE FOREST GARDEN?

In nature, forests maintain themselves beautifully. Your mini-orchard will mirror the layered vegetation and processes of this self-sustaining system, putting much of the maintenance burden onto Mother Nature's strong back. This approach significantly reduces maintenance because it:

- **Enhances Soil Health:** Diverse roots systems, leaf drop, and nutrient-accumulating plants create fertile, self-mulching soil that does not require ongoing fertilizing.
- **Retains Water:** The layered canopy and ground covers reduce water evaporation from the soil.
- **Promotes Biodiversity:** Each plant plays an interconnected role, contributing to the health of the entire system.
- **Naturally Discourages Pests and Weeds:** A diverse and dispersed plant mix reduces the prevalence of pests, diseases, and weeds.
- **Grows a Living Mulch:** Dense ground covers weave across the soil surface, keeping it cool and shaded, reducing erosion, suppressing weeds, and lessening the need for constant mulching. The plants can be dug and divided to propagate elsewhere, giving you free ground covers to expand your garden.

POTENTIAL CHALLENGES

Establishing a mini-orchard is a journey requiring a bit more time and investment than other projects in this book, but it's filled with nurturing rewards at every turn, and we've got you covered each step of the way. In three to five years, you'll be savoring the sweetest fruits, grown by your own hands, without the need for constant care. Your orchard will likely continue producing food for decades.

Growing fruits organically is similar to growing annual vegetables: both methods require healthy soil, adequate sunlight, and reliable moisture to thrive. These perennials, however, are a long-term investment, remaining in place for many years, unlike vegetables that can be swapped out each season. Because of this, certain factors, such as site selection, soil quality, and disease resistance, become even more critical for long-term success. While it may not be possible to tick every box perfectly, striving to meet as many of these criteria as possible sets the stage for a flourishing orchard. These potential problems are arranged to help you prioritize the biggest issues, with the most crucial ones listed first.

- **Sun and Water Needs:** Ensure your orchard has at least six hours of direct sunlight each day and is not located in a dry spot. Plants will yield more in full sun and with consistent soil moisture.
- **Soil Needs:** The majority of plant roots lounge in the top 18" (45.7cm) of soil. A mini-orchard needs to grow in rich, well-drained soil. Dig a hole and look for dark, crumbly soil to ensure roots can breathe and have room to stretch. If you find dense clay or sand, see "Build Healthy Soil: Testing and Improvement" (page 143) for solutions.
- **Disease Resistance:** Seek varieties that are bred for disease resistance or select plants native to your area for natural resistance. Specifically, look for fruit trees that are resistant to common diseases such as fire blight, apple scab, brown rot, and powdery mildew.
- **Pollination Needs:** Most apples, pears, and plums must be pollinated by another variety to maximize yields, so when purchasing, check the cross-pollination requirements to see if two trees are required. A nearby pollinator match could be in your own yard or in neighboring spaces. Include patches of pollinator habitat within or near your orchard to maximize fruit set.

After just three years of growth, this vibrant mini-orchard transforms a narrow hillside into a thriving edible forest garden. Tucked in beside a garage, it's proof that even small, sloped spaces can become bountiful and beautiful with thoughtful design.

This lush orchard ground cover—featuring creeping thyme, wild strawberry, and ground ivy—keeps soil cool, moist, and weed-free. These plants can be gently dug and divided to expand your garden.

Harvesting sour cherries on a warm summer day is one of the many joys that come with growing your own orchard. With a little time and care upfront, your mini-orchard will offer harvests like this for decades, building confidence and ease with every season.

- **Pruning Needs:** Many fruit trees and berry bushes can grow quickly and benefit from annual pruning to stay healthy and compact. It may feel counterintuitive to cut back abundance, but thoughtful pruning encourages better fruit and stronger branches. See "Pruning for Health and Harvest: Fruit Trees and Berry Bushes" (page 165) for tips.
- **Pest Pressure:** Fruits often attract birds, chipmunks, deer, and other nibblers. If they get too greedy, you may need to integrate deterrents like fencing or lightweight netting. Damage to a young fruit tree's bark can be fatal, so wintertime trunk guards are important.
- **Wind Considerations:** Most plants have higher yields when protected from constant strong winds.
- **Nutrient Needs:** Periodically topdress with a 1" (2.5cm) layer of compost, and cover bare soil with woodchip mulch. Interplant a few nutrient-accumulating companion plants.
- **Patience for Production:** Most fruiting plants take a few seasons to mature before yielding large harvests. While waiting, you can underplant with quick-growing vegetables and edible ground covers to make the space productive right away.

Thinning peaches helps produce larger, healthier fruit while preventing branches from breaking under the weight. Choosing small trees, like this semi-dwarf peach, keeps fruit within easy reach and makes harvesting safer and more enjoyable.

ENJOY THE FRUITS OF YOUR LABOR

The more you enjoy harvesting and eating your bounty, the more likely you are to visit and care for the plants. Select plants so they match your:

- **Harvesting Height:** Consider the mature height of fruit trees, especially if children will help with the harvest or you don't want to use ladders or harvesting tools. Select dwarf fruit trees, which grow only 10'–12' (3–3.7m) wide and tall, to ensure fruit is within easy reach. Shorter and narrower trees will also allow you to fit more trees into a smaller space.
- **Harvesting Times:** When will you have time to harvest, prepare, savor, and store your bounty? Consider annual vacations that may happen when fruits are ripe; maybe that fruit tree isn't the right choice for your garden.
- **Palate:** It won't matter how much food a plant yields if you don't like its taste. When possible, sample different varieties at a local orchard to find your favorites.

GOOD COMPANION PLANTS

Understory herbs can grow additional food, attract pollinators, discourage pests, accumulate nutrients, develop loamy soil, crowd out weeds, and conserve soil moisture. Interplanting these hardy plants near or around fruit trees and berry bushes will enhance growth and yields:

	Chives	Chives are flavorful, nutrient-accumulating companions with striking blooms that attract pollinators and beneficial insects. They also add zest to your meals.
	Clover, Dutch White	Dutch white clover is a common, drought-tolerant, clumping ground cover that feeds nutrients to nearby plants, supports pollinators, covers bare ground with ease, and makes a nourishing tea. It's simple and inexpensive to establish by seed and thrives with little care.
	Rhubarb	Rhubarb makes an excellent orchard companion, shading out weeds while offering tart, delicious stalks just a few feet from your fruit trees. Plant it 2'–4' (0.6–1.2m) away from the base of fruit trees and berry bushes.
	Thyme, Creeping	Creeping thyme softens edges with its fragrant blooms. It's tough, drought-tolerant, and thrives even in high-traffic areas. The flowers of this fragrant, spicy, clumping ground cover are beloved by beneficial insects.
	Wild Strawberry	This Midwest native creeping ground cover rapidly fills in bare spots to conserve soil moisture. Don't expect too much flavor from the small, mealy berries. While the berries are modest, wild strawberry plays a big role in orchard groundcover.

STEP-BY-STEP DESIGN

The sweetest reward for all your design and establishment work: a crisp, sun-warmed apple picked straight from your own mini-orchard. It's worth the wait and every nurturing step.

Designing your mini-orchard is an exciting journey. Try approaching each step with a sense of curiosity and enjoyment, envisioning the transformation of your space into a thriving haven of fruitfulness and ease.

1. **Choose the Perfect Spot:** Perennial orchard plants tend to grow with less hands-on care than annual vegetables and herbs, so your mini-orchard doesn't need to be immediately outside your door. Still, location matters. Choose a spot that receives at least six hours of full sun and has steady soil moisture to support strong growth and generous harvests. Nestling the orchard along a wall or fence can provide a tidy backdrop or visual screen, but if space allows, leave room for pathways on both sides to make pruning, harvesting, and general upkeep much more accessible over time.
2. **Discover and Dream:** Your orchard can be more than fruit trees—it can be a story of seasons, family traditions, and personal pleasure. Use "Fruit Favorites" (page 196) to explore what's possible, then dream beyond the practical. Which fruits evoke joy or memory? Is this a quiet place to watch bees and butterflies? A nourishing berry harvest for kids? A pantry full of preserves? Use the Plant Matchmaker sheet (page 187) to make a list of the fruits that speak to your senses and values. Then, think practically rank them based on how well they'll adapt to your growing conditions and available space.
3. **Layer Your Garden's Story:** Next, create a list of your chosen plants, categorizing them by natural layers: trees, vines, shrubs, herbs, and ground covers. See "Layer to Maximize Growth" (page 60) for ideas and details.
4. **Draw the Base Map:** Take a pencil, graph paper, and a measuring tape outside and draw your space to scale. See "Begin with a Sketch" (page 48) for details.
5. **Sketch Your Dream:** Now let your creativity flow. Use a pencil to sketch your design, erasing and correcting as you go. Tracing paper works well for this step, as it provides freedom to brainstorm while keeping your base map tidy.
    - **Trees:** Start with the backbone of your orchard: the trees. Place them so their mature canopies will have 1'–3' (30.5–91.4cm) of space between them. This spacing gives understory plants the needed sunlight for them to thrive.
    - **Vines:** Sketch in vines alongside arbors or other structures they will climb. Be aware that allowing vines to climb into trees will not work well; in addition to everything being harder to harvest, the plants will compete for sunlight and yields will decline.
    - **Shrubs:** Add shrubs next, ensuring they do not overlap more than 6" (15.2cm) at maturity.
    - **Herbs:** Sprinkle in herbs at the edge of your orchard or among the shrubs. Like all the other plants, draw them at their mature size, allowing for a little overlap.
    - **Ground Covers:** You don't need to sketch ground covers. Just imagine their gentle spread across your orchard's floor, connecting all elements.
6. **Bring the Sketch to Life:** With your blueprint in hand, step into your yard and lay out your design using whatever you have available: hoses, ropes, tape measures, sticks, or lawn chairs. This is a playful and practical way to visualize your dream in the real world.
7. **Live with Your Layout:** If possible, let your layout sit for a few days or weeks. Visit it when you can, pretending to water, weed, and harvest. Adjust as needed and play with different designs. This is a great way to bond with your future oasis while ensuring it aligns with the sun's path and your personal aesthetics.
8. **Set the Stage:** Finally, pound in stakes or sticks to identify bed edges, trees, shrubs, and herbs. With the layout in place, you can now wait as long as desired to establish your dream.

STEP-BY-STEP ESTABLISHMENT

ESSENTIAL MATERIALS

- **Contractor's Paper or Cardboard:** Smother existing vegetation.
- **Compost.**
- **Woodchip Mulch.**
- **Plants and Seeds.**

OPTIONAL MATERIALS

- **Edging.**
- **Garden Stakes:** Lay out beds and mark plant locations.
- **Tall Steel Stakes:** Support dwarf apple and pear trees.
- **Tree Strap:** Soft, flexible tie to secure a dwarf fruit tree to a stake without damaging the bark.

See "Materials Planning" (page 265) for details about quantities.

ESSENTIAL TOOLS

- **Garden Gloves:** Protect your hands.
- **Shovel, Trowel, or Hori Hori Knife:** Digging and transplanting.
- **Steel Rake:** Smooth soil, compost, and mulch.
- **Measuring Tape:** Lay out trees and shrubs.
- **Utility Knife:** Open bags of compost and woodchip mulch. Cut cardboard when sheet mulching.
- **Watering Can or Hose:** Keep plants hydrated.
- **Pruners, Loppers, and Tree Saw:** Prune trees and shrubs.

OPTIONAL TOOLS

- **Rubber Mallet or Hammer:** Drive in garden stakes when laying out planting locations.
- **Flat-Bladed Spade:** Create clean bed edges.
- **Large Bucket:** Keep bare root trees and shrubs hydrated just before planting.
- **Stirrup Hoe:** Remove weeds.
- **Post Pounder:** Drive in steel stakes.
- **Wheelbarrow:** Haul materials.
- **Pitchfork:** Loosen and aerate soil.

See "Garden Toolbox" (page 262) for details about each tool.

Establishing your mini-orchard weaves patience with excitement, providing flexibility to go at a pace that works for you. These steps embody best practices to streamline your energy and maximize success, ensuring a thriving orchard with the least effort.

1. **Lay the Foundation:** Begin by establishing hardscape elements, such as edging or arbors. This is the canvas upon which your mini-orchard will come to life, so take your time and enjoy the early crafting process.
2. **Prepare the Soil:** Let's ensure the soil is ready to support your plants. If the soil is not a dark brown and crumbly loam, follow the simple guidelines in "Build Healthy Soil: Testing and Improvement" (page 143). Take time to feel the earth, examine its inhabitants, and know that you're preparing a healthy home for your plants and soil allies.
3. **Sheet Mulch:** In summer or early fall, smother existing vegetation by following steps outlined in "Sheet Mulching: Prepare and Revive Garden Beds" (page 145). This simple method naturally converts existing grass and weeds into nutrient-rich soil.
4. **Procure Plants:** Spring often brings high demand for plants, making them hard to find. Order from a local nursery or online during winter, and arrange delivery or pickup just before planting to avoid extended care for bare-root or potted plants. This ensures you have the best selection and avoids the seasonal rush.
5. **Plant Trees and Shrubs:** Choose either spring or fall for planting to avoid the stressful summer heat. Our "Plant a Plant" section (page 160) will guide you through this process. As you plant, take moments to envision each tree and shrub taking root and growing to its full potential.
6. **Water Thoughtfully:** Give your plants a deep, thorough watering, spending 10–30 seconds with each plant. It might feel longer than you'd prefer, so imagine quenching the earth's thirst and connecting with your garden during this time. This mindful approach helps you and your plants stay healthy and vibrant.

7. **Spread Mulch:** The woodchips from your earlier sheet mulching may have broken down over time, so you might need to add more. Ensure the entire area is covered with 3"–6" (7.6–15.2cm) of woodchips, gently tucking your plants into a protective blanket that reduces watering and weeding chores. Take care not to pile the mulch against the trunks or stems, as this can lead to rot and other issues.
8. **Plant Herbs:** Introduce herbs to your mini-orchard after two to four seasons, once the mulch has settled and the plants are at less risk of being smothered.
9. **Establish Ground Covers:** Gently rake back mulch and plant or seed ground covers at the same time you establish herbs. These plants will knit your mini-orchard together, creating a lush, living tapestry underfoot.
10. **Consistently Care:** For the first two growing seasons, water all plants deeply when the soil feels dry 1" (2.5cm) below the surface. Pull any emerging weeds while they are still young. This attentive care can be a nurturing ritual, helping your garden establish strong roots.
11. **Annually Prune:** Each winter, prune your trees and shrubs to keep them healthy and shape their future. Refer to "Pruning for Health and Harvest: Fruit Trees and Berry Bushes" (page 165) for guidelines.

Planting a fruit tree in early spring or fall helps it establish strong roots before summer heat arrives.

STORY OF FRED'S YARD

Fred's least favorite outdoor task was mowing the lawn, especially on a hill. When he settled into his new home, he faced this challenge on a long stretch of sunny, sloping grass adjacent to his garage. Tired of wrestling the mower over this spot during his first summer, Fred had a tree trimmer deliver a large pile of woodchips to his nearby driveway. He envisioned transforming this area into a mini-orchard and wanted to prepare it for springtime planting.

With great satisfaction, Fred mowed the grass a final time, covered it with cardboard saved from storage boxes, and then blanketed the area with an 8" (20.3cm) layer of woodchips. Over the winter, as the soil marinated, Fred carefully sketched his orchard, taking the design outside to stomp out pathways and plant locations in each new snowfall to refine the vision.

When the design felt complete, he excitedly ordered three dwarf fruit trees: a peach, an apple, and a plum. In spring, when the trees arrived, he raked back circles of woodchips to reveal rich, dark soil free of grass and primed for planting, with no need for tilling or composting.

In the orchard's second year, Fred planted rhubarb and gooseberries between the trees. Creeping thyme, Dutch white clover, wild strawberry, chives, broadleaf sage, and yarrow were planted in thin patches of the decomposing mulch. These plants spread, creating a lush understory that buzzed with life.

While enjoying daily harvests of herbs for meals and teas, he does not mind occasionally pulling a weed or watering a bit. He transformed frustration into delight, happy knowing that his lawn mower was given to a friend.

While enjoying an increasing bounty with each year that passes, Fred continues to poke additional plants into bare spots, maximizing the diversity of this abundant space.

This sunny, south-facing slope once required constant mowing—a time-consuming task. A productive mini-orchard transforms the space into something more rewarding.

In its third summer, the orchard is thriving. Rhubarb offers tangy stalks for crisps, while savory herbs lend rich flavor to soups.

MINI-ORCHARD DESIGN

Fred's mini-orchard can serve as a template for creating a productive, small-scale orchard in a limited space. The bed measures 30 feet long and 3½ feet wide (9.1 x 1.1m).

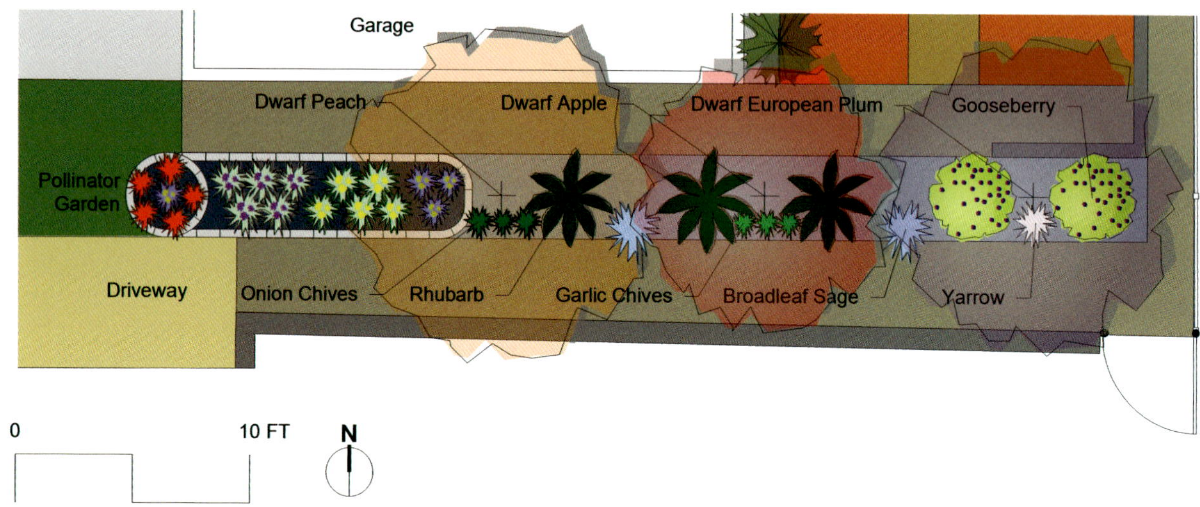

Fred's mini-orchard shows how thoughtful design can turn even a narrow space into a productive, low-maintenance food forest. With close tree spacing, an edible understory, and pollinator support, his layout offers a practical template for abundance in small yards.

Key features of Fred's mini-orchard design:

- **Narrow Bed:** The bed is only 3½' (1.1m) wide, providing easy reach into the space for harvesting, pruning, and weeding.
- **Slim Paths:** With limited space, the paths on either side of the bed are also 3½' (1.1m) wide. While wider paths would be ideal for accommodating a wheelbarrow, these slimmer paths are a practical solution for the small space. Fred chose to transform the paths from grass to herbal ground covers so he would not need to mow. Edging around the bed would have been required if he kept the pathways as grass.
- **Close Tree Spacing:** To make the most of the small area, Fred planted his dwarf fruit trees only 10' (3m) apart—the minimum recommendation of 10'–12' (3–3.7m). This compact spacing requires significant pruning at the end of each winter to prevent branches from overlapping, but Fred finds this task enjoyable and uses it as a happy milestone for warmer weather.

Gooseberries are tasty, low-maintenance, and often start yielding fruit in their first or second year of planting.

- **Cross-Pollination and Diverse Tree Neighbors:** Trees yield more fruit when they have another variety nearby, but to minimize the spread of diseases, Fred avoided planting similar fruit tree species next to each other. Instead, he created a more resilient orchard by establishing the other varieties in another area of his yard. For example, a Liberty apple variety grows in this orchard patch and an Enterprise is established in another patch.
- **Ground Covers:** After the woodchip mulch settled for a year, Fred established a variety of ground covers: creeping thyme, Dutch white clover, self-heal, and wild strawberry. Ground ivy (also known as creeping Charlie) crept its way into the mix, and within four years, the ground covers blanketed the entire area, helping repel weeds, build healthy soil, reduce erosion, and retain moisture.
- **Pollinator-Friendly Bed:** Next to the orchard, where an old gravel driveway once lay, Fred established a bed of native pollinator plants. This area attracts bees, wasps, and other beneficial insects, which help manage pests and boost fruit yields.

Now in its fourth year, the mini-orchard is thriving alongside a vibrant bed of Midwest native pollinator plants. Once a gravel driveway, this space now blooms with purple coneflower, butterfly milkweed, and more—welcoming beneficial insects that support the health and productivity of the orchard.

An overhead view reveals the power of plant diversity in a ground cover: wild strawberry runs, creeping thyme clumps, and oregano disperses seeds. Mixing runners, clumpers, and seed-dispersers creates a resilient, living mulch that fills space, suppresses weeds, and nurtures the soil.

Wild Edibles

You might love the idea of growing your own food but feel overwhelmed at the thought of tending a full-fledged vegetable garden or orchard. Maybe your schedule is packed, your budget is tight, or your space is limited. Still, wouldn't it be wonderful to step outside and find something delicious and nourishing—without the work?

If you've ever looked at the green tangle of plants in a natural area or your own backyard and wondered if any of it was edible, you're not alone. Many plants labeled as weeds or ignored entirely are edible and full of nutrients, all thriving without human intervention. Adding just a few of these low-maintenance wild edibles to your yard is one of the easiest and fastest ways to start enjoying homegrown food with almost zero effort.

Cheery dandelions grow freely in the grass pathways of the Iowa City Edible Classroom. They are a zero-maintenance, nutrient-dense edible hiding in plain sight.

WHY CHOOSE WILD EDIBLES?

While most of us humans rely on grocery stores for food—spending money, time, and travel to get it—all other critters see the world as a giant, free, zero-maintenance buffet. It's possible to shift a little closer to this effortless way of living by encouraging naturally resilient edibles in your landscape.

- **Food Foraging:** Foraging is often associated with forests and woodlands, but it's just as possible in an urban yard or suburban park. If your yard has unused, overgrown, or high-maintenance areas, wild edibles can help transform them into spaces that contribute to your well-being. Unlike traditional vegetables that require frequent care, many wild edibles mature quickly into self-sufficient providers. While you probably won't replace all your grocery runs, you can introduce these dependable food sources into your landscape and enjoy the health benefits of their self-sustaining nature.
- **A Living Laboratory:** Maybe a friend, book, or video introduced you to a hardy edible plant growing in a natural area. Since it's already thriving in your region, chances are high that it will grow in your yard just as easily. Or perhaps you brought home a few new plant friends or seeds from a nursery, farmers market, garden center, or park, but you aren't sure where to put them. Consider starting a "wild nursery" zone—a temporary bed where plants can take root while you decide on their permanent home. If they thrive, you might choose to let them stay and establish the space as a permanent wild patch, then start another nursery elsewhere. This space can also serve as a perfect testing ground for different planting techniques, allowing you to experiment on a small scale before applying what you learn to larger areas.

Foraging is often associated with wild places like forests. In this wild edibles foraging class taught by the authors, participants harvest mulberries along the wooded edge of a public park, uncovering an abundant, often-overlooked source of nourishment growing close to home.

These vibrant wild plums are a reminder that not all foods need tending. Wild edibles offer a delicious, low-effort way to enjoy homegrown abundance, no garden required.

- **Why Grow It If You Can't Eat It?** If an ornamental plant isn't pulling its weight—offering no food, no habitat, and little joy—you may be surprised to find an edible alternative that does all three. Consider these swaps:

Type	Ornamental Plant	Wild Edible Replacement
Tall Shrubs	Lilac, hydrangea, burning bush	Saskatoon serviceberry
Small Shrubs	Barberry, boxwood	Currant, gooseberry, goumi berry, raspberry
Vines	Clematis, English ivy	Grape
Herbaceous Plants	Hosta, coral bells, ornamental grasses	Anise hyssop, French sorrel, purple coneflower
Ground Covers	Turfgrass, ajuga, dead nettle, pachysandra	Self-heal, creeping thyme, wild strawberry, violet, Dutch white clover

- **Fill in Gaps:** If you have an open space in an existing garden bed, consider slipping in a wild edible or two. Gooseberry shrubs, dandelions, anise hyssop, self-heal, and violets can handle a wide variety of sun and soil conditions, making them excellent gap-fillers.
- **Trade Mowing for Munching:** Do you have an unused section of lawn that's a hassle to maintain? Turn it into a patch of edible wildness. A mix of edibles can create a lush, low-maintenance foodscape where you'd otherwise be pushing a mower.
- **Go Wild:** Nature flourishes in diverse, messy spaces. Unlike manicured landscapes that often restrict biodiversity, untamed areas weave together a rich tapestry of food, shelter, and safe havens where wildlife can thrive and reproduce. A patch of wild edibles and naturally unruly plants might be best placed in an area out of public view. Keep it somewhere you can easily observe, though, so you can enjoy the grateful birds, insects, mammals, and reptiles that will make this thriving habitat their home.

Serviceberries are a perfect example of an edible plant that offers food, beauty, and habitat; and they can be selected or swapped for a medium-sized ornamental tree or shrub that does far less.

Urban foraging at its finest—by late June, serviceberries offer a generous harvest of sweet, juicy fruit from trees planted for beauty but brim with abundance.

A young patch of springtime lambsquarters grows beneath a shrub in an overlooked corner of the yard. At this tender stage, the stems can go straight into soups and sautés—an easy way to add free nutrition to meals.

Gooseberries are small, hardy shrubs that can be tucked into garden gaps, offering delicious summer harvests with minimal effort.

POTENTIAL CHALLENGES

Wild edibles can offer carefree abundance but may come with a few considerations.

- **Aggressive Growth:** Some wild edibles can spread rapidly, outcompeting gentler garden companions. To keep them in check, harvest regularly, use edging or containers where needed, and remove unwanted ones before they take over.
- **Missed Harvests:** Many wild edibles are at their best during a brief seasonal window, and fruits often do not ripen all at once. Without close observation, ripe berries or tender leaves can quickly wither or turn bitter. Regular garden strolls and journaling harvest times can help you to monitor the abundance.
- **Aesthetic Preferences:** Wild plants don't always conform to tidy garden aesthetics. For those who prefer a neater appearance, consider grouping wild edibles in a designated area or bordering them with low-growing herbs or flowers.

Purple coneflower and anise hyssop thrive together in a vibrant patch, showing that hardy, adaptable edibles can be both beautiful and easy to grow in a wide range of soil and sun conditions.

STEP-BY-STEP DESIGN

Wild edible patches are often small and require little design work, utilizing more intuition and improvisation than the formal planning and design that is outlined for other projects in this book. By making small adjustments, you'll be surprised at how quickly your landscape can become a self-sustaining source of food and habitat.

1. **Identify Spaces That Could Work:** Look around your yard for existing plants or areas that aren't serving you—maybe they're high-maintenance, purely ornamental, bare, overgrown, or struggling to thrive. These areas might be perfect candidates for introducing wild edibles. Consider tips in "Put Your Garden Where You Roam" (page 55) to keep your edibles within easy reach.
2. **Choose the Right Wild Edibles:** Once you identify potential spots, find plants that will work well there using the steps in "Your Plant Matchmaking Guide" (page 180). Here are a few top considerations for tougher conditions:
    - **Shadier Spots:** Consider anise hyssop, violets, self-heal, or dandelions.
    - **Wet Areas:** Dandelions, lambsquarters, broadleaf plantain, and self-heal would work well.
    - **Dry, Tough Soil:** Goumi berries, gooseberries, French sorrel, purple coneflower, dandelions, mint, and Dutch white clover are resilient choices.
3. **Decide on Your Approach:** Start small and expand over time so your enthusiasm grows alongside your learning.
    - **Replace an Existing Plant:** If a plant in your landscape isn't serving you, swap it out for a wild edible that offers food, habitat, or both.
    - **Transform an Unused Patch:** Let an underutilized space go wild and observe what naturally appears, or jumpstart the process by planting or seeding edibles.
    - **Create a Wild Zone:** Designate a space to experiment with different wild edibles. This could be a tucked-away corner, a fence line, or a patch screened by a hedge.
    - **Fill a Gap:** If you notice an empty spot in a bed, tuck in a few wild edibles, keeping their mature size in mind to prevent overcrowding.

STEP-BY-STEP ESTABLISHMENT

MATERIALS

- **Contractor's Paper or Cardboard:** Smother existing vegetation.
- **Compost.**
- **Woodchip Mulch.**
- **Plants and Seeds.**

See "Materials Planning" (page 265) for details about quantities.

ESSENTIAL TOOLS

- **Garden Gloves:** Protect your hands.
- **Spade, Trowel, or Hori Hori Knife:** Digging and transplanting.
- **Steel Rake:** Smooth soil, compost, and woodchip mulch.
- **Watering Can or Hose:** Keep plants hydrated.

OPTIONAL TOOLS

- **Utility Knife:** Open bags of compost and woodchip mulch. Cut cardboard when sheet mulching.
- **Mattock or Flat-Bladed Spade:** Clear turf before planting.
- **Large Bucket:** Keep bare root trees and shrubs hydrated just before planting.
- **Pruners, Loppers, and Tree Saw:** Prune trees and shrubs.

See "Garden Toolbox" (page 262) for details about each tool.

Once you've chosen where to introduce wild edibles, it's time to help them take root. The beauty of wild edibles is that they're naturally resilient, so the process is usually simple. Whether you're swapping out an existing plant or seeding a new area, these guidelines will set you up for success with minimal effort.

A LITTLE PREP GOES A LONG WAY

Most wild edibles can adapt to a variety of conditions, but small improvements can make a big difference. Before planting or seeding, refer to "Build Healthy Soil: Testing and Improvement" (page 143) to see if any quick soil adjustments would be beneficial. Even a light dusting of compost can give your wild plants a strong, healthy start without adding much extra time or expense.

REPLACE AN EXISTING PLANT OR FILL A GAP

Swapping out an existing plant or filling an empty space in a bed with wild edibles is a simple way to make your landscape more edible and wildlife-friendly.

1. **Clear the Area:** Use a mower and steel rake to remove mulch, leaves, or other debris from the area to prevent them from falling into the planting hole.
2. **Dig It Out:** If replacing a plant, use a shovel to loosen the soil around the roots and carefully lift it out. If the plant is still healthy and useful, consider transplanting it elsewhere or gifting it to a friend.
3. **Plant the Wild Edible:** Refer to "Plant a Plant" (page 160) for detailed guidance on proper planting techniques.

Bee balm's vibrant blooms attract pollinators—and people too. With blossoms and leaves that make a fragrant, Earl Grey–flavored tea, it's a beautiful multipurpose plant that turns a grassy patch into a place worth lingering in.

Blend lambsquarters, oregano, and Egyptian walking onions with olive oil, then gently simmer to create a rich, flavorful Wild Edibles Pesto. It's a simple, nourishing way to make the most of your wild harvests.

SEED A GRASSY PATCH

Instead of seeing grass as a maintenance chore, why not turn a small section into something delicious and beneficial to wildlife? With a little preparation, you can easily transform a patch of lawn into a low-maintenance, edible habitat by broadcast seeding wild herbs and flowers. Some great choices include:

- **Anise Hyssop:** Fragrant, great for tea, friend to bees and birds.
- **Bee Balm:** Beautiful blooms, attracts pollinators, makes Earl Grey–flavored tea.
- **Broadleaf Plantain:** Tough, edible, medicinal, supports soil health.
- **Dandelion:** Highly nutritious, deep roots improve soil.
- **Dutch White Clover:** Builds soil, attracts bees, good in tea.
- **Purple Coneflower:** Pollinator favorite, medicinal.
- **Self-Heal:** Low-growing, edible, medicinal.
- **Violet:** Edible flowers and leaves, shade tolerant.

Violets and dandelions grow side by side in a former patch of lawn, now a low-maintenance edible habitat. Broadcasting seeds of wild herbs and flowers can turn grassy spaces into something beautiful and beneficial.

When seeding a patch of soil, choose the approach that matches your time, energy, and enjoyment. Good: Spread seeds onto bare soil. Better: Tamp them in for stronger seed-to-soil contact. Best: Add a light layer of soil or compost for optimal germination and growth.

Don't worry if the grass eventually grows back and integrates with your edibles; it's all part of creating a diverse, self-sustaining space. Start small, observe what works, and expand gradually to avoid wasting time, energy, or seed. Here's a step-by-step guide:

1. **Water Beforehand:** If the soil is dry, wait for a good rain or give the area a thorough watering the day before planting. Soft, damp soil is much easier to work with than dry, compacted earth.
2. **Knock Back the Grass:** Set your mower to its lowest setting and scalp the grass as low as possible. This gives wild edibles a chance to take root before the grass bounces back. If you have time, let the clippings dry in place for a few days to add fertility. For a more dramatic transformation (and a bit of a workout), use a mattock or flat-bladed spade to remove the turf entirely. Toss the grass into your compost bin or use it elsewhere as mulch.

3. **Rough Up the Soil:** Use a steel rake to lightly disturb the top 1" (2.5cm) of soil. This helps expose fresh earth, ensuring seeds make direct contact for better germination. If there's excessive grass or debris, rake it aside or compost it.
4. **Broadcast the Seeds:** Scatter the seeds evenly across the area. Don't stress about perfection—nature isn't precise, and a little randomness can help create a more natural look. If desired, lightly cover the seeds with a thin layer of compost or topsoil to help them settle.
5. **Press Them In:** Gently press the seeds into the earth for good seed-to-soil contact, which greatly improves germination. Lay down a piece of cardboard and lightly walk over the area. For a more grounding, sensory experience, press them in with your hands.
6. **Water Gently:** If no rain is expected, lightly water the area. A soft mist or gentle soak works best; too much force can dislodge the seeds.
7. **Optionally Mulch:** Spread a light layer of dried grass clippings or straw on the area to conserve moisture and reduce competition from weeds.
8. **Observe and Adjust:** Some seeds will sprout quickly, while others take their time. Be patient and let the space evolve naturally. If certain plants aren't thriving or some patches remain bare, try adding a few more seeds over time to fill in the gaps.
9. **Occasionally Trim:** If grass becomes too tall or seems to be overcrowding your herbs, use a weed trimmer to thin the entire area. Once established, most wild herbs can tolerate occasional trimming.

Relaxing Sensory Garden

Imagine stepping into a garden where time slows and your senses awaken—where the gentle rustling of leaves harmonizes with birdsong, the fragrance of sun-warmed herbs lingers in the air, and the soft embrace of foliage brushes against your fingertips. Whether you're beginning a new space or enriching a garden you've tended for years, any patch can become a sensory retreat. By thoughtfully adding plants and features that engage your senses, your garden becomes more than a place of cultivation, it becomes a space of immersion and presence.

A sensory garden is both a refuge for you and a sanctuary for the wildlife it welcomes. Butterflies flutter through blossoms, bees hum as they gather nectar, and birds flit between branches, adding their own rhythm to the garden's symphony. Whether you are sipping tea in the morning light, trailing your fingers through feathery grasses, or breathing deeply as you stroll along a path of fragrant ground covers, this garden embraces you with ease and restoration.

This small circular healing garden at Prairiewoods Franciscan Spirituality Center in Hiawatha, Iowa, invites you to pause, unwind, and reconnect with your senses. Peaceful and welcoming, it's a comfortable retreat where beauty, fragrance, and stillness gently converge.

Create a sensory garden that feels safe and welcoming. It is an inviting space where you can relax, explore, and truly belong.

Brushing your fingers across the soft, textured leaves of sage releases its earthy aroma—a simple act that invites you to slow down and engage your senses. In a sensory garden, touch isn't just allowed, it's essential.

WHY CHOOSE A SENSORY GARDEN?

A sensory garden is more than a collection of plants. It is a space intentionally designed to nourish body, mind, and spirit. By incorporating time-tested principles from horticultural therapy, trauma-informed landscape design, and Attention Restoration Theory, you can create a deeply personal sanctuary that fosters relaxation, engagement, and renewal. See "We All Need a Way to Recharge" (page 33) for more background inforation on why gardens are so restorative.

- **Safe and Inviting:** A well-designed sensory garden offers a sense of security and ease, allowing you to fully enjoy it without feeling overwhelmed. Thoughtful design choices—such as clear pathways, gently defined boundaries, and comfortable seating—help create a safe and predictable environment that encourages relaxation and a sense of belonging.
- **A Refuge for Mental Clarity:** Nature has a way of restoring the mind, especially when designed with gentle, flowing elements that invite effortless attention. Softly moving grasses, the shimmering light on leaves, the hum of pollinators, and the trickling sound of water all provide a quiet yet stimulating environment that encourages focus without demanding it. Whether you need a space for quiet contemplation, a backdrop for creative thought, or a peaceful retreat after a long day, a sensory garden naturally supports cognitive restoration and emotional balance.

Tucked into the corner of a small backyard, this newly established sensory garden blends comfort, beauty, and privacy. With a shaded table, swinging chair, and beds for herbs and flowers, it's thoughtfully designed to meet the diverse needs of a small family, offering a welcoming retreat just steps from the back door.

Vibrant bursts of white, orange, pink, and red brighten this street-side border, drawing in walkers, drivers, pollinators, and birds. This colorful bed creates habitat for everyone, inviting life to linger and thrive.

- **An Invitation to Slow Down:** In a world that constantly demands your attention, a sensory garden offers a rare invitation to pause. Unlike conventional landscapes that require frequent upkeep, this space is designed for presence rather than labor. It invites you to move at nature's pace, where a patch of chamomile waits to release its citrusy scent under your touch, and the steady hum of pollinators offers calm observation.

  Integrating a sensory garden into daily life invites you to explore the world through touch, a contrast to the usual "don't touch" warnings of everyday life. Soft lamb's ear begs to be stroked, fragrant sage releases its aroma with a simple brush, and sun-warm strawberries welcome eager fingers to pluck and taste. In this space, curiosity is encouraged and learning is hands-on, fostering both mindfulness and a deep-rooted connection to nature.

The pink petals of the lily magnolia tree blanket the grass in a stunning spring display, while blooming bluebells circle the base. Sensory experiences like these may already be present in your landscape, waiting to be enjoyed.

- **Your Personal Sanctuary:** A sensory garden is more than a collection of plants; it is a space that supports emotional well-being. Research consistently shows that engaging the senses through nature can lower stress hormones, regulate emotions, and foster a sense of safety. Raised beds, tall containers, and accessible pathways ensure that tending the space remains a joy rather than a strain. It offers a place where tension softens and clarity returns with each deep breath of earth-infused air.

  For urban dwellers with limited space, even a small balcony or patio can become a sanctuary. A container of chamomile provides a soothing scent, a pot of mint offers a refreshing aroma, and a cascading nasturtium vine creates a sense of enclosure. They all work together to create a restorative space within the constraints of city life.

  For parents of neurodivergent children, a sensory garden can be designed with predictability and comfort in mind. Gentle textures, fragrant plants, and enclosed seating areas offer a structured, engaging environment that fosters relaxation without overwhelming the senses.
- **A Habitat for Wildlife:** A sensory garden doesn't just nourish those who plant it—it supports the local ecosystem as well. A thoughtfully designed space includes nectar-rich flowers for pollinators, fruiting plants for birds, and a mix of textures and heights that provide shelter for small creatures. By choosing resilient, native species, the garden becomes a self-sustaining habitat that thrives with minimal intervention.
- **Let the Sensing Begin:** A sensory garden does not require a green thumb, a complete transformation, a perfect plan, or even extra time in your schedule. It begins with noticing what is already present. The rustling of leaves in a nearby tree, the warmth of the sun on a patio, the scent of soil after rain: these are all invitations to engage your senses before a single new plant is in place.

  Take a moment to explore your space as it is now. Are there flowers already drawing in pollinators? A cool, shaded nook that invites rest? A patch of grass or ground cover that feels soft beneath your bare feet? By tuning in to existing sensory elements in your landscape, you may find that your garden is already offering moments of ease and connection.

  The process of creating a sensory garden is as valuable as the garden itself. Every choice, from selecting plants with calming scents to arranging pathways that encourage wandering, becomes an opportunity to cultivate beauty alongside a deeper sense of presence.

STORY OF THE PRAIRIEWOODS HEALING GARDEN

Within the serene landscape of Prairiewoods Franciscan Spirituality Center in Hiawatha, Iowa, a unique healing garden emerged through a collaborative effort with EarthMind Practice. This small, circular sanctuary was conceived through a hands-on class aimed at teaching participants the principles of designing and establishing healing gardens.

The garden's design centers around a simple bench, inviting visitors to sit and reflect amid a thoughtfully arranged collection of sensory herbs. Interspersed among the greenery are various statues, each chosen to represent different aspects of healing and contemplation, adding layers of meaning to the tranquil space.

This initiative aligns with Prairiewoods' mission to integrate ecology and spirituality, providing a tangible example of how intentional design can create spaces that nurture both the land and the human spirit.

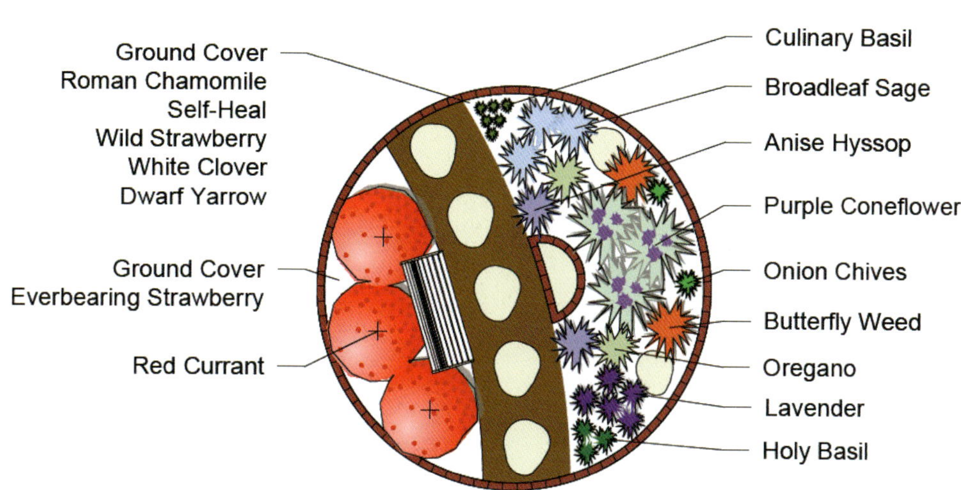

This detailed drawing maps out the healing garden, showing the placement of plants.

Clusters of potted sensory plants wait to be planted by class participants, eager to bring the healing garden to life.

After laying down cardboard to smother existing vegetation and topping it with compost, participants arranged potted plants where they would soon take root.

Symbols of healing and contemplation nestle among blooming anise hyssop, purple coneflower, and other herbs, inviting quiet moments of connection between spirit, soil, and self.

POTENTIAL CHALLENGES

While sensory gardens offer beauty and relaxation, they come with a few unique considerations.

- **Maintenance:** Fragrant herbs and blooming flowers often benefit from regular pruning, deadheading, or harvesting to stay at their best. While optional, regular touch-ups will help preserve the sensory experience. However, some gardeners may find this upkeep to be too much work for their liking.
- **Seasonal Gaps:** Some sensory plants bloom only briefly or have peak fragrance during specific times. For a year-round experience, take time to integrate a variety of plants with staggered bloom times, interesting winter textures, and evergreens.
- **Accessibility Considerations:** For full enjoyment and easy navigation, extra space may be needed for wide pathways, comfortable seating, and large containers.

A brilliant spring display of tulips and grape hyacinths greets visitors just outside this front door, showing how color and placement can create a visual invitation. Thoughtfully arranged blooms awaken the sense of sight and bring everyday beauty into focus.

A close look at oregano reveals more than just texture; rub the leaves between your fingers to release their bold, savory scent. Aromatic herbs like this turn everyday moments in the garden into rich sensory experiences.

DESIGNING FOR THE SENSES

Every garden offers sensory experiences, but when you make time to fully engage with them, those experiences become even more alive and enhanced. The crunch of a freshly harvested radish, the gleam of cherries heavy with morning dew, the hum of bees weaving between flowers. Even the feel of tall grasses brushing against your skin or the shifting scents of a garden after rainfall can free the mind from constant thoughts, creating an experience where stress fades and ease settles in.

Enhancing these experiences involves intentional design choices that encourage full sensory engagement, shaped to support well-being. Whether through color, scent, texture, sound, or taste, every garden has the potential to create moments of joy, calm, and restoration.

- **Sight:** Vision is often the first sense to greet us in a garden, and it can be cultivated to inspire wonder, ease, or excitement. Vibrant blooms in clustered arrangements create a classic palette of color, while a diverse mix of native wildflowers offers a confetti-like effect. Sunflowers follow the arc of the sun, butterfly weeds burst into striking orange, oregano and thyme flowers vibrate with bees. Seasonal changes offer a visual rhythm: spring's bright greens, summer's lush fullness, autumn's golden hues. Consider mixing plants that shift color throughout the year. Tall plants and trellised vines can frame views, directing attention toward inviting spots.
- **Sound:** Sound, often overlooked in garden design, has a profound effect on relaxation and mental clarity. A small fountain or gentle windchime can mask urban noise and offer a meditative backdrop. The whisper of wind through tall grasses, the rustle of leaves, and the soft crackling of dried seed heads add dynamic sound elements. A habitat rich in diversity brings another layer of sound—bees buzzing at blooms and songbirds singing from nearby branches.
- **Smell:** Scent has a direct line to memory and emotion, making it one of the most evocative elements of a garden. While flowers are a classic choice, there are many other ways to introduce aromatic layers. The crisp scent of pine needles, the spice of bee balm, and the earthy fragrance of damp soil all create a sensory experience that changes throughout the day and across the seasons.

  Herbs offer some of the most interactive scents. Creeping thyme releases a calming aroma when stepped on, while mint and oregano leave their fragrance on your fingers when rubbed. Anise hyssop carries a hint of licorice, and yarrow's feathery leaves exude a soft herbal scent when crushed. For the most immersive experience, plant fragrant varieties near walkways or seating areas, where even a light brush stirs scents into the air.
- **Touch:** The textures within a garden create a tactile landscape that invites exploration. Lamb's ear offers a velvety softness, while chamomile's fine, feathery leaves beg to be run through the fingers. Coneflowers have bristly, spiky centers that contrast with their smooth

Feathery and aromatic, the leaves of German chamomile invite gentle touch and close attention.

It's hard to beat the simple joy of a sun-warmed strawberry, which offers a perfect sensory moment where taste, warmth, and sweetness blend together.

A dandelion bloom dipped in chocolate is a playful, delicious way to experience the garden from a new perspective. Nutrient-packed dandelions paired with this touch of rich sweetness strike a joyful balance between earthy connection and indulgence that lifts the spirit.

petals. The delicate tendrils of climbing peas curl around fingertips, while the sturdy leaves of rhubarb offer a cool and solid surface.

Let touch be more than a passing experience; pause to gently press palms to the soil, brush a hand along swaying grass, or feel the temperature shift between a sun-warmed stone and the shaded underside of a leaf.

- **Taste:** Taste can be woven into any design for simple, delightful moments even in gardens not focused on growing an abundance of food. Fresh herbs are the easiest to incorporate: pluck a sprig of mint for an instant refresh, nibble a chive for a sharp bite, or roll a basil leaf between your fingers before tasting its rich, peppery warmth. Bee balm, anise hyssop, and chamomile can all be steeped into tea right in the garden, offering a slow, sensory ritual.

  For an even deeper sensory experience, challenge yourself to eat like a visiting critter—no hands, just mouth! Plucking a berry straight from the bush with your lips or leaning down to nibble dill fronds can engage taste in a playful way.

STEP-BY-STEP DESIGN

Every garden project, whether in this book or beyond, can be enhanced to heighten the sensory experience. But why wait until the plants are in the ground to begin that journey? The design process itself can be a deeply immersive and nourishing experience, filled with opportunities to engage your senses and cultivate a sense of ease, joy, and connection before a single seed is sown.

Too often, efficiency is prioritized over presence, with tasks framed as something to get through and check off. But gardening, especially sensory gardening, is not about rushing to an endpoint. The simple act of engaging with a space, experimenting with possibilities, and delighting in small discoveries can be just as restorative as the garden itself. And your landscape may already be offering sensory gifts—ones you can enjoy right now while you dream, plan, and create.

Before you sketch a single line or choose a single plant, let yourself simply be in the space. Linger. Listen. Breathe it in. Your senses will gently reveal what your garden wants to become.

CHOOSE THE PERFECT SPOT

If you've read "Put Your Garden Where You Roam" (page 55), you may already have a couple of locations in mind for your sensory garden. Instead of jumping straight into planning, spend time in those spaces and let them reveal possibilities to you. Find a comfortable seat, perhaps a cushion or folding chair, and settle in with your favorite warm beverage. Let yourself linger. Close your eyes. What scents drift through the air? What layers of sound can you detect, from the closest rustle to the farthest bird call? Does the feel of the breeze on your skin invite the thought of adding wind-loving grasses or chimes? Does the soft shade of a tree inspire a seating nook where you can relax? Does the distant sound of a chickadee lead you to include a bird bath or feeder? Does the drifting movement of clouds suggest a hammock or a shaded cot?

Once you've spent time in one spot, explore another—even one you hadn't considered. Different times of day and weather conditions offer new perspectives. A light summer rain might reveal the soothing rhythm of raindrops on leaves. An early morning sunrise might cast a warm glow over an unexpected nook, making it the perfect place for quiet reflection. A breezy autumn afternoon might show how movement through plants creates dynamic beauty. A twilight moment under the stars could inspire soft, glowing lights or a grassy stargazing spot.

Even before you begin designing, nature has already gifted you with these experiences. Enjoy them.

When shopping for plants, take a moment to touch the leaves and smell the flowers. You'll start connecting with them before they even come home.

DISCOVER AND DREAM

Allow the process of choosing plants and design elements to be as immersive as the garden itself. The "Plant Profiles" section (page 206) will guide you, but don't limit yourself to books; visit a local plant nursery, a community garden, or a wild natural area. If you can, attend seasonal plant sales or farmers markets where local growers offer plants suited to your climate. Wander, pause, and interact with the plants—run your hands through the leaves and stop to smell those flowers. Not only will you gather ideas, but you'll also begin forming a connection to the plants before they even enter your space. Use tips in "Your Plant Matchmaking Guide" (page 180) to continue the exploration and record your favorites.

3

RECORD YOUR VISION THROUGH SENSORY MEMORY

Once you've spent time in your future garden space and explored plant possibilities, reflect on the experiences that felt the most profound, joyful, or calming. Instead of making a list of what you "need," start by writing about how you want to feel in your garden.

Try using a present tense statement to make the vision feel alive even before it's built: "Each time I visit my garden, the bubbling water from a small fountain and the movement of vibrant colors remind me of an urban park I explored as a child, where I spent hours gathering wildflowers and watching the stream flow. After just five minutes, I feel relaxed, calm, and grounded." Pair this with "Maximize Ease with Location and Layout" (page 55) to align your desired emotions with what your landscape naturally offers.

A bee visits the vibrant purple bloom of anise hyssop—a plant that delights every sense. Its flowers draw pollinators, its leaves smell of licorice, its square stems invite touch, and it brews into a calming tea, making it a perfect addition to a sensory-rich garden.

CHOOSE FOR ALL SENSES

Where possible, select plants and features that engage all your senses. Even a small raised bed or container garden can overflow with sensory delight when designed with multipurpose in mind.

- **Anise Hyssop:** A pollinator favorite with vibrant purple flowers, its leaves release a licorice-like aroma, its square stem is fun to roll between fingers, and it brews into a soothing tea.
- **Raspberry Canes:** These catch the eye with their changing foliage, offer a rich scent when warmed by the sun, provide a tactile experience when brushed against, draw in songbirds, and of course, offer a sweet-tart summer snack.
- **Ornamental Grasses:** Their feathery fronds sway in the wind, their rustling sound adds an auditory element, their foliage provides year-round texture, and they soften visual boundaries in the space.

Textured pots, smooth pebbles, or rough bark mulch can also add many layers of sensation.

5

MINDFULLY LAY OUT

As you reach the layout step—using pots, stakes, string, or sticks to visualize the placement of features—staying present and mindful of moments can make the process immersive and restorative, even if you're short on time.

- Feel the rhythm of hammering in stakes—the deep sound, the vibration in your hands.
- Lie down in an empty raised bed or a pile of straw mulch to observe clouds, birds, and the sway of trees.
- Pause with a container before placing it, running your hands over its shape and feeling its weight.

6

LIVE WITH YOUR LAYOUT

Once your garden layout is in place, spend time with it before planting. Sit in different locations, experience it in different weather conditions, and explore how it interacts with your daily rhythms:

- **Morning Light:** Does the spot you imagined for your tea-drinking nook receive light from the golden sunrise?
- **Midday Buzz:** What activity do the birds and pollinators bring during a warm afternoon?
- **Evening Stillness:** Does your chosen seat catch a cool evening breeze?
- **Post-Rain Renewal:** How does the scent of soil shift after a gentle rainfall?

THE 5-4-3-2-1 SENSORY GROUNDING EXERCISE

This simple horticultural therapy exercise helps calm the mind and reconnect you with the present moment by engaging all five senses. Try it while sitting in your garden or during a slow stroll through your plants. This grounding activity is a wonderful alternative to traditional meditation, providing a natural reset for busy minds while deepening your connection to your garden.

5: Look around and name five things you can see. Notice the details: a delicate flower petal, a bee hovering, or the shifting colors of leaves.

4: Touch four different textures. Feel the cool soil, the rough bark, the velvety sage leaves, or a smooth garden stone.

3: Listen for three distinct sounds. Tune in to the rustling of leaves, chirping birds, or the gentle hum of pollinators.

2: Breathe in and identify two scents. Inhale the freshness of damp earth or the fragrance of nearby herbs and flowers.

1: Savor one taste. Nibble a fresh mint leaf or a sun-warmed berry.

The delicate bloom of an alpine strawberry is a reminder to slow down and notice the small wonders. With flowers that appear throughout the season, it's a perfect plant to support sensory grounding—inviting sight, scent, and taste into your landscape.

Now that your garden design is ready, it's time to bring it to life. But instead of rushing toward completion—like so many of your other tasks—why not treat it as an opportunity to slow down, engage your senses, and find joy in each step? Every moment spent in the act of building, planting, and tending is a chance to nourish body, mind, and spirit.

STEP-BY-STEP ESTABLISHMENT

ESSENTIAL MATERIALS

- **Compost.**
- **Straw or Woodchip Mulch.**
- **Plants, Seeds, or Seedlings.**
- **Tongue Depressors and Permanent Marker:** Label plants and seeds.
- **Contractor's Paper or Cardboard:** Smother existing vegetation
- **Containers.**
- **Container Mix:** Lightweight, well-draining mix designed for containers
- **Arbors or Trellises:** Support vining plants.

OPTIONAL MATERIALS

- **Garden Stakes:** Lay out beds and mark plant locations

See "Materials Planning" (page 265) for details about quantities.

ESSENTIAL TOOLS

- **Garden Gloves:** Protect your hands.
- **Shovel, Trowel, or Hori Hori Knife:** Digging and transplanting.
- **Utility Knife:** Open bags. Cut cardboard when sheet mulching.
- **Pruning Snips or Scissors:** Pruning and harvesting herbs.
- **Watering Can or Hose:** Keep plants hydrated.

OPTIONAL TOOLS

- **Measuring Tape:** Lay out beds and planting rows.
- **Rubber Mallet or Hammer:** Drive in stakes for laying out beds.
- **Flat-Bladed Spade:** Create clean bed edges.
- **Hand Rake:** Smooth small areas of soil and incorporate compost.
- **Steel Rake:** Smooth soil, compost, and mulch.

See "Garden Toolbox" (page 262) for details about each tool.

Feel the earth between your fingers, breathe in its mood-lifting scent, and watch the small creatures at work. These simple moments make gardening as rewarding as the harvest.

PREPARE SOIL WITH PRESENCE

Soil is the foundation of any garden, but it's also an invitation to engage deeply with the earth itself. Whether you're filling containers with a rich soil mix, improving the ground using tips from "Build Healthy Soil: Testing and Improvement" (page 143) or layering organic matter following tips from "Sheet Mulching: Prepare and Revive Garden Beds" (page 145), each action offers a chance to connect with the textures, scents, and life within the soil.

Take time to feel the texture of the earth between your fingers. Notice how it changes as you add water—does it crumble easily or hold together in a soft, spongy mass? Breathe in the scent of damp soil, a fragrance that has been scientifically shown to have mood-lifting properties. Observe the tiny creatures that call the soil home: pill bugs roll into tight balls, worms tunnel deeper, and beetles scurry under layers of mulch. These small moments of observation ground you in the present, making the process as rewarding as the results.

Place seed packets in a dry, visible spot to build anticipation for planting day.

WELCOME PLANTS

A garden begins the moment you bring plants or seeds into your life—not just when they take root in the soil. Nurture your excitement and build a connection with your new plants before they find their permanent home.

- Keep seed packets in a visible, dry spot indoors where you'll see them daily, letting anticipation grow as you await planting day.
- Place potted plants in high-traffic areas—by the front step, along a patio, or on a balcony—so you can enjoy their presence, scent, and beauty before they're in the ground.

Smelling a pot of flowers while planting, this gardener takes a moment to fully savor the experience. Planting isn't just a task, it's a chance to slow down, connect with your senses, and be present with the life you're helping to grow.

SAVOR THE PLANTING PROCESS

Let planting be a slow and grounding experience, one that invites all your senses into the moment.

- **Prepare the Bed with Intention:** Gently pull back straw mulch to reveal the rich, dark soil beneath. Feel the temperature of the earth, inhale the deep, grounding scent of loam, and listen to the rustle of shifting mulch.
- **Bask in the Moment:** Before planting, gather your seeds and seedlings around you like cherished companions. Sit with them for a moment, feeling the warmth of the sun on your skin, listening to the sounds of the garden, breathing slowly and deeply, and appreciating the life about to take root.
- **Sow Seeds Mindfully:** As you plant each seed, imagine the life held within them and the transformation that will soon unfold. Feel the texture of different seeds—smooth, round peas; tiny, fine basil; and firm, ridged sunflowers.
- **Set Transplants with Care:** Cradle the delicate roots of seedlings for a moment before placing them in the ground. Gently firm soil around them, setting an intention with each pat.

When planting is treated as an experience rather than a hurried task, it becomes an act of presence and restoration rather than just another step in a process.

Turn watering into a simple ritual—watch the soil drink, feel the cool splash on your skin, and listen as life stirs. It is nourishment for both plant and gardener.

RITUAL WATERING

Watering is essential in the early stages of growth, and it can become an opportunity to connect with the rhythm of your garden. When time is available, try turning it into a simple, mindful ritual.

- **Notice How the Water Moves:** Watch as water beads on leaves, sinks into the soil, or creates tiny rivulets in soil.
- **Feel the Temperature Change:** Let cool water flow across your skin on a warm day.
- **Listen to the Sounds:** The gentle splash of water hitting soil and mulch, the soft gurgle of a watering can, the hum of pollinators drawn to moisture.

Fast-growing seedlings invite frequent visits. Use all your senses to track their progress—notice color changes, feel the texture of the leaves, and nibble a tender piece as you follow their journey.

MINDFULLY MONITOR

Along with regular watering, periodic garden check-ins are a good way to detect pests, diseases, or nutrient deficiencies before they cause any major problems. Instead of seeing these inspections as a chore, approach them as an opportunity to be fully immersed in your space.

- **Use All Your Senses:** Instead of a quick glance, take a few extra moments to really engage with your plants. Observe subtle color shifts; run your fingers along the leaves, and check their underside; notice any sticky oils or residues left on your skin; then breathe in the lingering scent.
- **Observe Patterns:** Which flowers are attracting the most pollinators? Are leaves shifting toward the light? What birds or beneficial insects are appearing?
- **Greet New Growth:** When the first row of seedlings emerges, don't contain your excitement—embrace it! If you're able, get low and notice how they push through the soil, unfurl their first leaves, lean toward the light, and sway with the breeze as they settle into their new world. If the greens are edible—such as radish, lettuce, beet, Swiss chard, or culinary herbs—pluck a few, enjoy their fresh, tender flavors, and savor the abundance to come.

Even five minutes of slow, intentional observation can calm your nervous system and be restorative.

In the corner of this yard, two blooming serviceberries signal the arrival of spring with delicate white flowers. From fragrant blossoms and sweet summer berries to fiery autumn foliage, these shrubs offer a changing tapestry of sensory experiences to enjoy in every season.

ENJOY THE HARVEST

When the time comes to harvest, it's easy to focus only on gathering the yield, but this moment can also be a deeply immersive sensory experience.

- Feel the weight of a sun-warmed tomato in your palm.
- Listen to the crisp snap of a bean pulled from the vine.
- Run your fingers through feathery dill fronds before plucking a handful.
- Breathe in the peppery scent of basil leaves before snipping them for pizza.
- Nibble on a freshly picked serviceberry, letting the sweet juice linger on your tongue.

Harvesting is about food, but it's also about connecting with the season, the plants, and the abundance of the moment. The more you engage your senses, the more fulfilling each harvest becomes.

STORY OF THE GUIDELINK CENTER

The GuideLink Center in Iowa City, Iowa, provides immediate, on-site assessment and stabilization for individuals experiencing a mental health or substance-use crisis, who might seek support outside of a hospital. This vital community resource offers a safe and caring environment for clients as they explore the next steps in their treatment, whether they stayfor a few hours or a few days. Recognizing the need for access to fresh air and a calming outdoor space, the center includes an enclosed courtyard abundant with sunshine.

However, the initial conditions of the courtyard posed significant challenges: compacted clay soil from construction equipment, an imposing metal fence enclosing the space, and rock mulch that radiated heat rather than offering relief. These factors hindered plant growth and made it difficult for clients and staff to find respite there. The space remained underutilized, falling short of its potential as a place of restoration.

Seeking a solution that would be both effective and mindful of the needs of those in crisis, the center hired EarthMind Practice to reimagine the courtyard into a welcoming, interactive environment. Rather than undertaking costly and lengthy soil remediation, a container sensory garden was established, ensuring that the space could immediately offer a therapeutic experience while remaining adaptable to future needs.

Containers of varying sizes were arranged to encourage exploration and enhance visual appeal. Some were grouped near seating areas for prolonged interactive experiences, while others were placed throughout the space to invite movement and mindful engagement. The plant selection was curated with sensory stimulation in mind: ornamental grasses with soft, flowing textures, aromatic herbs like chamomile and mint that invited touch and scent, dangling vines for visual intrigue, and edible plants like cherry tomatoes and culinary herbs to encourage interaction.

Before the sensory enhancements, this courtyard offered safety, sunlight, and ample seating—but it lacked the natural elements that support deep comfort and restoration. With compacted soil, heat-retaining rock mulch, and limited plant life, the space remained underused, waiting for its next stage of growth.

This visual representation of the GuideLink Center's courtyard, created by EarthMind Practice, was used to communicate the design vision. It illustrates how sensory-rich plantings and thoughtful features could transform the space into a welcoming, restorative environment.

To bring nature's healing closer to hand, EarthMind Practice introduced a container sensory garden filled with herbs like dill, yarrow, chamomile, and lavender. Placed within easy reach of a bench, these aromatic plants invite visitors to see, touch, and smell—offering calm, comfort, and gentle engagement with the natural world.

Large containers filled with vibrant flowers and soft-textured grasses were placed at the garden entrance to soften the expanse of river rock and create a more inviting feel.

Additional elements, including rocking chairs, wall-mounted artwork, a solar-powered fountain, and shaded seating, were introduced to create a multisensory and comfortable respite. These features, guided by horticultural therapy principles, offer clients and staff the opportunity to ground themselves in the present moment, engage their senses, and find solace in nature. Mindfulness exercises, often centered around sensory awareness, are now integrated into the space, providing clients with a tangible, calming experience to help regulate their nervous system.

For many, the act of engaging with plants evokes positive memories—gardening with family members, childhood moments in nature, or the simple pleasure of nurturing a living thing. These connections foster hope, joy, and a sense of agency. Clients often describe how the colors of the flowers, the rustling of the grasses, and the presence of insects like bees and butterflies create an environment where they feel a renewed sense of hope.

Staff members also find relief in the garden, stepping outside for brief moments of respite from their emotionally demanding roles. The presence of nature—even in a small courtyard—has transformed the space into a place of shared healing, where both clients and caregivers can take a breath, reconnect, and find balance.

By applying trauma-informed landscape principles, EarthMind Practice helped transform the GuideLink Center's outdoor space into more than just a garden; it is now a therapeutic sanctuary, a living extension of the center's mission to provide compassionate, holistic care.

Art was added to soften the stark metal walls, bringing warmth and a touch of nature for a more welcoming, calming environment.

The gentle trickle of water from a solar fountain evokes an ancestral sense of safety and calm, offering a soothing presence that helps quiet the mind and ease the nervous system.

A collection of small, colorful stones painted with simple messages invites visitors to pause and reflect on how they're feeling. This gentle act of naming emotions can help regulate the nervous system, offering a step toward emotional grounding and a greater sense of control.

Whimsical touches like garden gnomes and uplifting hand-drawn messages help create a sense of safety, calm, and connection. These elements offer moments of lightness to support emotional regulation and invite clients to express care for themselves and others.

Compost for Free Fertilizer

Turning food scraps and garden clippings into rich, dark compost might just be the closest thing to magic in the gardening world. With nothing more than a simple bin, a tumbler, or even a hole in the ground, nature gets to work, transforming everyday waste into free, organic fertilizer. No fancy equipment, no complex steps—just a slow, natural process that gives back to the soil, feeding plants and improving your garden's vitality.

For those of us who want all the benefits of composting but without a big commitment, an easy, low-maintenance setup can be as simple as tossing scraps into a bin and letting time do the work. Even if you do not stir or turn your compost regularly, decomposition still happens—just at its own pace. Whether you choose a shallow pit, bin, or tumbler, the result is the same: a rich, soil-building amendment packed with nutrients that your plants will love.

A simple compost pit filled with leaves sits beside a compact tumbler—proof that there's no single right way to compost. Having two systems allows for flexibility: one pile can decompose while the other collects new scraps, making it easier to create rich, garden-loving compost with minimal effort.

WHY CHOOSE COMPOST?

Composting is nature's recycling program, a continuous loop of growth, decay, and renewal. By setting up a simple compost system, you create a way to turn everyday waste—vegetable peels, coffee grounds, and garden trimmings—into a nutrient-dense soil booster that keeps your garden thriving. Here's what composting does for you and your plants:

- **Feeds the Soil:** Compost provides a steady, slow-release source of nutrients, reducing the need for external fertilizers. It fosters a thriving underground ecosystem where soil bacteria, fungi, earthworms, and other soil-builders break down organic matter, cycling nutrients in a way that plants can readily absorb.
- **Improves Soil Texture:** Whether your soil is heavy clay or too sandy, compost helps create a crumbly, well-draining, loamy structure that makes planting and growing easier.
- **Holds Moisture:** Compost-rich soil retains water like a sponge, reducing the need for frequent watering.
- **Reduces Waste:** Every kitchen scrap and garden clipping you compost is one less thing headed to the landfill.

Best of all, composting doesn't have to be hard. Even an ignored pile will eventually break down into gardener's gold.

WHAT TO COMPOST

Anything organic will eventually break down, but for a well-balanced, efficient compost pile, some materials work better than others. To keep things simple, focus on plant-based materials that decompose easily. Here are great compost ingredients:

- **Fruit and Vegetable Scraps:** Apple cores, banana peels, potato peels, and any other fruit or veggie leftovers.

While anything organic will eventually decompose, focus on adding plant-based kitchen scraps for a balanced, efficient compost pile that breaks down smoothly.

- **Coffee Grounds and Tea Leaves:** These quickly decompose.
- **Eggshells:** A great source of calcium, though they take a while to break down.
- **Dried Leaves and Grass Clippings:** Dry leaves add carbon, while fresh grass clippings add nitrogen. Spread green clippings thinly to prevent matting.
- **Torn-Up Newspaper and Cardboard:** As long as it's not glossy or coated, paper products are a great carbon source.
- **Garden Trimmings:** Plant cuttings, old flowers, and wilted greens.
- **Hay and Straw:** Excellent for aeration, but avoid hay with weed seeds.
- **Woodchips and Sawdust:** These take longer to break down but can add structure to a pile in small amounts.

A simple ring of leaves held in place by stacked sticks creates a natural compost system. No turning, no bins—just letting nature do what it does best, slowly enriching the soil beneath the tree.

WHAT TO AVOID

Some materials are technically compostable but can cause more problems than they're worth.

- **Oily or Fatty Foods:** These take too long to break down and can attract pests.
- **Dairy and Meat:** They will compost eventually, but they tend to smell and attract animals.
- **Glossy or Coated Paper:** Magazines, wax-coated cartons, and plastic-lined cardboard contain chemicals that shouldn't go into the soil.
- **Diseased Plants and Plants with Mature Seeds:** These can survive the composting process, and the harvested compost can spread unwanted plants in your garden.
- **Pet Waste:** Waste can carry harmful pathogens, making it unsafe for garden compost.
- **Anything Treated with Herbicides:** Grass clippings or straw that was sprayed with herbicides can contaminate your compost and harm plants.

Bacteria, fungi, pill bugs, millipedes, earthworms, and more transform organic matter into rich compost in dark, moist, and well-aerated spaces.

HOW TO COMPOST

Nature is composting all the time, breaking down leaves, fallen branches, and grass clippings without any help from you. Composting simply speeds up that process by creating optimal conditions for decomposition. You can be as active or as inactive as you like; decomposition happens either way. You can simply rake leaves under shrubs or around a tree, and this can be considered composting. Over time, those leaves will break down naturally, feeding the soil and supporting the life above it.

Bacteria, fungi, pill bugs, millipedes, and earthworms are nature's clean-up crew, working together to break down material into dark, nutrient-rich compost. These soil-building organisms thrive in places that are dark, moist, and full of loose organic matter with plenty of oxygen: under a pile of leaves, at the base of a rotting log, or beneath a layer of mulch.

If you want to speed up the process, you can emulate these ideal conditions. A well-maintained compost pile is like a buffet for decomposers; the more inviting the setup, the faster they'll work and replicate. But even if you never stir or turn it, your compost will eventually break down, just at a slower pace.

To encourage decomposition, consider what composting organisms need most.

- **Moisture:** Compost that feels like a wrung-out sponge is about right—damp but not dripping.

- **Oxygen:** Turning the pile helps prevent smelly, airless conditions and speeds up decomposition.
- **Balance of Greens and Browns:** Green materials—such as kitchen scraps and fresh grass clippings—provide nitrogen, while brown materials—such as dried leaves, straw, and cardboard—provide carbon. Roughly aim for a ratio of one-part green to two- to three-parts brown by volume to keep the compost balanced, odor-free, and steadily decomposing.

COMPOST TROUBLESHOOTING

Composting is a natural process, but sometimes it needs a little nudge to keep things running smoothly. If your compost pile isn't breaking down as expected, here are symptoms and how to get it back on track.

- **Smells Bad:** A rotten or ammonia-like odor means too much nitrogen and not enough carbon. Mix in dry materials like straw, dry leaves, or shredded newspaper and turn the pile to aerate.
- **Too Slow:** Large pieces, not enough air or moisture, or an imbalance of greens (kitchen scraps) and browns (dry leaves, paper) can stall decomposition. Chop bulky items—aim for about 1:2 or 1:3 greens to browns—water lightly if dry, and turn the pile to boost airflow.
- **Attracting Pests:** Meat, dairy, or large exposed scraps can invite rodents and flies. Stick to plant-based scraps, bury food waste under dry materials, and keep bins covered.
- **Mold or Fungus Growth:** Some fungi are normal, but excessive mold signals too much moisture or poor aeration. Stir the pile and adjust moisture by adding dry materials as needed.

An old plastic colander or bowl makes a perfect kitchen compost container. Lining it with newspaper or brown paper keeps things tidy and adds a helpful "brown" layer when you empty your scraps into the pile.

COMPOSTING STRUCTURES

There are plenty of ways to compost, but some methods require more effort than others. If you're the type of gardener who wants rich, nutritious compost but doesn't want to spend much time turning piles or fine-tuning moisture levels, then use the small-scale composting structures that are the simplest to establish and maintain.

Each option allows you to be an "inactive" composter, meaning you can toss in your scraps and let time do the work. You don't need fancy setups or intensive management, just a place for nature to work its magic.

PIT

This is as basic as composting gets: a simple hole in the ground where scraps are tossed. Occasional stirring and turning will speed up decomposition, but that step is optional.

A compost pit is as simple and frugal as it gets—just toss scraps into a hole and let nature do the work. Stirring speeds things up, but patience is all you really need.

PROS:

- **Extremely Simple:** No structure to build, no bin to purchase.
- **Virtually Invisible:** It blends into the garden once covered with soil, leaves, or straw.
- **Low Maintenance:** Great for those who want to compost without much effort.

CONS:

- **Can Attract Critters:** Animals may dig through the pile if food scraps aren't buried deep enough.
- **Potential Odors:** Without aeration, anaerobic decomposition can become smelly.
- **Slow:** Decomposition happens slowly, especially if materials are not frequently mixed.

WHY CHOOSE THIS?

If you value frugality and simplicity, and want to begin immediately, a compost pit is a great option. This method works well if you want to keep composting nearly invisible and don't mind a potentially slow decomposition process. If you have pets, active wildlife, or limited digging ability, you may prefer a contained system.

WIRE BIN

This is a simple structure made by forming a circle or square with wire mesh or fencing to contain composting materials. If desired, remove the bin to stir and turn the compost, then put it back in place.

A wire bin offers a simple, affordable way to keep compost contained while allowing airflow.

PROS:

- **Inexpensive and Easy Set Up:** A simple section of sturdy wire mesh or fence is all that's needed.
- **High Capacity:** Allows for larger quantities of material than a pit.
- **Encourages Airflow:** The open sides help speed up decomposition.

CONS:

- **Untidy:** The open structure means scraps are often visible.
- **Can Attract Critters:** Without a secure lid, animals may be tempted.
- **Bulky:** May not be ideal for smaller spaces.

WHY CHOOSE THIS?

A wire bin is great for those who want an easy, expandable composting setup without a lot of upfront cost. It's slightly more structured than a pit but still requires only minimal effort to maintain.

PLASTIC BIN

This is a store-bought, dome-shaped bin with a lid on top for adding scraps and a sliding panel at the bottom to access finished compost. To stir, lift and move the entire bin next to the pile and then scoop the pile back into the bin.

It can be tricky to harvest finished compost from plastic compost bins, but they are compact and pest-resistant.

PROS:

- **Compact and Tidy:** Keeps compost contained and out of sight.
- **Breaks Down Weed Seeds:** If the bin is black and sits in full sun, high heat might help break down plants with mature weed seeds.
- **Discourages Animals:** A lid keeps pests out.

CONS:

- **Difficult to Retrieve Compost:** The bottom access panel is often impractical; lifting the entire bin off the pile works better.
- **Requires Watering:** Unless the top is left open, rainwater doesn't reach the compost, so moisture may need to be added.
- **Slow:** Because of limited aeration access, decomposition will take longer.
- **Limited Capacity:** Not ideal for high-volume composting.

WHY CHOOSE THIS?

This is a great choice if you want a tidy, enclosed composting system that keeps pests at bay. It works well in smaller yards and urban spaces where an open pile isn't ideal.

TUMBLER

A compost tumbler is a raised, rotating bin that allows you to aerate compost by spinning it.

A tumbler is a good option if you prefer a low-maintenance, contained system and are willing to invest a bit more for convenience.

PROS:

- **Fast:** Regular turning provides oxygen, which speeds decomposition.
- **Compact and Tidy:** Keeps compost contained and out of sight.
- **Discourages Animals:** A lid keeps pests out.
- **Reduces Odor:** Aeration prevents smelly anaerobic decomposition.

CONS:

- **Expensive:** Costs more than other methods.
- **Requires Watering:** Rainwater doesn't reach the compost, so moisture may need to be added.
- **Limited Capacity:** Not suited for high-volume composting.

WHY CHOOSE THIS?

A tumbler is ideal if you want a more structured, faster composting system and don't mind giving it a quick spin now and then. If you can afford it, the tumbler offers a good balance between convenience, tidiness, and efficiency.

STEP-BY-STEP ESTABLISHMENT

Setting up any of these composting structures is easy, and the best placement depends on how you garden. Ideally, keep it near your garden bed or kitchen, so scraps can be easily tossed in, and finished compost is within easy reach. If you're planning a future garden space, placing compost there now can enrich the soil before planting.

DIVIDE AND DECOMPOSE

If you have room, establishing two or three spots can make composting easier.

1. **Active Spot:** This is where you toss fresh scraps, leaves, and garden clippings.
2. **Inactive Spot:** Keep a second spot next to the first. Once your active pile is full, let it sit undisturbed while the second new pile starts. This allows for an easier, "set-it-and-forget-it" approach.
3. **Weedy and Disease Spot:** If you want to compost diseased plants or plants with mature weed seeds, set up a separate pile. Placing it in a shady area away from your garden, such as under a hedge, helps prevent weed seeds from sprouting and spreading. Avoid mixing diseased or weedy plants into your main pile to prevent spreading problems in your garden.

If you only have space for one active spot, that's fine too. You'll just need to sift out materials that haven't fully broken down when harvesting the compost.

SETTING UP DIFFERENT COMPOSTING METHODS

- **Pit:** Dig a shallow hole, toss in scraps, and cover with soil. Occasional stirring and turning helps, but it's optional.
- **Wire Bin:** Form a circle or square with sturdy wire mesh or fencing.
- **Plastic Bin:** Place the bin on level ground, ensuring airflow through bottom or side vents.
- **Tumbler:** Position it on level ground where you can spin it every few days.

HARVESTING THE GOLD

There's something deeply satisfying about lifting a forkful of compost and watching it crumble into rich, dark earth. What once was a heap of kitchen scraps and wilted leaves has transformed into something unrecognizable—soft, fragrant, and teeming with life. If you pause for a moment, you might catch a glimpse of the underground world at work: pill bugs scurrying, earthworms wriggling, millipedes curling into hidden tunnels. The soil is alive, and you've helped create it.

The simplest way to harvest compost is to scoop from the bottom or center of the pile, where the most finished material collects. If you're using a bin, you can lift it and set it aside to expose the compost underneath for easier access. When you come across a few half-decomposed scraps, no need to worry; soil organisms will happily finish the job right where they land. For a finer texture, sift the compost through a metal mesh screen into a container or wheelbarrow, setting aside larger, unfinished bits to return to the active pile.

Here's a surprising part—you don't need to harvest at all. A full compost bin, tumbler, or pile breaks down much more than you'd expect, shrinking into a fraction of its original size. You might go years before feeling the need to scoop any out. And if you never do? That's just fine too. In an undisturbed pile, your compost will quietly enrich the soil beneath it, providing a thriving habitat and feeding the ecosystem in its own slow, steady way.

Scoop rich compost from the bottom of the pile where decomposition is most complete. Optionally, sift it for a finer texture, tossing unfinished bits back into the pile to break down further.

PART III:

NURTURE YOUR GARDEN WHILE IT NURTURES YOU

Once your garden is in place, it becomes a living companion. This section shows you how to care for it in ways that feel sustainable for both you and the land. Your time in the garden can be flexible, forgiving, and deeply restorative, thus shifting with the seasons, your energy, and your needs.

CHAPTER 08: MANAGE YOUR SPACE WITH THE RHYTHMS OF NATURE

Planting a seedling can be more than a task, it can be a moment of connection and grounding. Gardening invites you to slow down, engage your body and mind, and find calm through simple, purposeful care.

Your garden is an invitation, not an obligation. Sometimes you may have hours to enjoy it, and other times all you can spare is a few minutes to run your fingers through fragrant herbs while on your way to the next task. Let it be a living, breathing relationship—one that adapts to your life as the seasons unfold.

Gardening as Self-Care

The caretaking tasks of a garden—planting, watering, weeding, pruning, harvesting—are opportunities to engage deeply with the rhythms of the natural world. Gardening is one of the few activities that engages both the body and the mind in a way that is calming, purposeful, and rewarding. Tending your garden offers:

- **Physical Grounding:** The gentle motion of weeding, the rhythm of harvesting, and the pressure of soil between your fingers—each act is a form of active meditation that anchors you in the present.
- **Emotional Restoration:** Repetitive, soothing tasks—watering, spreading mulch, harvesting herbs—reduce stress and quiet anxious thoughts.
- **Sense of Accomplishment:** Seeing a small patch cleared of weeds, a row of seedlings standing strong, or a basket of fresh herbs ready for your kitchen reinforces progress and connection.
- **Tactile Engagement:** The sensory experience of gardening—textures, scents, warmth, and moisture—brings deep satisfaction and reduces mental fatigue.

Recognizing these benefits can transform even the most basic garden tasks into conscious moments of purpose, connection, and renewal.

ALIGN YOUR GARDEN WITH YOUR LIFE

Your time in the garden will look different depending on the day, the season, and your energy level. Some days, you may find yourself deeply engaged, hands in the soil for hours, shaping, tending, and losing your sense of time. Other days, your only interaction might be stepping outside for a breath of fresh air, allowing nature to briefly embrace and support you.

Instead of seeing gardening as a rigid responsibility, let it be flexible—a space where you can choose how to engage based on what you need in the moment. Your time can be task-oriented, purely restorative, or a blend of both. Some days you may prefer intentional caretaking, checking off a few seasonal to-dos. Other times, you may simply want to be in the garden, sitting quietly, observing, and unwinding. Most often, you'll find yourself moving fluidly between the two, allowing the space to guide you.

Consider these flexible timeframes as a guide:

- **Five Minutes for a Quick Reset:** Step outside and let the garden greet you. Touch a leaf, water a single container, or nibble a sprig of mint. If you're here just to be, notice the feel of the air on your skin, the sway of branches, the scent of soil, or the song of a nearby bird. Even the briefest pause can restore your sense of calm.
- **Fifteen Minutes of Simple Connection:** Gently weed a small section, deadhead flowers, or turn compost with slow, rhythmic motions. Plant a single seedling with care, noticing the feel of the soil. Harvest a handful of berries or greens, appreciating their textures and scents in your hands. If your focus is restoration, walk slowly through the space, pausing when something catches your eye: a bee hovering over a blossom, the light filtering through leaves, a tiny new seedling unfurling toward the sun.
- **Thirty Minutes of Intentional Engagement:** Transplant a few seedlings, refresh mulch in a key area, or prune a small tree with care. Feel the connection between your hands and the plants, noticing how your actions shape their growth. If you're here to simply be, find a comfortable spot to sit, close your eyes for a moment, and listen to birds calling, wind shifting, and the soft rustling of branches.
- **Sixty Minutes of Full Immersion:** Weed, water, or tend to the soil, all while listening to the buzz of pollinators, feeling shifting temperatures on your skin, and observing the small lives that make a home in your garden. Move at a natural pace, savoring the rhythm of your work. Use this time to complete a full harvest: gathering ripened tomatoes, filling a basket with herbs, or cutting armfuls of leafy greens for a meal. If stillness calls, lay on the grass or a blanket, rest on a garden bench, or lean against a tree to absorb the calm and quiet satisfaction of a task fulfilled.

Harvest a handful of currants for a moment of simple connection. Feel the smooth berries, take in their vibrant color, and savor the sweet-tart bursts of flavor.

A generous harvest of tomatoes is the reward for unhurried time in the garden.

Transplant a few seedlings with intention to deepen your connection to the garden.

- **Ninety Minutes or More to Flow with the Garden:** Shift intuitively from one task to another, letting the garden guide your movements—watering here, harvesting there, tidying a corner that catches your eye. The steady rhythm of caretaking clears the mind and grounds the body. If your focus is restoration, settle into a cozy nook with a journal or sketchbook, sip tea beneath a tree, or even take a nap in the shade. Let curiosity lead you; walk barefoot, eyes closed, brushing your hands across fragrant herbs and bark.

This flexibility honors both your needs and the needs of your space. Some days, all it takes is a single nibble of fresh basil or a quiet moment of gratitude for a new blossom. Other times, you may find comfort in the slow, steady rhythm of watering, weeding, or harvesting. Each interaction, no matter how brief, strengthens the bond between you and your garden.

As you step away, take a moment to notice how you feel compared to when you arrived. Did you feel tension release in your neck and shoulders? Did your breath slow and your thoughts soften? These shifts, however small, are the garden's quiet gifts.

Your Seasonal Garden Guide

Gardening offers a rhythm that moves with the seasons, providing both practical rewards and personal renewal. As the garden shifts through growth, dormancy, and renewal, so do we. Some months call for hands-on tending, while others invite observation and quiet appreciation. This guide offers a periodic approach to thriving alongside your space as you both awaken, grow, and bloom.

Walk through your garden in early spring to spot early signs of life, like blooming daffodils.

In early spring, rake straw mulch off vegetable beds and into pathways to let the soil warm up.

EARLY SPRING: AWAKENING AND PREPARATION

The garden stirs as daylight increases and temperatures rise. Early spring is a time for preparing the soil, starting new plantings, and embracing slow emergence.

1. **Observe and Plan:** Walk through your space and notice what is waking up. Sketch a rough plan for the growing season, considering what worked well last year and what changes you'd like to make.
2. **Move Straw Mulch:** Rake straw mulch from vegetable beds onto pathways to warm up the soil in the returning sunshine.
3. **Tend Soil Life:** Lightly aerate compacted areas with a pitchfork.
4. **Refresh Soil:** Turn compost, top off raised beds and containers with soil mix, and add a layer of compost to all beds. In mini-orchards, apply mulch to bare patches.
5. **Plant Cold-Hardy Crops:** Sow the seeds of these cool-season champions directly into the soil: beet, cilantro, dill, kale, lettuce, peas, radish, spinach, and Swiss chard.
6. **Prune Trees and Shrubs:** Thin dense branches on fruit trees and berry bushes.
7. **First Harvests:** Perennial herbs like French sorrel, Egyptian walking onion, dandelion, chives, and thyme may already be offering new growth. Snip lightly to encourage more.

The thick layer of straw in pathways can be used to mulch around seedlings as they grow.

Snip early growth from perennial herbs like French sorrel to encourage new, tender leaves for continuous harvests.

Dandelions are packed with nutrients, and their early spring growth is milder and less bitter. The entire plant is edible—flowers, leaves, and roots—though the stems tend to be quite bitter and best left uneaten.

MID-SPRING: GROWTH AND ABUNDANCE

During this period, the garden comes alive, stretching toward the sun. The focus shifts to transplanting, tending young plants, and enjoying the vibrancy of the season.

1. **Check for Early Blossoms:** In sensory gardens and mini-orchards, look for pollinators on early blooms.
2. **Transplant:** Plant seedlings when temperatures are stable and frosts are unlikely.
3. **Offer Support:** Install trellises for climbing vegetables and windbreaks for tender plants.
4. **Savor Sensory Experiences:** Fragrant herbs, crunchy greens, the hum of returning bees, and warm afternoons invite mindful moments in the garden.

Enjoy the early blossoms of fruit trees, such as this plum, and delight in the sight of pollinators busy at work.

LATE SPRING: THE GARDEN SETTLES IN

Everything is growing now, and the garden begins to move toward balance. This is a time to observe, adjust, and enjoy the momentum.

1. **Weed with Ease:** Snip young weeds before they have time to form deep roots.
2. **Mulch Seedlings:** Move mulch from pathways to around seedlings once they are strong and sturdy.
3. **Sow Again:** Plant the seeds of beans, squash, and other heat-lovers. Successive plantings of radishes and cilantro will extend harvests into summer.
4. **Water Mindfully:** As days warm, water deeply but infrequently to encourage strong roots.
5. **Snip Flower Heads from Herbs:** Pinch off flower buds from basil, mint, oregano, and other herbs to promote bushier growth and keep flavors bright and tender.
6. **Harvest Early Crops:** Snap peas, spring greens, and early strawberries reach their peak. Harvest herbs regularly to keep plants producing.

Use the cut-and-come-again method to harvest lettuce: trim the top leaves and let the plants regrow for multiple harvests.

SUMMER: ABUNDANCE AND LIGHT MAINTENANCE

As temperatures climb, the focus turns to harvesting, light tending, and enjoying nature's work.

1. **Harvest in the Morning:** Pick leafy greens and herbs when nutrients are at their peak.
2. **Stay on Top of Watering:** Water deeply in the morning to minimize evaporation and ensure plants are dry by nightfall.
3. **Prune Tomatoes:** Thin dense tomato foliage to prevent disease and guide energy toward fruits.
4. **Prioritize Weed Flowers:** If weeds seem overwhelming, focus on snipping off their flower heads before they set seed. Even a quick trim can prevent future spread and buy you time.
5. **Berry Harvest:** Berry bushes share their abundance with you and wildlife.

LATE SUMMER: TRANSITION AND SUCCESSION PLANTING

The height of summer ushers in change. Some plants wane while others prepare for a second round of productivity.

1. **Succession Planting:** Replace beans with fast-growing arugula, or follow summer squash with cool-weather greens. Sow carrots and beets for a fall harvest.
2. **Tidy Up:** Remove spent plants, refresh mulch in bare spots, and add compost where needed.
3. **Start a New Bed:** Let soil-building microbes and mulch work for you by layering cardboard, compost, and organic matter onto a new bed. See "Sheet Mulching: Prepare and Revive Garden Beds" (page 145) for step-by-step guidance.
4. **Monitor Fruit Ripening:** Fruit trees begin bearing. Use a gentle twist to check if the fruit releases.

Harvest leafy greens like Swiss chard in the cool morning hours for peak flavor and nutrition.

Gather ripe berries and enjoy them fresh, baked into muffins, or added to your favorite seasonal recipes, such as these delicious serviceberry muffins.

FALL: PREPARING FOR REST

The garden shifts into a quieter, reflective stage, offering the final harvests before dormancy.

1. **Plant Garlic and Bulbs:** Settle garlic and spring-blooming bulbs into the soil for an early start next year.
2. **Harvest and Preserve:** Gather fruits, vegetables, herbs, and hardy greens before the first frost. Dry, freeze, or infuse herbs for winter use.
3. **Cut Back Selectively:** Let seed heads remain for birds and beneficial insects, but remove diseased plants to prevent future problems.
4. **Protect the Soil:** Cover exposed beds with straw or a thick layer of leaves to insulate soil-builders, encouraging them to continue their good work.
5. **Protect Trees:** Place guards around the bottoms of trees to protect them from rabbits.

Plant garlic bulbs in fall to give them a head start for next spring's growth.

Use a pitchfork to gently dig and harvest potatoes before the first frost to ensure they stay firm and store well.

Blending fallen leaves into straw adds insulation and enriches the soil as it breaks down.

Cover garden beds with straw and fallen leaves to protect soil health through winter and to feed microbes as they break down.

A simple layer of straw shields soil from winter weather, helping preserve moisture, structure, and life below.

Cure garlic by drying it in a cool, shaded spot for long-term storage.

Wrap tree guards around trunks to prevent rabbits from damaging bark during winter.

WINTER: REST, REFLECT, AND PLAN

In winter, the garden enters dormancy, but care continues in quieter ways.

1. **Observe the Land:** Winter reveals the bones of your garden. Notice where snow lingers in cool pockets, where water pools, and where you might add new elements next season.
2. **Plan for Next Year:** Sketch ideas for spring, order seeds, and dream about what you'd like to grow.
3. **Tend to Tools:** Clean and sharpen pruners, oil wooden handles, and organize materials for next year.
4. **Enjoy Stored Harvests:** Brew a pot of homegrown mint tea or cook with dried herbs, bringing the garden's warmth into the colder months.

Store potatoes and other root crops in a cool, dark, dry place to enjoy throughout winter months.

CHAPTER 09: DAILY AND PERIODIC GARDEN TASKS

Planting this seedling in early spring sets roots up for success and helps your garden thrive with less effort.

You and your garden thrive when efficiency and enjoyment are balanced. This section offers top tips on timing, techniques, and tools to help you care for your space with ease and confidence. Knowing when to do a task can make all the difference: start a new bed a month in advance of planting, water early to help foliage stay dry, remove weeds when they're small, and plant at the right time to improve success. Whether you're nourishing the soil, tucking seeds or transplants into place, pruning for health and harvest, or tending your space in small, regular bursts, these foundational skills are simple and rewarding.

Build Healthy Soil: Testing and Improvement

You've followed the guidelines from "Put Your Garden Where You Roam" (page 55) and found the perfect spot for your garden—hooray! But before you dive into planting, it's worth taking a moment to test the soil. Think of it like moving into a new house: you wouldn't settle in without first checking the foundation, right? The same goes for your garden. Testing your soil helps you understand where your plants will be living so you can set them up for success.

Dig a 12"–18" (30.5–45.7cm) hole to check your soil's health: look for dark, crumbly texture that signals rich, loamy soil ready to support strong plant growth.

CHECK FOR SIGNS OF HEALTHY SOIL

Are plants thriving in this spot? If you see a mix of bare soil and sparse, unhappy plants or struggling grass, that's a red flag. It could be a sign of poor soil, which means your garden might be better off elsewhere.

However, if the spot seems promising, it's time for a soil check. Ideally, do this when the soil isn't bone dry (slightly moist is best). Grab a spade and dig a hole 12"–18" (30.5–45.7cm) deep; 18" (45.7cm) is ideal, as that's where most plant roots grow. You're looking for soil that's dark brown and crumbles easily. This is the sign of healthy, loamy soil, which has the right balance of air and moisture for plants and soil-building organisms to thrive.

If the top few inches of soil are crumbly, that's a good sign, but deeper loamy soil is even better.

Roll moist soil into a ribbon to assess texture. This simple test reveals whether you're working with loam, clay, silt, or sand. The rich, crumbly soil shown here is a classic example of loam.

THE SOIL RIBBON TEST

Now, it's time to get your hands dirty (in the name of science!). If the soil you dug out isn't already moist, add a little water to it. Picture yourself as a kid again, making mud pies—except this time, you're making a cigar. Roll the moistened soil into a cigar shape about 6" (15.2cm) long. Press the end of the cigar between your thumb and forefinger and gently try to make a ribbon. The ribbon is an indicator of soil texture:

- Loamy soil is ideal and will ribbon out to about 2" (5.1cm).
- Clayey soil will form a ribbon longer than 2" (5.1cm), and it will feel heavy and sticky.
- Silty soil will form a short ribbon (less than 2" [5.1cm]), and it will feel smooth or powdery, almost like flour when dry.
- Sandy soil will break easily and feel gritty, with little to no ribbon.

IMPROVING SOILS

If your soil is sandy, silty, or clayey, don't worry—you can improve it and turn it into the loam plants love. Below are two effective ways to transform it.

DEEP SHEET MULCH: SLOW AND NATURAL

To build healthy soil over time, double or triple the amount of compost in your sheet-mulching process. This approach works great if you don't have a tiller or prefer to work slowly with nature. Your newly planted plants will thrive in this rich top layer of compost, while soil-building microbes break down the lower layers over the course of several years.

ONE-TIME TILLING: INSTANT AND EFFECTIVE

While we recommend avoiding repeated, long-term tilling, a one-time tilling event can work wonders when your soil needs quick improvement. Here's how to do it:

1. Spread compost evenly across the soil, aiming for 4"–12" (10.2–30.5cm). The poorer your soil, the more compost you'll need.
2. Use a tiller to mix the compost into the soil. The deeper, the better. But don't go overboard—just mix it until the compost is fully incorporated.
3. Let the soil rest for about a week to settle and allow the compost to blend with the soil. This gives it time to fully integrate and be ready for planting.

You don't need to own a tiller. Local garden centers or tool libraries may offer affordable rentals, or neighbors may have one to share.

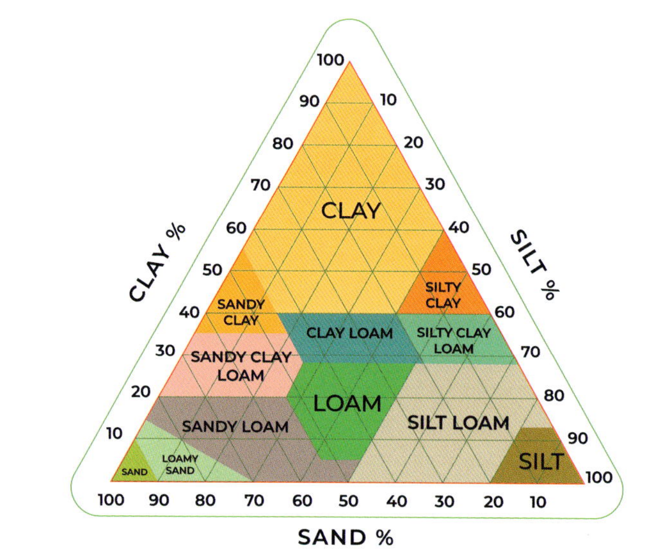

SOIL TYPES AND WHAT THEY MEAN

After assessing the balance of sand, silt, and clay, use the soil texture triangle to pinpoint your soil type. Loamy soil is the goal because it provides the optimal texture for thriving vegetables and fruits.

- **Loamy Soil:** Dark brown and crumbly all the way through. Loamy soil is ideal for gardening.
- **Clayey Soil:** Gray or tan, heavy, sticky, and often clumpy. If dry, it's hard to break into smaller pieces. Clayey soil holds lots of water and nutrients but may be too dense for plant roots to breathe.
- **Silty Soil:** Soft and powdery when dry, smooth and slippery when wet. Silty soil holds water better than sandy soil, but it can become compacted, making it harder for roots to penetrate.
- **Sandy Soil:** Loose and gritty, with individual grains visible. Sandy soil drains quickly and doesn't hold nutrients well.

Sheet Mulching: Prepare and Revive Garden Beds

Soil preparation is the cornerstone of a low-maintenance garden that brings long-term enjoyment rather than constant weeding and watering. Sheet mulching, also called "lasagna gardening," is a simple no-till technique that works with nature, emulating its process of creating fertile soil (also known as humus). Think of how forests build lush, thriving ecosystems: they blanket the ground with fallen leaves, branches, and organic debris. Sheet mulching replicates this method by layering biodegradable materials over the soil, creating a rich foundation for your plants.

Sheet mulch your bed with layers of cardboard, compost, and mulch to suppress weeds, build fertile soil, and create a foundation for low-maintenance planting.

Whether you're starting a new garden or rejuvenating an old bed, sheet mulching offers several benefits:

- **Suppresses Weeds:** It smothers existing grass and weeds while preventing new ones from sprouting.
- **Builds Fertile Soil:** As materials decompose, they enrich the soil with organic matter and soil-building organisms.
- **Conserves Moisture and Regulates Temperature:** This protective mulch layer reduces water evaporation and keeps soil cool in summer.

This technique works best in areas with fair to good soil. If your soil is overly compacted or poor, see "Build Healthy Soil: Testing and Improvement" (page 143) for additional guidance.

TIMING

Sheet mulching can be done year-round, but for best results, aim to complete it three to six months before planting. This allows the layers to break down, transforming into humus-rich soil that your plants will love. Summer or early fall is an ideal time, letting materials decompose over winter for spring planting.

WHY SKIP THE TILLER?

The rototiller is a popular tool for turning over soil, but it has significant downsides that make sheet mulching a better choice:

- **Disrupts Soil Structure:** Tilling destroys the natural arrangement of soil layers, which nature has been perfecting for over 400 million years to grow plants. It also disrupts the happy homes of soil-builders like fungi, worms, and beneficial microbes, whose intricate networks are essential for healthy, thriving plants.
- **Activates Weed Seeds:** Tilling stirs up dormant weed seeds, exposing them to air, water, and sunlight—the perfect recipe for germination.
- **Soil Compaction Risk:** The tiller can compact lower soil layers over time, making it harder for plants to establish healthy roots.
- **Noisy and Stressful:** Wrestling with a tiller can disrupt the peaceful rhythm of gardening.

Sheet mulching sidesteps these issues by building your garden on top of the soil, leaving weed seeds dormant and soil structure intact.

Tilling can provide an initial boost to plant growth by quickly mixing organic matter and oxygen into the soil, but this benefit is short-lived. Disruption releases a flush of nutrients as soil microbes break down organic matter rapidly, but this burst depletes the soil's long-term fertility. Over time, tilled soil becomes compacted, less productive, and more prone to erosion. Sheet mulching, in contrast, sustains long-term fertility and resilient soil health, helping ensure your plants thrive year after year.

STEP-BY-STEP ESTABLISHMENT

If possible, give yourself the gift of time to truly savor this process. As you bend, kneel, lift, and rake, imagine the vibrant community of life you are creating beneath your feet. Worms, pill bugs, fungi, beetles, bacteria, and countless other soil friends will call this space home—an area where much less life existed before. These tiny, mighty allies will work alongside you to help your plants thrive.

Before starting your sheet-mulching project, gather tools and materials nearby. Keeping everything within reach makes the process easier, more efficient, and more enjoyable.

MATERIALS & TOOLS

See "Materials Planning" (page 265) for details about quantities.

- **Contractor's Paper or Cardboard:** Smother existing vegetation.
- **Compost:** Use 2"–8" (5.1–20.3cm), depending on soil quality.
- **Mulch:** Use 2"–6" (5.1–15.2cm). Straw for vegetables and herbs; woodchips for mini-orchards.
- **Organic Matter:** Grass clippings, leaves, kitchen scraps, coffee grounds, vegetable garden waste, and other seed- and disease-free organic material.

See "Garden Toolbox" (page 262) for details about each tool.

- **Garden Gloves:** Protect your hands.
- **Lawn Mower or Weed Trimmer:** Cut grass and vegetation.
- **Loppers or Pruners:** Cut back woody plants.
- **Mattock:** Dig edges along perimeter of bed.
- **Steel Rake:** Smooth compost and mulch.
- **Leaf Rake:** Move leaves onto the bed.
- **Stirrup Hoe:** Remove weeds.
- **Utility Knife:** Open bags of compost and woodchip mulch. Cut cardboard when sheet mulching.
- **Watering Can or Hose:** Hydrate soil and dampen layers of weed barrier.

INSTRUCTIONS

1

Lay Out the Area: Define the bed's boundaries using stakes, string, a garden hose, or sticks.

2

Prepare the Area: Mow grass as low as possible, and trim larger vegetation with loppers or a stirrup hoe. Leave cuttings in place to feed the soil.

3

Hydrate the Soil: If the soil is very dry, consider watering the area thoroughly or wait for a heavy rain. Let the water soak in overnight to minimize compaction from your footsteps.

4

Define the Edge: Optionally dig a shallow trench around the bed using a mattock or flat-bladed spade. This helps keep mulch neatly in place and can double as a space for edging if desired.

5

Lay the Weed Barrier: Cover the area with cardboard, contractor's paper, or 8–12 sheets of newspaper. Overlap edges by 6" (15.2cm) to block weeds. Lightly water to hold it down. If using edging, place it on top of the barrier along the perimeter.

6

Spread Compost: Evenly cover the barrier with compost. Use more if your soil needs improvement, or skip it if your soil is healthy. For extra nutrients, top with leaves or garden trimmings.

7

Top with Mulch: Spread straw (for vegetable gardens) or woodchips (for mini-orchards and woody plants). Optionally mix in leaves for extra nutrients.

8

Celebrate: Step back and admire your work! You've laid the foundation for thriving plants and healthy soil.

Water Smart: Make Every Drop Count

Watering is one of the simplest yet most important ways to support a thriving garden. With some easy techniques, watering becomes less about checking off a task and more about building resilience in your garden while finding a moment of calm.

MAKING WATERING EASIER

- **Set Up a System:** If your water source is far from your garden, reduce the hassle: run a standard hose to a convenient location and attach an on-off switch at the end. From there, connect a collapsible hose, which is easy to hold and store in a small bucket. While collapsible hoses are less durable than traditional ones, handling them gently will extend their lifespan.
- **Use a Watering Wand:** A wand makes watering easier, reduces bending, and directs water exactly where it's needed—at the base of plants. Misting newly planted seeds and young plants also helps settle loosened soil without washing them away.
- **Mark Plants:** Ramblers like squash can make it difficult to see where the base of the plant is sited. When they are young, mark their base with a small stick or flag to make watering more precise later in the season.

Use a watering wand to deliver water precisely where it's needed.

WHEN AND HOW TO WATER

- **Water Deeply and Infrequently:** Deep, infrequent watering encourages strong root growth, making plants more self-sufficient over time. Rather than watering on a schedule, check the soil by pressing a finger 1" (2.5cm) deep—if it feels dry, it's time to water.
- **Water in the Morning:** This allows plants to absorb moisture before the heat of the day increases evaporation. Watering early also reduces the risk of fungal diseases that thrive in cool, damp nighttime conditions.
- **Aim for the Soil, Not the Leaves:** Watering foliage can encourage fungal diseases, especially if soil is splashed onto the leaves. Avoid sprinklers, which waste water and increase disease risk by dampening foliage.
- **Observe Plant Responses:** If you see droopy leaves in the afternoon heat, but the soil is still damp, the plant is likely just conserving moisture and will recover by evening. If leaves are wilted during cooler parts of the day, however, the plant likely needs watering.

Water deeply, focusing on the base of plants. This prevents diseases by keeping foliage dry.

LET WATERING REWARD YOU

Rather than rushing through watering, use it as a time to check in with your plants—and yourself.

- Take deep breaths as you watch the water soak into the soil.
- Listen to the buzzing of pollinators, the rustling of leaves, and cheerful birdsong.
- On a warm day, run water over your arms or legs, enjoying being watered alongside your plants.
- While watering, snip a few weeds, nibble fresh herbs, or gather produce for the next meal.

SOAKER HOSES: MORE HASSLE THAN HELP?

Soaker hoses seem like a great idea at first, and for densely planted rows, they can work well. But if your garden includes large, spread-out plants like tomatoes or squash, you may find them more frustrating than helpful. The water tends to pool in some spots, leaving areas soaked where there are no roots and dry patches on the opposite side of plants, meaning you'll probably end up bringing out the hose anyway to fill in gaps.

They also require more upkeep than you might expect. They kink easily, can be accidentally punctured by garden tools, and by the end of the season, they're often covered in caked-on mud that's tough to clean. Storing them over the winter takes up space, and even with the best care, most only last a few growing seasons before cracking or clogging.

Despite these negatives, if you have a long bed with dense rows of plants, try a soaker hose and see if it fits your setup. Simply turning on the spigot for a few hours can give you more time to enjoy your garden.

Weeding: Stay Ahead Without the Struggle

Regardless of what society says, weeds are not your enemy. They're nature's way of healing the land; weeds are pioneering plants that quickly cover bare soil to retain moisture, prevent erosion, and feed underground life like microbes, fungi, and beneficial insects. A patch of weeds often means damaged soil is alive and doing its best to recover.

By definition, a weed is simply a plant growing where it's not wanted. It's not always about the species itself, it's about context. Dandelions, for instance, are nutrient-rich edibles to some and an unwelcome guest to others. Bee balm might be a cherished pollinator magnet in one garden and labeled "too aggressive" in another due to its spreading nature. Over time, you'll notice which plants compete with your favorites or dominate more space than you'd like.

A well-maintained garden isn't about eradicating every stray plant or following rigid rules. Think of weeding as part of developing a relationship with your garden, learning its rhythms and deciding what works best for your goals and your plants. Weeds will always be part of the garden, but they don't have to control your time or your energy. With a few simple strategies, you can keep weeding to a minimum and even make it a peaceful, rewarding part of your time in the garden.

PREVENT WEEDS BEFORE THEY START

- **Mulch Heavily:** A thick layer of wood chips, straw, shredded leaves, or grass clippings smothers weed seeds, preventing them from germinating. If you see bare soil, add more mulch.
- **Densely Plant Your Crops:** Instead of widely spaced rows, plant vegetables and herbs closely so they shade the ground, leaving little room for weeds to take hold.
- **Use Ground Covers:** In an orchard, low-growing plants like Dutch white clover, creeping thyme, and chamomile act as living mulch, shading the soil and preventing weeds while adding nutrients.
- **Apply Corn Gluten Meal:** This natural pre-emergent herbicide suppresses weed seed germination by drying out emerging roots. Scatter it in early spring just before weeds sprout or in late summer for fall-germinating weeds. Water it lightly. Avoid using it where you plan to sow seeds for desired plants, as it prevents them from sprouting too.

Plant greens and herbs close together, like these rows of lettuce and kale, to shade the soil, suppress weeds, and boost your harvest in less space.

Apply a thick layer of mulch to lock in moisture, block weeds, and feed the soil as it breaks down.

Plant ground covers like creeping thyme to create a living mulch that suppresses weeds, retains moisture, and supports healthy soil.

WEEDING EFFICIENTLY

Shear young weeds at soil level to keep weed seeds buried and let roots decompose into nutrients.

- **Use Plant Markers:** If you're growing plants from seed, use labels to remind yourself what was planted where. Weeds can sometimes resemble seedlings at first, so watch them closely; if they look different from your planted crops, remove them.
- **Identify Weeds by Scent:** Many herbs release a distinct smell when crushed, even as seedlings. If you're unsure whether a sprout is a weed or an herb, rub a leaf between your fingers to check.
- **Remove Weeds While They're Small:** Tiny weeds are easy to snip and haven't had time to spread. A few minutes spent removing small weeds is far easier than wrestling with large, well-established ones.
- **Cut, Don't Uproot:** For young or shallow-rooted weeds, minimize soil disturbance by snipping weeds at the base with a sharp hoe, hori hori knife, or pruning snips. Cutting preserves soil structure, keeps dormant weed seeds buried, and allows soil organisms to break down roots into nutrients.
- **Chop and Drop:** If a weed has not produced seeds and is not diseased, cut it and leave it in place as mulch. This suppresses future weeds while returning nutrients to the soil.
- **Collect Weeds Efficiently:** If weeds have gone to seed, are diseased, or are too large to break down quickly, gather them in a bucket or box rather than leaving them in random small piles that must be gathered up later. Dispose of them in a yard waste bin or a "weedy" compost pile.

MAKING WEEDING MANAGEABLE (AND MAYBE EVEN ENJOYABLE)

Mark off a small area to weed at a time. Stay focused, avoid getting overwhelmed, and celebrate progress without exhausting yourself.

- **Weed While You're There:** Instead of setting aside a separate time for weeding, make it part of your regular garden visits. While harvesting, watering, nibbling, or simply enjoying your space, take a moment to snip a few weeds here and there. This casual weeding might be just enough to keep weeds managed, so it doesn't feel like a chore.
- **Weed in Small Sections:** Instead of tackling an entire garden in one exhausting session, break it up into small, manageable areas. Mark a section with sticks, a string, or even a hula hoop to keep the task focused. Once you've finished weeding that area, give yourself permission to stop and enjoy your garden in another way.
- **Get Comfortable:** A kneeling pad, sun hat, gloves, and lightweight clothing can make a big difference in how enjoyable the task feels.
- **Weed at the Right Time:** The cooler hours of morning or evening are much more comfortable than weeding in the heat of midday.
- **Make It Mindful:** Approach weeding as a moment to slow down, connect with your garden, and restore you from the rush of daily life. Even if you're short on time, try to enjoy the textures, scents, and sounds around you. Notice the soil beneath you, the warmth of the sun or the coolness of the breeze, the quiet hum of insects, and the chirping of birds. As you clear space for your plants to thrive, consider what in your life might benefit from a little weeding or pruning too.
- **Reclaim Overgrown Areas with Mulch:** If a patch becomes overrun with weeds, don't fight it—repurpose it. Instead of letting weeds continue to grow and spread seeds, cut everything down, including any struggling vegetables or herbs. Smother the area with mulch or a weed-suppressing cover, following the tips in "When Weeds Won't Quit" (page 153). This prevents future weed growth while allowing the soil to rebuild, turning a problem spot into a nutrient-rich space for future planting.

When Weeds Won't Quit

Whether you're preparing a new garden bed in a weedy area or reclaiming a weed-infested section of your existing garden, persistent weeds need a different approach, especially if the weeds are well-rooted perennials. Expansive and dispersive weeds—such as thistle, quackgrass, crabgrass, poison ivy, and daylilies—will quickly compete with your desired plants if not properly managed. Instead of endless weeding, you can let soil organisms do the work by smothering weeds and naturally breaking down unwanted growth. With a little patience, this strategy turns weedy areas into fertile ground, making gardening easier for seasons to come.

SMOTHERING FOR LONG-TERM SUCCESS

Sheet mulching is an excellent way to tackle tough weeds, but it needs time to transform those weeds and their seeds into fertile soil.

- **Start Early:** Begin sheet mulching in spring and plan to plant the following spring. Giving a full year ensures weed roots are starved of sunlight, depleting the energy they reserve for growth and expansion.
- **Double Up:** Apply an extra layer or two of weed barrier—such as cardboard or contractor's paper—and double the mulch thickness. You really can't overdo it. The more layers you add, the more difficult it is for those persistent weeds to poke through and find sunlight to regenerate.
- **Stay on Top of It:** If you spot a weed poking out, snip or pull it right away. This prevents it from recharging its energy and spreading further.
- **Test for Weeds:** When you think the area is ready, test a small strip for lingering weeds by planting a few fast-growing crops like lettuce or radishes along the edges. If weeds frequently pop up, add another layer of weed barrier and give it more time.

If your bed is full of weeds, skip the labor-intensive pulling. Smothering with cardboard and mulch is often a simpler, easier solution that lets nature do the cleanup for you.

For stubborn weeds, add two or more layers of cardboard to block sunlight and deprive them of the energy they need to regrow. The extra thickness provides a longer-lasting barrier.

Lift a corner of your old sheet mulch and take a peek. Worms, fungi, and other soil builders will have turned weeds and grass into dark, crumbly, plant-ready soil.

TIPS FOR STAYING PATIENT

It's tempting to jump in and plant right away, and waiting for a newly smothered garden bed to marinate can be an exercise in patience. However, this waiting period gives you a chance to connect with your garden in a more mindful way while laying the foundation for long-term success.

- **Keep the Big Picture in Mind:** While you wait, remember that your soil buddies—worms, fungi, microbes—are working tirelessly beneath the surface. They're breaking down weeds, improving soil structure, and building a thriving ecosystem. Their work may not be visible right away, but they are laying the groundwork for a healthier garden.
- **Start a Container Garden:** Use this waiting time to start a container garden in the space with easy-to-grow herbs like basil, mint, or dill. These plants will help you immediately enjoy the space by providing fresh herbs or flowers that benefit your kitchen and senses. For ideas, see "Compact Container Garden" (page 70). Your presence will also help you spot and pull any weeds that pop up, ensuring they do not recharge and expand.
- **Celebrate the Journey:** Gardening is a journey, not a race. Use this time to plan your garden layout, research companion planting, or explore new plants you're excited to grow. The more you learn now, the more rewarding the gardening experience will be in the future.

Persistent weeds may slow you down a bit at first, but the time and care you invest will pay off in a healthier, easier-to-maintain garden for years to come.

Sow a Seed

Seeds are alive and each one holds the potential for a thriving plant. Note that the early stages of sowing a seed are crucial, and providing extra care at the start will help the seedlings establish strong roots, leading to healthier plants that require less attention throughout the growing season.

SEEDS OR SEEDLINGS: WHICH ONE IS BEST FOR YOU?

If you're gardening on a budget, involving kids, or simply enjoy watching life unfold day by day, sowing seeds can be an incredibly rewarding experience. Many vegetables and culinary herbs like lettuce, spinach, radish, peas, and cilantro are especially well-suited to direct sowing. These crops germinate quickly and grow fast.

For others, especially warm-weather crops like tomatoes and basil, buying seedlings provides a helpful head start. Transplants are great when you want quicker harvests or a confidence boost as you learn the rhythms of the season.

In many gardens, a mix of both works beautifully: sow fast-growing greens and herbs from seed, and supplement with a few store-bought seedlings for plants that take longer to mature. For each plant, find guidance on the best method—sow directly or transplant seedlings—in the "Plant Profiles" section (page 206) and on seed packets. When in doubt, start with what's easiest.

SEEDS

PROS:

- Much more affordable. One packet can yield dozens (or even hundreds) of plants.
- More varieties available, including rare heirlooms and region-specific varieties.
- Better root development when direct-sown. No transplant shock.
- Easy to store for several years.

CONS:

- Requires patience and consistent watering until sprouted.
- Some seeds need special conditions (like warm soil).
- Can be harder to tell what's a weed and what's a seedling when things start sprouting.

SEEDLINGS

PROS:

- Instant gratification. No waiting for germination.
- Useful for slow-starting plants (like tomatoes and chives).
- Easier to visualize spacing and layout in the garden.

CONS:

- More expensive, especially if buying organic or larger quantities.
- Transplant shock of larger plants can slow growth.
- Fewer varieties available.

WHEN SEEDS AREN'T AN EASY START

Not every plant is an ideal candidate for seed-starting—at least not without some extra effort. While fruit trees, berry bushes, and flowers can be grown from seed, they often require longer growing seasons, specific germination conditions, or indoor setups with grow lights and heat mats. For many new gardeners or those with limited time and space, starting with store-bought plants may be more practical for these types of plants.

BEST TIMES TO SOW SEEDS

Seeds sown when the temperature is too cold or too hot often struggle to establish. The less time seeds spend sitting in soil, waiting for favorable conditions, the lower the risk of rotting or being eaten by hungry soil organisms. By planting at the right time, you give your seedlings the best chance for strong, healthy growth.

A traditional way to determine when to sow seeds has been by using the first and last frost dates for your area. These dates mark the average range of dates each year when freezing temperatures typically begin and end in your region based on historical weather data. However, with climate change causing increasing unpredictability, these once-reliable markers are shifting. Some years, a warm spell may arrive weeks earlier than expected, while in others, an unexpected cold snap can delay the growing season. To determine your frost dates, consult the Plant Hardiness Zone Map (page 276). You can also check local extension services or online resources that provide frost date estimates. Using frost dates as a flexible guide rather than a strict rule will help you make informed decisions about when to plant seeds and seedlings. Blend this knowledge with weather forecasts to give confidence in your timing.

COOL TEMPERATURES, 45°F–60°F (7°C–15.5°C)

Early to mid-spring and late fall.

- Beet
- Blooming Bulbs (fall planting)
- Cilantro
- Collard Greens
- Garlic (fall planting)
- Kale
- Lettuce
- Peas
- Potato
- Radish
- Spinach
- Swiss Chard
- Tatsoi
- Violet

MODERATE TEMPERATURES, 60°F–70°F (15.5°C–21°C)

Mid-spring to early summer and late summer to early fall.

- Beet
- Beans
- Chamomile
- Cilantro (best when cooler)
- Dandelion
- Dill
- Kale
- Lambsquarters
- Lettuce (best when cooler)
- Onion, Egyptian Walking
- Plantain, Broadleaf
- Self-Heal
- Sorrel, Creeping Wood
- Swiss Chard
- Tatsoi
- Violet

WARM TEMPERATURES, 70°F–85°F (21°C–29.5°C)

Summer to early fall.

- Beans
- Clover, Dutch White
- Cosmos
- Cucumber
- Nasturtium
- Squash, Summer and Winter
- Sunflower

HOW LONG DO SEEDS LAST?

Seed longevity varies depending on storage conditions. Keep seeds cool, dry, and dark for the best results. Here's how long they typically remain viable:

SHORT LIVED (1–2 YEARS)

- Spinach

MODERATE (3–4 YEARS)

- Beans
- Beet
- Peas
- Swiss Chard

LONG LIVED (5+ YEARS)

- Basil
- Chamomile
- Cilantro
- Clover, Dutch White
- Collard Greens
- Cosmos
- Cucumber
- Dandelion
- Dill
- Kale
- Lambsquarters
- Lettuce
- Nasturtium
- Plantain, Broadleaf
- Radish
- Self-Heal
- Sorrel, Creeping Wood
- Sunflower
- Tatsoi
- Violet

Test old seeds by placing them in a damp paper towel in a warm spot to check for germination. Large seeds, like these peas, can be planted once they sprout.

SEED VIABILITY TEST

You can easily test older seeds for viability before planting them.

1. Dampen a napkin or paper towel and place it on a plate.
2. Lay out 5–10 seeds, spaced apart.
3. Fold the napkin over the seeds, place it in an open plastic bag, and set them in a warm spot (65°F–75°F [18°C–24°C]), such as the top of your refrigerator.
4. Check daily and mist if the napkin is drying out.
5. If over 50 percent germinate within the sprouting time on the packet, then the seeds are good to plant.

SOIL-BUILDING WITH OLD SEEDS

If you have a bunch of old seeds, simply toss them into a bare patch of soil for an entertaining way to see what comes up. Even if no decent food or flowers materialize, anything that germinates will enhance the soil in that spot.

SOWING SEEDS

Seeds are alive and each one holds the potential for a thriving plant. Note that the early stages of sowing a seed are crucial, and providing extra care at the start will help the seedlings establish strong roots, leading to healthier plants that require less attention throughout the growing season.

1

Make Labels: It's surprisingly easy to forget what you planted where. Gather your seed packets, tongue depressors, and a permanent marker, then settle into a cozy spot indoors or out. Label each marker with the plant name and date. This simple step brings peace of mind later, especially when all the seedlings start looking alike.

2

Prepare a Seed Topping: If your soil is dense or clayey, mix equal parts sifted soil and compost, seedling mix, or container mix to lightly cover the seeds. This creates a softer, nutrient-rich layer that supports germination and makes it easier to see where you've planted.

3

Mark Your Layout: Head out to your prepared garden bed and place labels in the soil to visualize spacing before you plant. Most seed packets include helpful guidance for spacing and depth, but if yours doesn't, check the "Plant Profiles" section (page 206) or do a quick online search. When in doubt, provide extra room to prevent overcrowding, which can lead to competition and increased disease risk. For tidy rows, use a measuring tape, stakes, and string.

4

Create a Furrow or Mound: For row planting, use your finger, stick, or tool to create a shallow trench at the recommended depth. If planting in clusters, make a low mound.

5

Firm the Furrow: Lightly press down the soil at the bottom of the furrow to create an even, consistent surface where seeds can rest and make good contact with the soil.

6

Sow the Seeds: Space seeds according to the packet instructions. Large seeds, such as beans and peas, are easy to place individually into the furrow or mound. For small seeds, such as kale or radishes, roll them between your thumb and first two fingers. Tiny seeds, such as chamomile and lettuce, can be sprinkled lightly on the surface—no need for spacing perfection.

7

Tuck Them In: Gently pat the seeds into the soil to ensure each seed has good contact and stays in place.

8

Cover: Sprinkle soil or your prepared seed topping over the seeds, covering them to the recommended depth.

MATERIALS & TOOLS

See "Materials Planning" (page 265) for details about quantities.

- **Seed Packets.**
- **Tongue Depressors and Permanent Marker:** Label seeds.
- **Mix of Sifted Soil and Compost:** When soil is too rough for small seeds.
- **Stakes and String:** Make straight rows.
- **Lightweight Board, Burlap, or Light Fabric:** Optional for covering seeds.

See "Garden Toolbox" (page 262) for details about each tool.

- **Trowel or Hori Hori Knife:** Digging and transplanting.
- **Measuring Tape:** Lay out planting rows.
- **Watering Can or Hose:** Keep plants hydrated. If using a hose, consider a wand with a gentle spray attachment to avoid disturbing soil.

9

Press to Settle: Give the soil a final gentle pat to settle everything in place.

10

Water Gently: Gently water in the seeds, ensuring they remain undisturbed in their new home. If available, misting works best for the initial watering, settling the soil before using a heavier watering method. If it doesn't rain, water them every day until they sprout. Once they've sprouted, reduce watering to every other day unless temperatures are particularly high.

11

Optional Covering: To retain moisture, consider covering the newly seeded area with a lightweight board, burlap, or light fabric for three to four days. Check regularly and remove once sprouts appear.

WHAT ABOUT STARTING SEEDS INDOORS?

You've likely come across countless books, articles, and social media posts singing the praises of indoor seed starting. If you're drawn to the idea of nurturing tiny seedlings from the very start, then go for it! It can be a rewarding way to extend your gardening practice, experiment with unique varieties, and gain a sense of accomplishment when transplanting your homegrown seedlings outdoors.

That said, seed-starting indoors is its own adventure—one that requires time, space, and a bit of an investment upfront. Unlike direct-sowing or buying seedlings, starting seeds indoors requires a few extra tools, including grow lights, heating mats, seed trays, and a seedling-friendly potting mix. While these tools and materials may eventually save you money by reducing the need to buy seedling plants, the real cost is in the patience and care required.

Even with a sunny, south-facing window, starting seeds indoors often calls for a full-spectrum grow light to ensure strong, healthy growth.

Indoor seedlings are like young pets: you must check on them regularly, keep their environment just right, and gradually harden them off before introducing them to the outdoors. If you enjoy hands-on, detailed gardening tasks, it's a great way to become even more connected to your plants. However, if you prefer a lower-maintenance approach, you may find that direct-sowing resilient plants and purchasing robust, ready-to-go seedlings is the better fit.

No matter which route you take, the goal remains the same: grow a thriving, abundant garden in the ways that work best for you.

Plant a Plant

Planting something new, whether a leafy green seedling or a sturdy young tree, is an act of hope. With each plant, you're nurturing both your garden and yourself, aiming for a future of abundance. While there's a bit of technique involved, once you do it right the first time, the process becomes second nature.

GENERAL RULES OF THUMB

A few best practices apply to all plants, whether you're tucking in vegetable seedlings or planting a fruit tree. We'll cover those first, then move into specifics for different types of plants.

PRE-PLANTING PAMPERING

Give your plants a little love and protection before they even go in the ground.

- **Keep Them Moist:** Small container plants dry out quickly. Water them daily and store them in a partially shaded, wind-protected spot.
- **Bottom-Watering Trick:** Place potted plants in a shallow tray of water and let them soak up moisture from the bottom for an hour or two. Just be sure they don't stay waterlogged, as most plants dislike consistently soggy roots.

PICK THE RIGHT TIME

Nature can lend a hand in helping new plants settle. When possible:

- Pick an overcast, cool day to reduce transplant shock.
- Avoid the hottest part of the day—early morning or late afternoon is best.
- Plant just before rain is predicted. Rainwater is gentler on roots and richer for soil life, though city water works fine.

SITE PREPARATION

A little preparation goes a long way in ensuring your plants thrive.

- **Check the Soil:** If needed, remediate it using guidance from the "Preparing Problem Soils" section.
- **Clear the Area:** Remove sticks, rocks, and debris, then smooth the surface with the back of a steel rake. If mulch is present, push it aside.

Every seedling planted is a collaboration with nature's rhythms of growth and renewal.

DIGGING THE RIGHT HOLE

There's an old saying in gardening: for a $1 plant, dig a $10 hole. Plants are pricier nowadays, but the intention is solid: provide a high-quality home for your plant at the start.

- **Size It Up:** Dig the hole approximately twice the width of the root ball to encourage root expansion, especially in compacted or clay soils.
- **Depth Matters:** A too-deep hole can lead to stem rot, while too shallow can leave plants unstable. When in doubt, err on the side of planting slightly shallow—the soil will likely settle, and mulch will emulate the stabilizing and insulating effects of soil.
    - **Trees and Shrubs:** Identify the root flare, which is the point where the trunk widens and the roots begin. This should sit right at ground level.
    - **Large Perennials:** For plants like sage and coneflower, plant at the same depth as in their nursery container. Keep the base of the stem, where it meets the roots, level with or slightly above the soil.
    - **Seedlings:** Most should be planted at the same depth as in their container. (Tomatoes are the exception; bury them deeply to encourage extra root growth.)
- **Rough the Edges:** Smooth hole walls can cause roots to circle rather than spread. Use a garden fork or trowel to break up the sides and create a deeply roughed surface.
- **Skip Compost in the Hole:** It's tempting to enrich the planting hole with compost, but this encourages roots to stay put rather than spread outward in search of nutrients and water. Instead, place the same soil back into the hole and topdress the area with compost.

When planting trees and shrubs, locate the root flare—the trunk's widening into roots—and set it at ground level. Too deep invites rot; too shallow risks instability.

THE GREAT UNPOTTING

It's time to free your plant. Think of it as giving your new green companion a gentle hug before setting it into its forever home.

- Gently squeeze the container to loosen the soil. For small seedlings, this may be enough.
- For larger pots, lay them on their side and firmly press the sides. If needed, tap the bottom or slide a knife around the edges to release stubborn roots.
- Never yank the plant out by the stem or trunk—this can cause damage. Instead, let gravity do the work by turning it upside down and tapping the bottom while holding the soil in place.

When unpotting a seedling, gently squeeze the container and tap the bottom to release it. Avoid pulling the plant out by the stem, which can damage it.

UNBOUNDING ROOTS

- A well-rooted plant will have visible, healthy roots in loose soil.
- Snip away dead or diseased roots with clean pruners.
- Use your fingers to gently tease apart roots so they spread outward in the hole.
- If the roots are tightly coiled or circling the base, the plant is "pot-bound" and needs extra attention. Use a utility knife or pruners to make three to four vertical cuts through the outer layer of roots and then spread them outward. This may seem harsh, but the tough love helps prevent circling roots that can choke the plant over time.

Gently separate the roots of seedlings to help them grow outward. If the plant is pot-bound with dense, circling roots, make cuts to loosen them.

PLANTING TREES, SHRUBS, AND OTHER LARGE PERENNIALS

At planting time, larger plants require extra care to ensure they thrive for years to come. Take your time. This is an opportunity to slow down and connect with your new longtime friend.

INSTRUCTIONS

1

Prepare the Plants: If using potted plants, move them to the garden site. For bare root plants, place them in a large bucket of water nearby to keep them hydrated while you dig.

2

Mark Locations: Use spacing recommendations on plant labels or from the "Plant Profiles" section (page 206) to determine placement. Use a tape measure to stake out the spots before digging to visualize spacing and prevent overcrowding. Labeling stakes can help if planting multiple species.

3

Remove Vegetation: If grass or other vegetation exists, remove it with a mattock or flat-bladed spade.

4

Outline the Hole: Use your shovel to deeply score an outline in the soil before digging. This helps visualize the final size and shape of the hole, ensuring it's wide enough for the root system.

5

Dig the Hole: Dig one hole at a time, adjusting its size and depth based on the root system of each plant. Place removed soil onto cardboard, a tarp, plywood, or a bucket to keep it clean for backfilling. Break up large clumps to make refilling easier.

6

Rough the Edges: Use a shovel, pitchfork, or trowel to rough up the walls of the hole, creating a textured surface that encourages outward root growth.

7

Place Stakes: For dwarf apples and pears, drive a tall, sturdy, permanent steel stake into the ground 3"–6" (7.6–15.2cm) from the trunk's future location, ensuring it's buried at least 24" (61cm) deep. This support prevents the tree from tipping, protecting its weak root system from strain under the weight of heavy fruit.

8

Position the Plant: Remove the plant from its container or retrieve the bare root plant from the water. Identify the root flare, then lay a shovel handle across the hole to check the correct depth. Spread bare root plant roots outward and adjust the hole size as needed.

MATERIALS & TOOLS

See "Materials Planning" (page 265) for details about quantities.

- **Plants.**
- **Stakes and String:** Make straight rows.
- **Steel Stakes:** Keep trellises in place and dwarf apples and pears upright.
- **Cardboard, Plywood, Tarp, or Bucket:** Hold soil from dug holes.
- **Compost.**
- **Woodchip Mulch.**

See "Garden Toolbox" (page 262) for details about each tool.

- **Shovel, Trowel, or Hori Hori Knife:** Digging and transplanting.
- **Rubber Mallet or Hammer:** Drive in garden stakes for planting locations.
- **Measuring Tape:** Lay out planting rows.
- **Post Pounder:** Drive in steel stakes.
- **Large Bucket of Water:** Keep bare root plants hydrated while planting.
- **Watering Can or Hose:** Keep plants hydrated.

9

Backfill Carefully: Hold the plant steady while adding soil in layers, ensuring roots remain spread out and tamping gently every 3"–4" (7.6–10.2cm) to eliminate air pockets. When the hole is half full, water moderately to settle everything. Gently lift the plant up and down to ensure all air pockets are removed. Ensure the plant is straight and is still at the correct depth before adding the remaining soil.

10

Water Thoroughly: Optionally, create a shallow moat around the plant with a ridge of tamped soil to direct water toward the roots. Water deeply to saturate the soil.

11

Add Compost: If desired, spread 1"–3" (2.5–7.6cm) of compost around the base of the plant to give it a nutrient boost and support healthy soil life.

12

Add Mulch: Spread 3"–4" (7.6–10.2cm) of woodchip mulch over the entire planting area. Keep mulch away from the plant's base to prevent rot and pest damage.

13

Celebrate: Take a moment to appreciate this milestone—your plant is settling into its forever home. Over the next few weeks, check the soil moisture regularly; if it feels dry 1" (2.5cm) below the surface, water deeply to support strong root growth.

PLANTING VEGETABLE AND HERB SEEDLINGS

Each small plant you place in the soil sets the stage for a season of growth, nourishment, and abundance.

MATERIALS & TOOLS

See "Materials Planning" (page 265) for details about quantities.

- **Plants.**
- **Tongue Depressors and Permanent Marker:** Label plants.
- **Stakes and String:** Make straight rows.
- **Cardboard, Plywood, or Bucket:** Hold soil from dug holes.
- **Compost.**

See "Garden Toolbox" (page 262) for details about each tool.

- **Trowel or Hori Hori Knife:** Digging and transplanting.
- **Rubber Mallet or Hammer:** Drive in garden stakes for planting locations.
- **Measuring Tape:** Lay out planting rows.
- **Watering Can or Hose:** Keep plants hydrated.

INSTRUCTIONS

1

Make Labels: If your plants didn't come with labels, make them using wooden tongue depressors and a permanent marker.

2

Mark Your Layout: Head to your prepared garden bed or container. Use plant spacing recommendations from the "Plant Profiles" section (page 206) or the plant packet. Place your labels in the soil before planting to visualize spacing. When in doubt, provide extra room to prevent overcrowding, which can lead to competition and increased disease risk. For tidy rows, use stakes and string.

3

Dig the Hole: Use a trowel or hori hori to dig a hole. If the hole has smooth sides, gently rough them up to encourage outward root growth.

4

Remove the Plant: Gently squeeze the sides of the container to loosen the soil. Turn the pot upside down while supporting the plant with your other hand, and tap the bottom until the seedling slides out. Avoid pulling on the stem, as this can damage delicate roots.

5

Position the Plant: Place the plant in the hole, move soil around it, and gently pat it down. If desired, spread a ¼" (6.4mm) layer of compost around the seedlings to provide additional nutrients.

6

Water Deeply: Water thoroughly after planting. If it doesn't rain, continue watering daily for the first week—preferably in the morning—to encourage strong root establishment.

Pruning for Health and Harvest: Fruit Trees and Berry Bushes

Pruning a fruit tree or berry bush can feel a little intimidating. What if you cut off too much? What if you remove the wrong branch? What if you ruin the plant's chances of producing fruit? The good news is that pruning isn't as complicated as it seems, and trees and bushes are incredibly forgiving. Your job is just to help them along their way.

This guide will walk you through the why, when, and how of pruning, offering simple step-by-step instructions. By the end, you'll feel confident wielding your pruners and loppers, knowing that each cut is an act of care for your plants and your future harvests.

WHY PRUNE?

Imagine a tree or bush that has never been pruned. Its branches sprawl in every direction, competing for light, bending under their own weight, and forming dense tangles where air can't circulate. Left unchecked, such a plant can develop several problems:

- **Poor Fruit:** Struggles to produce high-quality fruit; the ones yielded are often small or misshapen.
- **Fosters Problems:** Becomes more susceptible to disease and pests, as lack of airflow creates a damp environment where fungi and bacteria thrive.
- **Dense Foliage:** Grows in a way that makes harvesting difficult, forcing you to reach through dense or tangled branches.
- **Wastes Energy:** Produces excessive branches instead of channeling nutrients into fruit production.

Pruning may seem intimidating at first, but it's easy to learn. It's also a simple way to guide your fruit trees and berry bushes toward healthier growth and better harvests.

There are many benefits to pruning:

- **Stronger Branches:** Encourages strong, well-spaced branches that can support the weight of healthy fruit.
- **Improves Air Circulation:** Reduces disease and promotes even ripening.
- **Better Fruit:** Allows sunlight to reach all parts of the plant, ensuring sweet, flavorful fruit.
- **Ease:** Shapes the plant for easy harvesting and maintenance.

It may feel counterintuitive to trim something that's thriving, especially if your heart leans toward letting nature's intelligence take its course. But in the wild, natural pruning happens all the time—branches break in storms, animals nibble off tips, and old wood dies back. You are emulating these natural disturbances with a thoughtful, nurturing hand.

The biological goal of a fruit tree and bush is to reproduce. Left alone, it will often create a flood of small fruits with viable seeds, hoping sheer quantity ensures the next generation. By selectively pruning, we gently guide energy toward fewer, higher-quality fruits.

Pruning isn't about forcing a plant into submission; it's about guiding its natural growth to help it flourish. It's a conversation between you and your tree or shrub, a way to observe its structure, understand its needs, and gently shape its future. Your presence, care, and thoughtful hands become just as helpful as the rain, pollinators, and soil organisms.

Pruning guides your plants toward abundance, health, and beauty. When you stand in front of bare branches with pruners in hand, know that you're shaping the summer's harvest. Trust the process, observe how your plant responds, and remember: no tree or shrub is ever pruned perfectly, and that's okay. The more you practice, the more natural it will feel.

WHEN TO PRUNE

For most fruit trees and berry bushes, the optimal time to prune is during their dormant period, typically in late winter to early spring (February, March, or April). Pruning during dormancy offers several benefits:

- **Reduced Stress:** With no active growth, plants experience less stress.
- **Efficient Healing:** As plants emerge from dormancy, they can quickly heal pruning wounds and direct energy toward new, fruit-bearing growth.
- **Clear Visibility:** The absence of leaves allows you to easily identify and remove dead, damaged, or crossing branches, improving the plant's structure.

Adjust pruning times based on your local climate conditions. In regions with severe winters, delayed pruning may be beneficial to avoid cold damage.

HOW TO PRUNE

This easy-to-follow pruning method applies to all fruit trees and bushes, whether you're shaping a young one or revitalizing an older one.

Use a hand saw for large limbs, loppers for thicker branches, and sharp bypass pruners for small ones. Keep tools clean with isopropyl alcohol to prevent the spread of disease.

MATERIALS

- **Isopropyl Alcohol and Rag:** Clean tools between cuts (a spray bottle works well).

See "Materials Planning" (page 265) for details about quantities.

TOOLS

- **Sharp Bypass Pruning Shears:** Cut small branches.
- **Loppers:** Cut branches over ½" (1.3cm) thick.
- **Hand Saw:** Cut larger limbs.
- **Gloves:** Protect your hands.
- **Stepladder or Sturdy Stool:** Reach into tall trees.

See "Garden Toolbox" (page 262) for details about each tool.

1. OBSERVE YOUR TREE OR SHRUB

Before making any cuts, step back and look at your plant. Ask yourself:

- What shape do I want this plant to take?
- Are there dead, damaged, or diseased branches?
- Are branches crossing or rubbing against each other?
- Is the center of the plant too dense, blocking light and air?

2. REMOVE THE THREE D'S

Removing unhealthy wood is the first and most important step in pruning, as it prevents disease from spreading and allows the plant to focus its energy on healthy growth. Remember the three *D*s: dead, damaged, diseased.

- **Where to Cut:** Make clean cuts just above a bud or branch collar—the slightly swollen, wrinkled area where a branch meets the trunk or another branch. This promotes faster healing and reduces disease risk.
- **Avoid Leaving Stubs:** The plant will struggle to heal them, creating an entry point for pests and pathogens.
- **Cut Out Dead or Broken Branches:** Do this first. If you are unsure whether a branch is alive, gently scratch the bark with your thumbnail. If the wood beneath is green, it's alive; if it's brown, it's dead.
- **Indicators of Disease:** Remove any branches with dark, sunken, or oozing spots, which may indicate disease.

A light scratch on the bark reveals green wood underneath. This branch is alive and healthy.

If a scratch reveals brown wood, the branch is dead and can be removed.

3. THIN FOR AIRFLOW AND LIGHT

Well-spaced branches allow for better air circulation, reducing disease risk and ensuring even sunlight exposure for healthy fruit development.

- **Eliminate Crossing Branches:** When two branches rub against each other, they create wounds that invite disease. Remove the weaker of the two.
- **Open the Center:** Prune inward-growing branches to allow light to penetrate and air to move freely.
- **Prevent Overcrowding:** Maintain 6"–12" (15.2–30.5cm) of space between main branches. This ensures each branch receives adequate sunlight.
- **Remove Suckers:** These are the vigorous shoots emerging from the base or roots. They sap energy from the tree and should be cut as close to the base as possible.
- **Prune Out Water Sprouts:** These are thin, vertical shoots that grow straight up from branches. They block light, reduce airflow, and divert nutrients away from fruit production.

Crossing branches rub against each other, creating wounds that invite pests and disease.

Position pruners at the base of the branch, just outside the collar, for a clean cut that supports fast healing.

A proper pruning cut leaves the branch collar intact, allowing the tree or shrub to seal the wound naturally and stay resilient against disease.

4. SHAPE THE PLANT

When shaping your fruit tree or berry bush, aim for a strong, well-balanced structure that supports good airflow, easy harvesting, and healthy growth. Start by observing how the plant naturally wants to grow.

Fruit Trees: Begin with a central leader (a single, dominant trunk) if the tree supports it naturally. If the tree tends to spread outward with multiple strong branches, consider shaping it into an open center (vase shape) instead.

Berry Bushes: Focus on maintaining an open, airy form by removing older, unproductive branches and allowing room for new, fruit-bearing growth.

Guidelines for shaping:

- **Strength:** Select strong, well-angled branches and remove weak ones. A strong branch forms a wide angle (45–60 degrees) where it meets the trunk or main stem. A weak branch has a narrow, V-shaped crotch, which is prone to splitting and breaking.
- **Pruning Cuts:** Make the cut just above an outward-facing bud at a slight angle. This directs new growth outward instead of inward, preventing overcrowding in the center of the plant.
- **Height:** Keep the plant at a manageable height for easy care and harvesting.
    - **Fruit Trees:** Limit height to what you can comfortably reach.
    - **Berry Bushes:** Regularly remove the oldest branches (typically three or more years old) to encourage fresh, productive growth while keeping the plant compact.

5. STEP BACK AND ASSESS

After your first round of pruning, take a step back and evaluate your work. Viewing the entire tree or bush from a distance helps ensure that your cuts create a balanced, open structure rather than removing too much from one area.

- Does the plant maintain an even, well-proportioned shape?
- Can sunlight reach the center of the tree or bush?
- Is there enough space between branches for good airflow?

Pruning tends to be an iterative process. You may need to make a second or third pass, thinning and shaping a little more where necessary.

If you worry that you've cut too much, don't panic. Plants are resilient and will regrow. Next year, you'll have the chance to refine and shape further, gently guiding the plant toward stronger, healthier growth.

CHAPTER 10: NATURALLY ADDRESS COMMON PESTS AND DISEASES

Chickadees and other feathered visitors are a natural pest control, feasting on caterpillars and insects before they damage your plants.

Step into your garden, and you'll notice something wonderful—this isn't a still life painting or an untouched landscape. It's a living, breathing, buzzing world. Birds dart through the air, butterflies pause for a sip of nectar, and ladybugs patrol the leaves, keeping tiny pests in check. A garden full of life is a good thing.

Your Garden's Built-In Helpers

Many of the visitors to your garden aren't there to cause trouble. They're helping to keep things in balance:

- **Birds:** Many—such as chickadees, warblers, and wrens—feast on caterpillars, cabbage worms, and moths before they turn leaves into lace.
- **Ladybugs:** These little insects are aphid assassins, each one devouring hundreds of those sap-sucking pests in its lifetime.
- **Toads and Frogs:** They keep slugs, snails, and mosquitoes in check. A small water source can turn them into loyal garden guardians.
- **Pollinators:** Bees and butterflies do more than just look pretty. They ensure flowers turn into fruits and veggies by moving pollen where it needs to go.

SHARING, NOT SURRENDERING

A nibbled leaf or a missing strawberry here and there is part of the deal when gardening alongside nature. If you tried to eliminate every bug or critter, you'd risk losing the good ones too. Instead of aiming for a perfectly untouched garden, it's helpful to decide the level of sharing you're comfortable with. A few bites? No big deal. A whole crop wiped out? Time to take action.

WHEN TO LET GO: HONORING YOUR WELL-BEING IN THE GARDEN

If you find yourself knee-deep in pest battles—spraying, squishing, and stressing—take a pause. A garden is meant to be a place of joy and renewal, not frustration and exhaustion.

Sometimes, despite our best efforts, cabbage worms love our kale a little too much, blight overtakes our tomatoes, or a hungry mother deer decides our chard is the perfect snack. When that happens, it can be easy to feel like we've lost a fight. But here's the truth: it was never a fight to begin with.

Instead of seeing these challenges as failures, try reframing them as nature's way of guiding you. Maybe this season, your garden is doing more for wildlife than for you, and that's okay. That hungry deer? She needed the meal to feed her fawns. The kale riddled by cabbage worms? Those caterpillars and the moths fed chickadees, wrens, and other birds. Even blighted tomatoes return to the soil, enriching it for next year. Nothing is ever truly lost in a garden; it just changes form.

When pests take over, sometimes the best approach is to let go. A few chewed-up leaves can feed wildlife and remind us that a garden's purpose isn't perfection—it's balance.

If a plant is beyond saving and if caring for it no longer brings you peace, it's okay to let it go. Cut it back and toss down some quick-growing radish seeds, or simply mulch over the area and take a well-earned break. Your garden will be there next season, ready to grow alongside you.

Because in the end, the most important thing your garden nurtures isn't just plants. It's you.

The Most Common Garden Challenges

When something is causing too much trouble, there's usually a simple way to nudge things back into balance. We'll cover the most common pests, diseases, and animal visitors, plus practical, low-maintenance ways to handle them without turning your garden into a battleground.

SAP-SUCKING INSECTS

Culprits: Aphids, Thrips, Whiteflies, Leafhoppers
These tiny insects feed on plant juices, weakening stems and causing curled, yellowing leaves. If you find sticky residue or see ants marching up your tomatoes, lettuce, or fruit trees, you might have an aphid party happening. Whiteflies often flutter up in a cloud from squash or kale, while thrips leave silvery streaks on onions or peas.

Simple Fix: A strong blast of water from the hose often knocks them off for good. If they persist, lightly spray leaves with soapy water (just a few drops of dish soap in a spray bottle). If aphids keep returning, it's a sign that your garden is missing ladybugs. Wait to see if they appear to take over the job.

Aphids sucking sap from tender leaves can weaken plants and attract ants, but they also attract helpful ladybugs and other predators ready to restore balance.

LEAF-CHEWING INSECTS

Culprits: Cabbage Worms, Tomato Hornworms, Colorado Potato Beetles, Flea Beetles
These hungry munchers love kale, tomatoes, and potatoes; basically, all the good stuff. Flea beetles leave behind tiny pinprick holes, turning leaves into delicate lace. If you spot these holes in your greens, or caterpillars camouflaged on tomato stems, it's time for action.

Simple Fix: Pick or brush them off into a container of soapy water.. It can be oddly satisfying. If they keep coming, scatter straw mulch around plants. It confuses egg-laying moths and beetles along with suppressing weeds and conserving moisture.

BORERS AND STEM PESTS

Culprits: Squash Vine Borer, Peach Tree Borer
Nothing's more frustrating than a squash plant collapsing overnight or a peach tree weeping sap from bore holes. These pests burrow inside stems and fruits, cutting off water and nutrients. Zucchini, pumpkins, and stone fruit trees are common victims.

Simple Fix: If a squash vine suddenly wilts, slice into the base of the stem with a sharp knife and remove the culprit, then bury the stem in soil to encourage new roots. If it's too far gone, pull the plant and compost it. For fruit trees, rub affected bark with a soft brush to remove eggs before they hatch.

SLIMY PLANT PREDATORS

Culprits: Slugs, Snails, Earwigs, Pill Bugs
If you've ever found ragged holes in your lettuce or chewed-up strawberries, slugs and their companions may be to blame. These moisture-loving grazers thrive in damp conditions, feeding at night and hiding under mulch or debris by day.

Simple Fix: Reduce damp hiding spots by raking back old mulch in early spring and letting the soil dry for a few weeks before replacing it with fresh mulch. Keep mulch away from the base of fragile seedlings until they've grown and toughened enough to be less palatable to the chewers. Water plants in the morning to reduce nighttime moisture. Hand-pick slugs at night. Place shallow, beer-filled containers around the garden to trap them. Encourage natural predators like ground beetles and toads.

Cabbage worms love leafy greens. Spotting early damage gives you a chance to step in before they take too much.

Squash vine borers silently burrow into stems, cutting off water and nutrients, often before you know they're there.

Slugs leave ragged holes in greens, feeding at night and hiding by day. A little mulch management and nighttime inspections can help keep them in check.

FUNGAL DISEASES

Culprits: Powdery Mildew, Downy Mildew, Blight, Rust
Fungal issues thrive in humid conditions, creating white powdery coatings on squash, yellow lettuce leaves, or dark blight spots on tomatoes. Blight can take out an entire crop in days, especially in damp weather.

Simple Fix: Fungus thrives in moisture, so dry leaves are your best defense. Space plants so they don't touch, prune to boost airflow, mulch heavily with straw to prevent soil splash, and water at the base, not the leaves. At the first sign of trouble, snip off affected foliage and clean your pruners with isopropyl alcohol between cuts to avoid spreading spores. Some plants—like zucchini and tomatoes—can still offer a decent harvest even while affected, so don't panic. But if the disease progresses, it's okay to remove the plant entirely, mulch over the area, and try something different in that spot next season. Do not compost it, as fungal pathogens may survive in the pile.

BACTERIAL DISEASES

Culprits: Fire Blight, Black Rot, Bacterial Leaf Spot
Bacterial issues cause blackened, wilting branches (fire blight in pears and apples) or dark, wet-looking spots on greens and brassicas (black rot). Unlike fungal diseases, these spread fast and can wipe out an entire plant before you notice.

Simple Fix: Prune out affected areas immediately and sterilize your pruners with isopropyl alcohol between cuts. If it spreads, remove the plant and don't compost it. Like fungal diseases, keeping plants spaced so they do not touch and ensuring leaves dry out quickly is the best prevention.

Powdery mildew thrives in humid weather, coating leaves in a white film and weakening plants. Good airflow and pruning can help prevent fungal outbreaks.

Fire blight causes leaves and branches to turn brown and wilt, often striking suddenly. Prompt pruning of affected areas can help contain the spread and safeguard the health of nearby trees.

VIRAL DISEASES

Culprits: Mosaic Viruses, Tomato Spotted Wilt Virus
Viral infections cause warped, yellow-streaked leaves and stunted growth, often in cucumbers, tomatoes, and peppers. Sadly, there's no cure. Viruses spread through insect bites or infected seeds.

Simple Fix: If just one plant is affected, pull it before it spreads. Next year, try to buy disease-resistant plants.

WILDLIFE DAMAGE

Culprits: Deer, Rabbits, Birds, Squirrels
Animals are part of the garden experience, and while we love them, they sometimes take more than their share. Rabbits mow down tender lettuce and beans, squirrels dig up bulbs, deer browse fruit trees, and birds snatch berries before you can enjoy them. Before jumping to defenses, consider this: if they're only taking a little, it's part of a healthy

ecosystem—a sign that your garden is thriving. A biodiverse space attracts natural predators like owls, hawks, and foxes, which help keep populations in check over time.

- **Simple Fix:** If damage becomes excessive, here are a few simple, nature-friendly solutions:
- **Deer:** Hang wind chimes, scented soap in a sock, or strips of reflective tape near plants to startle them. Rotating deterrents works best; deer get used to static objects. Products like Deer Scram or dried blood meal also repel deer by mimicking predator scents.
- **Rabbits:** A wire mesh barrier at least 18" (45.7cm) high and buried 6" (15.2cm) deep is a long-term fix. For a quick deterrent, sprinkle dried blood meal around plants.
- **Birds:** Sometimes, all it takes is a well-stocked bird feeder nearby. Full bellies mean fewer stolen berries. Lightweight mesh draped over fruit bushes is also a simple solution.
- **Squirrels:** Lay ½" (1.3cm) wire mesh over bulbs, securing it with stakes or rocks. Planting daffodils nearby can also help—squirrels hate them.

Mosaic virus causes yellow-streaked, twisted leaves and stunted plants. There's no cure, but removing infected plants early can help protect the rest of your garden.

Rabbits might nibble your plants, but it's also a sign of a healthy, welcoming ecosystem. A little sharing is part of gardening with nature, not against it.

Natural deterrents like blood meal and pepper flakes can help keep nibbling wildlife at bay—no harsh chemicals needed—and your soil gets a boost too.

SIMPLE NATURAL REPELLENTS

Watching plants you've nurtured disappear overnight can be frustrating, but there's no need for harsh chemicals. A few simple, natural ingredients can help deter hungry deer, rabbits, and squirrels.

- **Blood Meal:** Smells like a predator has been nearby, making herbivores uneasy. Bonus: It enriches the soil with nitrogen.
- **Crushed Red Pepper Flakes or Cayenne Pepper:** Unpleasantly spicy, making it an instant turn-off for nibblers.

HOW TO USE THEM:

- **On Fruit Trees and Berry Bushes:** Lightly dust lower branches and leaves, or mix with water to create a spray that sticks.
- **Around Vegetables:** Since no one wants a surprise burst of spice in their salad, sprinkle repellents around plant bases instead of directly on leaves. This creates a scent barrier without affecting your harvest.
- **Reapply After Rain or Watering:** Moisture washes the scent away, so refresh the area after each downpour.

CHAPTER 11: EVOLVE WITH YOUR GARDEN

Embrace nature's imperfections. Let your garden reflect life's beautiful, unfinished edges—progress, not perfection.

Gardens are always changing. This chapter invites you to work with those changes rather than against them by layering on mulch as a simple way to reset and enhance the soil, letting parts of your garden grow a little wild or gradually expanding your growing space in ways that feel doable.

Adapt with Life's Changes

Life, like nature, is unpredictable. No matter how carefully you plan or how diligently you follow low-maintenance gardening principles, unforeseen challenges will inevitably arise. Sometimes, the reality of maintaining a garden just doesn't match up to the enthusiasm you felt when you began. Nature has its ebbs and flows, and so do you. Seasons shift, energy fluctuates, and life outside the garden demands attention. There will be weeks, or even seasons, when you can't visit your garden as often as you'd like. If your garden starts to look a little ragged, don't worry about getting it back in shape with a rigid plan. Nature is highly adaptable, and you can be too.

When life gets busy, let mulch do the work. A thick layer of straw gives you, and your garden, a restful, soil-building break.

MULCH: YOUR REJUVENATING ALLY

Mulch is a powerful ally in any garden. Spread it over bare soil to suppress weeds and reduce watering needs. But if life starts to feel overwhelming and a break from garden maintenance is necessary, consider this an opportunity to let both you and your space rest. Cover the garden with a thick blanket of straw and declare a "soil-building year." The overgrown plants will break down into nutrient-rich soil, with help from the bacteria, worms, pill bugs, and other grateful organisms. When you're rejuvenated, you'll find that your garden is ready too.

EMBRACE THE NATURAL DISORDER

One of the most powerful tools for navigating life's ups and downs is embracing the natural disorder that comes with growth. After all, nature is never perfect, and there's beauty in its wildness. If your life feels chaotic and messy, let your garden be a safe space that mirrors your experience. Consider even making a sign that says, "Life in Progress." Research shows that accepting imperfection can be a significant step in healing and personal growth.

A TIME FOR REFLECTION

Rather than viewing a less-than-perfect garden as something to fix, try shifting your mindset and embracing it as a place for reflection. Your plants may be trying to show you something important. Maybe an overgrown patch is a sign that you've taken on too much and are feeling overwhelmed. Perhaps wilting herbs are a gentle reminder to focus on self-care and rest. Overgrown vines or unruly branches might signal that it's time to prune other aspects of your life. Birds and insects visiting your garden may be quietly encouraging you to reach out for support, reminding you that it's okay to lean on others when needed.

SENSORY SOLUTION

Wildlife thrives in gardens where diversity reigns. If you've ever felt peace while wandering a hiking trail or sitting beside a forest edge, you've already experienced the beauty of untamed, living systems. Natural areas are rarely tidy, and if your yard weren't shaped by societal pressure to control and contain it, it might look more like those beloved places. Resist rigid standards of what's considered "beautiful," and instead view your garden through nature's lens. A so-called "messy" garden is often far more vibrant and full of life than a neat, manicured one.

Engage fully with the sensory richness of your diverse space: feel the varied textures of leaves, listen to plants rustling in the breeze, observe shifting patterns of light and shadow, breathe in layered fragrances, and notice the ever-changing colors around you. This multisensory experience helps root you in the present moment, deepen your connection to the environment, and restore your sense of calm.

With its layered plantings and gentle wildness, this mini-orchard echoes the edge of a woodland—rich in scent, texture, taste, and sound. What may seem messy is deeply familiar to the brain, offering a sense of safety and grounding as you wander the path, immersed in sensory delight.

Expand Slowly

We recommend starting small. It's much easier to build on success than to rein in feeling overwhelmed. You don't need a plan for your entire landscape to get started. Nature begins with small patches of fast-growing plants, gradually expanding over time with longer-lasting perennials. This method has been refined over 400 million years, so it makes sense to follow this age-old wisdom in your gardens.

Expand your garden space as your knowledge and soil improve. This is the no-fail way to ensure that every step of your gardening journey is enjoyable and sustainable without pushing you beyond your limits. Below are a few simple ways to expand your garden gradually, allowing it to grow as naturally as the spaces it emulates.

Start small and let your garden grow at your pace. When the time and energy felt right, this long, curved front yard bed was extended to hold a few extra shrubs.

ADD PLANTS

As you gain more experience, you'll discover which plants bring you the most joy—whether through their taste, texture, scent, beauty, or the wildlife they attract. Consider adding a few new plants each year in the same space, or experiment with new arrangements of your tried-and-true favorites.

Let joy guide your planting. Add snapdragons or others that delight you with vibrant color, sweet scents, tasty harvests, or visiting wildlife.

GO VERTICAL

Vertical expansion is another great option. Adding a trellis or other vertical structure allows you to grow plants like pole beans, peas, cucumbers, nasturtiums, and other climbers without needing additional ground space. See "Layer to Maximize Growth" (page 60) for more tips on how to use vertical space effectively.

ADD CONTAINERS

Expanding a garden doesn't always mean growing its physical footprint. Adding a few containers to your existing space can be a simple and rewarding way to expand; plus, they require less weeding and protection. Containers at the edge of a garden allow you to create new space without committing to major changes in your layout.

Growth isn't always about adding space. Tuck containers, like these herbs in a mini-orchard, into existing areas for a simple, flexible way to expand your garden.

GROW THE EDGES

Instead of starting a whole new bed, consider simply expanding upon an existing one. You can do this by growing the edges and adding more space incrementally. In the fall, use the sheet-mulching method (page 145) on the outer edge or end of a bed, covering it with layers of cardboard, newspaper, and compost. This process will prepare the area for new planting in the spring without the need for intensive soil preparation.

PART IV:

MEET YOUR NEW BEST FRIENDS

A resilient garden grows from strong relationships between you, the soil, and the plants. This section introduces trusted companions chosen for their ease of care, adaptability, and generosity. Each one yields something meaningful: beauty to lift your spirits, food to nourish your body, habitat to support wildlife, or healing for both land and soul.

CHAPTER 12: YOUR PLANT MATCHMAKING GUIDE

Beautiful, medicinal, soil-building, and a magnet for pollinators: purple coneflower is the kind of friend every garden (and gardener) deserves.

All plants featured in this book are low-maintenance stars that thrive in temperate climates (Hardiness Zones 4–8), reward you with bountiful yields, and require minimal effort. You won't find high-maintenance divas here—like blueberries that demand acidic soil and consistent watering—or fussy crops like cauliflower that sulk in temperamental weather. Nor will you encounter hard-to-harvest challenges, like those that make you wrestle with thorns or dig for deep, elusive roots.

The Collaborative Garden

Every gardener dreams big, but how do you make sure your dreams don't overwhelm you? We're here to help you create a garden that aligns with your goals and your busy life, whether you're growing fresh food, creating a serene retreat, supporting pollinators, or building a wildlife habitat. With thoughtful choices, you will create a space that collaborates with you and your garden visitors.

Before diving into the plant profiles, let's start by capturing your thoughts and inspirations. This is your chance to imagine and explore. What plants bring you happiness through their beauty, their scent, their taste, or the memories they spark? For each garden area—whether it's a raised bed vegetable garden, container garden, a mini-orchard, or a sensory patch—print a dedicated Plant Matchmaker sheet (page 187) to capture your plant ideas for that particular space.

With blank sheets and big ideas in hand, prepare your favorite herbal tea, settle into a cozy chair, and get to dreaming. The following steps will guide you through the process and explain how to make the most of the Plant Matchmaker sheet.

1. KNOW THY BED

Plants flourish with minimal effort when they're in the right environment, exactly like we do. Before you start matching plants to your space, take a moment to get to know your area. This step defines your garden characteristics to ensure it will be a happy home for your plant friends.

- **Name Your Bed:** Try something fun or sentimental: Salsa Spot, Nibble Patch, Berry Bliss, Herbal Retreat, or Pollinator Paradise.
- **Visits per Week:** Estimate how often you naturally pass by or check in on this bed. Spots you visit daily are great for plants that need regular harvesting or watering, while areas you visit less often may be better suited to hardy perennials.
- **Other Characteristics:** Note anything else that might affect your plants: proximity to a water spigot, strong winds, curious pets, a nearby play area, or a view you want to frame or preserve.
- **Scout the Space:** Head outside, trowel in hand, and take notes on those characteristics:
    - **Sunlight:** How much direct light does this spot get each day during the growing season?
    - **Soil Moisture:** Is it typically dry, wet, or somewhere in between?
    - **Soil Composition:** Dig a hole and feel the soil. Is it sandy, clay-like, sticky silt, or rich loam?

Refer to "Put Your Garden Where You Roam" (page 55) for details about evaluating the best spot for your garden.

2. DREAM BIG

Now let your imagination run wild. Think of this step as a plant party where everyone is invited—no need to be practical just yet! Simply jot down the plants that call to you without overthinking where they'll fit. A garden with a diverse mix of plants is more than just beautiful, it's naturally more resilient, attracting beneficial insects, preventing soil depletion, and reducing pest issues. Aim for a variety of heights, root depths, bloom times, and functions to create a balanced, thriving ecosystem.

For inspiration, start with the tried-and-true options in "The Plant Explorer" (page 188) and let these prompts help you dream big. It's okay to have the same plant on two or more Plant Matchmaker sheets—this means that plant is a possibility for more than one spot.

- **Memory Lane:** Which plants bring back happy memories? Maybe the scent of mint from your grandmother's garden or the apple tree you climbed as a child?
- **Catalog Crushes:** Flip through seed or plant catalogs, and write down anything you've circled or dog-eared.
- **Online Inspiration:** Did you see something on social media or a favorite gardening blog?
- **Friendly Suggestions:** What plants do friends, family, or neighbors rave about?
- **Wild Encounters:** Ever been on a walk and spotted a plant that made you pause and smile?
- **Favorite Senses:** Think of plants that delight your senses: vivid blooms, calming scents, or delicious flavors.
- **Impulsive Delights:** You walked into the nursery just to browse, but a plant caught your eye and came home with you. Your heart knows a match when it sees one.

Feel free to leave most of the columns on your Plant Matchmaker sheet blank for now; this is about capturing ideas, not organizing them. Quickly jot down just enough information to remember the reason you chose this plant as a potential buddy.

Let curiosity guide you before practicality kicks in. A resilient, vibrant garden begins with imagination and the freedom to explore what excites you.

Leave seed and plant catalogs where you'll see them often, and let inspiration bloom every time you flip through their pages.

PLANT SHOPPING: DECODING PACKETS AND TAGS

Embarking on a plant shopping adventure is always exciting, but selecting the right plant involves more than just love at first sight. Whether you are choosing seedlings from a nursery or browsing through seed packets, understanding the information provided ensures you pick plants suited for your space and growing conditions. See "Plant and Seed Sources" (page 274) for additional information about finding and choosing high-quality plants and seeds.

DECIPHERING SEED PACKETS

Seed packets contain a wealth of information beyond just the plant variety. Learning to interpret them will help you select seeds that fit your growing conditions and gardening goals.

- **Variety Name and Type:** Look for details on whether the seed is a hybrid (F1) or heirloom:
    - **Hybrid (F1):** These are crossbred for disease resistance, uniformity, and high yields. Hybrids are vigorous and reliable, but seeds saved from them won't produce identical plants if you replant them.
    - **Open-Pollinated (OP):** All heirlooms are OP, but not all OP seeds are heirlooms. OP varieties reproduce true to type, meaning saved seeds will grow like the parent plant—if they don't cross-pollinate. Seed packets may not always say "OP," but if a variety isn't labeled hybrid or F1, it's usually open-pollinated.
    - **Heirloom:** A subset of open-pollinated seeds, heirlooms have been passed down for over 50 years and are prized for flavor and genetic diversity. Seeds can be saved and replanted. Some may be less disease-resistant than hybrids.
- **Germination Time and Planting Depth:** This tells you how long it takes for the seeds to sprout and how deep to plant them.
- **Days to Maturity:** The number of days from planting to harvest. This is especially helpful in short-season climates.
- **Spacing Requirements:** Guides how far apart to plant seeds to prevent overcrowding and ensure good air circulation.
- **Disease Resistance Codes:** Some seed packets include resistance abbreviations, such as VFN (Verticillium, Fusarium, and Nematode resistance) or PM (Powdery Mildew resistance).
- **All-America Selections (AAS) Winner:** Seeds labeled with "AAS Winner" have been rigorously trialed across the country and selected for outstanding performance.
- **Perennial vs. Annual:** Perennial plants live for multiple years within their specified growing zone, while annuals live for only a single growing season.

READING PLANT TAGS

- **Common and Scientific Name:** Provides both common and botanical names, helping you research and understand your plant better.
- **Hardiness Zone:** Shows the zones where the plant can survive year-round.
- **Mature Size:** Lists the expected height and width at maturity, which is crucial for planning space in your garden.
- **Light Requirements:** Indicates whether the plant prefers full sun, partial shade, or full shade.
- **Water Needs:** Specifies the plant's moisture preferences, from drought-tolerant to needing consistently moist soil.
- **Bloom Time:** Tells you when to expect flowers, aiding in planning for continuous garden color.
- **Special Features:** Notes attributes like fragrance, edibility, disease- and pest-resistance, or wildlife attraction.

Before you fall for a pretty picture, flip the packet. Reading the back helps ensure the plant you choose will thrive in your space and growing conditions.

Before bringing a plant home, take a moment to read the tag. It's full of tips to help ensure it will be a good match for you and your space.

3. REALITY CHECK

Now that you've dreamed big, it's time to refine your list. To ensure you and your plants are set up for a harmonious and rewarding relationship, let's dig a little deeper to see which ones truly belong in this particular space while making sure they fit your life and heart.

This process may involve a little research. Use the "Plant Profiles" (page 206) in this book, browse through other gardening resources, or search online for additional details. This exploration, and a little intuition, will help you fill in the Love Factor, Ease Factor, and Fit Factor columns for each entry on your Plant Matchmaker sheet. Take your time and sip that tea—it's worth the effort to find your perfect matches.

LOVE FACTOR

Answer this question: How much do you adore its beauty, scent, or taste?

This is where your emotions come into play. A plant that brings joy, beauty, or delicious flavors is more likely to keep you happily visiting the garden with enthusiasm. Plant what you love.

- **Palate Check:** If you're aiming for edibility, a plant's productivity doesn't matter much if you don't enjoy eating it. Whenever possible, sample specific varieties before committing. For instance, try a sweet cherry tomato like Super Sweet 100 at the farmers market before taking three months to grow it.
- **Memories and Senses:** Does the plant remind you of cherished childhood moments? Do you love its fragrance or the sight of its blooms swaying in the breeze?
- **Local Favorite:** If a plant caught your eye (or nose) in a local park or garden, it's likely to thrive in your area—and bring you just as much joy at home.

SCORE:

- **1** = It's okay.
- **5** = I can't imagine my garden without it.

EASE FACTOR

Answer this question: How easy it is to grow and care for?

Even the loveliest plants can become burdensome if they require constant attention. Evaluate how easy it is to grow, harvest, and maintain each plant.

- **Harvesting Times:** Will the plant's peak harvest align with your availability and vacation schedule? Summer squash, for example, can't wait—they need frequent picking in summertime to stay yummy and productive.
- **Harvesting Preferences:** Avoid plants that clash with your style. If you dislike digging, skip root crops. If tall ladders make you uneasy, go for dwarf fruit trees.
- **Disease Resistance:** Research common diseases in your area. For example:
    - Tomatoes are often plagued by blight in humid conditions with little airflow. Choosing resistant varieties like Defiant or Mountain Magic can improve success.
    - Apple trees may battle apple scab in certain regions, making resistant varieties like Liberty or Enterprise excellent options.

SCORE:

- **1** = High-maintenance diva.
- **5** = Practically takes care of itself.

FIT FACTOR

Answer the question: How well does it suit the area?

This is where practicality meets planning. The better the fit, the less work required to keep the plant happy.

- **Environmental Match:** Plants, like people, thrive in the right environment. Does the plant suit the sunlight, soil moisture, and soil composition of your chosen garden bed? For example, basil loves full sun and well-drained soil, while mint tolerates partial shade and wetter conditions.
- **Soil Adjustments:** If the soil is not a good match for your plant, consider amending the soil or placing this particular plant in a raised bed or container to create an ideal foundation.
- **Space Constraints:** If a plant seems too large for your space, search for compact varieties and you might be pleasantly surprised to discover a smaller version that fits perfectly.

SCORE:

- **1** = Not a great fit.
- **5** = Perfect fit.

4. SPOTLIGHT YOUR STARS

Congratulations! You've made it through the brainstorming and reality-check phases, and now it's time for the final round of auditions for your garden's cast of characters.

Add up the Love Factor, Ease Factor, and Fit Factor for each plant to calculate its Total Score (3–15). This number will help identify your top picks. You have a couple options to make the final list.

OPTION A: HIGHLIGHT FAVORITES DIRECTLY

If your list is tidy and you love seeing everything in one place, grab highlighters or colored markers to spotlight your top plants:

- **Green (Must Grow):** Scores 12–15. These plants are your garden's VIPs; they bring the most joy and the least hassle.
- **Yellow (Maybe Grow):** Scores 8–11. These plants have potential but might need extra care.
- **Red (Save for Later):** Scores 7 or below. These aren't rejects, but they might fit better in another garden bed, during another year, or after more planning.

OPTION B: TRANSFER TO A CLEAN SHEET

If your list feels a little chaotic, start fresh. Create a new Plant Matchmaker sheet with plants ranked in order of their scores and categories:

- **Must Grow:** Scores 12–15. The "Love It, Let's Do It!" plants.
- **Maybe Grow:** Scores 8–11. The "Tempting, but Plan to Pamper" plants.
- **Save for Later:** Scores 7 or below. The "Another Bed or Another Year" plants.

5. REFLECT AND CELEBRATE

Take a deep breath and look over your list. This is more than numbers—it's about plants that feel like friends, ones that will grow alongside you to help create your ideal garden space. These plants and the space where they'll reside reflect your tastes, memories, and values.

With your prioritized list in hand, it's time to start turning dreams into reality. Flip to "Simple, Low-Maintenance Garden Spaces" (page 68) for step-by-step guidance on placing and nurturing your new friends. Whether you're setting up a raised bed, planning a sensory retreat, or growing a mini-orchard, you're on your way to creating a garden that feels like home.

Plant Matchmaker

Bed Name Spud & Sprig Spot **Visits Per Week** 5 **Other Characteristics** ____

Daily Sunlight: Full Sun 6+ Hours | (Part Sun 4–6 Hours) | Part Shade 2–4 Hours | Full Shade <2 Hours

Soil Moisture: Dry | (Medium) | Wet

Soil Composition: (Loam) | Clay | Sand | Silt

Plant Name	Where You Found It	Why You Love It	Yields	Wildlife Supported	Lifecycle	Notes	Love Factor	Ease Factor	Fit Factor	Total Score
Include the variety, if known	(**M**)emory, (**C**)atalog, (**B**)ook, (**F**)riend, (**S**)tore, (**O**)nline	(**B**)eauty, (**T**)aste, (**S**)cent, (**N**)ostalgia	(**E**)dible, (**M**)edicinal, (**S**)ensory	(**P**)ollinators, (**Bu**)tterflies, (**B**)irds, (**I**)nsects, (**T**)oads	(**A**)nnual, (**B**)iennial, (**P**)erennial	Ideal conditions, challenges, companion plants	**Scale: 1–5** How much do you adore its beauty, scent, or taste?	**Scale: 1–5** How easy it is to grow and care for?	**Scale: 1–5** How well does it suit the area?	Add scores from the previous columns (ranges from 3–15)
Chives (common garlic)	M, F	T, N	E, S	P	P	self-spreads	5	5	5	15
Cilantro	F	T	E		A		3	5	5	13
Potato (Yukon gold)	M, C	T	E		A					
Tatsoi	O				A		5	4	1	10

This is just an example. Fill out as much info as you want, and make as many versions as you like!

Downloadable copies can be found at www.EarthMindPractice.org

Plant Matchmaker

Bed Name ________________________ **Visits Per Week** ____________ **Other Characteristics** ____

Daily Sunlight				Soil Moisture			Soil Composition			
Full Sun 6+ Hours	Part Sun 4–6 Hours	Part Shade 2–4 Hours	Full Shade <2 Hours	Dry	Medium	Wet	Loam	Clay	Sand	Silt

Plant Name	Where You Found It	Why You Love It	Yields	Wildlife Supported	Lifecycle	Notes	Love Factor	Ease Factor	Fit Factor	Total Score
Include the variety, if known	(**M**)emory, (**C**)atalog, (**B**)ook, (**F**)riend, (**S**)tore, (**O**)nline	(**B**)eauty, (**T**)aste, (**S**)cent, (**N**)ostalgia	(**E**)dible, (**M**)edicinal, (**S**)ensory	(**P**)ollinators, (**Bu**)tterflies, (**B**)irds, (**I**)nsects, (**T**)oads	(**A**)nnual, (**B**)iennial, (**P**)erennial	Ideal conditions, challenges, companion plants	**Scale: 1–5** How much do you adore its beauty, scent, or taste?	**Scale: 1–5** How easy it is to grow and care for?	**Scale: 1–5** How well does it suit the area?	Add scores from the previous columns (ranges from 3–15)

Downloadable copies can be found at www.EarthMindPractice.org

The Plant Explorer

You've likely started using the Plant Matchmaker to identify your garden's needs, now let's find plants that fit you and your space. These charts highlight trusted options that are perfect for a solid, low-maintenance foundation; of course, you can always include other plants. Scan the tables for potential matches, explore their attributes, and read their profiles for more details.

HOW TO READ THE CHARTS

While most of the attributes are easy to understand, we've included explanations for any that might need a little extra context.

HEIGHT AND WIDTH

Most plants have a range listed for how tall or wide they can grow. That's because plant size often depends on how well it likes its environment. When given the right combination of soil, sunlight, moisture, and nutrients, a plant will likely reach the higher end of its size range. In less ideal conditions, it may stay smaller.

Some self-sowing or sprawling ground covers don't have a fixed boundary—they'll happily wander wherever space allows. In those cases, you'll see "Indef." listed for width, meaning indefinite spread.

PAMPERING NEED

Pampering describes the level of effort and attention a plant needs from you to thrive from planting to harvest. Some plants take care of themselves, while others need more love and attention. Here's how the scale works:

- **5 (Very Easy):** These plants are the stars of low-maintenance gardening. Once planted, they need little to no help to thrive. Plant it, forget it, and let nature do the work.
- **4 (Easy):** These plants require some upfront care, such as planting, watering, and occasional weeding. But after the first month, they mostly look after themselves. Monthly pest checks and light pruning are usually all that's needed.
- **3 (Moderate):** A bit more attention is required to keep these plants happy. Expect to water consistently (two to four times a week) and check regularly for pests or diseases. Pruning or trellising branches may also be necessary a few times a year.

None of these plants are 2 (Difficult) or 1 (Very Difficult) because these are all low-maintenance.

HARVEST EASE

Harvesting ease refers to how simple or time intensive it is to gather the fruits, vegetables, or other parts of a plant. Factors include accessibility, the need for tools, and whether the harvest is quick or spread out over time.

- **5 (Very Easy):** The ultimate in convenience! Fruits and vegetables are low, clumped, and easy to access, making harvests quick and satisfying. Great when you're busy or need quick snacks from the garden.
- **4 (Easy):** Harvesting takes a little more time. Fruits or greens may be dispersed across the plant, require minor tools (like scissors or a knife), or involve destemming.
- **3 (Moderate):** These plants require some effort when harvesting. Fruit might be out of reach or hidden within dense or prickly foliage, and root crops may need digging. Harvests might also be spread out over a longer period.

None of these plants are 2 (Difficult) or 1 (Very Difficult) because these are low-maintenance plants.

NATURALLY DISEASE AND PEST RESISTANT

Plants with natural disease and pest resistance are tough and low-maintenance. Disease-resistant plants fend off common issues like fungal or bacterial infections, while pest-resistant plants deter deer, rabbits, and insects with strong aromatic oils or unappetizing foliage. These traits mean less work for you and a healthier, more resilient garden.

HARVEST PERIOD

A green mark in the box indicates the months when a plant is typically ready to harvest. Some plants have a generous harvest window, others may offer only a brief moment of abundance, and some have several harvests throughout the year. Keep in mind that the timing may vary slightly depending on your local climate, your growing zone, and seasonal shifts.

GROWTH RATE

Growth rate refers to how quickly a plant matures and begins to provide yields of food, scents, or blooms.

- **5 (Very Fast):** Yields within 30 days. These are the quick achievers, perfect for when you're looking for instant gratification.
- **4 (Fast):** Yields within one to three months. These are an excellent choice for busy gardeners.
- **3 (Moderate):** Yields within three months to two years. These plants require a bit more patience.
- **2 (Slow):** Yields within two to five years. These perennial plants demand a longer-term investment but reward you with significant yields and lasting beauty.
- **1 (Very Slow):** Takes over five years to yield. These are the patient gardener's companions, offering steady growth and eventual abundance.

LIFECYCLE

Lifecycle describes how long a plant lives and produces.

- **A (Annual):** These plants complete their entire life cycle—germinating, flowering, producing seeds, and dying—in a single growing season. They're perfect for quick rewards and adding seasonal variety to your garden.
- **B (Biennial):** These plants grow tasty leaves and roots in their first year, then flower, set seed, and die in their second. Since second-year growth is often tough and bitter, they're usually grown as annuals.
- **P (Perennial):** These plants live for many years and tend to need less pampering with age. They're ideal for creating long-lasting, low-maintenance spaces.

SUPERSTAR VEGETABLES AND HERBS

These are go-to garden champions: high-yield, easy to grow, and perfect for getting started. They'll give you fast, delicious harvests with minimal fuss.

Common Name	Height	Width	Light	Soil Moisture	Parts Used
Basil	1'–3' (30.5–91.4cm)	6" (15.2cm)	Full Sun	Medium	Flowers, Leaves
Beans	1' (30.5cm)	1' (30.5cm)	Full Sun	Medium	Pod, Seeds
Bee Balm	3'–4' (0.9–1.2m)	2'–6' (0.6–1.8m)	Full Sun, Part Shade	Dry, Medium	Flowers, Leaves
Beet	8"–12" (20.3–30.5cm)	6"–12" (15.2–30.5cm)	Full Sun	Medium	Leaves, Root
Chamomile	6"–12" (15.2–30.5cm)	Indef.	Full Sun	Dry, Medium	Flowers, Leaves
Chives	18" (45.7cm)	1' (30.5cm)	Full Sun, Part Shade	Dry, Medium	Bulb, Leaves
Cilantro	12"–14" (30.5–35.6cm)	6"–12" (15.2–30.5cm)	Full Sun, Part Shade	Medium	Leaves
Clover, Dutch White	4"–10" (10.2–25.4cm)	6"–36" (15.2–91.4cm)	Full Sun, Part Shade	Dry, Medium	Leaves, Flowers
Collard Greens	18"–24" (45.7–61cm)	12"–18" (30.5–45.7cm)	Full Sun, Part Shade	Medium	Leaves
Coneflower, Purple	3'–4' (0.9–1.2m)	18" (45.7cm)	Full Sun, Part Shade	Dry, Medium	Flowers, Leaves, Root
Cucumber	3'–7' (0.9–2.1m)	Indef.	Full Sun	Dry, Wet	Flowers, Leaves, Root
Dandelion	6"–12" (15.2–30.5cm)	6"–8" (15.2–20.3cm)	Full Sun, Full Shade	Medium, Wet	Fruit

Pampering Need:
5 = Very Easy
4 = Easy
3 = Moderate

Harvest Ease:
5 = Very Easy
4 = Easy
3 = Moderate

Growth Rate:
5 = Very Fast
4 = Fast
3 = Moderate
2 = Slow
1 = Very Slow

Lifecycle:
A = Annual
B = Biennial
P = Perennial

Pampering Need	Harvest Ease	Disease Resistant	Pest Resistant	HARVEST PERIOD Apr	May	June	July	Aug	Sept	Oct	Nov	Growth Rate	Lifecycle	Sensory Experience
4	4					■	■	■	■	■		5	A	Scent, Taste
4	5						■	■	■	■		5	A	Taste
5	4		■			■	■	■	■			3	P	Scent, Taste
3	4					■	■	■	■	■	■	5	A	
5	3	■	■	■	■	■						4	A, P	Scent, Sight, Taste
5	5	■	■	■	■	■	■	■	■	■		3	P	Taste
4	4					■	■	■	■	■		5	A	Scent, Taste
5	4	■				■	■	■	■			3	P	
4	5						■	■	■	■	■	4	A	
4	5	■	■		■	■	■	■	■	■		3	P	Sight
4	5						■	■	■	■		4	A	
5	4	■	■	■	■	■	■	■	■	■		4	P	

SUPERSTAR VEGETABLES AND HERBS

Common Name	Height	Width	Light	Soil Moisture	Parts Used
Dill	2'–3' (61–91.4cm)	6" (15.2cm)	Full Sun, Part Shade	Medium	Leaves
Garlic	18" (45.7cm)	4" (10.2cm)	Full Sun, Part Shade	Dry	Bulb, Leaves
Hyssop, Anise	2'–4' (0.6–1.2m)	1'–2' (30.5–61cm)	Full Sun, Part Shade	Dry, Medium	Flowers, Leaves
Kale	2' (61cm)	1' (30.5cm)	Full Sun, Part Shade	Medium, Wet	Leaves
Lambsquarters	1'–2' (30.5–61cm)	12"–18" (30.5–45.7cm)	Full Sun, Part Shade	Dry, Wet	Leaves
Lettuce	1' (30.5cm)	1' (30.5cm)	Full Sun	Medium	Leaves
Mint	8"–24" (20.3–61cm)	Indef.	Full Sun, Part Shade	Medium, Wet	Leaves
Nasturtium	1"–18" (2.5–45.7cm)	12"–18" (30.5–45.7cm)	Full Sun	Medium	Flowers, Leaves
Onion, Egyptian Walking	2' (61cm)	6" (15.2cm)	Full Sun	Medium	Bulb, Leaves
Oregano	8"–10" (20.3–25.4cm)	1'–4' (0.3–1.2m)	Full Sun	Dry, Medium	Leaves
Parsley	1' (30.5cm)	9"–12" (22.9–30.5cm)	Full Sun, Part Shade	Medium	Leaves
Peas	3'–7' (0.9–2.1m)	Indef.	Full Sun, Part Shade	Medium	Pod, Seeds
Plantain, Broadleaf	6"–10" (15.2–25.4cm)		Full Sun, Part Shade	Dry, Wet	Leaves
Potato	1'–2' (30.5–61cm)	18" (45.7cm)	Full Sun	Medium	Root

Pampering Need:
5 = Very Easy
4 = Easy
3 = Moderate

Harvest Ease:
5 = Very Easy
4 = Easy
3 = Moderate

Growth Rate:
5 = Very Fast
4 = Fast
3 = Moderate
2 = Slow
1 = Very Slow

Lifecycle:
A = Annual
B = Biennial
P = Perennial

Pampering Need	Harvest Ease	Disease Resistant	Pest Resistant	HARVEST PERIOD								Growth Rate	Lifecycle	Sensory Experience
				Apr	May	June	July	Aug	Sept	Oct	Nov			
5	**5**											4	A	Scent, Sight, Taste
4	3											3	A	
5	**5**											4	P	Scent, Sight, Taste
4	**5**											4	A or B	
5	**5**											5	P	
3	4											5	A	
5	4											4	P	Scent, Taste
5	**5**											4	A	Sight, Taste
5	**5**											3	P	
5	**5**											3	P	Scent, Taste
3	**5**											3	B	Scent, Taste
4	**5**											4	A	Taste
5	4											4	P	
5	3											3	A	

SUPERSTAR VEGETABLES AND HERBS

Common Name	Height	Width	Light	Soil Moisture	Parts Used
Radish	8" (20.3cm)	6" (15.2cm)	Full Sun	Medium	Leaves, Root
Rhubarb	3'–5' (0.9–1.5m)	3'–5' (0.9–1.5m)	Full Sun, Part Shade	Medium	Stalks
Sage, Broadleaf	18"–30" (45.7–76.2cm)	30"–36" (76.2–91.4cm)	Full Sun	Dry, Medium	Leaves
Self-Heal	6"–12" (15.2–30.5cm)	Indef.	Full Sun, Part Shade	Medium, Wet	Flowers, Leaves
Sorrel, Creeping Wood	2"–4" (5.1–10.2cm)	Indef.	Full Sun, Part Shade	Dry, Medium	Flowers, Leaves
Sorrel, French	1'–3' (30.5–91.4cm)	10"–12" (25.4–30.5cm)	Full Sun, Part Shade	Dry, Medium	Leaves
Spinach	6"–12" (15.2–30.5cm)	6"–8" (15.2–20.3cm)	Full Sun, Part Shade	Medium	Leaves
Squash, Summer	18" (45.7cm)	4' (1.2m)	Full Sun	Medium	Fruit
Squash, Winter	18" (45.7cm)	Indef.	Full Sun	Medium, Wet	Fruit
Strawberry	10" (25.4cm)	Indef.	Full Sun, Part Shade	Medium	Berries, Leaves
Sunflower	3'–15' (0.9–4.6m)	1' (30.5cm)	Full Sun	Medium	Seeds
Swiss Chard	1'–2' (30.5–61cm)	1' (30.5cm)	Full Sun	Medium	Leaves, Stalks
Tatsoi	6" (15.2cm)	8"–12" (20.3–30.5cm)	Full Sun, Part Shade	Medium	Leaves
Thyme	4"–12" (10.2–30.5cm)	4"+ (10.2cm)+	Full Sun, Part Shade	Dry, Medium	Leaves
Tomato	2'–10' (0.6–3m)	3'–5' (0.9–1.5m)	Full Sun	Medium	Fruit
Violet	6"–12" (15.2–30.5cm)	Indef.	Full Sun, Part Shade	Medium	Flowers, Leaves
Yarrow	2'–3' (61–91.4cm)	Indef.	Full Sun, Part Shade	Dry	Flowers, Leaves

Pampering Need:	**Harvest Ease:**	**Growth Rate:**	**Lifecycle:**
5 = Very Easy 4 = Easy 3 = Moderate	5 = Very Easy 4 = Easy 3 = Moderate	5 = Very Fast 4 = Fast 3 = Moderate 2 = Slow 1 = Very Slow	A = Annual B = Biennial P = Perennial

Pampering Need	Harvest Ease	Disease Resistant	Pest Resistant	HARVEST PERIOD								Growth Rate	Lifecycle	Sensory Experience
				Apr	May	June	July	Aug	Sept	Oct	Nov			
5	4			■	■	■	■	■	■	■	■	5	A	
5	5	■	■		■	■	■					2	P	
4	5	■	■		■	■	■	■	■	■		3	P	Scent, Taste
5	3	■	■	■	■	■	■	■	■	■	■	3	P	
5	4	■	■		■	■	■	■	■	■		4	P	
5	5	■	■	■	■	■	■	■	■	■	■	3	P	Taste
3	4					■			■	■		4	A	
3	5							■	■			4	A	
4	4									■		3	A	
5	4					■	■	■	■	■		3	P	Taste
5	3											5	A	Sight
4	5					■	■	■	■	■	■	4	A or B	
4	4				■	■	■	■	■	■		5	A	Taste
5	4	■	■	■	■	■	■	■	■	■	■	3	P	Scent, Sight, Taste
3	5						■	■	■	■		3	A	Taste, Sight
5	3	■	■	■	■	■						3	P	Sight
5	5	■	■			■	■	■	■	■		3	P	Scent, Sight, Taste

FRUIT FAVORITES

These plants are the gift that keeps on giving. While they take a little patience to establish, you'll be rewarded year after year with homegrown sweetness.

Common Name	Height	Width	Light	Soil Moisture	Parts Used
Apple	5'–12' (1.5–3.7m)	5'–12' (1.5–3.7m)	Full Sun	Medium	Fruit
Cherry, Sour	8'–10' (2.4–3m)	8'–10' (2.4–3m)	Full Sun	Medium	Fruit
Cherry, Sweet	6'–8' (1.8–2.4m)	8'–15' (2.4–4.6m)	Full Sun	Medium	Fruit
Currant, Clove	6'–12' (1.8–3.7m)	6'–8' (1.8–2.4m)	Full Sun, Part Shade	Dry, Medium	Berries
Currant, Red	3'–5' (0.9–1.5m)	4'–5' (1.2–1.5m)	Full Sun, Part Shade	Medium	Berries
Gooseberry	3'–5' (0.9–1.5m)	3'–5' (0.9–1.5m)	Full Sun, Part Shade	Dry, Medium	Berries
Goumi Berry	5'–6' (1.5–1.8m)	5'–6' (1.5–1.8m)	Full Sun, Part Shade	Dry, Medium	Berries
Grape	15'–20' (4.6–9.1m)	15'–20' (4.6–9.1m)	Full Sun	Dry, Medium	Fruit
Peach	12'–15' (3.7–4.6m)	12'–15' (3.7–4.6m)	Full Sun	Medium	Fruit
Pear, European	8'–15' (2.4–4.6m)	8'–15' (2.4–4.6m)	Full Sun	Medium	Fruit
Plum, European	10'–12' (3–3.7m)	10'–15' (3–4.6m)	Full Sun	Medium	Fruit
Raspberry	4'–6' (1.2–1.8m)	Indef.	Full Sun	Medium	Berries, Leaves
Serviceberry, Saskatoon	6'–15' (1.8–4.6m)	4'–10' (1.2–3m)	Full Sun	Medium	Berries
Strawberry	10" (25.4cm)	Indef.	Full Sun, Part Shade	Medium	Berries, Leaves

Pampering Need:
5 = Very Easy
4 = Easy
3 = Moderate

Harvest Ease:
5 = Very Easy
4 = Easy
3 = Moderate

Growth Rate:
5 = Very Fast
4 = Fast
3 = Moderate
2 = Slow
1 = Very Slow

Lifecycle:
A = Annual
B = Biennial
P = Perennial

Pampering Need	Harvest Ease	Disease Resistant	Pest Resistant	HARVEST PERIOD Apr	May	June	July	Aug	Sept	Oct	Nov	Growth Rate	Lifecycle	Sensory Experience
4	3						■	■	■	■		2	P	Taste
5	3					■	■					2	P	Taste
5	3						■					2	P	Taste
4	3					■						3	P	Scent, Taste
5	5					■						3	P	Taste
5	3						■					3	P	Taste
5	4	■	■		■	■						3	P	Taste
4	5							■	■			2	P	Taste
4	3						■	■	■			2	P	Taste
4	3							■	■			1	P	Taste
4	3							■	■			2	P	Taste
4	3						■	■	■	■	■	3	P	Taste
5	3					■						3	P	Taste
5	4					■	■	■	■	■		3	P	Taste

SENSORY DELIGHTS

While any edible plant can offer a sensory experience, these stand out for their especially inviting textures, fragrances, or flavors. They naturally encourage you to pause, engage, and savor, making them ideal for a sensory-focused garden.

Common Name	Height	Width	Light	Soil Moisture	Parts Used
Basil	1'–3' (30.5–91.4cm)	6" (15.2cm)	Full Sun	Medium	Flowers, Leaves
Bee Balm	3'–4' (0.9–1.2m)	2'–6' (0.6–1.8m)	Full Sun, Part Shade	Dry, Medium	Flowers, Leaves
Blooming Bulbs	3'–5' (0.9–1.5m)	1'–3' (30.5–91.4cm)	Full Sun, Part Shade	Medium	
Butterfly Weed	2' (61cm)	2' (61cm)	Full Sun	Dry, Medium	
Chamomile	6"–12" (15.2–30.5cm)	Indef.	Full Sun	Dry, Medium	Flowers, Leaves
Chives	18" (45.7cm)	1' (30.5cm)	Full Sun, Part Shade	Dry, Medium	Bulb, Leaves
Cilantro	12"–14" (30.5–35.6cm)	6"–12" (15.2–30.5cm)	Full Sun, Part Shade	Medium	Leaves
Coneflower, Purple	3'–4' (0.9–1.2m)	18" (45.7cm)	Full Sun, Part Shade	Dry, Medium	Flowers, Leaves, Root
Cosmos	2'–7' (0.6–2.1m)	2' (61cm)	Full Sun, Part Shade	Dry, Medium	
Currant, Clove	6'–12' (1.8–3.7m)	6'–8' (1.8–2.4m)	Full Sun, Part Shade	Dry, Medium	Berries
Dill	2'–3' (61–91.4cm)	6" (15.2cm)	Full Sun, Part Shade	Medium	Leaves
Hyssop, Anise	2'–4' (0.6–1.2m)	1'–2' (30.5–61cm)	Full Sun, Part Shade	Dry, Medium	Flowers, Leaves
Lamb's Ear	6"–12" (15.2–30.5cm)	Indef.	Full Sun, Part Shade	Dry, Medium	
Mint	8"–24" (20.3–61cm)	Indef.	Full Sun, Part Shade	Medium, Wet	Leaves
Nasturtium	1"–18" (2.5–45.7cm)	12"–18" (30.5–45.7cm)	Full Sun	Medium	Flowers, Leaves

Pampering Need:
5 = Very Easy
4 = Easy
3 = Moderate

Harvest Ease:
5 = Very Easy
4 = Easy
3 = Moderate

Growth Rate:
5 = Very Fast
4 = Fast
3 = Moderate
2 = Slow
1 = Very Slow

Lifecycle:
A = Annual
B = Biennial
P = Perennial

Pampering Need	Harvest Ease	Disease Resistant	Pest Resistant	HARVEST PERIOD								Growth Rate	Lifecycle	Sensory Experience
				Apr	May	June	July	Aug	Sept	Oct	Nov			
4	4											5	A	Scent, Taste
5	4											3	P	Scent, Taste
5												3	P	Sight
5												3	P	Sight
5	3											4	A, P	Scent, Sight, Taste
5	5											3	P	Taste
4	4											5	A	Scent, Taste
4	5											3	P	Sight
5												4	A	Sight
4	3											3	P	Scent, Taste
5	5											4	A	Scent, Sight, Taste, Touch
5	5											4	P	Scent, Sight, Taste
5												3	P	Touch
5	4											4	P	Scent, Taste
5	5											4	A	Sight, Taste

SENSORY DELIGHTS

Common Name	Height	Width	Light	Soil Moisture	Parts Used
Oregano	8"–10" (20.3–25.4cm)	1'–4' (0.3–1.2m)	Full Sun	Dry, Medium	Leaves
Parsley	1' (30.5cm)	9"–12" (22.9–30.5cm)	Full Sun, Part Shade	Medium	Leaves
Peas	3'–7' (0.9–2.1m)	Indef.	Full Sun, Part Shade	Medium	Pod, Seeds
Sage, Broadleaf	18"–30" (45.7–76.2cm)	30"–36" (76.2–91.4cm)	Full Sun	Dry, Medium	Leaves
Sorrel, French	1'–3' (30.5–91.4cm)	10"–12" (25.4–30.5cm)	Full Sun, Part Shade	Dry, Medium	Leaves
Strawberry	10" (25.4cm)	Indef.	Full Sun, Part Shade	Medium	Berries, Leaves
Sunflower	3'–15' (0.9–4.6m)	1' (30.5cm)	Full Sun	Medium	Seeds
Sweet Potato, Ornamental	8" (20.3cm)	3'–5' (0.9–1.5m)	Full Sun, Part Shade	Dry, Medium	
Tatsoi	6" (15.2cm)	8"–12" (20.3–30.5cm)	Full Sun, Part Shade	Medium	Leaves
Thyme	4"–12" (10.2–30.5cm)	4"+ (10.2cm)+	Full Sun, Part Shade	Dry, Medium	Leaves
Tomato	2'–10' (0.6–3m)	3'–5' (0.9–1.5m)	Full Sun	Medium	Fruit
Yarrow	2'–3' (61–91.4cm)	Indef.	Full Sun, Part Shade	Dry	Flowers, Leaves

Pampering Need:
5 = Very Easy
4 = Easy
3 = Moderate

Harvest Ease:
5 = Very Easy
4 = Easy
3 = Moderate

Growth Rate:
5 = Very Fast
4 = Fast
3 = Moderate
2 = Slow
1 = Very Slow

Lifecycle:
A = Annual
B = Biennial
P = Perennial

Pampering Need	Harvest Ease	Disease Resistant	Pest Resistant	HARVEST PERIOD Apr	May	June	July	Aug	Sept	Oct	Nov	Growth Rate	Lifecycle	Sensory Experience
5	**5**	■	■	■	■	■	■	■	■	■	■	3	P	Scent, Taste
3	**5**						■	■	■	■		3	B	Scent, Taste
4	**5**					■			■	■		4	A	Taste
4	**5**	■	■		■	■	■	■	■	■		3	P	Scent, Taste
5	**5**	■	■	■	■	■	■	■	■	■	■	3	P	Taste
5	4					■	■	■	■	■		3	P	Taste
5	3											4	A	Sight
4												3	A	Sight
4	4				■	■	■	■	■	■		5	A	Taste
5	4	■	■	■	■	■	■	■	■	■	■	3	P	Scent, Sight, Taste
3	**5**					■	■	■	■	■		3	A	Taste, Sight
5	**5**	■	■			■	■	■	■	■		3	P	Scent, Sight, Tast

GROUND COVER GUARDIANS

Low-growing and hardworking, these plants build your soil, conserve moisture, block weeds, and keep your garden looking lush.

Common Name	Height	Width	Light	Soil Moisture	Parts Used
Chamomile	6"–12" (15.2–30.5cm)	Indef.	Full Sun	Dry, Medium	Flowers, Leaves
Clover, Dutch White	4"–10" (10.2–25.4cm)	6"–36" (15.2–91.4cm)	Full Sun, Part Shade	Dry, Medium	Leaves, Flowers
Lamb's Ear	6"–12" (15.2–30.5cm)	Indef.	Full Sun, Part Shade	Dry, Medium	
Mint	8"–24" (20.3–61cm)	Indef.	Full Sun, Part Shade	Medium, Wet	Leaves
Oregano	8"–10" (20.3–25.4cm)	1'–4' (0.3–1.2m)	Full Sun	Dry, Medium	Leaves
Self-Heal	6"–12" (15.2–30.5cm)	Indef.	Full Sun, Part Shade	Medium, Wet	Flowers, Leaves
Strawberry	10" (25.4cm)	Indef.	Full Sun, Part Shade	Medium	Berries, Leaves
Sweet Potato, Ornamental	8" (20.3cm)	3'–5' (0.9–1.5m)	Full Sun, Part Shade	Dry, Medium	
Thyme	4"–12" (10.2–30.5cm)	4"+ (10.2cm)+	Full Sun, Part Shade	Dry, Medium	Leaves
Violet	6"–12" (15.2–30.5cm)	Indef.	Full Sun, Part Shade	Medium	Flowers, Leaves

Pampering Need:
5 = Very Easy
4 = Easy
3 = Moderate

Harvest Ease:
5 = Very Easy
4 = Easy
3 = Moderate

Growth Rate:
5 = Very Fast
4 = Fast
3 = Moderate
2 = Slow
1 = Very Slow

Lifecycle:
A = Annual
B = Biennial
P = Perennial

Pampering Need	Harvest Ease	Disease Resistant	Pest Resistant	HARVEST PERIOD Apr	May	June	July	Aug	Sept	Oct	Nov	Growth Rate	Lifecycle	Sensory Experience
5	3											4	A, P	Scent, Sight, Taste
5	4											3	P	
5												3	P	Touch
5	4											5	P	Scent, Taste
5	5											3	P	Scent, Taste
5	3											3	P	
5	4											3	P	Taste
4												3	A	Sight
5	4											3	P	Scent, Sight, Taste
5	3											3	P	Sight

CAREFREE WILD EDIBLES

These resilient plants often thrive on their own, needing little to no care. If they're not already in your yard, they're easy to tuck into empty spaces or use as low-maintenance swaps.

Common Name	Height	Width	Light	Soil Moisture	Parts Used
Bee Balm	3'–4' (0.9–1.2m)	2'–6' (0.6–1.8m)	Full Sun, Part Shade	Dry, Medium	Flowers, Leaves
Clover, Dutch White	4"–10" (10.2–25.4cm)	6"–36" (15.2–91.4cm)	Full Sun, Part Shade	Dry, Medium	Leaves, Flowers
Coneflower, Purple	3'–4' (0.9–1.2m)	18" (45.7cm)	Full Sun, Part Shade	Dry, Medium	Flowers, Leaves, Root
Currant, Clove	6'–12' (1.8–3.7m)	6'–8' (1.8–2.4m)	Full Sun, Part Shade	Dry, Medium	Berries
Currant, Red	3'–5' (0.9–1.5m)	4'–5' (1.2–1.5m)	Full Sun, Part Shade	Medium	Berries
Dandelion	6"–12" (15.2–30.5cm)	6"–8" (15.2–20.3cm)	Full Sun, Full Shade	Dry, Wet	Flowers, Leaves, Root
Gooseberry	3'–5' (0.9–1.5m)	3'–5' (0.9–1.5m)	Full Sun, Part Shade	Dry, Medium	Berries
Goumi Berry	5'–6' (1.5–1.8m)	5'–6' (1.5–1.8m)	Full Sun, Part Shade	Dry, Medium	Berries
Grape	15'–20' (4.6–9.1m)	15'–20' (4.6–9.1m)	Full Sun	Dry, Medium	Fruit
Hyssop, Anise	2'–4' (0.6–1.2m)	1'–2' (30.5–61cm)	Full Sun, Part Shade	Dry, Medium	Flowers, Leaves
Lambsquarters	1'–2' (30.5–61cm)	12"–18" (30.5–45.7cm)	Full Sun, Part Shade	Dry, Wet	Leaves
Onion, Egyptian Walking	2' (61cm)	6" (15.2cm)	Full Sun	Medium	Bulb, Leaves
Plantain, Broadleaf	6"–10" (15.2–25.4cm)		Full Sun, Part Shade	Dry, Wet	Leaves
Raspberry	4'–6' (1.2–1.8m)	Indef.	Full Sun	Medium	Berries, Leaves
Self-Heal	6"–12" (15.2–30.5cm)	Indef.	Full Sun, Part Shade	Medium, Wet	Flowers, Leaves
Serviceberry, Saskatoon	6'–15' (1.8–4.6m)	4'–10' (1.2–3m)	Full Sun	Medium	Berries
Sorrel, Creeping Wood	2"–4" (5.1–10.2cm)	Indef.	Full Sun, Part Shade	Dry, Medium	Flowers, Leaves
Sorrel, French	1'–3' (30.5–91.4cm)	10"–12" (25.4–30.5cm)	Full Sun, Part Shade	Dry, Medium	Leaves
Strawberry	10" (25.4cm)	Indef.	Full Sun, Part Shade	Medium	Berries, Leaves
Thyme	4"–12" (10.2–30.5cm)	4"+ (10.2cm)+	Full Sun, Part Shade	Dry, Medium	Leaves
Violet	6"–12" (15.2–30.5cm)	Indef.	Full Sun, Part Shade	Medium	Flowers, Leaves

Pampering Need:
5 = Very Easy
4 = Easy
3 = Moderate

Harvest Ease:
5 = Very Easy
4 = Easy
3 = Moderate

Growth Rate:
5 = Very Fast
4 = Fast
3 = Moderate
2 = Slow
1 = Very Slow

Lifecycle:
A = Annual
B = Biennial
P = Perennial

Pampering Need	Harvest Ease	Disease Resistant	Pest Resistant	HARVEST PERIOD Apr	May	June	July	Aug	Sept	Oct	Nov	Growth Rate	Lifecycle	Sensory Experience
5	4		■			■	■	■	■			3	P	Scent, Taste
5	4	■				■	■	■	■			3	P	
4	**5**	■	■		■	■	■	■	■	■		3	P	Sight
4	3					■						3	P	Scent, Taste
5	**5**					■						3	P	Taste
5	4	■	■	■	■	■	■	■	■	■		4	P	
5	3						■					3	P	Taste
5	4	■	■		■	■						3	P	Taste
4	**5**							■	■			2	P	Taste
5	**5**	■	■			■	■	■	■	■		4	P	Scent, Sight, Taste
5	**5**	■	■				■	■	■	■		5	P	
5	**5**	■	■	■	■	■	■	■	■	■		3	P	
5	4	■	■	■	■	■	■	■	■	■	■	4	P	
4	3						■	■	■	■	■	3	P	Taste
5	3	■	■	■	■	■	■	■	■	■	■	3	P	
5	3					■						3	P	Taste
5	4	■	■		■	■	■	■	■	■		4	P	
5	**5**	■	■	■	■	■	■	■	■	■	■	3	P	
5	4					■	■	■	■	■		3	P	Taste
5	4	■	■	■	■	■	■	■	■	■	■	3	P	Scent, Sight, Taste
5	3	■	■	■	■	■						3	P	Sight

CHAPTER 13: PLANT PROFILES

Every harvest begins with a relationship. These cherry tomatoes are more than just food—they're the result of care, timing, and choosing the right plant partners.

By now, you've seen how plants can bring your garden to life, offering beauty, resilience, and nourishment. You've learned how to place them with intention, making your garden feel less like a chore and more like a space that gives back. Now it's time to meet the plants themselves.

Each one was chosen because it's easy to care for and because it offers something meaningful in return. Like any good companion, these plants nourish you, soothe you, attract helpful wildlife, and help guide your garden toward natural balance. As you explore each profile, you'll get to know their unique characteristics: how they grow, what they offer, where they thrive, and where they may need a little support. Like any good friendship, you'll come to appreciate their quirks and strengths.

Let's get to know your new best friends.

Apple

When people dream of growing fruit, they often think of apples—a timeless classic that brings crisp autumn harvests to the garden.

QUICK REFERENCE

Type: Tree
Lifecycle: Perennial (Zones 3–8)
Applications: Orchard
Sensory Experiences: Taste
Disease Resistant: No
Pest Resistant: No
Pampering Need: 4 (Easy)
Harvest Ease: 3 (Moderate)
Parts Used: Fruit
Harvest Period: July–October

Personality: Your wise, steadfast friend that grows sweeter with time, offering gifts of crisp, juicy fruit and the comfort of seasonal rhythm year after year.

Description: This time-honored tree has been at humanity's side for millennia, symbolizing everything from wisdom to abundance. In your garden, it offers more than sustenance; it creates a connection to the changing seasons and a moment of quiet joy. A couple dwarf trees can thrive in small spaces, making them perfect for urban or suburban gardens.

Unless another apple or crabapple tree is within 100' (30.5m), you'll need to plant two compatible varieties to ensure cross-pollination. Choose varieties that bloom at the same time. Nursery tags or fruit tree pollination tables can guide you in finding the perfect pair, setting the stage for bountiful harvests every year.

Apples are a delight to grow, but they can be prone to certain diseases. Choosing a disease-resistant variety ensures your tree rewards your patience with years of fruitful harvests instead of heartbreak from common ailments.

Botanical Name: *Malus* spp.

Top Varieties: Crimson Crisp, Enterprise, Gold Rush, Jonafree, Liberty, Williams Pride

Care: Plant your apple tree in a sunny spot with well-draining soil, and give it plenty of space to spread its branches. Permanently stake dwarf trees at planting to ensure the weight of future abundant fruit does not topple it. Consistent watering is crucial during the first two years while the roots establish. Surround the base with a wide ring of compost and woodchip mulch each spring to nourish the soil and keep the tree thriving.

Prune in winter, removing dead or crossing branches to improve airflow and encourage fruiting. Keep an eye out for common pests; natural sprays or encouraging predatory insects can keep them in check.

Harvest/Enjoyment: Apples are ripe when they detach easily from a gentle twist, typically in late summer to fall. When the time comes, take a moment under its branches to savor the crisp bite of your first apple. Each harvest is a reminder of the care and patience you've shared with this tree.

PLANNING AND GROWING

Light: Full Sun
Soil Moisture: Medium
Height and Width: 5'–12' (1.5–3.7m) x 5'–12' (1.5–3.7m)
Growth Rate: 2 (Slow)
Time to Harvest: 3+ years
Common Pests and Diseases: Codling moth, aphid, fire blight, and apple scab (fungal disease that causes leaf spots and fruit lesions). Deer may eat foliage and rub antlers on trunks.

PLANTING INSTRUCTIONS

Period: Early spring (45°F–65°F [7°C–18°C])
Method: Transplant
Depth: Set the base of the trunk at ground level.
Spacing: Check the mature width of the tree and leave at least 12" (30.5cm) of space beyond that from other trees or structures.

Basil

More than just a kitchen staple, basil fills your garden with fragrance, flavor, and charm. It's an easygoing companion that's as delightful to touch as it is to taste.

QUICK REFERENCE

Type: Herb
Lifecycle: Annual
Applications: Container, Raised Bed, In-Ground Garden, Sensory Garden
Sensory Experiences: Scent, Taste
Disease Resistant: No
Pest Resistant: No
Pampering Need: 4 (Easy)
Harvest Ease: 4 (Easy)
Parts Used: Flowers, Leaves
Harvest Period: June–October

Personality: Your vibrant and zesty summer companion, ready to brighten your garden and flavor your meals.

Description: Basil brings more than just culinary flair to your garden. It's a sensory experience and a symbol of warmth, well-being, and tradition. Whether you're brushing past sweet basil for that familiar, mouthwatering aroma or steeping tulsi leaves for a calming herbal tea, basil offers something for both body and soul. In many cultures, tulsi is cherished as a sacred plant known for promoting resilience and balance—perfect for a self-care garden.

Beyond its flavors and soothing properties, basil is a cheerful companion plant, known to help deter pests like aphids and mosquitoes. Its compact size and love of sunshine make all types of basil ideal for containers, raised beds, or tucked between tomatoes. Tulsi tends to self-seed freely, spreading to nearby areas.

Botanical Names: *Ocimum basilicum*, *Ocimum tenuiflorum* (tulsi/holy basil)

Top Varieties: Genovese, Thai, Tulsi (Holy Basil)

Care: Basil is a sunbather, thriving in as much sun as it can get. Plant it in nutrient-rich, well-draining soil and water consistently to keep its roots happy. If you're growing basil in a container, use a high-quality potting mix and feed it with a diluted organic fertilizer or a sprinkle of compost every couple of weeks. Basil loves warmth, so keep it indoors or cover it when the temperature dips below 50°F (10°C).

Harvest/Enjoyment: Begin harvesting once your basil plant has several sets of leaves. Snip leaves or stems just above a node (the place where leaves meet the stem) to encourage bushier growth. Pinch off edible flower buds as they appear to keep it focused on growing lush, flavorful leaves. Use the fresh leaves in your cooking, such as bruschetta and salad, or brew them into a calming tea. For a simple, garden-fresh treat, wrap a leaf around a cherry tomato and enjoy the explosion of flavor right there in the garden.

PLANNING AND GROWING

Light: Full Sun

Soil Moisture: Medium

Height and Width: 12"–36" (30.5–91.4cm) x 6" (15.2cm)

Growth Rate: 5 (Very Fast)

Time to Harvest: 6–8 weeks

Common Pests and Diseases: Aphids and downy mildew.

PLANTING INSTRUCTIONS

Period: Mid- to late spring (65°F–85°F [18°C–29.5°C])

Method: Transplant

Depth: Plant at the same depth as in the pot.

Spacing: Transplant one plant every 6"–12" (15.2–30.5cm).

Beans

Dragon tongue beans are so tasty, they rarely make it indoors, which is perfect for gardeners (and kids) who love to snack while harvesting. Easy, abundant, and fun to grow.

QUICK REFERENCE

Type: Vegetable

Lifecycle: Annual

Applications: Container, Raised Bed, In-Ground Garden

Sensory Experiences: Taste

Disease Resistant: No

Pest Resistant: No

Pampering Need: 4 (Easy)

Harvest Ease: 5 (Very Easy)

Parts Used: Pod, Seeds

Harvest Period: July–October

Personality: The tireless provider of your garden, offering abundant harvests while quietly nurturing the soil.

Description: Beans are a marvel of nature—fast-growing, nutritious, and easy to grow in even the smallest of spaces. These humble plants enrich the soil by infusing it with nitrogen, creating a healthier foundation for their garden companions. Whether climbing a trellis or forming neat rows in a bed, beans are a versatile addition to any garden. A symbol of resilience and abundance, they remind us that consistent effort yields great rewards.

Beans come in two main forms: bush and pole. Bush beans are compact and low-growing, perfect for tidy garden rows or large containers (at least 12" [30.5cm] in diameter and depth for a single plant). Pole beans are the climbers, requiring a trellis, teepee, or arbor that's at least 6'–8' (1.8–2.4m) tall. Make sure the lowest rungs are close to the soil so seedlings can easily find their way upward without your help. Watching their delicate tendrils grasp for support is a delight, showcasing nature's determination and symbolizing your own growth.

Botanical Name: *Phaseolus vulgaris*

Top Varieties:

- **Bush:** Contender, Dragon Tongue, Provider
- **Pole:** Blue Lake, Fortex, Kentucky Wonder

Care: Beans thrive in warm, sunny spots with well-draining soil. Sow seeds directly into the ground or container once the weather is consistently warm (above 60°F [15.5°C]). Optionally, soak the seeds for 8–12 hours to accelerate germination, but avoid exceeding 24 hours to prevent seed damage or rot. Plant immediately after soaking. Add a layer of compost at planting, and water consistently to keep the soil evenly moist but not soggy. Once bush beans reach 4"–5" (10.2–12.7cm) tall, add a light mulch of straw to retain moisture and reduce weeds.

For pole beans, provide sturdy vertical support. You may need to guide their young shoots to the trellis during their first weeks, but after that help, they'll climb happily on their own, reaching for sunlight and producing pods along the way.

Harvest/Enjoyment: Harvest bush beans when pods are firm, crisp, and about 4"–6" (10.2–15.2cm) long. Pick them regularly to encourage continued production. Pole beans will produce over a longer period, giving you a steady supply. Snap a fresh bean off the vine and savor its crunch right in the garden as a delicious reminder of your care.

After bush beans deliver their first generous harvest, they often slow down. You can leave the plants in place for a smaller, occasional yield, or remove them entirely by clipping the stems at soil level with pruners. Leaving the roots in the soil allows them to decompose naturally, enriching it with nitrogen as a gift for your future crops. To protect your soil-building allies and keep weeds down in the cleared space, mulch it with straw and the chopped bean foliage (a simple and effective chop-and-drop technique). If you still have time in the growing season, consider planting quick-growing crops like radishes, leaf lettuce, or cilantro to nibble new friends and keep your garden vibrant.

If pods grow too large and tough, let them dry on the plant. Collect them in the fall for dried beans, a pantry staple perfect for soups or stews. To separate the beans from their pods, place them in a pillowcase and stomp on it gently to loosen the beans. Sift the mixture through a wire mesh screen to separate the beans from the chaff.

PLANNING AND GROWING

Light: Full Sun
Soil Moisture: Medium
Height and Width: 1' x 1' (30.5 x 30.5cm)
Growth Rate: 5 (Very Fast)
Time to Harvest: 7–8 weeks
Common Pests and Diseases: Aphids and bean rust (fungal disease that causes reddish-brown leaf spots). Deer and rabbits may eat foliage and pods.

PLANTING INSTRUCTIONS

Period: Mid- to late spring (60°F–85°F [15.5°C–29.5°C])
Method: Seed
Depth: Bury seeds 1" (2.5cm) deep.
Spacing: Plant one seed every 4" (10.2cm), with rows 8" (20.3cm) apart.

Bee Balm

Rub bee balm to release its signature spicy-sweet scent. Its vibrant blooms and fragrance beckon both you and pollinators.

QUICK REFERENCE

Type: Herb
Lifecycle: Perennial (Zones 3–9)
Applications: Container, Orchard, Sensory Garden, Wild Edible
Sensory Experiences: Scent, Taste
Disease Resistant: No
Pest Resistant: Yes
Pampering Need: 5 (Very Easy)
Harvest Ease: 4 (Easy)
Parts Used: Flowers, Leaves
Harvest Period: June–September

Personality: A spirited, cheerful healer that graces your garden with beauty and lures pollinators with vibrant blooms and irresistible charm.

Description: Bee balm is the heart of any pollinator-friendly garden, drawing bees, butterflies, and hummingbirds to its vivid, tubular flowers. This native perennial adds a touch of wild beauty to sunny borders or partially shaded spots. Its aromatic leaves and flowers have been cherished for centuries in teas and traditional remedies. Blend the leaves with black tea for a flavor reminiscent of Earl Grey. Bee balm readily spreads by seed, making it a wonderful choice for naturalizing areas or filling large bare spots with ease. However, its enthusiastic self-seeding nature means it may need a little management in small beds or yards to keep its cheerful chaos contained.

Botanical Name: *Monarda fistulosa*

Top Varieties: Bee balm (wild bergamot) is a natural, untamed variety perfect for native gardens. Petite Delight is a compact variety with soft pink blooms, ideal for small spaces or containers.

Care: Bee balm thrives in full sun, but will tolerate partial shade, especially in hotter climates. Plant it in well-draining, dry-to-medium soil, and water deeply, allowing the soil to dry between watering sessions. This sun-loving perennial appreciates occasional grooming—trim back spent blooms to encourage a second flush of flowers and prevent excessive self-seeding if you prefer a more controlled spread.

Its seeds can germinate easily, so if you want to manage its reach, deadhead flowers before they dry and release seeds. For areas where you'd like it to spread naturally, leave a few seed heads to provide a new burst of blooms the following year. To maintain healthy, vigorous plants, divide clumps every two to three years, which also helps prevent overcrowding.

Bee balm is naturally resilient but can develop powdery mildew, especially in humid conditions or spots with poor air circulation. While it doesn't significantly harm the plant, it does affect the aesthetic and edibility of the leaves. If you spot powdery mildew, skip using those leaves in teas or cooking. To minimize powdery mildew, ensure wide spacing between plants to improve airflow, and avoid overhead watering, which can create the damp conditions the fungus loves. Regularly prune the plant to remove overcrowded or shaded foliage. To work around the condition, harvest leaves early in the season, while they're fresh, yummy, and vibrant.

Harvest/Enjoyment: Harvesting bee balm is as enjoyable as growing it. Snip flowers for vibrant bouquets or scatter petals into teas for a soothing treat. Its peppery leaves can substitute for oregano in savory dishes, adding a unique twist to your meals. Take a moment to savor its wild essence: pluck a single petal, taste its light spice, and connect with the natural rhythm of your garden.

On warm afternoons, pause to watch the dance of bees, butterflies, and hummingbirds around your bee balm. This cheerful healer fosters life and beauty in your garden while reminding you to slow down and enjoy the small, joyful moments of shared care.

PLANNING AND GROWING

Light: Full Sun, Part Shade

Soil Moisture: Dry, Medium

Height and Width: 3'–4' (0.9–1.2m) tall

Growth Rate: 3 (Moderate)

Time to Harvest: 10–12 weeks

Common Pests and Diseases: Powdery mildew.

PLANTING INSTRUCTIONS

Period: Early spring (60°F–75°F [15.5°C–24°C])

Method: Transplant

Depth: Plant at the same depth as in the pot.

Spacing: Transplant one plant every 24" (61cm).

Beet

Beets bring color, flavor, and nutrition to the table, offering sweet roots and leafy greens in one easy-to-grow package.

QUICK REFERENCE

Type: Vegetable

Lifecycle: Annual

Applications: Container, Raised Bed, In-Ground Garden

Disease Resistant: No

Pest Resistant: No

Pampering Need: 3 (Moderate)

Harvest Ease: 4 (Easy)

Parts Used: Leaves, Root

Harvest Period: June–November

Personality: The earthy artist of the garden, beets create bold, nutritious treasures beneath the soil while offering leafy greens to brighten your plate.

Description: Beets are a dual-purpose wonder, providing sweet, earthy roots and nutrient-rich greens. These fast-growing vegetables are reliable and rewarding, thriving in sunny beds with medium moisture. Roasted, pickled, or sliced fresh into salads, beets are a versatile feast for the senses. They're celebrated as a colorful superfood. If you prefer mess-free meal prep, golden varieties offer all the flavor without the notorious red stains.

Botanical Name: *Beta vulgaris*

Top Varieties: Bull's Blood, Chioggia, Cylindra, Detroit Dark Red, Golden Beet, Touchstone Gold

Care: Beets are quiet, industrious creators, turning sunlight and water into vibrant roots and lush greens. Start seeds in loose, fertile soil, free of rocks or debris that can distort their growth. Space the seeds 1"–2" (2.5–5.1cm) apart, then thin the seedlings once they reach about 2" (5.1cm) tall, leaving 3"–4" (7.6–10.2cm) between plants to allow the roots to develop fully. Beet seeds are actually clusters that may sprout multiple plants, which is why thinning is essential for proper growth.

Keep the soil consistently moist, as beets need even watering to grow tender roots. A layer of straw mulch can help retain moisture and suppress weeds. Midway through the growing season, give your plants a boost by spreading compost or an organic fertilizer on top of the soil around them. Beets grow well in cooler weather, making them a perfect choice for spring and fall planting.

If your garden has limited space, consider companion planting with cilantro or lettuce, as their shallow roots won't compete with the deeper-growing beets.

Harvest/Enjoyment: Beets are ready for harvest when their roots reach about the size of a golf ball; they are perfectly tender and sweet at this stage. Gently pull one from the soil, slice it open, and marvel at the vibrant color inside—it's like unearthing a hidden gem. If left in the ground longer, they'll continue to grow, and while larger roots may become a bit tougher and starchier, they're still excellent for roasting or adding to hearty soups.

Roast beets to caramelize their natural sugars, slice them raw for an earthy crunch, or pickle them for a tangy treat. Don't overlook their greens; they're close relatives of Swiss chard and can be steamed, sautéed, or added to soups for a nutritious boost. Harvest the leaves sparingly while the plant is still growing, ensuring you leave enough for continued root development.

PLANNING AND GROWING

Light: Full Sun

Soil Moisture: Medium

Height and Width: 8"–12" (20.3–30.cm) x 6"–12" (15.2–30.5cm)

Growth Rate: 5 (Very Fast)

Time to Harvest: 7–10 weeks

Common Pests and Diseases: Leaf miners (insects creating tunnels in leaves) and Cercospora leaf spot (fungal disease that causes circular spots). Rabbits may eat foliage.

PLANTING INSTRUCTIONS

Period: Early spring to late summer (50°F–75°F [10°C–24°C])

Method: Seed

Depth: Bury seeds ½" (1.3cm) deep.

Spacing: Plant one seed every 2" (5.1cm) in rows 12" (30.5cm) apart.

Blooming Bulbs

Daffodils brighten early spring with cheerful blooms, then quietly return nutrients to the soil as they fade, adding beauty and enriching your garden's ecosystem year after year.

QUICK REFERENCE

Type: Herb

Lifecycle: Perennial (generally Zones 3–8, but varies by species)

Applications: Orchard, Sensory Garden

Sensory Experiences: Sight

Disease Resistant: Yes

Pest Resistant: Yes

Pampering Need: 5 (Very Easy)

Personality: Meet the cheerful treasures of early spring! These resilient plants awaken your garden with vibrant color, nourish pollinators, and quietly enrich the soil, making them the perfect companions for your eco-friendly haven.

Description: Spring-blooming bulbs are nature's early risers, transforming bare winter landscapes into cheerful, colorful gardens. Known as spring ephemerals, these bulbs grow early and bloom quickly, taking advantage of open spaces and abundant sunlight before tree canopies fill in. By emerging early, they act as nature's breakfast buffet for awakening pollinators while absorbing vital soil nutrients before spring rains wash them away. As their blooms fade and leaves die back in summer, they return those nutrients to the soil, enriching your garden's ecosystem.

These small flowers will become joyful harbingers of warming weather and the start of the spring growing season, returning reliably with little effort. Their vibrant bursts of color and the lively hum of pollinators they attract signal the awakening of both you and your garden. They invite you to simply enjoy their beauty, wander among their blooms, and take comfort in knowing they're quietly enriching the soil and fostering a healthier ecosystem.

These bulbs thrive beautifully alongside other perennials in orchards and sensory gardens. They can be interplanted with them since their growing seasons are different, maximizing space and adding layered interest to your landscape.

Characteristics of Bulb Types:

- **Allium:** With striking globe-shaped flowers atop tall, slender stems, alliums are garden showstoppers. Blooming later in spring, they provide continued interest as other bulbs finish. These pest-resistant bulbs are perfect for adding height and structure to your garden.

- **Crocus:** One of the earliest bloomers, crocuses often peek through snow to brighten gardens with jewel-toned flowers. Their small size makes them ideal for naturalizing in lawns or along paths, where their delicate blooms can shine.
- **Daffodil:** The classic symbol of spring, daffodils boast trumpet-shaped blooms in shades of yellow, white, and orange. Their cheerful flowers naturalize easily and are highly pest-resistant, making them a timeless favorite.
- **Grape Hyacinth:** These tiny, bell-shaped blooms resemble clusters of grapes, adding a touch of whimsy to borders and underplantings. Grape hyacinths spread easily and create lush carpets of color over time.
- **Hyacinth:** Renowned for their sweet fragrance and dense clusters of flowers, hyacinths are perfect for compact spaces or containers. Their scent and vibrant colors make them a sensory garden staple.
- **Snowdrop:** Delicate white, bell-shaped flowers dangle gracefully from slender stems, symbolizing hope and renewal. Snowdrops thrive in shaded areas, making them ideal for woodland gardens.

Botanical Names: *Allium* spp. (allium), *Crocus* spp. (crocus), *Narcissus* spp. (daffodil), *Muscari* spp. (grape hyacinth), *Hyacinthus orientalis* (common hyacinth), *Galanthus* spp. (snowdrop)

Top Varieties:

- **Allium:** Purple Sensation, Star of Persia
- **Crocus:** Cream Beauty, Ruby Giant
- **Daffodil:** February Gold, Mount Hood
- **Grape Hyacinth:** Armeniacum, Blue Spike
- **Hyacinth:** Blue Jacket, Carnegie
- **Snowdrop:** Giant Snowdrop, Flore Pleno

Care: Spring-blooming bulbs share similar planting needs and low-maintenance care requirements:

- **Planting:** Plant bulbs in the fall in well-drained soil, tucking them in at a depth that's roughly two to three times the height of the bulb. For smaller bulbs, such as crocuses and snowdrops, plant about 2"–3" (5.1–7.6cm) deep and 2"–4" (5.1–10.2cm) apart. Larger bulbs, such as daffodils, alliums, and hyacinths, do best planted 6"–8" (15.2–20.3cm) deep, spaced 4"–6" (10.2–15.2cm) apart to give them room to grow.
- **Light:** Most bulbs enjoy full sun to partial shade, but you'll need to consider the amount of sun that will be available when these early growers are popping up. Snowdrops prefer partial to full shade.
- **Soil:** Bulbs thrive in loose, nutrient-rich soil.
- **Watering:** Water deeply after planting to help the bulbs establish strong roots. During their first spring growing season, provide additional water during dry spells, but ensure the soil remains well-drained and never soggy. Once established, these bulbs are drought-tolerant.
- **After Blooming:** Allow the foliage to die back naturally after flowering, which is necessary to feed the bulbs for next year. You can tidy up once the leaves turn yellow and wither.
- **Dividing Bulbs:** To refresh crowded clumps of spring-blooming bulbs, wait until their leaves have turned yellow and crisp, usually by late summer. Then, gently lift the bulbs with a garden fork, being careful not to spear them. Brush off the soil and separate the baby bulbs (called offsets) from the parent bulb by hand. Discard any soft or damaged ones, and replant the healthy bulbs right away, nestling them two to three times as deep as the bulb is tall, with the pointy end facing up. Water well and envision the new springtime beauty you've just brought to your yard.

Unique Care Notes:

- **Allium:** Space generously to prevent overcrowding and leave the dried flower heads for whimsical interest.
- **Crocus:** These bulbs naturalize beautifully in lawns, but avoid mowing until the foliage dies back completely.
- **Daffodil:** Ideal for mass planting, daffodils will spread and form stunning drifts over time.
- **Grape Hyacinth:** This enthusiastic spreader thrives in borders or under taller bulbs but may require thinning if it becomes too dense.
- **Hyacinth:** Plant near paths or patios to enjoy their fragrance. Wear gloves when handling bulbs, as they may cause skin irritation.
- **Snowdrop:** These bulbs prefer moist, shaded areas and benefit from a mulch layer to retain moisture in early spring.

PLANNING AND GROWING

Light: Full Sun, Part Shade

Soil Moisture: Medium

Height and Width: 3'–5' (0.9–1.5m) x 1'–3' (0.3–0.9m)

Growth Rate: 3 (Moderate)

Common Pests and Diseases: Narcissus bulb fly and basal rot (fungal disease that causes bulb decay). Daffodils are generally avoided by deer, rabbits, and squirrels, but other bulbs may be dug up.

PLANTING INSTRUCTIONS

Period: Late fall to early spring (40°F–60°F [4.5°C–15.5°C])

Method: Bulb

Depth: Bury bulbs 2"–8" (5.1–20.3cm) deep.

Spacing: Plant bulbs 4"–6" (10.2–15.2cm) apart in clusters for a natural look.

Snowdrops are the first to wake, pushing through frost to welcome pollinators and offer delicate charm when little else is in bloom.

Hyacinths fill the air with rich fragrance and bold color, creating a sensory celebration that feeds both you and early pollinators.

Crocus flowers burst through late snow, offering vital nectar to awakening bees and a splash of vibrant color to sleepy spring gardens.

Butterfly Weed

Beloved by monarchs, butterfly weed offers vibrant color and vital habitat, bringing beauty and resilience with less spreading habits of common milkweed.

QUICK REFERENCE

Type: Herb
Lifecycle: Perennial (Zones 3–9)
Applications: Container, Raised Bed, In-Ground Garden, Sensory Garden
Sensory Experiences: Sight
Disease Resistant: Yes
Pest Resistant: Yes
Pampering Need: 5 (Very Easy)

Personality: The butterfly's best friend, adorned with fiery orange blooms, bringing life and resilience to your garden.
Description: Butterfly weed is a stunning perennial native to much of North America, celebrated for its vibrant orange flowers and vital role in supporting monarch butterflies and other pollinators. Its deep roots make it drought-tolerant and easy to grow in sunny, well-drained locations. Butterfly weed tends to self-seed freely, spreading to nearby areas. Symbolizing transformation and resilience, this hardy plant adds visual appeal while enriching the ecosystem by providing nectar for pollinators and food for monarch caterpillars.
Botanical Name: *Asclepias tuberosa*
Top Varieties: The native, uncultivated species is an excellent choice.
Care: Butterfly weed thrives in full sun and dry-to-medium, well-drained soil. It is highly drought-tolerant once established, making it a perfect choice for low-maintenance gardens. It is slow to emerge in spring, so be patient. To promote fuller growth and more blooms, trim spent flowers during the growing season, though leaving some seed pods intact will encourage self-seeding and support wildlife.
Harvest/Enjoyment: Butterfly weed is a plant that brings joy in every season. Its fiery orange blooms attract butterflies, bees, and other pollinators, creating a vibrant, fluttering garden scene that feels alive with gratitude. Monarch caterpillars munching on its leaves remind you of the critical role your garden plays in sustaining life.

As the blooms fade, butterfly weed produces fun, fuzzy seed pods that are as delightful as the flowers themselves. These pods can be left on the plant for autumn charm or harvested for a bit of whimsy—kids and adults will enjoy releasing the fluffy seeds into the wind, watching them float away like tiny parachutes.

PLANNING AND GROWING

Light: Full Sun
Soil Moisture: Dry, Medium
Height and Width: 2' x 2' (61 x 61cm)
Growth Rate: 3 (Moderate)
Common Pests and Diseases: Generally pest-free; occasional aphids.

PLANTING INSTRUCTIONS

Period: Early spring (60°F–75°F [15.5°C–24°C])
Method: Transplant
Depth: Plant at the same depth as in the pot.
Spacing: Transplant one plant every 18"–24" (45.7–61cm).

Chamomile

Chamomile soothes both garden and gardener, whether self-seeding through sunny beds or weaving fragrant ground cover along pathways.

QUICK REFERENCE

Type: Herb
Lifecycle: Annual (German), Perennial (Roman) (Zones 4–9)
Applications: Container, Raised Bed, In-Ground Garden, Sensory Garden, Ground Cover
Sensory Experiences: Scent, Sight, Taste
Disease Resistant: Yes
Pest Resistant: Yes
Pampering Need: 5 (Very Easy)
Harvest Ease: 3 (Moderate)
Parts Used: Flowers, Leaves
Harvest Period: April–June

Personality: A soothing companion with delicate blooms that calm your senses.
Description: Chamomile is a timeless addition to any garden, offering beauty, relaxation and even soil support. It's daisy-like flowers are ideal for a calming and relaxing tea. It thrives in sunny conditions and has a long history as a medicinal plant.

- **German Chamomile:** An annual herb that self-seeds readily, filling your garden with cheerful blooms year after year. It grows upright, reaching 1'–2' (30.5–61cm) tall and its self-seeding nature makes it perfect for naturalizing areas or filling garden gaps year after year.
- **Roman Chamomile:** A perennial ground cover, weaving a low, fragrant mat of feathery foliage and flowers. It is perfect for borders or lightly traveled pathways. Roman spreads slowly by above-ground roots. While its flowers are smaller than its German cousin, they are equally fragrant and useful for tea-making.

Botanical Names: *Matricaria recutita* (German chamomile), *Chamaemelum nobile* (Roman chamomile)
Top Varieties:

- **German Chamomile:** Bodegold, German Improved, Zloty Lan
- **Roman Chamomile:** Dwarf Roman, Treneague (a nonflowering lawn alternative)

Care: Chamomile is as low maintenance as it is rewarding. Both varieties prefer full sun and well-drained soil, but Roman chamomile tolerates partial shade, especially in hotter climates. Water moderately, allowing the soil to dry slightly between drinks, as overwatering can cause root issues. German chamomile self-seeds readily, so thin seedlings if it becomes too dense.
Harvest/Enjoyment: Flowers and foliage can both be enjoyed simply for their beauty, so don't feel obligated to harvest them all. To harvest from them, gently pick the blooms from their stems, ideally in the morning when their essential oils are at their peak. The leaves are also edible and can be used in tea, adding a subtle herbaceous note to your brew. Both flowers and foliage can be dried for later.

Chamomile can be used to unwind after a long day while also nurturing the wildlife in your garden. Its graceful foliage will bring a sense of peace and gentle beauty to any landscape.

- **German Chamomile:** Its upright habit makes flowers easy to gather in bulk for tea or dried arrangements. Harvest flowers often to encourage prolonged blooming. The foliage can also be harvested in small amounts for tea.
- **Roman Chamomile:** Enjoy its dual role as a fragrant ground cover and tea herb. Harvest flowers and foliage sparingly to keep its mat-forming habit lush and full, allowing it to continue spreading gracefully across your garden.

PLANNING AND GROWING

Light: Full Sun
Soil Moisture: Dry, Medium
Height and Width: 6"–12" (15.2–30.5cm) tall
Growth Rate: 4 (Fast)
Time to Harvest: 6–10 weeks
Common Pests and Diseases: Generally pest-free; occasional aphids.

PLANTING INSTRUCTIONS

Period: Mid- to late spring (60°F–75°F [15.5°C–24°C])
Method: Seed, Transplant
Depth: Scatter seeds on soil surface; press gently.
Spacing: Scatter seeds lightly, rake them in, and pat down. Space clumps every 6"–8" (15.2–20.3cm).

Cherry, Sour

A single sour cherry tree can fill bowls like this year after year. With minimal care, these hardy trees offer abundant harvests perfect for pies, preserves, and sharing.

QUICK REFERENCE

Type: Tree
Lifecycle: Perennial (Zones 4–6)
Applications: Orchard
Sensory Experiences: Taste
Disease Resistant: No
Pest Resistant: No
Pampering Need: 5 (Very Easy)
Harvest Ease: 3 (Moderate)
Parts Used: Fruit
Harvest Period: June–July

Personality: The tart little charmer, bringing bold flavor to your kitchen, vibrant beauty to your garden, and the simplest care of all fruit trees.
Description: Sour cherry trees are the unsung heroes of fruit orchards, offering tangy, versatile cherries that are perfect for pies, preserves, and sauces. These compact, low-maintenance trees thrive in sunny locations with medium soil moisture, making them ideal for small orchards or as a front yard focal point. With their rich history symbolizing renewal and beauty, sour cherries are as meaningful as they are delicious. Their early spring flowers and bright-red fruit also support wildlife, offering a treat for birds and pollinators.
Botanical Name: *Prunus cerasus*
Top Varieties: Meteor (natural dwarf), Montmorency, North Star (natural dwarf), Surefire
Care: Sour cherry trees are the lowest-maintenance option among fruit trees, making them perfect for gardeners seeking simplicity and reliability. There's no need for permanent staking—unlike dwarf apples and pears, sour cherries naturally grow strong and stable. Natural dwarf varieties like North Star and Meteor are bred to grow shorter and sturdier without requiring a dwarf rootstock. If you're selecting a tree that isn't a natural dwarf, choose one grafted onto a dwarf rootstock for a manageable, space-saving option that's easy to prune and harvest. Prune sour cherry trees in late winter, focusing on removing dead or crossing branches to maintain an open shape.

Plant your cherry tree in a sunny location with well-drained soil, as sour cherries thrive on abundant sunlight. Water regularly during the first two years to establish a strong root system, then reduce watering as the tree matures. Mulch around the base where soil is exposed to retain moisture and suppress weeds. Fertilize in early spring with compost or an organic fruit-tree fertilizer to support healthy growth and fruiting.
Harvest/Enjoyment: Sour cherries are ready to harvest when their color deepens to a rich red and the fruit feels slightly soft to the touch. A taste test is the best way to determine their perfect tartness. Enjoy them fresh for a zingy burst of flavor, or turn them into pies, jams, or syrups to savor their tangy-sweet essence all year long. As the easiest fruit tree to grow, sour cherries connect you to the joys of low-maintenance gardening and the delight of harvesting your own fresh, flavor-rich fruit.

PLANNING AND GROWING

Light: Full Sun
Soil Moisture: Medium
Height and Width: 8'–10' (2.4–3m) x 8'–10' (2.4–3m)
Growth Rate: 2 (Slow)
Time to Harvest: 3+ years
Common Pests and Diseases: Cherry fruit fly and brown rot (fungal disease that causes fruit decay). Deer may eat foliage and rub antlers on trunks. Birds may eat fruit.

PLANTING INSTRUCTIONS

Period: Early spring (45°F–65°F [7°C–18°C])
Method: Transplant
Depth: Set the base of the trunk at ground level.
Spacing: Check the mature width of the tree and leave at least 12" (30.5cm) of space beyond that from other trees or structures.

Cherry, Sweet

Sweet cherries reward attentive care with juicy, irresistible fruit, bringing beauty and flavor to the right sunny spot.

QUICK REFERENCE

Type: Tree
Lifecycle: Perennial (Zones 5–7)
Applications: Orchard
Sensory Experiences: Taste
Disease Resistant: No
Pest Resistant: No
Pampering Need: 5 (Very Easy)
Harvest Ease: 3 (Moderate)
Parts Used: Fruit
Harvest Period: July

Personality: A sweet, petite delight that fills your garden with joy, beauty, and irresistible flavor.
Description: Sweet cherry trees are a delicious and beautiful addition to your garden, offering juicy bursts of flavor and a touch of elegance with their spring blossoms and vibrant fruit. Like all fruit trees, they thrive in full sun and well-drained soil.

Sweet cherries are bit less durable than their sour counterparts and require more attentive care to thrive. They are more sensitive to climate and soil conditions, favoring well-drained, slightly sandy soil and areas with mild winters. They are less cold-tolerant than sour cherries, often struggling in zones with late frosts or severe winters, and they can be more prone to cracking during heavy rain conditions. Despite these quirks, with the right care and location, sweet cherries reward you with their irresistible flavor and abundant harvests.
Botanical Name: *Prunus avium*
Top Varieties: Benton, Blackgold, Kristin, Lapins, Ulster
Care: Consistent watering is essential during their first two years to establish a strong root system, but be careful not to overwater, as they dislike soggy conditions. Mulch around the base of the tree to retain moisture and regulate soil temperature, keeping the mulch a few inches away from the trunk.

Add compost or an organic fertilizer in early spring to promote healthy growth and fruit growth. They also benefit from a permanent stake to keep them upright under the weight of heavy fruit. Prune in late winter or early spring to remove dead or crossing branches, shape the tree, and improve airflow, which helps prevent fungal diseases.
Harvest/Enjoyment: Sweet cherries are ready to harvest when the fruit feels plump and firm, and their color deepens to a glossy, rich red or dark purple, depending on the variety. Taste testing is the best way to determine peak ripeness. Enjoy sweet cherries fresh off the tree for their luscious, sun-kissed flavor, or use them in desserts, preserves, or salads.

PLANNING AND GROWING

Light: Full Sun
Soil Moisture: Medium
Height and Width: 6'–8' (1.8–2.4m) x 8'–15' (2.4–4.6m)
Growth Rate: 2 (Slow)
Time to Harvest: 3+ years
Common Pests and Diseases: Cherry fruit fly and brown rot (fungal disease that causes fruit decay). Deer may eat foliage and rub antlers on trunks. Birds may eat fruit.

PLANTING INSTRUCTIONS

Period: Early spring (45°F–65°F [7°C–18°C])
Method: Transplant
Depth: Set the base of the trunk at ground level.
Spacing: Check the mature width of the tree and leave at least 12" (30.5cm) of space beyond that from other trees or structures.

Chives

With slender, tubular leaves and cheerful lavender-pink blooms, onion chives add mild flavor to your meals, accumulate nutrients, and help build soil, making them as useful as they are beautiful.

QUICK REFERENCE

Type: Herb
Lifecycle: Perennial (Zones 3–9)
Applications: Container, Raised Bed, In-Ground Garden, Orchard, Sensory Garden
Sensory Experiences: Taste
Disease Resistant: Yes
Pest Resistant: Yes
Pampering Need: 5 (Very Easy)
Harvest Ease: 5 (Very Easy)
Parts Used: Bulb, Leaves
Harvest Period: April–October

Personality: A lively, low-maintenance herb that jazzes up dishes with fresh flavor and brightens your garden with edible blooms.
Description: Chives are versatile, zero-maintenance, and flavorful herbs that bring a mild onion or garlic taste to your kitchen and a cheerful charm to your garden. Onion chives produce slender, tubular leaves with lavender-pink flowers, while garlic chives boast

flat, grass-like leaves and delicate white blossoms. Garlic chives bloom later than onion chives, producing clusters of white flowers in late summer to early fall, extending the visual and culinary interest of your garden.

Both varieties attract pollinators, thrive in sunny-to-lightly shaded spots, and are perfect for containers, raised beds, or borders.

Botanical Names: *Allium schoenoprasum*, *Allium tuberosum* (garlic chives)

Top Varieties: Common Garlic, Common Onion, Giant Siberian Chives, Siberian Garlic Chives

Care: Chives are delightfully low-maintenance and thrive with minimal effort. Choose a sunny-to-partially shaded spot with well-draining soil. They adapt well to various soil types but prefer soil rich in organic matter. Water regularly after initial planting, but once established, chives are drought-tolerant. Divide clumps every two to three years to prevent overcrowding and encourage fresh, vigorous growth.

Chives tend to self-seed, spreading naturally around your garden. If you'd like more plants, let some flowers mature and set seed; or trim them back to focus the plant's energy on producing fresh, flavorful leaves.

Harvest/Enjoyment: Chives are simple to harvest and use, adding fresh flavor and charm to your kitchen creations. Snip leaves as needed, cutting just above the base to keep the plants producing continuously. Both the leaves and flowers are edible, offering endless culinary possibilities. Add the delicate onion flavor of onion chives to soups, salads, or eggs, or enjoy the subtle garlic taste of garlic chives in stir-fries, dumplings, or herbal butters.

The lavender-pink flowers of onion chives make beautiful garnishes, can be infused into vinegars, or dried for decorative arrangements, while the white blossoms of garlic chives—harvested in late summer or early fall—provide their own peak of flavor.

With every cut, chives remind you how easily food can be grown while still being simple, flavorful, and full of life. Watch them thrive and consider how they generously provide for you season after season.

PLANNING AND GROWING

Light: Full Sun, Part Shade

Soil Moisture: Dry, Medium

Height and Width: 18" x 12" (45.7 x 30.5cm)

Growth Rate: 3 (Moderate)

Time to Harvest: 6–12 weeks

Common Pests and Diseases: Generally pest-free; occasional onion thrips.

PLANTING INSTRUCTIONS

Period: Early spring (50°F–70°F [10°C–21°C])

Method: Transplant

Depth: Plant at the same depth as in the pot.

Spacing: Transplant one plant every 8"–12" (20.3–30.5cm).

Garlic chives grow flat, grass-like leaves and delicate white blooms that appear late in the season—extending beauty, attracting pollinators, and adding a subtle garlicky kick to your kitchen creations.

Cilantro

Cilantro grows fast, delivers fresh flavor, and even leaves you with coriander seeds, making it an easy, two-for-one herb.

QUICK REFERENCE

Type: Herb

Lifecycle: Annual

Applications: Container, Raised Bed, In-Ground Garden, Sensory Garden

Sensory Experiences: Scent, Taste

Disease Resistant: No

Pest Resistant: No

Pampering Need: 4 (Easy)

Harvest Ease: 4 (Easy)

Parts Used: Leaves

Harvest Period: June–October

Personality: A fresh, citrusy dynamo that adds zest to your garden and dishes, bringing flavor and vitality to every bite.

Description: Cilantro is a fast-growing, annual herb that delivers bold, citrusy flavor to salsas, salads, and countless dishes. Its delicate, lacy foliage and fragrant leaves make it a standout in the garden. Thriving in sunny and partially shaded areas with medium soil moisture, it's an easy-to-grow favorite for gardeners who love fresh, homegrown flavor. In ancient cultures, cilantro symbolized vitality and health, making it a fitting addition to any eco-friendly garden.

Botanical Name: *Coriandrum sativum*

Top Varieties: Calypso, Cruiser, Santo

Care: Cilantro thrives in morning sun and benefits from afternoon shade in hot climates to prevent early bolting (flowering and setting seed). Bolting is cilantro's natural tendency to produce seed, especially in warm weather. When it does, the leaves become sparse, tough, and less flavorful. You can clip the stem at soil level and start anew or let it flower, feeding pollinators with its delicate blossoms. Once the flowers mature into seeds, you'll have coriander—a versatile spice to add to your kitchen. Keep the soil consistently moist, but not waterlogged, and sow a new batch of seeds every few weeks to maintain a steady supply of fresh leaves.

Harvest/Enjoyment: Pick cilantro leaves regularly to encourage bushier growth and prevent bolting. The more you harvest, the more it gives, rewarding your care with bursts of fresh flavor. Crush a leaf between your fingers and inhale its citrusy aroma—a simple yet joyful sensory experience. The leaves can be used to brighten up salsas, soups, or salads, and its seeds are the spice coriander, doubling its culinary value. When the plant bolts, collect the seeds to expand your spice rack.

PLANNING AND GROWING

Light: Full Sun, Part Shade

Soil Moisture: Medium

Height and Width: 12"–14" (30.5–35.6cm) x 6"–12" (15.2–30.5cm)

Growth Rate: 5 (Very Fast)

Time to Harvest: 4–6 weeks

Common Pests and Diseases: Aphids and leaf spot.

PLANTING INSTRUCTIONS

Period: Early spring to early summer (50°F–65°F [10°C–18°C])

Method: Seed

Depth: Bury seeds ¼" (6.4mm) deep.

Spacing: Scatter seeds thinly, about 1" (2.5cm) apart, in rows 8"–12" (20.3–30.5cm) apart.

Clover, Dutch White

This cheerful ground cover is an ecological powerhouse by feeding pollinators; enriching soil; and keeping lawns, paths, and orchards healthy and vibrant with little effort.

QUICK REFERENCE

Type: Herb

Lifecycle: Perennial (Zones 3–10)

Applications: Orchard, Wild Edible, Ground Cover

Disease Resistant: Yes

Pest Resistant: No

Pampering Need: 5 (Very Easy)

Harvest Ease: 4 (Easy)

Parts Used: Leaves, Flowers

Harvest Period: June–September

Personality: The soil's secret fixer-upper, spreading cheer while feeding bees, enriching soil, and brightening lawns.

Description: Dutch white clover is a hardworking yet charming perennial ground cover that brings beauty, resilience, and ecological benefits to your garden. Its small white flowers attract bees and other pollinators, while its nitrogen-fixing roots naturally enrich the soil for surrounding plants. Thriving in sunny and partially shaded spots with dry-to-medium soil, clover is perfect for orchards, lawns, or anywhere that needs a low-cost, ecological boost. Mix it with self-heal, wild strawberry, creeping thyme, violets, or even dandelions for a tough, soil-building ground cover that's full of life. Historically a symbol of luck, clover is truly magical in its ability to support biodiversity and soil health.

Seed it into bare patches of grass to enhance visual beauty with cheerful flowers, increase lawn resilience by boosting soil fertility, and provide a pollinator habitat. Unlike traditional grasses, clover stays green during droughts when cool-season lawns turn brown, ensuring your lawn and garden remain vibrant.

Botanical Name: *Trifolium repens*

Care: Clover is nature's little helper, requiring zero care once established. It happily thrives and spreads during wet and dry spells. Clover's flowers are a favorite for bees, so avoid mowing when it's in bloom to give pollinators a feast. In areas where blooms aren't desired, mowing or trimming before flowering can maintain a tidy appearance while still providing soil benefits.

Harvest/Enjoyment: Clover is more than just a ground cover; it's a versatile, edible plant. Both the leaves and flowers are edible with a mild, slightly sweet flavor. Add the fresh leaves to salads or steep the flowers for a light herbal tea.

Walk barefoot through a patch of clover and enjoy its soft, cushiony feel underfoot. Its tiny flowers bring charm to the garden, and its presence serves as a gentle reminder that even the smallest plants can make a big difference in creating balance and sustainability in your garden.

PLANNING AND GROWING

Light: Full Sun, Part Shade
Soil Moisture: Dry, Medium
Height and Width: 4"–10" (10.2–25.4cm) x 6"–36" (15.2–91.4cm)
Growth Rate: 3 (Moderate)
Time to Harvest: 6–10 weeks
Common Pests and Diseases: Rabbits may graze heavily on foliage.

PLANTING INSTRUCTIONS

Period: Early spring to late summer (50°F–75°F [10°C–24°C])
Method: Seed
Depth: Lightly cover with soil.
Spacing: Scatter seeds at 2oz (57g) per 1,000 ft.^{2} (92.9 m^2); rake in and pat down.

Collard Greens

Collards bring hearty, nutrient-packed leaves to your garden. They are easy to grow, frost-tolerant, and always ready to nourish body and soul.

QUICK REFERENCE

Type: Vegetable
Lifecycle: Biennial (grown as annual)
Applications: Container, Raised Bed, In-Ground Garden
Disease Resistant: No
Pest Resistant: No
Pampering Need: 4 (Easy)
Harvest Ease: 5 (Very Easy)
Parts Used: Leaves
Harvest Period: July–November

Personality: The southern soul of your garden, bringing hearty, nutrient-packed leaves that nourish both body and spirit.
Description: Collard greens are the backbone of a bountiful garden, offering large, nutrient-dense leaves perfect for traditional dishes or fresh, modern recipes. These frost-tolerant greens thrive in sunny and partially shaded areas with medium soil moisture, making them a dependable choice for raised beds, in-ground gardens, or container planting. Packed with vitamins and minerals, collards symbolize resilience and nourishment, bringing vibrant greens from your eco-friendly garden to your plate.
Botanical Names: *Brassica oleracea* var. *viridis*
Top Varieties: Champion, Flash, Georgia Southern, Morris Heading
Care: Collard greens thrive in full sun, but will tolerate partial shade, especially in hotter climates. Plant them in rich, well-drained soil, and keep the soil consistently moist for optimal growth. Mulch around the base of the plants with straw to retain moisture and suppress weeds. Fertilize with compost or an organic vegetable fertilizer at planting and again midway through the growing season to keep them thriving.

Regularly remove yellowing or damaged leaves to maintain the plant's vigor and direct its energy toward producing lush, healthy greens. Collards are frost-hardy and even sweeten after a light frost, making them an excellent choice for extending your harvest into cooler months.
Harvest/Enjoyment: Begin harvesting collard greens as soon as the leaves reach a usable size, usually 8"–10" (20.3–25.4cm) long. Pick from the bottom of the plant upward, leaving the crown intact to encourage continuous growth. For the best flavor, harvest early in the morning when the leaves are crisp and full of moisture.

Collards are versatile in the kitchen. Steam or sauté them with garlic for a quick, nourishing side dish. Their earthy, slightly sweet flavor deepens after frost, making them a seasonal favorite that connects you to the rhythm of your garden.

PLANNING AND GROWING

Light: Full Sun, Part Shade
Soil Moisture: Medium
Height and Width: 18"–24" (45.7–61cm) x 12"–18" (30.5–45.7cm)
Growth Rate: 4 (Fast)
Time to Harvest: 6–8 weeks
Common Pests and Diseases: Cabbage worms and downy mildew. Deer and rabbits may eat foliage.

PLANTING INSTRUCTIONS

Period: Early spring or late summer (50°F–75°F [10°C–24°C])
Method: Seed
Depth: Bury seeds ½" (1.3cm) deep.
Spacing: Transplant one seedling every 18" (45.7cm) in rows 24"–36" (61–91.4cm) apart.

Coneflower, Purple

One of the easiest native prairie plants to grow, purple coneflower stands tall with bold blooms that feed pollinators, brighten your garden, and never flops into pathways.

QUICK REFERENCE

Type: Herb
Lifecycle: Perennial (Zones 3–9)
Applications: Orchard, Sensory Garden, Wild Edible
Sensory Experiences: Sight
Disease Resistant: Yes
Pest Resistant: Yes
Pampering Need: 4 (Easy)
Harvest Ease: 5 (Very Easy)
Parts Used: Flowers, Leaves, Root
Harvest Period: May–October

Personality: A resilient prairie native that brings bold beauty to your garden while offering pollinators a feast and a boost to your herbal remedies.

Description: Purple coneflowers are iconic perennials known for their striking purple petals and prominent central cones. Native to North American prairies, these plants symbolize strength and healing, making them a perfect match for gardens that prioritize beauty, resilience, and ecological harmony. Thriving in sunny and lightly shaded areas with dry-to-medium soil, purple coneflowers attract bees, butterflies, and birds while also offering herbal benefits. Traditionally used to make immune-boosting teas and tinctures, this plant brings physical healing along with visual interest to your garden.

Botanical Name: *Echinacea purpurea*

Top Varieties: Green Jewel, Kim's Knee High, Magnus, PowWow Wild Berry, Purple Emperor

Care: Purple coneflowers are low-maintenance and highly adaptable, making them a favorite for new and experienced gardeners. Plant them in full sun for the best blooms, though they can tolerate light shade. They prefer well-drained soil but are forgiving of less-than-ideal conditions. Water regularly during their first growing season to establish strong roots, but once mature, they are drought-tolerant.

To encourage continuous flowering, deadhead spent blooms during the growing season. In the fall, leave some seed heads intact to provide winter food for birds and add structural interest to your garden. Every three to four years, divide clumps in early spring or late fall to maintain plant vigor and prevent overcrowding.

Harvest/Enjoyment: Purple coneflowers offer beauty and benefits in equal measure. Harvest flowers when they are in full bloom by cutting the stems just above a pair of leaves. This will encourage further blooms. The petals can be used fresh or dried to make herbal teas, traditionally believed to support immune health. To dry, hang small bundles of flowers in a cool, dark, well-ventilated area. Leaves can also be harvested and dried for tea or used fresh in herbal blends.

The roots of purple coneflowers are also edible and often used for their medicinal properties, but digging them up can be labor intensive. Consider harvesting roots sparingly and only from well-established plants that are at least three years old.

As fall approaches, let the seed heads mature to provide a natural food source for birds like goldfinches, and they will reward you with lively visits. Purple coneflowers bring more than blooms to your garden; they foster vitality and a sense of connection throughout the seasons.

PLANNING AND GROWING

Light: Full Sun, Part Shade
Soil Moisture: Dry, Medium
Height and Width: 3'–4' (0.9–1.2m) x 18" (45.7cm)
Growth Rate: 3 (Moderate)
Time to Harvest: 2–3 years
Common Pests and Diseases: Occasional aphids and aster yellows (bacterial disease that causes deformed growth).

PLANTING INSTRUCTIONS

Period: Early spring (60°F–75°F [15.5°C–24°C])
Method: Transplant
Depth: Plant at the same depth as in the pot.
Spacing: Transplant one plant every 18"–24" (45.7–61cm).

Cosmos

Effortlessly elegant, cosmos sway in the breeze, bringing pollinators, color, and carefree charm to your garden with almost no effort.

QUICK REFERENCE

Type: Herb
Lifecycle: Annual
Applications: Container, Orchard, Sensory Garden
Sensory Experiences: Sight
Disease Resistant: No
Pest Resistant: No
Pampering Need: 5 (Very Easy)

Personality: An elegant bloom that dances in the breeze, filling your garden with effortless charm and joy.
Description: These annual flowers thrive in sunny spots and are delightfully easy to grow. Cosmos germinate quickly, usually within a week, making them one of the easiest flowers to grow from seed. Known for attracting pollinators like bees and butterflies, cosmos bring life and harmony to your garden. In Victorian times, they symbolized order and serenity, qualities that radiate from their graceful presence in your eco-friendly space.
Botanical Names: *Cosmos bipinnatus*
Top Varieties:

- **Tall:** Bright Lights, Sensation Mix
- **Compact:** Cosmic Orange, Rubenza

Care: Plant them in full sun for the best blooms, though they can tolerate light shade. Cosmos prefer dry, well-drained soil and don't require fertilization; in fact, overly rich soil can result in fewer flowers. Scatter seeds directly on the soil after the last frost, gently rake them in, and water lightly to help them settle. Water sparingly, as they are drought-tolerant and actually prefer less moisture once established. If desired, deadhead spent flowers regularly to encourage new blooms.
Harvest/Enjoyment: Cosmos bring a sense of carefree beauty to your garden and home. Snip blooms for cheerful bouquets. They last several days in a vase and add a touch of elegance to any room. As the season winds down, leave some seed heads intact to attract birds. In warmer climates, they may self-seed for the next year.

PLANNING AND GROWING

Light: Full Sun, Part Shade
Soil Moisture: Dry, Medium
Height and Width: 2'–7' (0.6–2.1m) x 2' (0.6m)
Growth Rate: 4 (Fast)
Common Pests and Diseases: Aphids and powdery mildew.

PLANTING INSTRUCTIONS

Period: Early spring (65°F–85°F [18°C–29.5°C])
Method: Seed
Depth: Lightly cover with soil.
Spacing: Scatter seeds thinly, about 1" (2.5cm) apart, in clumps about 12" (30.5cm) apart.

Cucumber

Cucumbers thrive in heat and sunshine, delivering crisp, refreshing harvests all summer long that are perfect for snacking or pickling.

QUICK REFERENCE

Type: Vegetable
Lifecycle: Annual
Applications: Container, Raised Bed, In-Ground Garden
Disease Resistant: No
Pest Resistant: No
Pampering Need: 4 (Easy)
Harvest Ease: 5 (Very Easy)
Parts Used: Fruit
Harvest Period: July–October

Personality: The crisp and reliable friend of the garden, thriving in heat and sunshine, climbing high or staying compact to fit any space.
Description: Cucumbers are a refreshing favorite, perfect for pickling, salads, or snacking fresh from the vine. This versatile plant grows quickly, offering an abundance of hydrating fruits in the warm months. Historically symbolizing bounty and health, cucumbers are a practical and cheerful addition to any garden, making the most of sunny spots and bringing a touch of crisp coolness to your summer days.

Cucumbers come in two main forms: bush and vining. Bush cucumbers are compact and ideal for small spaces or container gardens (use a container that's at least 12" [30.5cm] wide and deep for a single plant). Vining cucumbers require a trellis, fence, or arbor for support, saving ground space and keeping the fruits clean, free from disease, and easy to harvest. Provide a trellis at least 5'–6' (1.5–1.8m) tall, and guide young vines toward the structure during the first few weeks.

Botanical Name: *Cucumis sativus*

Top Varieties:

- **Bush:** Bush Champion, Salad Bush
- **Vining:** Lemon Cucumber, Marketmore 76, Straight Eight, Sweet Slice

Care: Cucumbers thrive in warm, sunny locations with well-drained, fertile soil. Wait to plants seeds until the temperature is consistently above 60°F (15.5°C). Thin to one plant every 12" (30.5cm) for bush varieties and every 18"–24" (45.7–61cm) for vining types.

Water deeply and consistently, as cucumbers dislike drying out. Top with compost at planting and again midway through the growing season to boost fruit production. Once seedlings are 3"–4" (7.6–10.2cm) tall, mulch with straw around the base of the plant to retain moisture, regulate soil temperature, and suppress weeds.

Harvest/Enjoyment: Cucumbers are ready to harvest when they're firm, green, and the size specified on the packet for their variety. Pick frequently to encourage continued yields, as overripe cucumbers left on the vine become bitter and can slow down the plant. Neighbors and friends will thank you for the abundance.

During a hot day in the garden, munch on a freshly harvested cucumber and savor its crisp, refreshing crunch. Use bush varieties for salads and quick snacks, while vining varieties provide longer fruits that are great for pickling.

PLANNING AND GROWING

Light: Full Sun

Soil Moisture: Medium, Wet

Height and Width: 3'–7' (0.9–2.1m) tall

Growth Rate: 4 (Fast)

Time to Harvest: 6–9 weeks

Common Pests and Diseases: Cucumber beetles and powdery mildew. Deer may eat foliage and fruit.

PLANTING INSTRUCTIONS

Period: Mid- to late spring (65°F–85°F [18°C–29.5°C])

Method: Seed

Depth: Bury seeds 1" (2.5cm) deep.

Spacing: Plant two seeds per hill, with hills 3' (91.4cm) apart.

Currant, Clove

Clove currants fill the air with spicy spring fragrance before offering tart summer berries. It's an easy-care shrub that delights both senses and taste buds.

QUICK REFERENCE

Type: Shrub

Lifecycle: Perennial (Zones 3–8)

Applications: Orchard, Wild Edible, Sensory Garden

Sensory Experiences: Scent, Taste

Disease Resistant: No

Pest Resistant: No

Pampering Need: 4 (Easy)

Harvest Ease: 3 (Moderate)

Parts Used: Berries

Harvest Period: June

Personality: The aromatic berry bush that sweetens your garden with tart harvests and clove-scented spring blooms.

Description: Clove currants are a fragrant and versatile shrub, offering spice-scented yellow blossoms in spring and tart, black berries in summer. Thriving in sunny and partially shaded areas, they bring beauty and edibles to your garden while supporting pollinators with their nectar-rich flowers. Berries can be used for jams and syrups, or simply enjoyed fresh. These hardy bushes were once a staple in pioneer gardens for their easy care and adaptability.

Botanical Name: *Ribes odoratum*

Top Varieties: Crandall

Care: Clove currants thrive in full sun but tolerate partial shade, making them ideal for gardens with less-than-optimal light. Plant them in rich, well-drained soil, adding compost at planting to ensure a healthy start. Water regularly during their first year to establish strong roots, then reduce watering once the plants are established; they are drought-tolerant but appreciate occasional deep watering during dry spells.

Prune lightly in late winter or early spring, removing dead or older wood to encourage vigorous new growth and more berries.A topdressing of compost in early spring will fuel fragrant blooms and improve fruit yields.

Harvest/Enjoyment: Clove currant berries are ready to harvest when they turn deep red to black and are slightly soft to the touch. Their sweet-tart flavor adds a bright, distinctive note to jams, syrups, and sauces. Enjoy them fresh or freeze them for later use.

Beyond the harvest, clove currants bring sensory delight throughout the seasons. In spring, their golden blooms fill the air with a clove-like fragrance, creating a calming, nostalgic ambiance in your garden.

PLANNING AND GROWING

Light: Full Sun, Part Shade
Soil Moisture: Dry, Medium
Height and Width: 6'–12' (1.8–3.7m) x 6'–8' (1.8–2.4m)
Growth Rate: 3 (Moderate)
Time to Harvest: 1–2 years
Common Pests and Diseases: Currant borer and powdery mildew. Deer may eat foliage.

PLANTING INSTRUCTIONS

Period: Early spring (50°F–75°F [10°C–24°C])
Method: Transplant
Depth: Place where stems meet roots at ground level.
Spacing: Plant slightly closer than the mature width for a hedge effect. Stagger them in a zigzag pattern to catch more sunlight and make harvesting easier.

Currant, Red

Clusters of red currant berries beg to be plucked. Kids love them, and these cheerful shrubs deliver tart, abundant harvests year after year.

QUICK REFERENCE

Type: Shrub
Lifecycle: Perennial (Zones 3–7)
Applications: Orchard, Wild Edible
Sensory Experiences: Taste
Disease Resistant: No
Pest Resistant: No
Pampering Need: 5 (Very Easy)
Harvest Ease: 5 (Very Easy)
Parts Used: Berries
Harvest Period: June

Personality: The tart-yet-generous shrub that fills your garden with ruby-red berries and your summer with the taste of abundance.
Description: Red currants are a delightful addition to any edible landscape, producing clusters of translucent, jewel-like berries that are as beautiful as they are nutritious. These hardy shrubs thrive in sunny areas with medium soil moisture, offering a steady harvest of tart fruit that's perfect for preserves, desserts, or fresh snacking. Beloved in European gardens for centuries, red currants symbolize health and abundance. With their cheerful appearance and versatile fruit, they bring both beauty and productivity to your garden.
Botanical Name: *Ribes rubrum*
Top Varieties: Pink Champagne, Red Lake
Care: Red currants thrive in full sun, though they can tolerate partial shade, especially in warmer climates. Plant them in rich, well-drained soil, and mulch around the base to retain moisture and regulate soil temperature. These shrubs appreciate consistent watering, particularly during dry spells, to support healthy growth and fruiting.

Fertilize with a topdressing of compost in early spring to give the plants a boost as they awaken from dormancy. Prune annually in late winter or early spring, removing older wood (branches that are three years or older) to encourage new growth and improve air circulation. Focus on maintaining an open, vase-like shape to optimize sunlight exposure for all parts of the plant, which encourages better fruit yields.
Harvest/Enjoyment: Red currants are ready to harvest in mid-summer when the berries are translucent, vibrant, and firm. You can gently clip entire clusters from the shrub rather than pulling individual berries. Their tart, bright flavor makes them perfect for baked goods, savory sauces, jams, and syrups, while their striking appearance elevates desserts like pavlovas or fruit salads. Eat them fresh for a sharp burst of flavor or freeze them to enjoy throughout the year.

PLANNING AND GROWING

Light: Full Sun, Part Shade
Soil Moisture: Medium
Height and Width: 3'–5' (0.9–1.5m) x 4'–5' (1.2–1.5m)
Growth Rate: 3 (Moderate)
Time to Harvest: 1–2 years
Common Pests and Diseases: Currant borer and powdery mildew. Deer may eat foliage.

PLANTING INSTRUCTIONS

Period: Early spring (50°F–75°F [10°C–24°C])
Method: Transplant
Depth: Place where stems meet roots at ground level.
Spacing: Plant slightly closer than the mature width for a hedge effect. Stagger them in a zigzag pattern to catch more sunlight and make harvesting easier.

Dandelion

Dandelions nourish people, pollinators, and soil. They thrive anywhere while offering edible greens, sunny blooms, and deep roots that heal the earth.

QUICK REFERENCE

Type: Herb
Lifecycle: Perennial (Zones 3–9)
Applications: Orchard, Wild Edible
Disease Resistant: No
Pest Resistant: No
Pampering Need: 5 (Very Easy)
Harvest Ease: 4 (Easy)
Parts Used: Flowers, Leaves, Root
Harvest Period: April–October

Personality: The resilient underdog with a sunny disposition, offering edible greens, sunny flowers, and roots that dig deep into well-being.
Description: Often misunderstood, the dandelion is a remarkable plant that transforms "weedy" spaces into vibrant hubs of health, play, and ecological support. Beloved by children and playful adults for its sunny yellow blooms and whimsical, puffball seed heads, it adds magic and delight to any garden.

Beneath the surface, its deep taproots work tirelessly to improve soil structure, drawing up nutrients, loosening compacted ground, and naturally aerating the earth. This makes dandelions an excellent addition to orchard ground covers or pollinator-friendly lawns, where they help reduce the need for fertilizing and watering.

Every part of the dandelion—leaves, flowers, and roots—is nutrient-packed and versatile in the kitchen, earning its reputation as a superfood. Thriving in sunny to partially shaded areas with no care, dandelions are a true testament to resilience and resourcefulness. Once revered in folklore as symbols of wishes and dreams, this humble wildflower continues to inspire with its strength, adaptability, and playful beauty.
Botanical Names: *Taraxacum officinale*
Top Varieties: While a few cultivated varieties exist, the wild dandelions already growing in your yard are just as nutritious, versatile, and delightful.
Care: Dandelions thrive almost anywhere, making them a carefree addition to your garden. They prefer full sun but also enjoy partial shade and require no watering. If you'd like to encourage dandelions as part of a pollinator-friendly lawn or garden, avoid mowing where they grow and allow their bright yellow blooms to flourish.
Harvest/Enjoyment: Dandelions offer a bounty of nutritional and ecological benefits. Harvest leaves and flowers early in the season, ideally before the plant begins to flower, as old foliage tends to be bitter. In shady spots, dandelions often produce leaves with shallow, rounded lobes that are milder in flavor compared to those grown in full sun. If harvesting the nutrient-dense roots, dig deep and gently loosen the soil to avoid breaking the taproot, and give them a good scrub before use.

Tender young leaves are delicious in fresh salads or can be sautéed for a milder, spinach-like flavor. The sunny yellow flowers can be steeped into a lightly sweet tea, used in herbal infusions, or turned into homemade dandelion wine. The roots, while more labor-intensive to harvest, are packed with nutrients and can be roasted and brewed as a coffee substitute or added to soups for an earthy, rich flavor. While stems are technically edible, their bitter milky sap can be off-putting.

Beyond harvesting for the kitchen, dandelion leaves can be repeatedly pulled from the plant and used as fertilizer through chop-and-drop weeding. Simply lay the freshly pulled leaves around garden plants to enrich the soil, feeding your crops while naturally mulching the ground. Avoid spreading the flowers or seed heads unless you want a lot more dandelions.

And don't forget the playful magic of dandelions: blow on a puffball seed head, make a wish, and celebrate the joyful resilience this plant brings to your garden and spirit.

PLANNING AND GROWING

Light: Full Sun, Full Shade
Soil Moisture: Dry, Wet
Height and Width: 6"–12" (15.2–30.5cm) x 6"–8" (15.2–20.3cm)
Growth Rate: 4 (Fast)
Time to Harvest: 4–6 weeks
Common Pests and Diseases: Generally pest-free.

PLANTING INSTRUCTIONS

Period: Early spring to late summer (50°F–75°F [10°C–24°C])
Method: Seed
Depth: Scatter seeds on soil surface.
Spacing: Blow seed heads into the wind and let nature do the rest.

Dill

Dill's feathery fronds are fun to nibble as you garden, while its flowers attract pollinators.

QUICK REFERENCE

Type: Herb
Lifecycle: Annual
Applications: Container, Raised Bed, In-Ground Garden, Sensory Garden
Sensory Experiences: Scent, Sight, Taste, Touch
Disease Resistant: No
Pest Resistant: No
Pampering Need: 5 (Very Easy)
Harvest Ease: 5 (Very Easy)
Parts Used: Leaves
Harvest Period: July–October

Personality: A feathery, aromatic companion that flavors your kitchen and invites pollinators to your garden.
Description: Dill is a fragrant and fast-growing herb that brings fresh flavor to your meals and ecological benefits to your garden. Its feathery foliage adds texture and lightness, while its delicate yellow flowers attract pollinators and beneficial insects like ladybugs and hoverflies. Dill is also a host plant for swallowtail butterflies, meaning it provides an essential food source for their caterpillars. Thriving in sunny spots with dry-to-medium soil, dill is a versatile addition to culinary and pollinator gardens. Historically, it has symbolized luck and protection, making it a cherished choice for gardeners who value its beauty and utility.
Botanical Names: *Anethum graveolens*
Top Varieties: Bouquet, Fernleaf
Care: Dill loves full sun and well-drained soil, growing best when direct-sown outdoors after the last frost. Water moderately, keeping the soil moist but not soggy. For a steady supply of fresh foliage, sow seeds every two to three weeks throughout the growing season.

This herb tends to bolt quickly, especially in hot weather, but don't worry—its flowers are a feast for pollinators and the seeds are a flavorful bonus for your kitchen. To extend its leafy harvest, plant dill in a cooler, partially shaded spot during the heat of summer, or try a bolt-resistant variety like Fernleaf.
Harvest/Enjoyment: Pull and nibble dill leaves as you meander through your garden, choosing the youngest, most tender fronds for the freshest flavor. The more you harvest, the more it will grow. Dill seeds can be collected once they've dried on the plant; clip the seed heads and place them in a paper bag to catch the seeds as they fall.

Use fresh dill to add a bright, tangy twist to roasted vegetables, fish, or potato salads. Its feathery greens bring a touch of summer sunshine to every dish, and its seeds enhance pickles, breads, and even teas.

PLANNING AND GROWING

Light: Full Sun
Soil Moisture: Medium
Height and Width: 2'–3' (61–91.4cm) x 6" (15.2cm)
Growth Rate: 4 (Fast)
Time to Harvest: 6–8 weeks
Common Pests and Diseases: Aphids and powdery mildew.

PLANTING INSTRUCTIONS

Period: Early spring to early summer (50°F–75°F [10°C–24°C])
Method: Seed
Depth: Lightly cover with soil.
Spacing: Scatter seeds thinly, about 1" (2.5cm) apart, in rows 12" (30.5cm) apart.

Garlic

Garlic practically grows itself, offering bold flavor and a health-boosting harvest. Harvest garlic when lower leaves turn brown but a few green ones remain.

QUICK REFERENCE

Type: Vegetable
Lifecycle: Annual
Applications: Container, Raised Bed, In-Ground Garden
Disease Resistant: No
Pest Resistant: Yes
Pampering Need: 4 (Easy)
Harvest Ease: 3 (Moderate)
Parts Used: Bulb, Leaves
Harvest Period: July

Personality: The bold, spicy guardian of your garden, protecting plants from pests while adding robust flavor to every meal.
Description: Garlic is a multitasker: repelling pests, thriving with minimal care, and enriching dishes with its bold, unmistakable flavor. This hardy, perennial bulb grows easily in sunny areas with medium soil, making it a must-have for any garden. Its ability to grow through thick straw mulch makes it an excellent choice for beds prone to weeds, keeping maintenance low while producing a rewarding harvest. Garlic symbolizes health and strength, celebrated for centuries for its medicinal properties and culinary uses.
Botanical Names: *Allium sativum*
Top Varieties: Chesnok Red, German Extra Hardy, Music

Care: Garlic can be sourced from farmers markets, garden centers, online stores, or even grocery stores. For temperate climates, hardneck varieties are the easiest to grow, offering larger cloves and flavorful scapes, while softneck varieties thrive in warmer regions and store longer. If buying from the grocery store, choose organic garlic grown in the US to avoid possible treatments that hinder sprouting. Look for firm, healthy bulbs with large cloves, avoiding any that are dried out, shriveled, or moldy.

In fall, plant the largest cloves about a month before the ground freezes. Choose a sunny spot with well-drained soil and spread a generous layer of compost across the growing area. Bury each clove 2"–3" (5.1–7.6cm) deep, root side down, with 6" (15.2cm) between cloves. Cover with 3"–6" (7.6–15.2cm) of straw mulch to protect against winter cold and suppress weeds. Come spring, watch for green shoots emerging—gently help any that struggle to push through the mulch.

Water regularly during the growing season, ensuring the soil stays evenly moist but not waterlogged. Stop watering when the tops begin to yellow, signaling the bulbs are nearing harvest.

Harvest/Enjoyment: Garlic is ready to harvest in late summer when about two-thirds of the leaves have dried and turned brown. Use a pitchfork or trowel to gently loosen the soil around the bulbs before pulling them out by hand. Cure the harvested bulbs by brushing soil from the bulbls and laying them in a warm, dry, well-ventilated are out of direct sunlight for two to four weeks, allowing their skins to dry and harden for longer storage.

As you sort through your cured harvest, set aside the largest, healthiest bulbs to plant for next season. By saving your best cloves for seed, you'll create a self-sustaining garlic cycle, ensuring you never need to purchase garlic again if you grow enough each year.

If you're growing hardneck varieties, you'll be treated to scapes in late spring or early summer. These curling, edible flower stalks are a sign that your garlic is thriving. To direct the plant's energy toward bulb development, snip scapes early, as soon as they begin to curl. Enjoy them fresh in pestos, stir-fries, or as a garlicky addition to salads. Their unique flavor and tender texture are a gardener's bonus, adding to garlic's versatility.

PLANNING AND GROWING

Light: Full Sun, Part Shade

Soil Moisture: Dry

Height and Width: 18" x 4" (46.7 x 10.2cm)

Growth Rate: 3 (Moderate)

Time to Harvest: 5–7 months

Common Pests and Diseases: Onion maggot and white rot (fungal disease that causes bulb decay).

PLANTING INSTRUCTIONS

Period: Late fall (40°F–60°F [4.5°C–15.5°C]) or early spring (50°F–65°F [10°C–18°C])

Method: Bulb

Depth: Bury cloves 2" (5.1cm) deep, pointed side up.

Spacing: Plant bulbs 4"–6" (10.2–15.2cm) apart in rows 12" (30.5cm) apart.

Snip garlic scapes in early summer for a mild, savory treat. These curly shoots are delicious in pestos, stir-fries, or simply sautéed.

Gooseberry

Gooseberries thrive with little care, offering berries perfect for nostalgic summer snacking.

QUICK REFERENCE

Type: Shrub

Lifecycle: Perennial (Zones 3–8)

Applications: Orchard, Wild Edible

Sensory Experiences: Taste

Disease Resistant: No

Pest Resistant: No

Pampering Need: 5 (Very Easy)

Harvest Ease: 3 (Moderate)

Parts Used: Berries

Harvest Period: July

Personality: The thorny, tenacious bush that thrives with ease, offering sweet-tart berries perfect for pies, jams, and summer treats.

Description: Gooseberries are hardy, adaptable shrubs that produce clusters of jewel-like berries with a tangy flavor. Their resilience and ability to flourish with minimal care make them a charming and productive addition to any eco-friendly garden.

Botanical Name: *Ribes uva-crispa*

Top Varieties: Hinnonmaki Red, Invicta, Poorman

Care: Gooseberries are tough and adaptable, growing well in full sun or partial shade. They prefer moist, well-drained soil and benefit from a 2"–3" (5.1–7.6cm) layer of woodchip mulch to conserve moisture and suppress weeds. If planting in rows, space shrubs at least 4'–5' (1.2–1.5m) apart to ensure good airflow and make harvesting easier.

Prune annually in late winter or early spring to remove old wood and encourage fresh, fruit-bearing branches. Leather gloves and long loppers will help avoid sharp thorns.

Gooseberries are easy to propagate. To start a new plant for your garden—or to share with a friend—use a technique called "layering." Select a healthy, flexible branch and bury a portion of it under a few inches of soil, leaving the tip exposed. To hold down a springy branch, you may need put a rock or brick on top of the soil. After several months, the buried section will develop roots, and you can snip it from the parent plant and transplant it to a new location.
Harvest/Enjoyment: Gooseberries are ready to harvest in mid- to late summer. For a tangy, refreshing taste, pick them when they're firm and slightly underripe. If you prefer a sweeter flavor, allow them to ripen fully on the bush until they soften and turn a deeper shade. Enjoy gooseberries fresh from the garden or bake them into pies, crisps, and jams for a sweet-tart treat. Their unique flavor is a nostalgic reminder of simpler times, and their easygoing nature makes them a delightful addition to your garden's bounty.

PLANNING AND GROWING

Light: Full Sun, Part Shade
Soil Moisture: Dry, Medium
Height and Width: 3'–5' (0.9–1.5m) x 3'–5' (0.9–1.5m)
Growth Rate: 3 (Moderate)
Time to Harvest: 1–2 years
Common Pests and Diseases: Gooseberry sawfly and powdery mildew. Deer may eat foliage. Chipmunks may eat fruit.

PLANTING INSTRUCTIONS

Period: Early spring (50°F–75°F [10°C–24°C])
Method: Transplant
Depth: Place where stems meet roots at ground level.
Spacing: Plant slightly closer than the mature width for a hedge effect. Stagger them in a zigzag pattern to catch more sunlight and make harvesting easier.

Goumi Berry

Goumi berries deliver fruit while enhancing the soil. This beautiful shrub is as tasty as it is beneficial to your garden.

QUICK REFERENCE

Type: Shrub
Lifecycle: Perennial (Zones 4–9)
Applications: Orchard, Wild Edible
Sensory Experiences: Taste
Disease Resistant: Yes
Pest Resistant: Yes
Pampering Need: 5 (Very Easy)
Harvest Ease: 4 (Easy)
Parts Used: Berries
Harvest Period: May–June

Personality: The versatile berry shrub with silvery leaves and sweet-tart fruit, adding beauty, resilience, and bounty to your garden.
Description: A treasure in the garden, goumi berries produce an abundance of small, nutrient-rich fruits with a tangy flavor reminiscent of cherry with a hint of pear. The small, soft seeds are entirely edible, but if you prefer, you can simply enjoy the fruit and spit out the seeds. This hardy shrub is more than just a fruit producer—it also improves soil by fixing nitrogen, making it an ecological asset to any garden.

The goumi greets springtime with brilliant yellow blooms, brightening the landscape and inviting pollinators. As the seasons progress, its silvery-green leaves shimmer in the sun, adding texture and light to your garden. Tough yet elegant, goumi thrives in poor soil, dry conditions, and overlooked spaces. It offers beauty, resilience, and abundance all in one.
Botanical Name: *Elaeagnus multiflora*
Top Varieties: Red Gem, Sweet Scarlet, Tillamook
Care: Goumi berries are highly adaptable and low-maintenance. They thrive in full sun but can tolerate partial shade, making them versatile for various garden settings. Plant them in well-drained soil and water regularly during their first growing season to help establish strong roots. Once mature, goumi shrubs become drought-tolerant, requiring only occasional deep watering during extended dry periods.

Apply a layer of woodchip mulch around the base to retain moisture and suppress weeds. Goumi berries are naturally resistant to pests and diseases, further enhancing their low-maintenance appeal. Light pruning in late winter or early spring helps maintain their shape and encourages better air circulation, improving both plant health and fruit yields.

Harvest/Enjoyment: Goumi berries are ready to harvest when they turn soft and deep red, usually in late spring to early summer. Their tangy-sweet flavor is perfect for snacking straight off the bush or for creating jams, jellies, and desserts. While harvesting, take a moment to admire the shrub's silvery leaves shimmering in the sunlight; it's a little bit of magic that makes the experience even more enjoyable.

PLANNING AND GROWING

Light: Full Sun, Part Shade
Soil Moisture: Dry, Medium
Height and Width: 5'–6' (1.5–1.8m) x 5'–6' (1.5–1.8m)
Growth Rate: 3 (Moderate)
Time to Harvest: 1–2 years
Common Pests and Diseases: Generally pest-free; occasional leaf spot. Deer may eat foliage.

PLANTING INSTRUCTIONS

Period: Early spring (50°F–75°F [10°C–24°C])
Method: Transplant
Depth: Place where stems meet roots at ground level.
Spacing: Plant slightly closer than the mature width for a hedge effect. Stagger them in a zigzag pattern to catch more sunlight and make harvesting easier.

Goumi berries welcome spring with clusters of golden blooms, lighting up the landscape and drawing in pollinators.

Grape

Give your grapevine a sturdy trellis or fence, and it will reward you with cascading fruit and natural shade.

QUICK REFERENCE

Type: Vine
Lifecycle: Perennial (Zones 4–9)
Applications: Orchard, Wild Edible
Sensory Experiences: Taste
Disease Resistant: No
Pest Resistant: No
Pampering Need: 4 (Easy)
Harvest Ease: 5 (Very Easy)
Parts Used: Fruit
Harvest Period: August–September

Personality: The vigorous climber with cascading clusters of juicy fruit, bringing beauty and summer sweetness to your garden.
Description: Grapevines thrive in sunny spots and reward your care with flavorful clusters of fruit. Perfect for snacking and jellies, these native North American vines also attract pollinators and birds while offering natural shade and garden elegance. Grapes symbolize abundance and connection, making them a meaningful addition to your garden.
Botanical Name: *Vitis labrusca*
Top Varieties: Concord, Himrod, Mars, Reliance (all seedless)
Care: Grapes love full sun and dry-to-medium, well-drained soil. Choose a sturdy trellis, arbor, or fence to support their vigorous growth and allow for proper airflow and sunlight penetration. Space vines about 6'–10' (1.8–3m) apart to give them room to flourish without overcrowding. Water deeply after planting ensuring the soil dries slightly between waterings. Grapes are drought-tolerant, but appreciate consistent watering during long dry spells, especially when fruit is forming.

Pruning is key to managing their growth and maximizing fruit production. In late winter, cut back excess vines, focusing on leaving strong canes that will produce fruit-bearing shoots in the coming season. Prune aggressively. Grapevines thrive on hard pruning, which keeps them yielding and prevents them from becoming unmanageable.

Harvest/Enjoyment: Grapes are ready to harvest when they're full, juicy, and slightly firm, typically in late summer to early fall. Taste a few to ensure they've reached peak sweetness; different varieties fluctuate in ripeness timing. Use pruning shears to snip entire clusters cleanly from the vine. The young leaves are also edible and can be harvested earlier in the season for salads, wraps, or sautés.

As you harvest, pop a sun-warmed grape into your mouth and savor its burst of sweetness—it's summer captured in a single bite. Use fresh grapes for snacking or toss them into salads. Preserve your harvest by making jams, jellies, or maybe experimenting with homemade grape juice or wine.

PLANNING AND GROWING

Light: Full Sun
Soil Moisture: Dry, Medium
Height and Width: 15'–20' (4.6–6.1m) x 15'–20' (4.6–6.1m)
Growth Rate: 2 (Slow)
Time to Harvest: 3+ years
Common Pests and Diseases: Japanese beetles and powdery mildew. Deer may eat foliage and fruit.

PLANTING INSTRUCTIONS

Period: Early spring (50°F–70°F [10°C–21°C])
Method: Transplant
Depth: Place where stems meet roots at ground level.
Spacing: Transplant 6'–10' (1.8–3m) apart near a sturdy structure.

Hyssop, Anise

Anise hyssop fills your garden with a sweet licorice scent, vibrant blooms, a delicious tea, and year-round joy, nourishing both you and visiting wildlife.

QUICK REFERENCE

Type: Herb
Lifecycle: Perennial (Zones 4–9)
Applications: Orchard, Sensory Garden, Wild Edible
Sensory Experiences: Scent, Sight, Taste
Disease Resistant: Yes
Pest Resistant: Yes
Pampering Need: 5 (Very Easy)
Harvest Ease: 5 (Very Easy)
Parts Used: Flowers, Leaves
Harvest Period: June–October

Personality: The charming licorice-scented prairie sage that doubles as a pollinator magnet and herbal tea companion.

Description: With its sweet licorice aroma and tall, spiky purple flowers, anise hyssop is a garden favorite for pollinators, birds, and herbalists. Bees and butterflies flock to its long-blooming, nectar-rich flowers in summer, while birds enjoy its tiny black seeds through the winter. This perennial herb thrives in sunny and partially shaded spots with dry-to-medium soil. It is highly drought-tolerant once established. Traditionally used in teas and remedies, anise hyssop combines beauty, aroma, and utility, creating a calming and practical presence in your garden.
Botanical Name: *Agastache foeniculum*
Top Varieties: Black Adder, Blue Fortune, Golden Jubilee
Care: Once established, anise hyssop thrives with minimal care, requiring no supplemental watering or fertilizing, which is perfect for dry climates and busy gardeners. Its resilience and drought tolerance make it a true set-it-and-forget-it plant. It tends to self-seed freely, spreading to nearby areas.

If you desire a longer display of its pollinator-friendly blooms, deadhead flowers after their first flush to encourage a second round of blossoms into late summer. If its habit of self-seeding becomes too enthusiastic, simply remove the flowers before they fully mature. Every few years, divide the clumps to rejuvenate the plant and keep it thriving, or share divisions with friends to spread its charm.

Harvest/Enjoyment: Simply crush a leaf between your fingers as you pass by to release its sweet, calming scent—a momentary escape into tranquility. Harvest flowers and leaves just after the morning dew evaporates for full potency. Their subtle, licorice-like flavor adds a unique herbal note to teas, syrups, and desserts.

In fall and winter, leave seed heads intact and enjoy the sight of juncos, goldfinches, and other small birds feasting on them, bringing life and movement to your garden even in colder months. Anise hyssop is a year-round gift to your senses and the wildlife it nourishes.

PLANNING AND GROWING

Light: Full Sun, Part Shade
Soil Moisture: Dry, Medium
Height and Width: 2'–4' (0.6–1.2m) x 1'–2' (0.3–0.6m)
Growth Rate: 4 (Fast)
Time to Harvest: 6–8 weeks
Common Pests and Diseases: Generally pest-free; occasional root rot in poorly drained soils.

PLANTING INSTRUCTIONS

Period: Early spring (60°F–75°F [15.5°C–24°C])
Method: Transplant
Depth: Plant at the same depth as in the pot.
Spacing: Transplant one plant every 12"–18" (30.5–45.7cm).

Kale

Easy to grow and packed with nutrients, kale saves you money while filling your kitchen with leafy goodness.

QUICK REFERENCE

Type: Herb
Lifecycle: Biennial (grown as annual)
Applications: Container, Raised Bed, In-Ground Garden
Disease Resistant: No
Pest Resistant: No
Pampering Need: 4 (Easy)
Harvest Ease: 5 (Very Easy)
Parts Used: Leaves
Harvest Period: July–November

Personality: The cold-hardy powerhouse that nourishes your body and soul, thriving through fall and winter with leafy vitality.
Description: The champion of nutrient-dense greens, kale brings brightness and health to your garden and kitchen. Thriving in sunny to partially shaded spots, this fast-growing plant can provide a near-constant supply of vitamin-packed leaves. If you're watching your budget, kale is a savvy choice. Bunches may be pricey at the store, yet it's remarkably easy to grow in abundance at home.

Kale has a rich history of nourishing people during lean times, its resilience a reminder of how the garden and gardener care for each other. Blend it into a smoothie, sauté it with garlic, or simmer it in a hearty soup; kale is a steadfast, versatile companion in any space committed to well-being and sustainability.
Botanical Name: *Brassica oleracea* var. *acephala*
Top Varieties: Lacinato, Red Russian, Vates (compact), Winterbor
Care: Kale is incredibly versatile and forgiving, making it perfect for gardeners of all experience levels. It flourishes in well-drained soil. For strong growth through multiple harvests, water consistently, aiming to keep the soil moist but not waterlogged, and optionally apply a midseason layer of compost or organic fertilizer.

Kale is wonderfully easy to grow from seed. For tender baby greens, scatter seeds in shallow rows and harvest them as they grow. If you're aiming for mature plants, plant two to three seeds spaced 18"–24" (45.7–61cm) apart, thinning to the strongest seedling once they establish. For a pamper-free option, purchase young plants at a store or farmers market.

Watch for signs of cabbage worms. Those sneaky green caterpillars can quickly turn your kale leaves into lace. The first clue is often the telltale holes or ragged edges on the leaves. If you spot these, check the undersides of the leaves, where these tiny culprits often hide, blending in with the plant's green color. Gently inspect the entire plant and remove any worms you find by hand. Acting early prevents the problem from escalating. Kale is a tough and resilient plant, but a little vigilance ensures it stays healthy and productive, rewarding your care with a robust, continued harvest.

Harvest/Enjoyment: To enjoy kale as tender baby greens, harvest when leaves are 4"–5" (10.2–12.7cm) tall by cutting off one-third of their height. This encourages regrowth for continuous leaves. If some of these "babies" become taller "teenagers," you can leave them to become full-grown plants. For mature plants, harvest outer leaves as needed, leaving the central growing point intact to keep the plant productive.

When you need a quick handful, grab a leaf near the stem and strip the greens from the center rib in one motion. The result is a ready-to-use bounty perfect for tossing into salads, blending into smoothies, sautéing for a hearty meal, or stuffing into freezer bags for later use.

PLANNING AND GROWING

Light: Full Sun, Part Shade
Soil Moisture: Medium, Wet
Height and Width: 2' x 1' (61 x 30.5cm)
Growth Rate: 4 (Fast)
Time to Harvest: 6–8 weeks
Common Pests and Diseases: Cabbage worms and black rot (bacterial disease that causes leaf blackening). Deer and rabbits may eat foliage.

PLANTING INSTRUCTIONS

Period: Early spring or late summer (50°F–75°F [10°C–24°C])
Method: Seed
Depth: Bury seeds ¼" (6.4mm) deep.
Spacing: Plant one seed every 12" (30.5cm) in rows 18"–24" (45.7–61cm) apart.

Lamb's Ear

Lamb's ear softens your garden with silvery, velvety leaves, making it a low-maintenance ground cover that welcomes your touch.

QUICK REFERENCE

Type: Herb
Lifecycle: Perennial (Zones 4–8)
Applications: Sensory Garden, Ground Cover
Sensory Experiences: Touch
Disease Resistant: No
Pest Resistant: No
Pampering Need: 5 (Very Easy)

Personality: The soft-spoken ground cover, soothing your garden with velvety leaves and silvery-green elegance.
Description: Lamb's ear is a sensory delight, adding both visual and tactile charm to your garden. Its soft, fuzzy leaves shimmer with a silver-green hue, making it a standout addition to borders, pathways, or sensory gardens. Thriving in sunny locations with dry-to-medium soil, this low-maintenance perennial is a ground cover and a tactile beauty. Traditionally associated with comfort and healing, lamb's ear is as calming to your spirit as it is to your garden.
Botanical Name: *Stachys byzantina*
Top Varieties: Big Ears, Silver Carpet
Care: Lamb's ear thrives in full sun but tolerates light shade. It prefers well-drained soil and is highly drought-tolerant once established, requiring only occasional watering during prolonged dry spells.

To keep it looking its best, trim back old or damaged foliage in early spring, allowing fresh, velvety leaves to emerge. While lamb's ear can self-seed or spread vigorously in favorable conditions, it's easy to manage by removing unwanted clumps or runners. If growing in a humid climate, ensure good airflow around the plant to prevent rot or mildew on its fuzzy leaves.
Harvest/Enjoyment: Lamb's ear offers quiet beauty and tactile joy. Run your fingers over its soft, silvery leaves as you walk by—it's a gentle reminder of nature's comforting touch. In addition to its aesthetic charm, lamb's ear can also be used as a natural bandage in a pinch, as its leaves have a texture and absorbency ideal for small scrapes or wounds.

PLANNING AND GROWING

Light: Full Sun, Part Shade
Soil Moisture: Dry, Medium
Height and Width: 6"–12" (15.2–30.5cm) tall
Growth Rate: 3 (Moderate)
Common Pests and Diseases: Slugs and leaf spot.

PLANTING INSTRUCTIONS

Period: Early spring (60°F–75°F [15.5°C–24°C])
Method: Transplant
Depth: Plant at the same depth as in the pot.
Spacing: Transplant one plant every 12"–18" (30.5–45.7cm). Plant in a container to prevent spreading.

Lambsquarters

Why pamper greens when lambsquarters might already be growing for free? This "wild spinach" offers effortless, nutrient-rich harvests.

QUICK REFERENCE

Type: Herb
Lifecycle: Perennial (Zones 4–8)
Applications: Orchard, Wild Edible
Disease Resistant: Yes
Pest Resistant: Yes
Pampering Need: 5 (Very Easy)
Harvest Ease: 5 (Very Easy)
Parts Used: Leaves
Harvest Period: July–October

Personality: The wild, carefree forageable that grows wherever it pleases, adding earthy greens to your table and charm to your garden.
Description: Lambsquarters, often called "wild spinach," are a nutrient-packed powerhouse that grows effortlessly in sunny areas and even in less-than-ideal soil. This fast-growing annual has tender, earthy-flavored leaves perfect for salads, sautés, and soups. With its silvery, dusted leaves and rugged adaptability, lambsquarters are a true forager's favorite, connecting your garden to centuries of traditional use.
Botanical Name: *Chenopodium album*
Top Varieties: While a few cultivated varieties exist, the wild lambsquarters already growing in your yard are just as nutritious, versatile, and delightful.
Care: Lambsquarters are the epitome of resilience, thriving with no effort. It loves full sun but will grow happily in partial shade, and it adapts to a variety of soil types as long as they're well-drained. This hardy green will flourish on its own, often reseeding freely for future harvests.

Encourage it to grow in an area by simply scattering dried seed heads where you'd like it to appear. It doesn't require any special planting care. If you want to manage its spread, remove seed heads before they mature, but leave a few if you'd like to enjoy its abundance again next season.
Harvest/Enjoyment: For the best flavor, harvest lambsquarters when the leaves are young and tender, before flowering. The leaves have a mild, earthy taste that works beautifully when raw in salads or when cooked as a substitute for spinach in sautés and soups.

You might notice a silvery, powdery coating on the leaves—a unique feature of lambsquarters. This natural dust is completely harmless and acts as a protective layer, helping the plant retain moisture and resist pests. Simply rinse the leaves gently before eating to remove the coating if desired. Take a moment to admire the plant's dusted, silvery glow. It's a signature trait that sets lambsquarters apart as a hidden gem in your garden.

PLANNING AND GROWING

Light: Full Sun, Part Shade
Soil Moisture: Dry, Wet
Height and Width: 12"–24" (30.5–61cm) x 12"–18" (30.5–45.7cm)
Growth Rate: 5 (Very Fast)
Time to Harvest: 4–6 weeks
Common Pests and Diseases: Generally pest-free; occasional aphids.

PLANTING INSTRUCTIONS

Period: Early spring to early summer (50°F–75°F [10°C–24°C])
Method: Seed
Depth: Lightly cover with soil.
Spacing: Scatter seeds lightly and pat down.

Lettuce

Quick to grow and easy to harvest using the cut-and-come-again method, lettuce is a crisp, reliable staple.

QUICK REFERENCE

Type: Vegetable
Lifecycle: Annual
Applications: Container, Raised Bed, In-Ground Garden
Disease Resistant: No
Pest Resistant: No
Pampering Need: 3 (Moderate)
Harvest Ease: 4 (Easy)
Parts Used: Leaves
Harvest Period: May–June, September–October

Personality: A crisp, cool, quick-growing favorite that's always up for a fresh salad.
Description: Lettuce is the ultimate garden staple, thriving in sunny to partially shaded areas with rich, medium-moisture soil. This fast-growing annual offers a delightful range of textures, flavors, and colors that is perfect for elevating your salads and sandwiches. Easy to grow and quick to harvest, lettuce symbolizes abundance, simplicity, and the joy of cultivating fresh, healthy food right outside your door.
Botanical Name: *Lactuca sativa*
Top Varieties: Black Seeded Simpson, Buttercrunch, Deer Tongue, Garrison, Red Sails
Care: Lettuce thrives in the cool seasons of spring and fall, preferring rich, well-drained soil. Plant seeds just before the last frost and keep the soil consistently moist to encourage tender, flavorful leaves. Water gently and regularly, especially during warm spells, to prevent bolting. Experiment with multiple varieties in different rows or containers to create a diverse palette of colors, textures, and flavors for your garden and salad.

For cut-and-come-again harvesting, scatter seeds densely in shallow rows or broadcast them over a patch. If growing into full-sized heads, thin seedlings to allow room for growth. Be prepared to defend your crop against slugs and other garden critters that love tender greens as much as you do. Once plants are 2"–3" (5.1–7.6cm) tall, use straw mulch to keep soil moist and deter weeds.
Harvest/Enjoyment: For baby greens, harvest leaves when they are 5"–6" (12.7–15.2cm) tall by cutting off one-third of their height. This encourages regrowth for multiple harvests. Mature plants can be harvested by picking outer leaves as needed or cutting the entire head when fully grown. Once lettuce begins to bolt—that is, sending up a tall flower stalk in response to heat or lengthening days—the leaves quickly become bitter. At this stage, instead of eating them, you can chop and drop the plants right in place, enriching the soil with organic matter. Relish the crisp snap of a freshly picked leaf as you gather your lettuce. It's a reminder of the simple joys your garden brings.

PLANNING AND GROWING

Light: Full Sun, Part Shade
Soil Moisture: Medium
Height and Width: 1' x 1' (30.5 x 30.5cm)
Growth Rate: 5 (Very Fast)
Time to Harvest: 4–6 weeks
Common Pests and Diseases: Aphids and downy mildew. Deer and rabbits may eat foliage.

PLANTING INSTRUCTIONS

Period: Early spring to early summer (50°F–70°F [10°C–21°C])
Method: Seed
Depth: Bury seeds ¼" (6.4mm) deep.
Spacing: Plant one seed every 2"–4" (5.1–10.2cm) in rows 8" (20.3cm) apart.

Mint

Mint grows quickly and spreads eagerly if left unchecked, filling your garden with a refreshing scent. Perfect for teas, desserts, or a breath-freshening nibble.

QUICK REFERENCE

Type: Herb
Lifecycle: Perennial (Zones 3–9)
Applications: Container, Raised Bed, Sensory Garden, Ground Cover
Sensory Experiences: Scent, Taste
Disease Resistant: Yes
Pest Resistant: Yes
Pampering Need: 5 (Very Easy)
Harvest Ease: 4 (Easy)
Parts Used: Leaves
Harvest Period: May–November

PLANNING AND GROWING

Light: Full Sun, Part Shade
Soil Moisture: Medium, Wet
Height and Width: 8"–24" (20.3–61cm) tall
Growth Rate: 4 (Fast)
Time to Harvest: 6–12 weeks
Common Pests and Diseases: Occasional aphids and rust.

PLANTING INSTRUCTIONS

Period: Mid- to late spring (60°F–75°F [15.5°C–24°C])
Method: Transplant
Depth: Plant at the same depth as in the pot.
Spacing: Transplant one plant every 3' (91.4cm). Plant in a container to prevent spreading.

Personality: Mint is your spirited garden companion, ready to refresh with its invigorating scent and soothing flavor for teas.
Description: Mint is a fragrant, fast-growing herb that brings versatility and vigor to your garden. Perfect for teas, cocktails, desserts, or savory dishes, this hardy perennial thrives in sunny to partially shaded spots and is as delightful as it is useful. Its spreading nature makes it an excellent choice for containers or carefully managed spaces.
Botanical Name: *Mentha* spp.
Top Varieties: Apple Mint, Chocolate Mint, Peppermint, Spearmint
Care: Mint thrives in full sun to partial shade and adapts easily to a range of soils, though it prefers moist, well-drained conditions. Its rapid growth and spreading habit mean it's best planted in a container or an area controlled by wide borders or frequent mowing to prevent it from overtaking your garden.

If grown in a container, water occasionally to keep the soil consistently moist. Trim the plant frequently to prevent flowering, which encourages new, tender growth and keeps the flavor at its peak. Mint is forgiving, so even aggressive pruning will rejuvenate its growth.
Harvest/Enjoyment: Harvest mint by snipping stems as needed, ideally in the morning when the essential oils are most concentrated. Use the leaves fresh in teas, infuse them into water, or add them as a garnish to elevate any dish. For an instant pick-me-up, crush a leaf between your fingers and inhale its invigorating scent. It's a burst of refreshment for your spirit.

Nasturtium

Slow to start but vigorous by summer's end, nasturtiums sprawl with vibrant, edible blooms and peppery leaves that brighten both gardens and salads.

QUICK REFERENCE

Type: Herb
Lifecycle: Annual
Applications: Container, Raised Bed, In-Ground Garden, Sensory Garden
Sensory Experiences: Sight, Taste
Disease Resistant: No
Pest Resistant: No
Pampering Need: 5 (Very Easy)
Harvest Ease: 5 (Very Easy)
Parts Used: Flowers, Leaves
Harvest Period: July–October

Personality: The playful, peppery flower that loves to climb or sprawl, brightening your garden and salads with effortless charm.
Description: Nasturtiums are the cheerful multitaskers of the garden, offering vibrant, edible blooms and leaves that are tasty and beautiful. Thriving in sunny spots with dry-to-medium soil, these adaptable annuals come in two growth habits: compact bushy varieties are great for edging pathways, filling containers, or

creating tidy garden patches; and trailing vines are best for training up trellises, spilling over walls, or adding a sprawling glow to larger spaces. Their peppery flavor enhances salads and garnishes, while their colorful blooms attract pollinators. Historically a symbol of victory, nasturtiums are a low-maintenance addition to any garden.
Botanical Names: *Tropaeolum majus*
Top Varieties:

- **Compact:** Alaska, Dwarf Jewel
- **Vining:** Trailing Mix, Yeti

Care: Nasturtiums thrive in full sun and well-drained, nutrient-poor soil—too much fertilizer encourages leaf growth at the expense of blooms. Water sparingly, as they prefer to be slightly neglected once established. Deadhead spent flowers regularly to prolong blooming, though these self-sufficient plants will continue to delight even without much attention. In warmer climates or mild winters, seeds may overwinter and germinate for a springtime surprise.
Harvest/Enjoyment: Harvest flowers and leaves as needed, ideally in the morning when they're freshest. The leaves add a peppery kick to salads, while the flowers make vibrant garnishes for plates, cocktails, or desserts. You can also pickle the seeds as a caper substitute for a unique culinary twist.

Occassionally pause to savor their bright, cheerful blooms. They're like little bursts of sunshine reminding you of the simple joys your garden brings.

PLANNING AND GROWING

Light: Full Sun
Soil Moisture: Medium
Height and Width: 1"–18" (2.5–45.7cm) x 12"–18" (30.5–45.7cm)
Growth Rate: 4 (Fast)
Time to Harvest: 4–6 weeks
Common Pests and Diseases: Aphids and flea beetles.

PLANTING INSTRUCTIONS

Period: Mid- to late spring (65°F–85°F [18°C–29.5°C])
Method: Seed
Depth: Bury seeds 1" (2.5cm) deep.
Spacing: Plant one seed every 12" (30.5cm) in rows 18" (45.7cm) apart.

Onion, Egyptian Walking

These quirky onions "walk" around your garden, offering fresh greens with zero fuss and a bit of whimsy.

QUICK REFERENCE

Type: Herb
Lifecycle: Perennial (Zones 3–9)
Applications: Container, Orchard, Wild Edible
Disease Resistant: Yes
Pest Resistant: Yes
Pampering Need: 5 (Very Easy)
Harvest Ease: 5 (Very Easy)
Parts Used: Bulb, Leaves
Harvest Period: April–October

Personality: The quirky perennial onion that "walks" around your garden, providing greens year after year.
Description: Egyptian walking onions are the wanderers of the garden, leaning over to plant their bulblets as they "walk" to new spots. Thriving in sunny areas with medium, well-drained soil, these hardy perennials are perfect for low-maintenance gardeners who enjoy a touch of whimsy. With their spicy, oniony flavor and ability to effortlessly provide greens, they're both practical and entertaining. Historically valued for their resilience and uniqueness, these onions bring character and function to your garden.
Botanical Name: *Allium × proliferum*
Care: Plant Egyptian walking onions in full sun with well-drained soil, spacing them about 6"–8" (15.2–20.3cm) apart. Water regularly during active growth and frequent harvests. These onions are incredibly low-maintenance, self-propagating by producing clusters of bulblets (called top sets) at the end of their stalks.

As the top sets mature, the weight causes the stalks to bend toward the ground, planting the next generation for you. To control their spread, harvest some of the top sets before they root, or replant them in a designated area to manage their wandering nature. Mulch lightly with straw in late fall to supress weeds and for added protection in colder climates.
Harvest/Enjoyment: Enjoy Egyptian walking onions year-round by harvesting their different parts. In early spring and fall, snip young, tender greens for salads or garnishes; they're mild and flavorful, perfect for fresh eating. During summer, the greens may toughen, but they are still excellent for flavoring soups or stews. Harvest the small, flavorful bulbs at the base or the top sets for a burst of spicy onion flavor. While the small bulbs are delicious, they can be thick-skinned and require a bit of peeling.

Let their unique "walking" habit surprise and delight you—it's nature's way of keeping your garden dynamic and ever-growing.

PLANNING AND GROWING

Light: Full Sun
Soil Moisture: Medium
Height and Width: 2' (61cm) x 6" (15.2cm)
Growth Rate: 3 (Moderate)
Time to Harvest: 16–24 weeks
Common Pests and Diseases: Onion maggot and downy mildew.

PLANTING INSTRUCTIONS

Period: Early spring (50°F–70°F [10°C–21°C])
Method: Bulb
Depth: Bury bulb sets 1"–2" (2.5–5.1cm) deep.
Spacing: Plant bulbs 6" (15.2cm) apart in rows 12" (30.5cm) apart.

Oregano

Oregano fills your garden with earthy fragrance, feeds pollinators, and brings bold flavor to every meal. It's tough, timeless, and full of charm.

QUICK REFERENCE

Type: Herb
Lifecycle: Perennial (Zones 5–9)
Applications: Container, Raised Bed, Sensory Garden, Ground Cover
Sensory Experiences: Scent, Taste
Disease Resistant: Yes
Pest Resistant: Yes
Pampering Need: 5 (Very Easy)
Harvest Ease: 5 (Very Easy)
Parts Used: Leaves
Harvest Period: April–November

Personality: The hearty Mediterranean native that perfumes the air and brings depth to Italian dishes.
Description: A robust and aromatic herb, oregano is a culinary cornerstone, elevating savory dishes and infusing teas with its earthy warmth. This sun-loving perennial thrives in dry-to-medium soil and is exceptionally drought-tolerant. Its delicate flowers support pollinators, while its spreading nature ensures it can fill garden spaces with its resilience and charm. Revered in ancient Greece as a symbol of joy and good health, oregano brings flavor, history, and vitality to your garden.
Botanical Name: *Origanum vulgare* subsp. *hirtum*
Top Varieties: Common, Compactum (compact), Greek, Hot & Spicy, Italian
Care: Oregano thrives in full sun and well-drained soil, tolerating drought and heat with ease. Its Mediterranean roots prefer drier conditions, but overly humid environments can cause leaf spot. To avoid this, ensure good airflow around the plants and avoid overhead watering.

Prune oregano regularly to encourage bushy growth and prevent legginess. Its spreading habit makes it a great ground cover, but it may get a bit too unruly. To manage spreading, grow it in containers or trim back trailing stems and clip seed heads shortly after the flowers brown and pollinators have finished enjoying them.
Harvest/Enjoyment: Harvest oregano sprigs as needed, ideally before the plant flowers, when the leaves are at their most flavorful. To strip leaves from a stem, hold the tip and pull your fingers down toward the base, easily collecting a handful of leaves ready to use. In early spring, the stems are tender enough to chop and add to soups and sautés, but they grow woody as summer progresses.

Rub a leaf between your fingers and breathe in its spicy, earthy aroma. It's like capturing a moment of sun-soaked Mediterranean warmth.

PLANNING AND GROWING

Light: Full Sun
Soil Moisture: Dry, Medium
Height and Width: 8"–10" (20.3–25.3cm) tall
Growth Rate: 3 (Moderate)
Time to Harvest: 8–12 weeks
Common Pests and Diseases: Generally pest-free; occasional leaf spot.

PLANTING INSTRUCTIONS

Period: Early to mid-spring (60°F–75°F [15.5°C–24°C])
Method: Transplant
Depth: Plant at the same depth as in the pot.
Spacing: Transplant one plant every 12"–18" (30.5–45.7cm).

Parsley

Slow and steady, parsley rewards you with fresh sprigs for months while quietly feeding pollinators and swallowtail caterpillars.

QUICK REFERENCE

Type: Herb
Lifecycle Biennial (grown as annual)
Applications: Container, Raised Bed, In-Ground Garden, Sensory Garden
Sensory Experiences: Scent, Taste
Disease Resistant: No
Pest Resistant: No
Pampering Need: 3 (Moderate)
Harvest Ease: 5 (Very Easy)
Parts Used: Leaves
Harvest Period: July–October

Personality: The humble herb that grows slow and steady, rewarding you with endless fresh sprigs for your meals.
Description: Parsley is a versatile culinary and medicinal herb that brings a fresh, bright flavor to dishes while quietly supporting your garden's ecosystem. Thriving in sunny to partially shaded areas with rich, medium soil, this biennial is easy to grow in both beds and containers. Parsley is frost-tolerant, often providing generous yields late into the season, making it one of the last herbs to grace your garden.

Its foliage serves as a food source for swallowtail butterfly caterpillars while its delicate flowers attract beneficial insects, making it an essential part of a wildlife-friendly garden. To get the most out of parsley's versatility, consider growing two plants—one for regular harvesting and another that you let flower for the benefit of pollinators and wildlife.
Botanical Name: *Petroselinum crispum*
Top Varieties: Italian Flat-Leaf, Triple Curled
Care: Parsley thrives in partial to full sun with rich, well-drained soil. Water consistently to keep the soil moist, but not soggy, especially during hot weather, as dry conditions can cause leaves to turn bitter. A layer of straw mulch helps retain moisture and regulate soil temperature.

Parsley grows slowly at first, so patience is key. Regularly snipping sprigs encourages tender new growth and prevents the plant from becoming leggy. Its frost tolerance means it can be harvested well into fall and even early winter in some climates. In its second year, parsley will bolt, sending up flower stalks and yielding fewer leaves that have a stronger, less palatable flavor. Allowing one plant to flower supports pollinators and other beneficial insects while providing food for swallowtail butterfly caterpillars.
Harvest/Enjoyment: Harvest parsley by cutting outer stems close to the base, leaving the central ones to continue growing. Typically, a single plant will provide an abundant supply for garnishing and flavoring soups, salads, and sauces. The leaves can also be dried or frozen for use through winter.

Take a moment to admire its vibrant green sprigs, each one a reminder of the rewards of slow, steady growth. Parsley's frost-hardiness makes it a steadfast garden companion, bridging the seasons and delivering bright, grassy flavors long after other herbs have faded. With a little extra space for wildlife, you'll also enjoy the beauty of butterflies and the satisfaction of supporting your garden's ecosystem.

PLANNING AND GROWING

Light: Full Sun, Part Shade
Soil Moisture: Medium
Height and Width: 12" (30.5cm) x 9"–12" (22.9–30.5cm)
Growth Rate: 3 (Moderate)
Time to Harvest: 12–14 weeks
Common Pests and Diseases: Carrot flies and leaf spot.

PLANTING INSTRUCTIONS

Period: Early to mid-spring (50°F–75°F [10°C–24°C])
Method: Transplant
Depth: Plant at the same depth as in the pot.
Spacing: Transplant one plant every 8"–12" (20.3–30.5cm).

Pea

Peas climb eagerly in cool weather, offering sweet snap, tender snow, or plump shelling pods.

QUICK REFERENCE

Type: Vegetable
Lifecycle: Annual
Applications: Container, Raised Bed, In-Ground Garden, Sensory Garden
Sensory Experiences: Taste
Disease Resistant: No
Pest Resistant: No
Pampering Need: 4 (Easy)
Harvest Ease: 5 (Very Easy)
Parts Used: Pod, Seeds
Harvest Period: June, September–October

Personality: The sweet climber that loves cool weather and rewards you with tender pods to snack on fresh.

Description: Peas are the joyful harbingers of spring, thriving in sunny and partially shaded spots with medium soil. These versatile vines bring a vertical dimension to your garden and are packed with nutrients and whimsical beauty. Peas come in three delicious forms, each with its own charm and purpose. Seek snap and snow varieties that are "stringless," meaning they lack a tough, fibrous string along the pod's seam, making them easier to eat and prepare.

- **Snap:** These crunchy, sweet pods are eaten whole and are perfect for snacking or stir-fries.
- **Snow:** Flat, tender pods with a subtle sweetness, snow peas are ideal for salads and quick cooking.
- **Shelling:** Also known as garden peas, these are grown for the plump, flavorful peas inside the fibrous pods. While they require shelling, you don't need to grow them in bulk. Just a few plants can provide the simple pleasure of popping open pods to enjoy their taste.

Botanical Name: *Pisum sativum*

Top Varieties: The approximate height of the vine is shown next to each variety.

- **Snap:** Sugar Daddy (2' [61cm]), Sugar Snap (4'–6' [1.2–1.8m])
- **Snow:** Oregon Sugar Pod II (3' [91.4cm]), Snow Green (2' [61cm])
- **Shelling:** Dakota (2' [61cm]), Knight (3' [91.4cm]), Lincoln (3' [91.4cm])

Care: Peas love cool weather and are best sown directly into rich, well-drained soil as soon as it can be worked in early spring. Optionally, soak the seeds for 8–12 hours to accelerate germination, but avoid exceeding 24 hours to prevent seed damage or rot. Plant immediately after soaking. Spread a generous layer of compost onto the growing area and then sow seeds about 1" (2.5cm) deep and 2" (5.1cm) apart. Water consistently to keep the soil evenly moist, especially during flowering.

Provide support with a trellis, stakes, or netting to encourage vertical growth, which makes harvesting easier and keeps the vines healthy. Trellis heights depend on the variety. Compact types need only 2'–3' (61–91.4cm) of support, while taller varieties require 4'–6' (1.2–1.8m). Once plants are 3"–4" (7.6–10.2cm) tall, spread straw mulch around the base to retain moisture and suppress weeds. Peas are nitrogen-fixers, enriching your soil naturally, so they're as good for your garden as they are for your table.

Harvest/Enjoyment: For the best flavor, harvest snap and snow peas when the pods are plump but tender, before the seeds fully develop. Pick shelling peas when the pods are bright green and swollen, indicating the peas inside are ready. Harvest regularly to encourage continued yields, and don't overlook the fun of nibbling on young tendrils—they're tender, sweet, and add a unique touch to salads or as a whimsical garnish.

Pop a pod right off the vine and enjoy its sweet, garden-fresh flavor. It's a simple, tasty reward for your care. Share a pod with a friend or use them to top salads or stir-fries. Whether you're munching on snap peas, savoring the crispness of snow peas, or delighting in the buttery sweetness of fresh-shelled garden peas, this versatile climber will always remind you of the abundance your garden can bring.

PLANNING AND GROWING

Light: Full Sun, Part Shade

Soil Moisture: Medium

Height and Width: 3'–7' (0.9–2.1m) tall

Growth Rate: 4 (Fast)

Time to Harvest: 8–12 weeks

Common Pests and Diseases: Aphids and powdery mildew. Deer and rabbits may eat foliage and pods.

PLANTING INSTRUCTIONS

Period: Early spring (45°F–65°F [7°C–18°C])

Method: Seed

Depth: Bury seeds 1" (2.5cm) deep.

Spacing: Plant one seed every 1"–2" (2.5–5.1cm).

Peach

Peach trees overflow with juicy, sun-ripened fruit, bringing showy spring blooms and abundant summer harvests.

QUICK REFERENCE

Type: Tree

Lifecycle: Perennial (Zones 4–8)

Applications: Orchard

Sensory Experiences: Taste

Disease Resistant: No

Pest Resistant: No

Pampering Need: 4 (Easy)

Harvest Ease: 3 (Moderate)

Parts Used: Fruit

Harvest Period: July–September

Personality: The vibrant orchard charmer that gifts you with sweet, sun-kissed fruit at the height of summer.

Description: A fragrant symbol of summer, peach trees deliver and abundance of luscious, sun-ripened fruit. Thriving in sunny areas with medium soil, these fast-growing trees offer a double delight: showy spring blossoms that attract pollinators and juicy fruit in summer. Revered in folklore as symbols of immortality and renewal, peach trees bring beauty and bounty to your orchard.

Most peach trees are self-pollinating, meaning you only need one tree to enjoy a harvest of juicy fruit. However, planting two varieties can increase yields and extend your harvest window. Choose the type of peach based on how you plan to enjoy it: quick snacks, baking cobblers, or filling jars for winter treats.

- **Freestone:** The pit easily separates from the flesh, making freestone peaches ideal for fresh eating, slicing, and baking. If you want peaches for snacking or preparing with minimal effort, freestone is the way to go.
- **Semi-Freestone:** These peaches have flesh that partially clings to the pit. They combine the versatility of freestone with a firmer texture, making them great for fresh use or cooking.
- **Clingstone:** The flesh clings tightly to the pit, often making them more labor-intensive to prepare. However, their juiciness and firm texture are perfect for canning and preserves, as they hold their shape beautifully.

Botanical Name: *Prunus persica*

Top Varieties:

- **Freestone:** Contender, Reliance
- **Semi-Freestone:** Redhaven
- **Clingstone:** Babygold 5

Care: Peaches are the fastest-growing fruit trees, but their rapid growth leads to brittle wood, making them prone to damage from heavy fruit sets or ice storms. In colder climates, seek out cold-hardy varieties to avoid losing buds to an early frost and ensure a bountiful harvest. To keep your tree healthy and productive, prune it annually to manage its shape, remove weak or crowded branches, and improve air circulation, which helps prevent disease.

Water consistently, especially during the first two years, to establish a robust root system. Mulch with woodchips to conserve moisture and reduce weeds, but keep the mulch a few inches away from the trunk to prevent rot. Fertilize in early spring with compost or organic fruit-tree fertilizer to fuel growth and fruit yields.

To encourage the healthiest harvest, thin young fruits when they're about the size of a marble, leaving 4"–6" (10.2–15.2cm) between each one. This prevents overloading the branches, which could cause them to break, and ensures your peaches grow larger, sweeter, and more flavorful.

Harvest/Enjoyment: Peaches are ready to harvest when their color deepens to a rich blush and they yield slightly to gentle pressure. Pick them carefully to avoid bruising, and enjoy them fresh off the tree when they're warm from the summer sun. If you can resist eating them all right away, peaches make wonderful jams, cobblers, or even a simple dessert when sliced and served with cream.

PLANNING AND GROWING

Light: Full Sun

Soil Moisture: Medium

Height and Width: 12'–15' (3.7–4.6m) x 12'–15' (3.7–4.6m)

Growth Rate: 2 (Slow)

Time to Harvest: 3+ years

Common Pests and Diseases: Peach tree borer and peach leaf curl (fungal disease that causes leaf distortion). Deer may rub antlers on trunks.

PLANTING INSTRUCTIONS

Period: Early spring (50°F–70°F [10°C–21°C])

Method: Transplant

Depth: Set the base of the trunk at ground level.

Spacing: Check the mature width of the tree and leave at least 12" (30.5cm) of space beyond that from other trees or structures.

Pear, European

Graceful and slow to bear fruit, pear trees offer fragrant blooms and sweet, buttery harvests, proving that patience rewards you with lasting beauty and abundant bounty.

QUICK REFERENCE

Type: Tree

Lifecycle: Perennial (Zones 4–8)

Applications: Orchard

Sensory Experiences: Taste

Disease Resistant: No

Pest Resistant: No

Pampering Need: 4 (Easy)

Harvest Ease: 3 (Moderate)

Parts Used: Fruit

Harvest Period: August–September

Personality: The graceful orchard classic that gifts you with sweet, buttery fruit.

Description: A tree of quiet elegance, pears deliver crisp, luscious fruit while supporting pollinators with their fragrant spring blossoms. Thriving in sunny spots with medium soil, they grow slower than other fruit trees, making them easy to maintain in small spaces. To enjoy their bounty, plant two compatible varieties for cross-pollination, ensuring they bloom at the same time. Check nursery tags or fruit tree pollination tables for guidance. Revered as symbols of wisdom and generosity, pear trees offer nourishment for both you and the ecosystem.

Botanical Name: *Pyrus communis*

Top Varieties: Harrow Delight, Moonglow, Seckel, Warren

Care: Dwarf pears require permanent staking to support their slender frames and prevent leaning under the weight of their fruit. Choose a sunny spot with well-drained soil and water deeply and consistently during the first two seasons to establish strong roots.

Apply compost or organic fertilizer each spring to encourage healthy growth and fruiting. Prune lightly in late winter to shape the tree, improve air circulation, and remove dead or crossing branches. If the tree produces an abundance of fruit, thin clusters to leave one or two pears per spur for larger, healthier harvests. Spread woodchip mulch around the base to conserve moisture and suppress weeds, but keep the mulch a few inches from the trunk to prevent rot.

Harvest/Enjoyment: Pears are unique in that they ripen best off the tree. Harvest when the fruit lifts easily from the branch but is still firm. Allow pears to ripen indoors at room temperature until their skin softens and their aroma deepens. Slice one open and enjoy its buttery sweetness, or poach it with spices for a luxurious dessert. Fresh, preserved, or baked, pears are a testament to your patience and care.

PLANNING AND GROWING

Light: Full Sun

Soil Moisture: Medium

Height and Width: 8'–15' (2.4–4.6m) x 8'–15' (2.4–4.6m)

Growth Rate: 1 (Very Slow)

Time to Harvest: 3+ years

Common Pests and Diseases: Codling moth and fire blight. Deer may eat foliage and rub antlers on trunks.

PLANTING INSTRUCTIONS

Period: Early spring (50°F–70°F [10°C–21°C])

Method: Transplant

Depth: Set the base of the trunk at ground level.

Spacing: Check the mature width of the tree and leave at least 12" (30.5cm) of space beyond that from other trees or structures.

Plantain, Broadleaf

Nature's first aid: broadleaf plantain soothes bites and stings while thriving anywhere. It's an edible, healing ally often hiding in plain sight.

QUICK REFERENCE

Type: Herb

Lifecycle: Perennial (Zones 3–9)

Applications: Orchard, Wild Edible

Disease Resistant: Yes

Pest Resistant: Yes

Pampering Need: 5 (Very Easy)

Harvest Ease: 4 (Easy)

Parts Used: Leaves

Harvest Period: April–November

Personality: The resilient healer that soothes bites, nourishes meals and thrives where other plants can't.

Description: A humble yet powerful herb, broadleaf plantain is a perennial ground cover that thrives almost anywhere, from sunny lawns to shaded garden edges. Often dismissed as a "weed," this unassuming plant is a natural healer, offering ecological benefits and practical uses. Smaller plantain plants are typically found in lawns, but when left unmowed, they can grow up to 10" (25.4cm) in diameter, forming lush rosettes of edible, nutrient-rich leaves. Used for centuries in herbal remedies, its crushed leaves soothe cuts, insect bites, and stings, earning it a reputation as nature's first aid kit.

Botanical Name: *Plantago major*

Top Varieties: While a few cultivated varieties exist, the wild plantain already growing in your yard is just as reliable and beneficial.

Care: Plantain thrives in full sun to partial shade and adapts to almost any soil type, from compacted clay to sandy loam. It's incredibly drought-tolerant and requires no additional watering once established. Trim flower stalks to keep the plant tidy, or allow them to mature and scatter seeds for new plants next season. If you'd like plantain in a specific area, simply toss mature seed heads there in late summer or early fall and they'll sprout the following growing season.

Harvest/Enjoyment: Pick young leaves for tender greens, adding them to salads or sautéing as a nutritious side dish. Larger, tougher leaves are ideal for medicinal uses. To create a soothing salve, crush or chew the leaves to release their natural juices, then rub them directly onto cuts, bites, or stings.

Broadleaf plantain is a gentle, reliable presence in your garden, generously offering healing and nutrition without asking for anything in return.

PLANNING AND GROWING

Light: Full Sun, Part Shade

Soil Moisture: Dry, Wet

Height and Width: 6"–10" (15.2–25.4cm) tall

Growth Rate: 4 (Fast)

Time to Harvest: 4–6 weeks

Common Pests and Diseases: Generally pest-free; occasional leaf spot.

PLANTING INSTRUCTIONS

Period: Early spring to early summer (50°F–75°F [10°C–24°C])

Method: Seed

Depth: Lightly cover with soil.

Spacing: Scatter seeds lightly and pat down.

Plum, European

Sweet as candy, plums are like lumps of sugar on a tree. Beautiful spring blooms are followed by juicy, jewel-toned fruit.

QUICK REFERENCE

Type: Tree
Lifecycle: Perennial (Zones 3–8)
Applications: Orchard
Sensory Experiences: Taste
Disease Resistant: No
Pest Resistant: No
Pampering Need: 4 (Easy)
Harvest Ease: 3 (Moderate)
Parts Used: Fruit
Harvest Period: August–September

Personality: The candy-sweet plum tree—your orchard's little sugar factory—graces you with juicy, jewel-like fruit.
Description: A delightful addition to small orchards, European plum trees reward you with sweet, flavorful fruit and delicate spring blossoms that attract pollinators. Thriving in sunny spots with medium soil, this easy-to-care-for tree brings beauty and bounty to your garden.

Some plum tree varieties are self-pollinating, meaning you only need one to enjoy a harvest, but even self-pollinators produce better yields with a second tree nearby. Other varieties require two compatible trees for cross-pollination, so be sure to check nursery tags or fruit tree pollination tables to ensure their bloom times align.
Botanical Name: *Prunus domestica*
Top Varieties: Mount Royal, Stanley, Toka, Waneta
Care: Water young plum trees regularly during their first two years to establish strong roots. Mulch with woodchips each spring to retain moisture and reduce weeds, keeping the mulch a few inches away from the trunk to prevent rot. Fertilize with compost or organic fertilizer in early spring to encourage healthy growth and fruiting.

Prune in late winter to shape the tree, remove dead or crossing branches, and allow sunlight and air to reach fruit within the canopy. Thin fruit when they're marble-sized, leaving 3"–4" (7.6–10.2cm) between each plum to prevent branch stress and encourage larger, sweeter fruit.
Harvest/Enjoyment: Plums are ready to harvest when they're soft, fragrant, and come off the tree with a gentle tug. Savor one right there in the garden, its juice bursting in your mouth like a little chunk of sweet sunshine. Beyond fresh eating, plums can be dried into chewy treats or preserved as rich jams and syrups to enjoy the taste of summer all year long.

PLANNING AND GROWING

Light: Full Sun
Soil Moisture: Medium
Height and Width: 10'–12' (3–3.7m) x 10'–15' (3–4.6m)
Growth Rate: 2 (Slow)
Time to Harvest: 3+ years
Common Pests and Diseases: Plum curculio and black knot (fungal disease that causes black galls on branches). Deer may eat foliage and rub antlers on trunks.

PLANTING INSTRUCTIONS

Period: Early spring (50°F–70°F [10°C–21°C])
Method: Transplant
Depth: Set the base of the trunk at ground level.
Spacing: Check the mature width of the tree and leave at least 12" (30.5cm) of space beyond that from other trees or structures.

Potato

Potatoes are easy to grow and quietly generous. Tuck them under straw and they'll reward you with hearty autumn harvests.

QUICK REFERENCE

Type: Vegetable
Lifecycle: Annual
Applications: Container, Raised Bed, In-Ground Garden
Disease Resistant: No
Pest Resistant: No
Pampering Need: 5 (Very Easy)
Harvest Ease: 3 (Moderate)
Parts Used: Root
Harvest Period: September–October

Personality: The humble underground treasure that turns simple sunlight and soil into a feast of hearty, golden rewards.
Description: Potatoes are the reliable workhorse of the garden, growing quietly underground while their leafy tops bask in the sun. Perfect for sunny spots with medium soil, they thrive under a thick

layer of straw mulch, making them excellent for helping suppress weeds. Beloved across the globe for roasting, mashing, or soups, potatoes are a symbol of simple abundance and resilience.

Potatoes are grouped by how quickly they mature, letting you plan fresh harvests and winter storage effortlessly.

- **Early:** Maturing in 60–90 days, these small, thin-skinned varieties are perfect for fresh eating, but not ideal for long storage.
- **Midseason:** Maturing in 90–110 days, these versatile spuds offer a mix of fresh use and moderate storage potential.
- **Late:** Maturing in 110–135 days, late varieties have thicker skins, making them perfect for long-term storage and hearty meals all winter.

Botanical Name: *Solanum tuberosum*

Top Varieties:

- **Early:** Red Norland, Yukon Gold
- **Midseason:** Goldrush
- **Late:** Kennebec

Care: Potatoes thrive in full sun and loose, nutrient-rich soil. To prepare your seed potatoes, cut larger ones into pieces, ensuring each piece has at least two eyes. Let the cut surfaces dry and callous over for a day or two before planting to reduce the risk of rot. Smaller potatoes with multiple eyes can be planted whole.

Bury seed potatoes 4"–6" (10.2–15.2cm) deep, spacing them 12"–15" (30.5–38.1cm) apart, and then top with 1"–2" (2.5–5.1cm) of compost. As plants grow, hill soil or add straw mulch around the base to cover developing tubers and prevent them from turning green in the sunlight. Deep watering encourages strong growth, but let the soil dry slightly between waterings to avoid rot. To maximize yields, pinch off flowers if they appear, redirecting energy to tuber production. Keep an eye out for pests like potato beetles and remove them by hand or use organic controls.

Harvest/Enjoyment: Harvest potatoes when the plants yellow and die back. Use a pitchfork to gently loosen the soil and dig up your crop—it's a treasure hunt that kids will adore, finding the tubers like hidden Easter eggs. If left in the ground after the foliage dies, they'll wait patiently, but be sure to harvest before the first snowfall for a more comfortable experience.

Roast them with herbs, mash them into creamy comfort food, or turn them into hearty soups: potatoes bring warmth and nourishment to any meal. If you plan to enjoy them soon, give them a quick scrub under water for easy, ready-to-cook spuds when needed. For long-term storage, brush off soil without washing and place them in a cool, dry, dark area with good ventilation. With proper conditions, many varieties will keep for several months.

PLANNING AND GROWING

Light: Full Sun

Soil Moisture: Medium

Height and Width: 1'–2' (30.5–61cm) x 18" (45.7cm)

Growth Rate: 3 (Moderate)

Time to Harvest: 10–16 weeks

Common Pests and Diseases: Colorado potato beetle and late blight. Deer may eat foliage.

PLANNING AND GROWING

Period: Early spring (50°F–70°F [10°C–21°C])

Method: Tuber

Depth: Bury tubers 3"–4" (7.6–10.2cm) deep.

Spacing: Plant one tuber every 12" (30.5cm) in rows 36" (91.4cm) apart.

WHAT ARE SEED POTATOES?

Seed potatoes are simply potatoes with plenty of "eyes," or growth buds, that will sprout into new plants. These eyes are where the rooting magic happens, transforming a humble spud into a thriving potato plant.

You can purchase certified seed potatoes from garden centers or catalogs, which are full of eyes, free from diseases, and ready to plant. However, if you're looking for a budget-friendly option, you can use store-bought potatoes as long as you choose wisely:

- Look for potatoes with lots of visible eyes.
- Choose organic potatoes grown in the US, as they're less likely to be treated with sprout inhibitors.
- Avoid potatoes that are overly shriveled, moldy, or show signs of rot.

Radish

Radishes grow fast, add a peppery bite to meals, and deliver crisp roots and tasty greens.

QUICK REFERENCE

Type: Vegetable

Lifecycle: Annual

Applications: Container, Raised Bed, In-Ground Garden

Disease Resistant: No

Pest Resistant: No

Pampering Need: 5 (Very Easy)

Harvest Ease: 4 (Easy)

Parts Used: Leaves, Root

Harvest Period: April–November

Personality: The feisty garden sprinter that delivers spicy roots and versatile greens.
Description: Radishes are the ultimate quick crop, bringing peppery crunch to your meals and vibrancy to your garden. Perfect for sunny spaces with medium soil, these fast-growing annuals thrive in small gardens and containers. Cultivated since ancient times and symbolizing vitality, radishes are a reminder that even the simplest efforts can yield bold rewards.
Botanical Name: *Raphanus sativus*
Top Varieties: Black Spanish, Cherry Belle, Easter Egg, French Breakfast
Care: Radishes thrive in cool weather, making them perfect for early spring and fall planting. These quick growers love loose, well-drained soil and consistent watering, which helps keep their roots crisp and prevents them from splitting or becoming woody. Sow seeds directly into the soil, spacing them about 1" (2.5cm) apart, and thin seedlings to 2"–4" (5.1–10.2cm) once they sprout to allow roots room to develop.

For continuous harvests, sow a new round every two weeks. If a fall planting sounds exciting, radishes are excellent gap-fillers, quickly maturing in bare spots left by harvested plants like beans, tomatoes, or potatoes.
Harvest/Enjoyment: Harvest radishes when they're firm and about the size of a large marble to 1" (2.5cm) across. Pulling them too late can result in overly spicy or woody roots. Their leafy greens are also edible, though their bristly texture makes them less enjoyable raw. Sautée the leaves, add them to soups, or blend them into pesto for a nutrient-packed side.

Bite into a fresh radish for its peppery zing or thinly slice it to add crunch and spice to salads, sandwiches, or tacos. Radishes are a fun, fast way to brighten your meals and your garden.

PLANNING AND GROWING

Light: Full Sun
Soil Moisture: Medium
Height and Width: 8" x 6" (20.3 x 15.2cm)
Growth Rate: 5 (Very Fast)
Time to Harvest: 4–6 weeks
Common Pests and Diseases: Clubroot (fungal disease that causes swollen roots). Deer and rabbits may eat young foliage.

PLANTING INSTRUCTIONS

Period: Early spring to late summer (50°F–75°F [10°C–24°C])
Method: Seed
Depth: Bury seeds ½" (1.3cm) deep.
Spacing: Plant one seed every 2"–4" (5.1–10.2cm) in rows 6"–12" (15.2–30.5cm) apart.

Raspberry

Reliable and rewarding, cultivated raspberries deliver sweet-tart berries perfect for snacking, baking, or preserving.

QUICK REFERENCE

Type: Shrub
Lifecycle: Perennial (Zones 3–8)
Applications: Orchard, Wild Edible
Sensory Experiences: Taste
Disease Resistant: No
Pest Resistant: No
Pampering Need: 4 (Easy)
Harvest Ease: 3 (Moderate)
Parts Used: Berries, Leaves
Harvest Period: July–November

Personality: The resilient bramble that gifts you with sun-ripened jewels for snacking, baking, or preserving.
Description: A sweet, tangy perennial, raspberries thrive in sunny spots with medium soil. These vigorous plants produce versatile, nutrient-rich berries that are perfect for snacking, desserts, or homemade preserves. Raspberries have long symbolized kindness and remembrance, offering emotional abundance in your garden.

Raspberries come in two main types, each offering unique harvest times to suit your seasonal rhythms:

- **Summer Bearing:** These varieties produce a single, abundant crop in early to mid-summer on second-year canes (floricanes). Ideal if you prefer a large harvest for preserving or fresh eating during the summer months.
- **Fall Bearing (Ever Bearing):** Also known as primocane varieties, these plants yield two harvests: a primary crop in late summer to early fall on first-year canes; and a smaller, secondary crop the following early summer on the same canes. Perfect for gardeners seeking fresh raspberries over an extended season.

If you don't have space for these larger, spreading bushes in your garden, keep an eye out for their wild cousins along sunny forest edges and woodland trails, where you can forage berries with no planting or upkeep required.
Botanical Name: *Rubus idaeus*
Top Varieties:

- **Summer Bearing:** Boyne, Cascade Delight, Killarney
- **Fall Bearing:** Anne (yellow), Caroline, Heritage

Care: Raspberries thrive in full sun and rich, well-drained soil. Water them consistently, especially during fruiting, to ensure plump, juicy berries. Apply compost each spring to encourage strong, productive canes. Mulch with woodchips to suppress weeds and conserve moisture. To keep their underground roots from spreading too far, plant in a low raised bed or maintain wide, grass borders with regular mowing. Raspberry bushes need regular management to stay contained.

Organize your raspberry patch into 2'–3' (61–91.4cm) wide rows to reduce scratches while picking. Trellis the canes between two wires—like a mini-clothesline—to keep them upright for easier harvesting. Prune in late winter, removing spent canes and thinning new growth to improve airflow and prevent disease.

Harvest/Enjoyment: Harvest raspberries when they're plump, brightly colored, and come off the cane with a gentle tug. As you pick, feel free to snack on a few. There's nothing quite like a sun-warmed berry straight from the plant.

PLANNING AND GROWING

Light: Full Sun
Soil Moisture: Medium
Height and Width: 4'–6' (1.2–1.8m) tall
Growth Rate: 3 (Moderate)
Time to Harvest: 1–2 years
Common Pests and Diseases: Raspberry cane borer and anthracnose (fungal disease that causes cane lesions). Deer and birds may eat foliage and eat fruit.

PLANTING INSTRUCTIONS

Period: Early spring (50°F–70°F [10°C–21°C])
Method: Transplant
Depth: Place where stems meet roots at ground level.
Spacing: Transplant 2'–3' (61–91.4cm) apart in rows 8' (2.4m) apart.

Foraged wild black raspberries are woodland gems, bursting with flavor and a reminder that nature loves to share.

Rhubarb

Rhubarb is effortless food. Its bold stalks return year after year, ready to add tangy goodness to crisps, jams, and pies.

QUICK REFERENCE

Type: Vegetable
Lifecycle: Perennial (Zones 3–8)
Applications: Orchard
Disease Resistant: Yes
Pest Resistant: Yes
Pampering Need: 5 (Very Easy)
Harvest Ease: 5 (Very Easy)
Parts Used: Stalks
Harvest Period: May–July

Personality: The tart and sassy perennial that is always ready to brighten your pies and crisps.

Description: The bold and tangy giant of the garden, rhubarb offers striking red stalks and lush green leaves, creating a vibrant and eye-catching statement in any landscape. This low-maintenance perennial thrives in sunny to partially shaded areas with medium soil, returning year after year with little effort. Perfect for pairing with a mini-orchard, rhubarb flourishes between fruit trees, capturing sunlight that filters through the canopy while its broad leaves shade the ground, acting as a living mulch to conserve moisture for its neighbors.

Traditionally associated with rejuvenation, rhubarb brings a splash of nutrition and tangy flavor to pies, jams, and desserts.

Botanical Name: *Rheum × cultorum*

Top Varieties: Canada Red, Crimson Red, Timperley Early, Victoria

Care: Rhubarb thrives in full sun but tolerates light shade, especially in warmer climates. Plant it in well-drained, fertile soil, layered with plenty of compost for best results. Regular watering during the growing season helps the stalks grow thick and juicy, while a layer of woodchip mulch retains moisture and suppresses weeds.

To keep the plant productive, remove flower stalks as soon as they appear. This redirects the plant's energy into growing lush stems. Avoid harvesting in the first year after planting to allow the plant to establish strong roots. Once the plant is mature, divide the crown every five to seven years in early spring or late fall to rejuvenate the plant and share with friends or expand your patch.

Avoid harvesting more than half of the stalks at a time, ensuring the plant retains enough foliage for growth and to store energy for the next season. Stop heavy harvests before midsummer—around early August—so it can strengthen its root system and ensure a productive harvest the following year.
Harvest/Enjoyment: Harvest rhubarb stems when they're thick and brightly colored. To harvest, grab a stalk near the base, twist slightly, and pull upward; it should come away cleanly. Cut off the leaves, which are toxic due to their high oxalic acid content, and drop them as mulch around the base of the plant to recycle their nutrients.

Rhubarb's tart flavor shines in baked goods like pies and crisps, or simmer the stalks into a tangy-sweet salad dressing or compote to drizzle over yogurt or ice cream.

PLANNING AND GROWING

Light: Full Sun, Part Shade
Soil Moisture: Medium
Height and Width: 3'–5' (0.9–1.5m) x 3'–5' (0.9–1.5m)
Growth Rate: 2 (Slow)
Time to Harvest: 1–2 years
Common Pests and Diseases: Slugs and crown rot (fungal disease that causes plant collapse).

PLANTING INSTRUCTIONS

Period: Early spring (45°F–70°F [4.5°C–21°C])
Method: Transplant
Depth: Place where stems meet roots at ground level.
Spacing: Transplant 3' (91.4cm) apart in rows 4' (1.2m) apart.

Harvest stalks when they're thick and vibrant. Just twist and pull. Snip off the toxic leaves and let them fall as mulch, feeding the plant that feeds you.

Sage

With soothing scent and savory flavor, sage is a low-maintenance herb that calms the garden and elevates your cooking.

QUICK REFERENCE

Type: Herb
Lifecycle: Perennial (Zones 4–8)
Applications: Container, Raised Bed, In-Ground Garden, Sensory Garden
Sensory Experiences: Scent, Taste
Disease Resistant: Yes
Pest Resistant: Yes
Pampering Need: 4 (Easy)
Harvest Ease: 5 (Very Easy)
Parts Used: Leaves
Harvest Period: May–October

Personality: The wise, silver-haired sage that calms the spirit and elevates your kitchen creations.
Description: A soothing and steadfast companion, broadleaf sage is a perennial favorite for its culinary versatility and calming presence. With its soft, silver-green leaves, sage thrives in sunny spots with dry-to-medium soil, making it a low-maintenance star in orchards, raised beds, containers, or sensory gardens. Its strong, aromatic scent helps deters nibbling critters like deer and rabbits, making it both beautiful and useful.

Steeped in history, sage has long symbolized wisdom, protection, and healing. This resilient herb brings balance and quiet strength to your garden, grounding your mind with its soothing aroma and enhancing your cooking with savory, earthy flavor.
Botanical Name: *Salvia officinalis*
Top Varieties: Berggarten (compact), Common Sage, Purpurascens (purple)
Care: Sage thrives in full sun and well-drained soil, embodying a "less is more" attitude. Water sparingly, as this Mediterranean native is drought-tolerant and prefers dry conditions over soggy soil. If grown in a container, ensure excellent drainage and avoid overwatering. Prune lightly in summer to shape the plant and prevent it from becoming leggy, and cut back any woody stems each spring to keep it fresh and productive.
Harvest/Enjoyment: Harvest sage leaves as needed, pinching them just above a leaf node to encourage new growth. Younger leaves offer a more delicate flavor, while older ones are bolder and richer, making them perfect for roasting meats or adding to soups and stews. Dry leaves in bunches to preserve their flavor for tea or seasoning through the colder months.

Even if you're not harvesting, sage invites moments of mindfulness. Gently rub a leaf between your fingers as you walk by and let its calming, earthy aroma serve as a reminder to pause and take a deep, centering breath. In the garden, the plant's soft, silvery presence is a quiet and powerful anchor.

PLANNING AND GROWING

Light: Full Sun
Soil Moisture: Dry, Medium
Height and Width: 18"–30" (45.7–76.2cm) x 30"–36" (76.2–91.4cm)
Growth Rate: 3 (Moderate)
Time to Harvest: 6–12 weeks
Common Pests and Diseases: Powdery mildew.

PLANTING INSTRUCTIONS

Period: Mid- to late spring (60°F–75°F [15.5°C–24°C])
Method: Transplant
Depth: Plant at the same depth as in the pot.
Spacing: Transplant one plant every 18"–24" (45.7–61cm).

Self-Heal

Self-heal is easy to seed into lawns or mix with ground covers, bringing beauty, pollinator support, and a touch of healing to overlooked spaces.

QUICK REFERENCE

Type: Herb
Lifecycle: Perennial (Zones 4–9)
Applications: Orchard, Wild Edible, Ground Cover
Disease Resistant: Yes
Pest Resistant: Yes
Pampering Need: 5 (Very Easy)
Harvest Ease: 3 (Moderate)
Parts Used: Flowers, Leaves
Harvest Period: April–November

Personality: The herbalist's tiny friend with purple flowers and medicinal leaves for soothing cuts and sores.
Description: Known as the "healer of all ailments," self-heal is a modest yet mighty herb with a long history in herbal medicine. Thriving in sunny to partially shaded spots with medium soil, this resilient perennial offers edible leaves and flowers that are used in teas and salves. In addition, its small purple flowers attract pollinators, making it a subtle addition to your lawn and garden for both beauty and biodiversity. A symbol of resilience and renewal, self-heal offers quiet beauty and a touch of healing magic to your space.

Self-heal is an excellent ground cover for orchards and pairs beautifully with Dutch white clover, wild strawberry, and creeping thyme. Together, these plants create a lush, soil-building carpet that protects the ground, draws beneficial insects, and keeps your garden vibrant. Seed self-heal into bare patches of grass to replace thirsty, traditional lawns with this drought-tolerant alternative that stays green even when cool-season grasses turn brown.
Botanical Name: *Prunella vulgaris*
Top Varieties: Alba (white), Common
Care: Self-heal thrives in full sun to partial shade and moderately moist soil. Deadhead flowers to extend its blooming period and prevent excessive self-seeding. If it becomes too enthusiastic in spreading, it's easy to manage; simply pull up any unwanted clumps.
Harvest/Enjoyment: Harvest leaves and flowers for teas that soothe and restore. Let the plant's seed heads dry, then scatter them in bare areas to spread its healing beauty across your garden.

PLANNING AND GROWING

Light: Full Sun, Part Shade
Soil Moisture: Medium, Wet
Height and Width: 6"–12" (15.2–30.5cm) tall
Growth Rate: 3 (Moderate)
Time to Harvest: 1 year
Common Pests and Diseases: Generally pest-free; occasional powdery mildew.

PLANTING INSTRUCTIONS

Period: Early spring (60°F–75°F [15.5°C–24°C])
Method: Seed
Depth: Lightly cover with soil.
Spacing: Scatter seeds lightly and pat down.

Serviceberry, Saskatoon

Often planted for its beauty, urban serviceberries yield sweet, edible berries perfect for urban foraging if you know where to look.

QUICK REFERENCE

Type: Shrub
Lifecycle: Perennial (Zones 2–7)
Applications: Orchard, Wild Edible
Sensory Experiences: Taste
Disease Resistant: No
Pest Resistant: No
Pampering Need: 5 (Very Easy)
Harvest Ease: 3 (Moderate)
Parts Used: Berries
Harvest Period: June

Personality: The sugary-sweet shrub that delights through the seasons with blossoms, berries, and blazing autumn leaves.
Description: A multiseason marvel, the serviceberry brightens gardens with fragrant white flowers in spring, sweet berries in summer, and vibrant red foliage in fall. Known by several names—serviceberry, saskatoon, and juneberry—this versatile shrub's aliases hint at its origin and function. The name "juneberry" reflects the typical ripening time of its fruit, a sweet signal of the coming summer.

While often planted as an ornamental, many don't realize its berries are edible and delicious—and they're nutritional powerhouses too, rich in fiber, vitamin C, and potent antioxidants that match or exceed those in blueberries. Once you learn to spot them, you'll begin noticing serviceberries in parks, public spaces, and urban streetscapes. They can add beauty to your orchard, make a charming focal point or tall accent plant, or fit perfectly as a cluster of wild edibles in a corner of your yard.
Botanical Names: *Amelanchier* ssp. (serviceberry), *Amelanchier alnifolia* (Saskatoon berry)

PLANNING AND GROWING

Light: Full Sun
Soil Moisture: Medium
Height and Width: 6'–15' (1.8–4.6m) x 4'–10' (1.2–3m)
Growth Rate: 3 (Moderate)
Time to Harvest: 3+ years
Common Pests and Diseases: Generally pest-free; occasional rust. Deer may eat foliage and eat berries.

PLANTING INSTRUCTIONS

Period: Early spring (50°F–70°F [10°C–21°C])
Method: Transplant
Depth: Place where stems meet roots at ground level.
Spacing: Plant slightly closer than the mature width for a hedge effect. Stagger them in a zigzag pattern to catch more sunlight and make harvesting easier.

Top Varieties: Saskatoons come in a range of heights, so select a variety that suits your space: Honeywood (8'–10' [2.4–3m]), Martin (8'–10' [2.4–3m]), Northline (6'–10' [1.8–3m]), Smokey (10'–15' [3–4.6m]), Thiessen (10'–15' [3–4.6m]).
Care: Serviceberries are remarkably adaptable, thriving best in full sun or partial shade with moist, well-drained soil. Water consistently during the first two years to help establish strong roots. Spread a layer of woodchip mulch each spring to conserve moisture and nourish the soil. Prune lightly in late winter to shape the shrub and remove any dead or crossing branches.
Harvest/Enjoyment: Harvest serviceberries when they're deep purple, soft, and sweet, typically in early to mid-summer. Each berry carries a hint of almond flavor from its tiny edible seeds, adding a subtle nuttiness to their sweetness. Enjoy them fresh or use them in baked goods, jams, or pies. As you pick, take a moment to reflect on their role in sustaining humans and wildlife through the ages. They are a flavorful reminder of nature's simple generosity right in your garden.

Serviceberries are purplish-blue fruits with a distinctive crown. Their sweet flesh and tiny seeds deliver a hint of almond flavor, making them a uniquely delicious summer treat.

SASKATOON VS. SERVICEBERRY: SAME FAMILY, DIFFERENT FLAVORS

While Saskatoon berries and serviceberries are closely related, there are some key differences that make each unique.

- **Taste:** Saskatoon berries have a richer, sweet flavor with a hint of almond, while other serviceberries are typically milder and more tart.
- **Region:** Saskatoons are native to the western regions of North America and thrive in drier, prairie-like conditions. Other serviceberries are more widespread across North America, often found in forests and wetter climates.
- **Growth Habit:** Saskatoons grow as multistemmed shrubs or small trees, typically more compact than some taller serviceberry species.
- **Uses:** Both are excellent for fresh eating, baking, and preserving, but Saskatoon berries' denser flesh makes them particularly prized for pies and jams.

Sorrel, Creeping Wood

Known as the hiker's friend, creeping wood sorrel offers a refreshing lemony nibble wherever it pops up. No care needed, just enjoy.

QUICK REFERENCE

Type: Herb
Lifecycle Perennial (Zones 4–9)
Applications: Orchard, Wild Edible
Disease Resistant: Yes
Pest Resistant: Yes
Pampering Need: 5 (Very Easy)
Harvest Ease: 4 (Easy)
Parts Used: Flowers, Leaves
Harvest Period: May–October

Personality: The tangy, wild edible friend that reliably offers a lemony nibble as you explore your garden or a forest trail.
Description: Known as the "hiker's friend," creeping wood sorrel is a delicate, cheerful plant with tart, lemony leaves, seeds, and flowers. It thrives in sunny to partially shaded areas with medium soil and needs very little attention to flourish. This perennial is excellent for filling gaps or adding edible greenery to your orchard or sensory garden, tending to self-seed freely and spread to nearby areas. Associated with luck and happiness in folklore, sorrel brings both taste and charm to your space.
Botanical Name: *Oxalis corniculata*
Top Varieties: Wild creeping wood sorrel is just as nutritious, flavorful, and delightful as any cultivated variety.
Care: Creeping wood sorrel prefers partial shade and moist, well-drained soil. Its tendency to spread prolifically by seed can make it overly friendly in vegetable beds, so it's best suited for orchards or areas where its free-spirited nature is welcome. If you'd like to keep it in check, frequent and consistent harvesting for salads and snacks is an effective, and delicious, solution.
Harvest/Enjoyment: Every part of creeping wood sorrel—the leaves, flowers, and seeds—offers a tangy, lemony flavor. Harvest tender leaves to brighten salads, sprinkle the flowers over a dish for a pop of color and taste, or simply enjoy a nibble while walking through your garden. Its vibrant, zesty flavor is a refreshing treat that connects you to the wild abundance of nature.

PLANNING AND GROWING

Light: Full Sun, Part Shade
Soil Moisture: Dry, Medium
Height and Width: 2"–4" (5.1–10.2cm) tall
Growth Rate: 4 (Fast)
Time to Harvest: 4–6 weeks
Common Pests and Diseases: Generally pest-free; occasional leaf spot.

PLANTING INSTRUCTIONS

Period: Early spring to late summer (50°F–75°F [10°C–24°C])
Method: Seed
Depth: Lightly cover with soil.
Spacing: Scatter seeds lightly and pat down.

Sorrel, French

French sorrel's tangy leaves are perfect for garden nibbles or tossing into salads. It's easy to grow and one of the first greens to appear each spring.

QUICK REFERENCE

Type: Herb
Lifecycle: Perennial (Zones 4–9)
Applications: Orchard, Wild Edible, Sensory Garden
Sensory Experiences: Taste
Disease Resistant: Yes
Pest Resistant: Yes
Pampering Need: 5 (Very Easy)
Harvest Ease: 5 (Very Easy)
Parts Used: Leaves
Harvest Period: April–November

Personality: A tangy and reliable companion, French sorrel brightens your garden and meals all season long.
Description: A culinary classic with a bright citrus twist, French sorrel offers tender, tangy leaves that elevate soups, salads, and sauces. Often among the first greens to emerge in spring and the last to fade in fall, it's a steadfast presence in the garden. Thriving in sunny to partially shaded spots with medium soil, this perennial is easy to grow and highly productive. Loved since ancient times for its refreshing flavor and health-boosting properties, French sorrel is a delightful addition your orchard and wild edible landscape.
Botanical Name: *Rumex scutatus*
Top Varieties: Common, Round-Leaved
Care: French sorrel flourishes in sunny and partially shaded spots with rich, moist, well-drained soil. Trim flowering stalks as they appear to prevent bolting and extend the harvest season. If left to bolt, the plant's tall seed head can add a whimsical touch to the garden, but the leaves may toughen and lose some tanginess.
Harvest/Enjoyment: For the best flavor, harvest young leaves regularly throughout the growing season. Mature leaves can still be used, but their texture and taste are less delicate. After bolting, the tall seed heads can be cut back to encourage fresh leaf growth or left for visual interest. Add sorrel's lemony zing to salads, blend it into creamy soups, or use it to brighten a sauce—it's a versatile herb that brings a bold, refreshing flavor to any dish.

PLANNING AND GROWING

Light: Full Sun, Part Shade
Soil Moisture: Dry, Medium
Height and Width: 1'–3' (30.5–91.4cm) x 10"–12" (25.4–30.5cm)
Growth Rate: 3 (Moderate)
Time to Harvest: 4–6 weeks
Common Pests and Diseases: Generally pest-free; occasional leaf spot.

PLANTING INSTRUCTIONS

Period: Early spring to late summer (50°F–75°F [10°C–24°C])
Method: Transplant
Depth: Plant at the same depth as in the pot.
Spacing: Transplant one plant every 12" (30.5cm).

Spinach

Spinach loves cool weather and grows fast, delivering nourishing, tender greens before the summer heat.

QUICK REFERENCE

Type: Vegetable
Lifecycle: Annual
Applications: Container, Raised Bed, In-Ground Garden
Disease Resistant: No
Pest Resistant: No
Pampering Need: 3 (Moderate)
Harvest Ease: 4 (Easy)
Parts Used: Leaves
Harvest Period: June, September–October

Personality: A nutrient-rich, fast-growing companion that wilts at the mere thought of summer heat.
Description: The nutrient-packed champion of leafy greens, spinach is a cool-weather favorite that grows quickly and abundantly, thriving in sunny to partially shaded spots with rich soil. Spinach has been cherished since ancient times for its ability to invigorate and nourish, making it a cornerstone of any nutrient-dense garden. This versatile annual is perfect for salads, smoothies, and sautés.
Botanical Name: *Spinacia oleracea*
Top Varieties: Bloomsdale Long Standing, Red Kitten, Space, Tyee
Care: Spinach thrives in cool weather and fertile, well-drained soil. Sow seeds directly into the ground as soon as the soil is workable in early spring, or wait for the cool days of fall. Avoid summer planting, as heat causes spinach to bolt quickly, leading to bitter leaves. Water consistently to keep the soil evenly moist and the leaves tender. Once seedlings reach 2"–3" (5.1–7.6cm) tall, mulch lightly with straw to retain moisture and cool the soil. For continuous harvests, sow new seeds every two weeks while the growing season is cool.

Harvest/Enjoyment: Harvest spinach by picking outer leaves as needed, leaving the center to continue growing; or snip the entire plants when they are full and lush. For the sweetest flavor, harvest early in the morning when the leaves are cool and crisp. Enjoy the first tender leaves fresh in a garden salad, blend them into a smoothie for a nutrient-packed boost, or sauté them with garlic for a simple, savory side.

PLANNING AND GROWING

Light: Full Sun, Part Shade

Soil Moisture: Medium

Height and Width: 6"–12" (15.2–30.5cm) x 6"–8" (15.2–20.3cm)

Growth Rate: 4 (Fast)

Time to Harvest: 6–8 weeks

Common Pests and Diseases: Leaf miners (insects creating tunnels in leaves) and downy mildew. Deer and rabbits may eat foliage.

PLANTING INSTRUCTIONS

Period: Early spring (45°F–65°F [7°C–18°C])

Method: Seed

Depth: Bury seeds ½" (1.3cm) deep.

Spacing: Plant one seed every 2"–4" (5.1–10.2cm) in rows 12" (30.5cm) apart.

Squash, Summer

Zucchini goes wild when happy and healthy, thriving with little effort and filling your kitchen with more squash than you thought possible.

QUICK REFERENCE

Type: Vegetable

Lifecycle: Annual

Applications: Raised Bed, In-Ground Garden

Disease Resistant: No

Pest Resistant: No

Pampering Need: 3 (Moderate)

Harvest Ease: 5 (Very Easy)

Parts Used: Fruit

Harvest Period: August–September

Personality: The prolific garden comedian that grows fast, thrives with little fuss, and keeps your kitchen endlessly supplied all summer long.

Description: A garden favorite, summer squash is a low-maintenance and prolific yielder that thrives in sunny spots with medium-to-wet soil. This quick-growing annual is famous for its generous harvests and versatile fruit, ideal for grilling, sautéing, or baking. Several kinds of squash fall under this category—most notably, zucchini. It symbolizes abundance and resilience, making it a staple for gardens large and small, while its rapid growth and playful nature keep gardeners on their toes.

Botanical Name: *Cucurbita pepo*

Top Varieties: Black Beauty, Gold Rush, Spineless Perfection

Care: Summer squash thrives in full sun and fertile, well-drained soil. To prevent powdery mildew, choose resistant varieties and ensure good air circulation. Another method is to water deeply and less frequently, focusing on the soil rather than the leaves. Uneven watering can cause fruits to deform, so aim for steady moisture, especially during flowering and fruiting stages.

Sow seeds directly into the soil once the danger of frost has passed, spacing them 3'–4' (0.9–1.2m) apart. Plant seeds 1" (2.5cm) deep and keep the soil consistently moist until germination, which typically occurs within 5–10 days. Consider starting seeds in early July to avoid the squash vine borer's egg-laying season; you'll still get a bountiful harvest without worrying about these common pests. If your garden space is tight, consider staking your zucchini. Place a sturdy 2'–3' (61–91.4cm) stake next to the plant at the time of seeding and gently tie the main stalk to it with twine as it grows. This keeps the fruit off the ground, saves space, and improves airflow.

Once plants reach 3"–4" (7.6–10.2cm) tall, spread a deep layer of straw mulch around the base. This helps retain soil moisture, suppress weeds, and protect the fruit from direct contact with the soil, reducing the risk of rot. Add compost before applying straw and again mid-season to keep plants vigorous and productive.

Harvest/Enjoyment: Regular harvesting is key to maintaining bountiful yields. Pick zucchini when they're young and tender, typically 6"–8" (15.2–20.3cm) long. At this stage, their skin is soft, seeds are edible, and no peeling is required. Check daily. They grow fast, and missing a couple days could mean discovering a baseball bat. While larger zucchinis are still edible, they require peeling and deseeding, and their flavor is less sweet. Whether you're grilling, stuffing, or spiralizing, zucchini's versatility will keep your meals fresh and exciting all season long.

PLANNING AND GROWING

Light: Full Sun

Soil Moisture: Medium

Height and Width: 18" (45.7cm) x 4' (1.2m)

Growth Rate: 4 (Fast)

Time to Harvest: 7–9 weeks

Common Pests and Diseases: Squash bugs and powdery mildew. Deer may eat foliage and fruit.

PLANTING INSTRUCTIONS

Period: Mid- to late spring (65°F–85°F [18°C–29.5°C])

Method: Seed

Depth: Bury seeds 1" (2.5cm) deep.

Spacing: Plant two seeds per hill, with hills 3'–4' (0.9–1.2m) apart.

Squash, Winter

Compact honeynut squash climbs a trellis with ease, offering sweet, hearty harvests without letting vines take over your garden.

QUICK REFERENCE

Type: Vegetable

Lifecycle: Annual

Applications: Raised Bed, In-Ground Garden

Disease Resistant: No

Pest Resistant: No

Pampering Need: 4 (Easy)

Harvest Ease: 4 (Easy)

Parts Used: Fruit

Harvest Period: October

Personality: The patient provider that takes its time but offers sweet, hearty rewards to sustain you through the colder months.

Description: Winter squash is a dependable crop that turns a little patience into nutrient-rich, long-lasting fruit. Thriving in sunny spots with medium-to-wet soil, these sprawling annuals produce sweet, dense flesh that's perfect for roasting, soups, or pies. Pumpkins, a close cousin, add seasonal charm and culinary versatility. Symbolizing sustenance and abundance, winter squash is both a practical and comforting addition to your garden.

Botanical Name: *Cucurbita moschata*

Top Varieties:

- **Winter Squash:** Blue Hubbard, Bonbon, Butterscotch (miniature), Honeynut (miniature), Waltham Butternut
- **Pumpkin:** Baby Bear (miniature), New England Pie, Wee-B-Little (ornamental)

Care: Winter squash loves full sun and nutrient-rich, well-drained soil. Before seeding, layer on generous amounts of compost to provide the nutrients needed by these heavy feeders. Direct-sow seeds in late spring, after the danger of frost has passed, spacing them about 3'–4' (0.9–1.2m) apart for bush varieties or 6'–8' (1.8–2.4m) apart for vining types. Consider planting in early July to avoid the squash vine borer's egg-laying season. Just be sure to check the time to harvest on your seed packet to ensure there's still time for a full harvest before late fall.

Water deeply and consistently, focusing on the soil rather than the leaves to prevent fungal diseases like powdery mildew. Consistent moisture is especially important during flowering and fruit development to prevent splitting or irregular growth. Once plants reach 2"–3" (5.1–7.6cm) tall, mulch deeply with straw to retain soil moisture, suppress weeds, and protect the sprawling vines. If space is limited, train the vines onto a sturdy trellis. This saves room and keeps the fruit off the ground, reducing the risk of rot. Tie them to slings on the trellis to support heavy fruit and prevent stem breakage. Winter squash is largely self-sufficient once established.

Harvest/Enjoyment: Allow squash to fully ripen on the vine; they're ready to harvest when their rinds are tough and stems have dried and turned woody. Use pruners to cut the stem 2"–3" (5.1–7.6cm) from the fruit and handle them carefully to prevent bruising. Store your harvest in a cool, dry, well-ventilated place, and they'll keep for months, providing a steady supply of nourishing meals through winter.

PLANNING AND GROWING

Light: Full Sun

Soil Moisture: Medium, Wet

Height and Width: 18" (45.7cm) tall

Growth Rate: 3 (Moderate)

Time to Harvest: 12–15 weeks

Common Pests and Diseases: Squash vine borer and powdery mildew. Deer may eat foliage and fruit.

PLANTING INSTRUCTIONS

Period: Mid- to late spring (65°F–85°F [18°C–29.5°C])

Method: Seed

Depth: Bury seeds 1" (2.5cm) deep.

Spacing: Plant three seeds per hill, with hills 4'–5' (1.2–1.5m) apart.

Wee-B-Little pumpkins are so productive there's always extra to share, making them perfect for autumn gift-giving.

Strawberry

Sweet, juicy, and irresistible: garden strawberries bring classic flavor to beds or containers.

QUICK REFERENCE

Type: Herb
Lifecycle: Perennial (Zones 3–9)
Applications: Container, Orchard, Wild Edible, Sensory Garden, Ground Cover
Sensory Experiences: Taste
Disease Resistant: No
Pest Resistant: No
Pampering Need: 5 (Very Easy)
Harvest Ease: 4 (Easy)
Parts Used: Berries, Leaves
Harvest Period: June–October

Personality: A sweet and versatile friend, strawberries come in many forms, each offering unique beauty, flavor, and function to your garden.

Description: Strawberries are a delightful addition to any garden, providing delicious berries and aesthetic charm. The tiny, flavor-packed alpine strawberries; the juicy and iconic garden strawberries; and the spreading ground cover of wild strawberries are all adaptable and rewarding.

- **Garden Strawberry:** The classic strawberry thrives in sunny in-ground or raised beds, producing large, sweet berries beloved by gardeners. They can also thrive in containers, but keep them close to your travel paths and water spigot to ensure consistently moist soil. They may struggle to yield fruit in densely planted areas like orchards, so it's often best to give them a dedicated space. Garden strawberries are categorized by their bearing times:
    - **June Bearing:** They produce a single large crop in early summer (June), typically over two to three weeks. These are perfect if you want a large harvest for preserving, freezing, or enjoying fresh at a predictable time.
    - **Ever Bearing:** These strawberries provide two to three smaller harvests, usually in early summer, mid-summer, and early fall. They are low-maintenance and ideal if you prefer a few predictable harvests without frequent upkeep.
    - **Day Neutral:** They produce berries continuously throughout the growing season as long as temperatures remain between 35°F and 85°F (1.5°C and 29.5°C). Ever-bearing varieties may be a better choice if you prefer less constant management and harvesting.
- **Alpine Strawberry:** Compact and elegant, alpine strawberries are perfect for small spaces, bed borders, or pathways. They don't spread like other types, making them an ideal choice for a tidy, low-maintenance garden. Their tiny, sweet berries ripen continuously throughout the growing season, offering delightful treats for snacking or garnishing.
- **Wild Strawberry:** This tiny woodland gem is a resilient ground cover, spreading naturally to fill bare spaces while conserving moisture and building soil health. They grow wonderfully with Dutch white clover, self-heal, violets, and creeping thyme, contributing to a dense, moisture-conserving, soil-building, dynamic ground cover. Although their berries are often less flavorful, they add charm and functionality to your landscape, weaving effortlessly between plants without overwhelming them.

Botanical Name: *Fragaria* spp.

Top Varieties:

- **Garden:** Albion (day-neutral), Earliglow (early June-bearing), Lateglow (late June-bearing), Ozark Beauty (ever-bearing), Seascape (day-neutral), Surecrop (mid-season June-bearing), Tristar (ever-bearing)
- **Alpine:** Bowlenzauber, Pineapple Crush, Reine des Vallees
- **Wild:** No named varieties

Alpine strawberries stay neatly where you plant them, delivering tiny, sweet berries without the rambling habit of their wilder cousins.

Alpine strawberries add a burst of sweetness and elegance to salads all season long.

Care: Strawberries thrive in different settings but share some common care practices. Most strawberries prefer full sun, though alpine and wild varieties can tolerate partial shade. Plant in rich, well-drained soil, and mulch around plants to retain moisture and protect roots. Water deeply and consistently, but avoid wetting leaves to prevent fungal diseases.

- **Garden:** Feed garden strawberries with a generous layer of compost in spring and after the first harvest to encourage continued fruiting. To keep berries yields high, thin and separate plants every two to three years. Remove older plants and replant their young offshoots—small, rooted stems called "runners" that grow from the parent plant—in fresh soil to renew vigor.
- **Alpine:** These tidy plants require little maintenance beyond consistent watering and mulching. They don't spread by runners, making them ideal for tight spaces.

- **Wild:** Allow these strawberries to spread naturally and form a lush ground cover. They are exceptionally low-maintenance and thrive in less fertile soils.

Harvest/Enjoyment: Strawberries are a joy to grow, a treat to eat, and a way to observe nature as it happily meanders through your garden. In addition to delightful berries, the leaves of all three types are edible. They add a subtly earthy flavor to teas or can be used as a nutritious garnish.

- **Garden:** Pick plump, bright red berries at peak ripeness. Enjoy them fresh, turn them into jam, or freeze for later use.
- **Alpine:** Harvest tiny berries when fully red and fragrant. Pop one into your mouth for an intense burst of sweetness.
- **Wild:** While their berries are often mealy and bland, their lush foliage and spreading nature bring beauty to your garden while enhancing soil life for their overstory companions.

PLANNING AND GROWING

Light: Full Sun, Part Shade
Soil Moisture: Medium
Height and Width: 10" (25.4cm) tall
Growth Rate: 3 (Moderate)
Time to Harvest: 6–8 months
Common Pests and Diseases: Strawberry weevil and gray mold (fungal disease that causes fruit rot). Deer, rabbits, and birds may eat fruit and foliage.

PLANTING INSTRUCTIONS

Period: Early spring (50°F–70°F [10°C–21°C])
Method: Transplant
Depth: Plant at the same depth as in the pot.
Spacing: Transplant 6"–8" (15.2–20.3cm) apart in rows 12" (30.5cm) apart.

Sunflower

From towering giants to compact blooms for containers, sunflowers brighten any space while feeding pollinators, birds, and your spirit.

QUICK REFERENCE

Type: Herb
Lifecycle: Annual
Applications: Container, Raised Bed, In-Ground Garden, Sensory Garden
Sensory Experiences: Sight
Disease Resistant: No
Pest Resistant: No
Pampering Need: 5 (Very Easy)
Harvest Ease: 3 (Moderate)
Parts Used: Seeds

Personality: The sunny showstopper that dazzles with bold blooms and edible seeds.

Description: Sunflowers bring warmth and vibrance to your garden as towering giants or compact dwarfs. Thriving in sunny spots with medium soil, these annual favorites attract pollinators, delight birds, and provide a bounty of edible seeds. Watching birds acrobatically harvest seeds from the seed heads is entertainment for all ages. Symbolizing adoration and loyalty, sunflowers add a bold, cheerful presence while offering abundance to wildlife.

Botanical Name: *Helianthus annuus*

Top Varieties:

- **Full-Sized:** Autumn Beauty, Lemon Queen, Mammoth, Skyscraper, Titan
- **Dwarf:** Little Becka, Pacino, Sunspot, Teddy Bear

Care: Sunflowers thrive in full sun and well-drained soil, needing minimal maintenance once established. Sow seeds directly into the soil after the last frost, spacing them according to their variety: 2' (61cm) apart for tall types and closer for dwarfs. Water deeply during their early growth phase to help establish strong roots, but they'll tolerate dry conditions once mature.

Taller varieties may need staking to keep them upright, especially in windy areas. Adding compost mid-season can encourage impressive growth in full-sized varieties. Dwarf varieties are perfect for containers or smaller spaces, bringing the same sunny joy in a more compact form.

Sunflowers have a delightful habit of self-seeding, often gifting you with cheerful volunteers the following spring. Keep in mind that hybrid varieties are unlikely to produce offspring identical to the originals, but the surprises can add curious charm to your garden. Simply thin out unwanted seedlings early on, allowing the chosen ones to flourish. It's nature's way of sharing abundance, giving you the pleasure of sunflowers without the effort of replanting.

Harvest/Enjoyment: Harvest seeds when the flower heads droop and the seeds have fully darkened. Roast them for a delicious snack or let the birds enjoy them straight from the flower. Pause to appreciate the sunshiny joy these blooms bring, feeding appreciative birds and pollinators while brightening your garden.

PLANNING AND GROWING

Light: Full Sun
Soil Moisture: Medium
Height and Width: 3'–15' (0.9–4.6m) x 1' (0.3m)
Growth Rate: 4 (Fast)
Time to Harvest: 8–12 weeks
Common Pests and Diseases: Aphids and downy mildew. Deer may eat young plants. Birds eat seeds.

PLANTING INSTRUCTIONS

Period: Mid- to late spring (65°F–85°F [18°C–29.5°C])
Method: Seed
Depth: Bury seeds 1" (2.5cm) deep.
Spacing: Plant one seed every 12"–18" (30.5–45.7cm).

Sweet Potato, Ornamental

Ornamental sweet potato vines spill gracefully from containers or beds, adding vibrant color and lush texture wherever they grow.

QUICK REFERENCE

Type: Herb
Lifecycle: Annual
Applications: Container, Sensory Garden, Ground Cover
Sensory Experiences: Sight
Disease Resistant: No
Pest Resistant: No
Pampering Need: 4 (Easy)

Personality: The vibrant tropical charmer with cascading vines that brings color and elegance to any space.
Description: A captivating mix of beauty and utility, ornamental sweet potatoes feature stunning, colorful foliage that spills gracefully from containers or weaves across garden beds. Thriving in sunny spots with medium-to-dry soil, these vigorous growers make for an excellent ground cover or accent plant in hanging baskets and along walls.
Botanical Name: *Ipomoea batatas*
Top Varieties: Blackie, Marguerite, Tricolor
Care: Ornamental sweet potatoes thrive in full sun and loose, well-drained soil, soaking up warmth like the tropical beauties they are. Water consistently, especially during dry spells, but avoid overwatering, as soggy soil can lead to root rot. Mulch around the base to retain moisture, keep the soil cool, and suppress weeds. These vigorous vines grow quickly, so give them plenty of room to spread or train them to climb for added drama.
Harvest/Enjoyment: Ornamental sweet potatoes bring a dynamic dimension to your garden with their draping and meandering vines. Let them spill over the edges of containers, cascade down walls, or weave gracefully through garden beds. Their vibrant foliage adds layers of movement and texture to your space. Even as the growing season winds down, their flowing presence leaves a lasting impression of beauty and abundance.

PLANNING AND GROWING

Light: Full Sun, Part Shade
Soil Moisture: Dry, Medium
Height and Width: 8" (20.3cm) x 3'–5' (0.9–1.5m) trailing vines
Growth Rate: 3 (Moderate)
Common Pests and Diseases: Sweet potato weevil and fusarium wilt (fungal disease that causes plant wilting). Deer may eat foliage.

PLANTING INSTRUCTIONS

Period: Mid- to late spring (65°F–85°F [18°C–29.5°C])
Method: Transplant
Depth: Plant at the same depth as in the pot.
Spacing: Transplant one plant every 8"–12" (20.3–30.5cm).

Swiss Chard

Swiss chard's colorful stems and nutrient-rich leaves bring vibrant beauty and versatile nutrition to every meal.

QUICK REFERENCE

Type: Vegetable
Lifecycle: Biennial (grown as annual)
Applications: Container, Raised Bed, In-Ground Garden
Disease Resistant: No
Pest Resistant: No
Pampering Need: 4 (Easy)
Harvest Ease: 5 (Very Easy)
Parts Used: Leaves, Stalks
Harvest Period: June–November

Personality: The big-stemmed beauty that keeps your garden vibrant and your meals healthy.
Description: A dazzling and nutritious green, Swiss chard is the artist of the garden with its jewel-toned stems and leafy tops. Thriving in sunny to partially shaded spots with medium soil, this fast-growing biennial is ideal for gardens of any size. Historically celebrated as a symbol of vitality, Swiss chard is a versatile crop that nourishes both the body and the landscape, offering beauty, resilience, and endless culinary possibilities.
Botanical Name: *Beta vulgaris* subsp. *vulgaris*
Top Varieties: Bright Lights, Fordhook Giant
Care: Swiss chard is remarkably low-maintenance, thriving in full sun to partial shade and rich, well-drained soil. Sow seeds after the last frost. For baby greens, plant densely in rows, thinning as needed. Once seedlings reach 2"–3" (5.1–7.6cm) tall, spread straw mulch around them to conserve moisture and suppress weeds. Consistent watering keeps leaves tender and flavorful. A mid-season layer of compost fuels continued growth.
Harvest/Enjoyment: For baby greens, harvest when leaves are 4"–5" (10.2–12.7cm) tall and let missed ones mature into larger plants. When harvesting mature leaves, focus on the outer stalks, leaving the inner growth intact for continuous production. The stalks themselves are as delightful as the leaves—crunchy and vibrant, they can be dipped, chopped into soups, or sautéed.

Swiss chard's bright hues bring joy to your garden and your plate, serving as a cheerful reminder that healthy choices can also be beautiful and delicious.

PLANNING AND GROWING

Light: Full Sun
Soil Moisture: Medium
Height and Width: 1'–2' (30.5–61cm) x 1' (30.5cm)
Growth Rate: 4 (Fast)
Time to Harvest: 8–10 weeks
Common Pests and Diseases: Leaf miners (insects creating tunnels in leaves) and Cercospora leaf spot (fungal disease that causes circular spots). Deer and rabbits may eat foliage.

PLANTING INSTRUCTIONS

Period: Early spring to early summer (50°F–75°F [10°C–24°C])
Method: Seed
Depth: Bury seeds ½" (1.3cm) deep.
Spacing: Plant one seed every 6"–8" (15.2–20.3cm) in rows 12"–18" (30.5–45.7cm) apart.

Tatsoi

Tatsoi grows quickly into tender, spoon-shaped greens that are perfect for salads, stir-fries, and adding a mild, peppery flavor to your plate.

QUICK REFERENCE

Type: Vegetable
Lifecycle: Annual
Applications: Container, Raised Bed, In-Ground Garden, Sensory Garden
Sensory Experiences: Taste
Disease Resistant: No
Pest Resistant: No
Pampering Need: 4 (Easy)
Harvest Ease: 4 (Easy)
Parts Used: Leaves
Harvest Period: May–October

Personality: The mild-mannered rosette that grows quickly and offers tender, spoon-shaped greens with a gentle peppery bite.
Description: A compact and elegant Asian green, tatsoi thrives in sunny to partially shaded spots with medium soil, offering spinach-like leaves perfect for salads, stir-fries, or soups. Its fast-growing nature makes it a favorite for small spaces, containers, or as a

gap-filler in your garden. It is revered for its peppery, nutty flavor and beautiful rosette shape.
Botanical Name: *Brassica rapa* var. *rosularis*
Top Varieties: Common Tatsoi
Care: Tatsoi thrives in cool weather and rich, moist soil, making it a perfect addition to your spring and fall planting schedules. Sow seeds in shallow rows, spacing them about 1"–2" (2.5–5.1cm) apart. Thin seedlings to 4"–6" (10.2–15.2cm) to allow the rosettes to form fully. Mulch lightly to keep roots cool and retain moisture, especially during dry spells.

Avoid planting tatsoi during summer heat, as it bolts quickly, setting seed and getting less tasty in warm conditions. Water consistently to ensure tender leaves. Its shallow roots mean it's a great candidate for interplanting with taller crops or roots, as it won't compete for water or nutrients.
Harvest/Enjoyment: Harvest tatsoi by picking individual leaves as needed or by cutting the entire rosette at its base when it's full and lush. The leaves are tender and mild, perfect for adding to fresh salads or lightly wilting in stir-fries.

PLANNING AND GROWING

Light: Full Sun, Part Shade
Soil Moisture: Medium
Height and Width: 6" (15.2cm) x 8"–12" (20.3–30.5cm)
Growth Rate: 5 (Very Fast)
Time to Harvest: 6–8 weeks
Common Pests and Diseases: Flea beetles and downy mildew. Deer and rabbits may eat foliage.

PLANTING INSTRUCTIONS

Period: Early spring or late summer (50°F–70°F [10°C–21°C])
Method: Seed
Depth: Bury seeds ¼" (6.4mm) deep.
Spacing: Plant one seed every 4"–6" (10.2–15.2cm) in rows 12" (30.5cm) apart.

Thyme

Whether creeping as ground cover or standing tall as a culinary herb, thyme weaves fragrance and flavor into every corner of your garden.

QUICK REFERENCE

Type: Herb
Lifecycle: Perennial (Zones 5–9)
Applications: Container, Orchard, Wild Edible, Sensory Garden, Ground Cover
Sensory Experiences: Scent, Sight, Taste
Disease Resistant: Yes
Pest Resistant: Yes
Pampering Need: 5 (Very Easy)
Harvest Ease: 4 (Easy)
Parts Used: Leaves
Harvest Period: April–November

Personality: A fragrant companion that weaves beauty and flavor into your garden as a stout culinary herb or a resilient ground cover.
Description: Thyme is a versatile and aromatic perennial that earns its place in both your kitchen and your garden. With its woody stems and tiny, fragrant leaves, thyme offers culinary charm while supporting pollinators and improving your soil. Historically associated with courage and healing, this herb provides flavorful sprigs for cooking.

Creeping thyme forms a low, aromatic carpet, ideal for an orchard ground cover, pathway, or filling cracks between stepping stones. Culinary thyme stands upright, making it a bit easier to harvest. Together, they bring both practical and sensory delight to your garden.
Botanical Name: *Thymus* spp.
Top Varieties:
- **Creeping:** Caraway
- **Culinary:** English Thyme

Care: Both creeping and culinary thyme are hardy and low-maintenance, preferring full sun and thriving in poor soils where other plants may struggle. Water sparingly; thyme is drought-tolerant and overwatering can lead to root rot. Mulch lightly with gravel or coarse sand to improve drainage and keep plants happy.
Harvest/Enjoyment: Gently snip sprigs as needed, cutting just above a leaf node to encourage regrowth. Harvest leaves throughout the growing season for fresh flavor in soups, stews, and roasted dishes. As you harvest, crush a leaf between your fingers to release its signature earthy aroma—it's a small but powerful moment of sensory connection.

Creeping thyme is more than an edible ground cover. Its flowers attract bees and butterflies, adding life and movement to your garden. Walk upon this fragrant mat and enjoy the calming strength it brings, connecting you to the small joys of tending your garden.

PLANNING AND GROWING

Light: Full Sun, Part Shade

Soil Moisture: Dry, Medium

Height and Width: 4"–12" (10.2–30.5cm) tall

Growth Rate: 3 (Moderate)

Time to Harvest: 8–12 weeks

Common Pests and Diseases: Generally pest-free; occasional root rot in poorly drained soils.

PLANTING INSTRUCTIONS

Period: Early to mid-spring (60°F–75°F [15.5°C–24°C])

Method: Transplant

Depth: Plant at the same depth as in the pot.

Spacing: Transplant one plant every 8"–12" (20.3–30.5cm). Plant in a container to prevent spreading.

Tomato

Tomatoes come in every shape, size, color, and flavor. They offer endless possibilities for fresh snacking, sauces, and summer abundance.

QUICK REFERENCE

Type: Vegetable

Lifecycle: Annual

Applications: Container, Raised Bed, In-Ground Garden, Sensory Garden

Sensory Experiences: Taste, Sight

Disease Resistant: No

Pest Resistant: No

Pampering Need: 3 (Moderate)

Harvest Ease: 5 (Very Easy)

Parts Used: Fruit

Harvest Period: July–October

Personality: The summer superstar, bursting with juicy flavor and sunshine; and bringing abundance to every garden.

Description: Tomatoes are the heroes of the garden, offering bold flavors for everything from sauces to sandwiches to fresh-off-the-vine snacking. Thriving in sunny locations with fertile, well-drained soil, these fast-growing annuals are equally at home in containers and beds. A symbol of prosperity and health, tomatoes are a beloved staple, rewarding your care with vibrant harvests and a sense of connection to the rhythms of summer.

Tomatoes come in many shapes, sizes, and flavors, each perfect for different gardens and needs. If you feel overwhelmed by all the varieties available at the farmer's market or nursery, you're not alone. This plant often dominates the storefront stage due to its popularity and versatility. Use this simple guide to help you decide:

- **Fruit Size:**
    - **Cherry and Grape:** Small, snackable, and prolific. Perfect for fresh eating or salads with minimal prep.
    - **Saladette:** Medium-sized and versatile for fresh use or light cooking, such as salsas.
    - **Slicing:** Large, juicy tomatoes ideal for sandwiches or caprese salads.
    - **Paste:** Dense, meaty fruits with low water content. Great for sauces or canning.
- **Fruiting Time:**
    - **Determinate:** All fruit ripens at once. Great for preserving or if you prefer shorter harvest windows.
    - **Indeterminate:** Produces fruit continuously all season. Ideal for fresh harvests throughout the growing season.
- **Growth Size:**
    - **Dwarf/Patio:** Compact and perfect for containers or small spaces. Easy to manage.
    - **Full Size:** Larger plants needing support, which produces more fruit over time. Best for a large space with a trellis or cage.
- **Color and Flavor:**
    - **Red:** Balanced, classic tomato flavor. Perfect for all uses.
    - **Yellow/Orange:** Mildly sweet and low in acidity. Great for fresh eating.
    - **Purple/Black:** Rich, earthy flavor. Ideal for unique dishes.
    - **Green:** Tangy and zesty, perfect for salsas or frying.
    - **Striped/Bicolor:** Sweet and complex. Adds unique beauty to the garden and any dish.
- **Hybrid vs. Heirloom:**
    - **Hybrid:** Crossbred for disease resistance and consistent yields. Perfect for busy gardeners who want reliability with less effort.
    - **Heirloom:** Traditional varieties passed down through generations. Known for unique flavors and colors, but they may need a little more care to thrive compared to hybrids. Great for experimenting, but often less resilient than hybrids.
- **Other Tips:**
    - Look for disease-resistant and crack-resistant varieties to reduce maintenance and maximize yield. Hybrids often provide these traits, making them an excellent choice for a low-maintenance garden.
    - Start small with one or two types that suit your space and needs, then expand as you grow your confidence.

Botanical Name: *Solanum lycopersicum*

Top Varieties:

- **Cherry and Grape:**
  - **Full Size:** Sungold, Sweet 100
  - **Dwarf/Patio:** Sweet Baby Girl
- **Saladette:**
  - **Full Size:** Juliet, San Marzano
  - **Dwarf/Patio:** Dwarf Hannah's Prize, Dwarf Firebird Sweet, Dwarf Sweet Scarlet
- **Slicing:**
  - **Full Size:** Better Boy, Big Beef, Celebrity
  - **Dwarf/Patio:** New Girl

Care: Tomatoes thrive in full sun and fertile, well-drained soil. Space in-ground, full-sized tomatoes 3'–4' (0.9–1.2m) apart, while patio/dwarf varieties can be spaced about 2' (61cm) apart.

Unlike most plants that are planted at the same depth as their pot, tomatoes benefit from being buried deeply. Remove the bottom one or two branches of a tall seedling and bury the stem deeply, leaving 1"–2" (2.5–5.1cm) of space between the soil and the first remaining stem. The buried stem will develop additional roots, creating a stronger and more resilient plant.

After planting, top the soil with compost to fuel initial growth, and repeat mid-season to keep the plant vigorous. For patio or dwarf varieties, use a large container; 3 gallons (11.5L) is the absolute minimum, though 5 gallons (19L) or larger is ideal to ensure healthy root development. Apply a thick layer of straw mulch around the base of the plant to retain soil moisture, suppress weeds, and prevent soil from splashing onto leaves during watering or rain—a key step in reducing soil-borne diseases.

Provide sturdy support for your tomatoes. Full-sized plants need a heavy-duty trellis, large cage, or sturdy stake to accommodate their vigorous growth and heavy fruit. Avoid flimsy wire cages—they can buckle under the weight of a thriving tomato. If using stakes, plan to prune and tie regularly to keep the plant manageable.

Pruning helps direct energy toward fruit production and improves airflow, reducing the risk of disease. Start by removing the lowest branches once the plant reaches 1'–2' (30.5–61cm) tall to keep soil from splashing up onto the leaves. For full-sized tomatoes, consider removing "suckers"—the small shoots that grow between the main stem and branches—to focus the plant's energy on fewer, larger fruits. If pruning feels overwhelming, let your plant grow freely and you'll still enjoy a great harvest.

Water deeply at the base of the plant, avoiding wetting the leaves, which can encourage fungal diseases. Consistent watering is key to preventing cracked fruits. Tomatoes prefer a steady supply of moisture rather than irregular, heavy watering.

Harvest/Enjoyment: Harvest tomatoes when they are fully colored and firm, yet slightly yielding to the touch. For the freshest experience, pick them in the morning when they're juiciest. Slice one straight off the vine, sprinkle it with a pinch of salt, and savor the pure essence of summer in every bite. For an aromatic garden snack, wrap a slice in fresh basil, thyme, or oregano leaves; it's a simple, flavorful treat that connects you to the care that brought it to life.

Plant tomatoes deep by stripping lower leaves and setting seedlings in a deep hole to encourage strong roots and healthier growth.

Cover tomato stems well, leaving just the top above soil. Deep planting builds sturdy roots for a thriving, productive plant.

PLANNING AND GROWING

Light: Full Sun

Soil Moisture: Medium

Height and Width: 2'–10' (0.6–3m) x 3'–5' (0.9–1.5m)

Growth Rate: 3 (Moderate)

Time to Harvest: 9–12 weeks

Common Pests and Diseases: Tomato hornworm and blight. Deer may eat foliage and fruit.

PLANTING INSTRUCTIONS

Period: Mid- to late spring (60°F–85°F [15.5°C–29.5°C])

Method: Transplant

Depth: Transplant deep; bury two-thirds of the stem.

Spacing: Plant 3'–5' (0.9–1.5m) apart with sturdy cages or stakes.

Violet

Violets likely already brighten your lawn, but if not, they're easy to seed—adding beauty, a pollinator habitat, and edible blooms.

QUICK REFERENCE

Type: Herb
Lifecycle: Perennial (Zones 3–9)
Applications: Container, Orchard, Wild Edible, Ground Cover
Sensory Experiences: Sight
Disease Resistant: Yes
Pest Resistant: Yes
Pampering Need: 5 (Very Easy)
Harvest Ease: 3 (Moderate)
Parts Used: Flowers, Leaves
Harvest Period: April–June

Personality: The gentle groundcover that sprinkles your garden with bright edible blooms and timeless charm.
Description: Violets bring delicate beauty and edible versatility to your garden with their heart-shaped leaves and vibrant, sweetly scented flowers. Thriving in sunny to shaded areas with medium soil, these hardy perennials are low-maintenance, making them ideal for orchards, lawns, or anywhere needing a touch of whimsy.

Paired with Dutch white clover, self-heal, wild strawberry, or creeping thyme, violets form a dynamic, soil-building, protective ground cover that's as tough as it is enchanting.

Cherished through history as symbols of love and modesty, violets also provide vital support to pollinators, adding ecological value to their ornamental appeal.
Botanical Names: *Viola tricolor*, *Viola odorata*, *Viola sororia*
Top Varieties: Common Blue typically grows wild and works well. For added color and flair, try these edible varieties: Alba, Freckles, Helen Mount, Johnny Jump-Up, Queen Charlotte.
Care: Violets thrive in partial shade and moist, well-drained soil, though they are adaptable and resilient. Deadhead spent flowers to prolong blooming and allow them to spread naturally for a charming ground cover. Their self-sowing nature means they'll return year after year with minimal effort on your part.
Harvest/Enjoyment: Pick greens and blooms to nibble, garnish desserts, or mix into salads. Their subtle fragrance and vibrant petals are tiny reminders of nature's enduring grace and effortless resilience.

PLANNING AND GROWING

Light: Full Sun, Part Shade
Soil Moisture: Medium
Height and Width: 6"–12" (15.2–30.5cm) tall
Growth Rate: 3 (Moderate)
Time to Harvest: 10–12 weeks
Common Pests and Diseases: Aphids and powdery mildew. Rabbits may nibble on foliage.

PLANTING INSTRUCTIONS

Period: Early spring (50°F–70°F [10°C–21°C])
Method: Seed
Depth: Lightly cover with soil.
Spacing: Scatter seeds lightly and pat down.

Johnny Jump-Ups dazzle with purple and yellow blooms that bring cheerful color to gardens, salads, and desserts.

Yarrow

Yarrow offers reliable medicinal uses, pollinator-friendly blooms, and feathery foliage that strengthens both garden and gardener.

PLANNING AND GROWING

Light: Full Sun, Part Shade
Soil Moisture: Dry
Height and Width: 2'–3' (61–91.4cm) tall
Growth Rate: 3 (Moderate)
Time to Harvest: 10–12 weeks
Common Pests and Diseases: Occasional aphids and powdery mildew.

QUICK REFERENCE

Type: Herb
Lifecycle: Perennial (Zones 3–9)
Applications: Container, Raised Bed, In-Ground Bed, Orchard, Sensory Garden
Sensory Experiences: Scent, Sight, Taste
Disease Resistant: Yes
Pest Resistant: Yes
Pampering Need: 5 (Very Easy)
Harvest Ease: 5 (Very Easy)
Parts Used: Flowers, Leaves
Harvest Period: June–October

PLANTING INSTRUCTIONS

Period: Early spring (60°F–75°F [15.5°C–24°C])
Method: Transplant
Depth: Plant at the same depth as in the pot.
Spacing: Transplant one plant every 18"–24" (45.7–61cm). Plant in a container to prevent spreading.

Personality: The feathery healer that thrives on neglect, offering delicate flowers and ancient remedies.
Description: The hardy healer of the garden, yarrow is a drought-tolerant perennial that flourishes in sunny spots with dry-to-medium soil. Its soft, feathery leaves and cheerful clusters of tiny flowers attract beneficial insects, making it a favorite among pollinators and gardeners. Yarrow's rich history in herbal medicine—where it was used for everything from wound care to digestive aids—has earned it a reputation as a symbol of strength and protection. With its low-maintenance needs and timeless charm, yarrow is a resilient, beautiful companion for any garden.
Botanical Name: *Achillea millefolium*
Top Varieties: Common, Moonshine, Paprika, White Beauty
Care: Yarrow loves full sun and thrives in poor, well-drained soil, making it an ideal choice for tough spots in the garden. Once established, it's highly drought-tolerant and requires minimal care. If desired, deadhead spent flower stalks to encourage continuous blooms. Every few years, divide the clumps in early spring or fall to prevent overcrowding and maintain vigor.
Harvest/Enjoyment: Gather yarrow flowers in the morning just as they begin to bloom for the highest concentration of oils. They are perfect for fresh tea infusions, drying for future use, or creating beautiful arrangements. Its leaves can be crushed fresh and applied to minor cuts to help stop bleeding—a nod to its historical use as a battlefield remedy.

PART V:

RESOURCES

Even the most self-sufficient garden benefits from a few well-chosen tools and materials. This section helps you gather what you need—confidently and intentionally. With the right resources at hand, you'll be equipped to start strong, adapt easily, and enjoy the process from seed to harvest.

CHAPTER 14: GARDEN TOOLBOX

From raking and digging to weeding and watering, well-chosen tools help turn everyday tasks into satisfying moments, making time in the garden feel smoother, simpler, and more enjoyable.

The right tools make gardening easier and more enjoyable. Whether you're tending a few containers on a balcony or shaping a thriving, edible landscape, having the right tools at your fingertips ensures efficiency, reduces frustration, and prevents unnecessary strain on your body.

Stocking your tool shed, storage bin, or garden tote before you start planting will streamline your workflow. Instead of scrambling for a watering can or borrowing a shovel mid-season, everything you need will be ready when you need it.

While it may be tempting to grab the cheapest tools available, investing in the highest quality your budget allows will save you money and effort in the long run. Well-made tools last for years, while flimsy ones break or wear out quickly. Look for solid metal construction, particularly for trowels, hori hori knives, and rakes. A single piece forged (SPF) or full tang tool is far sturdier than one with welded joints that are prone to bending and rusting.

If you're on a budget or simply looking to reduce waste, consider buying secondhand tools. Garage sales, estate sales, consignment shops, and community-sharing platforms often offer well-crafted tools at a fraction of the cost. Many older tools were built to last and, with a little cleaning, can outperform their modern counterparts.

PROTECTION AND COMFORT

- **Garden Gloves:** Protect hands from blisters, thorns, and rough soil.
- **Garden Kneeling Pad:** Cushions knees while planting or weeding.
- **Garden Seat:** Reduces strain on the back and knees. Some models have wheels for easy mobility.

DIGGING

- **Trowel:** Digging, transplanting, and scooping soil.
- **Hori Hori Knife:** A sturdy, all-purpose, digging and transplanting tool. Opt for one with a full tang, stainless steel blade for durability.
- **Shovel:** A strong, multipurpose digging tool for planting trees, breaking up soil, and moving materials.
- **Flat-Bladed Spade:** Edging garden beds and precise digging tasks.

SOIL ENRICHMENT AND COMPOSTING

- **Compost Sifter:** Separates finished compost from larger, unfinished pieces.
- **Pitchfork:** Loosens compacted soil, incorporates organic matter, and helps turn compost piles.
- **Mulch Fork:** Designed specifically for efficiently scooping mulch.
- **Scoop Shovel or Snow Shovel:** Makes quick work of moving bulk materials like wood chips and compost on solid surfaces.
- **Broadfork:** A costly but worthwhile investment for large, in-ground beds. Its deep tines effectively loosen compacted soil without disturbing soil structure.

This low, wheeled garden chair might look simple, but it can make a big difference by reducing strain on your back and knees while keeping you comfortable during planting, weeding, or harvesting.

When possible, choose tools with single-piece construction—like this trowel—for strength and longevity.

The hori hori knife handles digging, cutting, planting, and weeding all in one sturdy tool.

WEEDING AND BED MAINTENANCE

- **Hand Rake:** Perfect for smoothing small areas of soil and spreading mulch in tight spaces.
- **Steel Rake:** Spread and level soil, compost, and mulch evenly.
- **Stirrup Hoe:** A push-pull hoe that excels at clearing weeds in beds and pathways with minimal effort. It is ideal for fast, efficient weeding in beds and paths. Replaceable blades extend its lifespan.

WATERING AND TRANSPORTING

- **Bucket:** A 3 or 5 gallon (11.5 or 19L) bucket is versatile for carrying tools, water, or harvested produce. They are often available for free at grocery stores.
- **Watering Can or Hose:** Provides deep watering, essential for young and established plants alike.
- **Watering Wand:** A hose attachment that reduces back strain and directs water to the base of plants. Look for a wand with a mist setting for settling soil on newly planted seeds and seedlings.
- **Wheelbarrow or Garden Cart:** Makes transporting soil, mulch, and plants easier. Two-wheeled carts provide better balance than traditional wheelbarrows.

Perfect for tight spaces, a hand rake helps smooth soil and spread mulch where larger tools can't easily reach.

A stirrup hoe is a sharp, push-pull tool that slices weeds at the root with minimal effort.

PRUNING AND HARVESTING

- **Pruning Snips or Scissors:** Precise for small pruning tasks and herb harvesting.
- **Bypass Pruners:** Essential for annual pruning and maintaining healthy trees and shrubs.
- **Bypass Loppers:** Cuts thicker branches than hand pruners and is useful for thorny shrubs like gooseberries.
- **Pruning Saw:** Handles large branches that are too thick for loppers.
- **Stepladder:** Reach upper branches of fruit trees.

MISCELLANEOUS HANDY TOOLS

- **Measuring Tape:** Ensures accurate spacing of beds and plants. For larger spaces, a flexible tape reel is helpful.
- **Utility Knife:** Easily open bags of soil, compost, and mulch. It's also useful for cutting cardboard when sheet mulching.
- **Rubber Mallet or Hammer:** Pound in garden stakes and level raised beds.
- **Post Pounder:** Drive in steel stakes.
- **Mattock:** Cut bed edges, remove turfgrass, and dig out deep-rooted plants.
- **Wire Brush:** Keep tools in good condition by removing dried soil and rust.
- **Wheeled Plant Dolly:** Makes it easy to reposition heavy containers to follow the sun or move them to shelter during extreme weather.

A sturdy plant dolly lets you move heavy pots with ease, which is ideal for chasing sunlight or tucking plants into protected spots for winter.

CHAPTER 15: MATERIALS PLANNING

A thriving garden starts with the right building blocks, from compost and mulch to seeds and plants. Gathering what you need becomes easy when you know what to look for and where to begin.

Whether you're starting fresh or expanding an existing garden, gathering the right materials, seeds, and plants can feel overwhelming. But don't worry, we'll walk through it together. Whether you're starting a compact container garden, refreshing an in-ground vegetable bed, or adding to an orchard, this section will help you determine what you need, how to calculate the right amounts, and where to source everything efficiently and confidently.

CONTAINER MIX

Container mix, also called potting mix, is specifically designed for plants grown in pots or other containers. It's lightweight, well-draining, and ensures plant roots get the perfect balance of moisture and oxygen. This mix contains organic materials, such as peat moss or coconut coir, which retain moisture without becoming waterlogged. Like raised bed mix, it often includes perlite or vermiculite, which helps improve aeration and drainage.

Avoid using soil from the garden and bagged topsoil. They are too dense for containers and often lead to poor drainage, compacted roots, and slow plant growth.

HOW MUCH DO YOU NEED?

The amount of mix you need depends on the size of your containers. Below are common container sizes with their approximate diameters:

- 1 quart (1L), 5"–6" (12.7–15.2cm) diameter
- 3 quarts (3L), 7"–8" (17.8–20.3cm) diameter
- 4 quarts/1 gallon (4L), 8"–9" (20.3–22.9cm) diameter
- 20 quarts/5 gallons (19L), 11"–12" (27.8–30.5cm) diameter
- 28 quarts/7 gallons (26.5L), 14" (35.6cm) diameter

Most container mix is sold in volumes of 8, 16, and 25 quarts (7.5, 15, and 24L). For example, a single 5 gallon (19L) pot (great for patio tomatoes or several herbs) requires about 20 quarts (19L) of mix, so one 25 quart (24L) bag would fill the pot with plenty left over for smaller containers.

WHERE TO FIND IT

Purchase it at garden centers, nurseries, or home improvement stores. Look for mixes labeled "potting soil" or "container mix." Avoid any labeled as "topsoil" or "garden soil," as these will be too dense for pots.

RAISED BED MIX

Raised bed mix shares similarities with container mix but is designed for larger, open-bottomed beds. It's typically heavier than container mix to anchor plants in place and support robust root systems. This mix contains organic materials like peat moss or coconut coir and compost, creating a nutrient-rich medium that retains moisture better than container mix. Like container mix, it often includes perlite or vermiculite, which help improve aeration and drainage.

HOW MUCH DO YOU NEED?

For a 4' x 8' (1.2 x 2.4m) raised bed that is 7" or 0.58' (17.8cm or 0.18m) tall, multiply the area by the depth to find the volume:

- **Area:** 4' (1.22m) x 8' (2.44m) = 32 ft.^{2} (3m^2)
- **Volume:** 32 ft.^{2} (3m^2) x 0.58' (0.18m) = 18.6 ft.^{3} (0.5m^3)

In this example, you'll need approximately 18.5 ft.^{3} (0.5m^3) of mix. Most raised bed mixes come in 1.5 ft.^{3} (0.04m^3) bags, so you'll need approximately 12 bags to fill your bed (18.5 ÷ 1.5 = 12.3 [0.5 ÷ 0.04 = 12.5]).

WHERE TO FIND IT

Purchase raised bed mix at garden centers, nurseries, or home improvement stores. Avoid any labeled as "topsoil" or "garden soil," as these will be too dense for a raised bed.

RAISED BED KIT

Purchasing a raised bed kit provides a ready-made solution to quickly establish your garden. These kits come in various sizes, styles, and materials, and you'll find them widely available at home improvement stores or online. Most kits can be assembled easily with just basic household tools—or sometimes no tools at all.

If you enjoy woodworking, crafting your own raised beds from cedar lumber or reclaimed materials is a wonderful DIY alternative. This allows you to tailor the design to fit your space, style, and planting dreams. For guidance on crafting the perfect raised bed for your unique space and goals—including size, materials, and placement—check out "Basic Raised Bed" (page 76), where you'll find step-by-step instructions.

For potted plants, choose a lightweight container mix to give roots the ideal balance of moisture, air, and drainage for healthy growth.

Raised bed mix provides stable support and nutrient-rich soil, which is perfect for thriving plants in raised beds of any size or height.

Gardening is always more fun with friends, and raised bed kits make it easy to build and grow together.

Crafting your own stacked raised beds adds a personal, stylish touch that fits the needs of your garden and life.

STRAW

Straw is an excellent mulch for vegetable gardens. It suppresses weeds, retains moisture, and gradually breaks down to enrich the soil. Bonus: It also works well for mulching pathways.

HOW MUCH DO YOU NEED?

For a vegetable garden, apply straw at a depth of 4" (10.2cm). A single straw bale typically covers 40–50 ft.^{2} (3.7–4.6m^2) at this depth.

Remember: A 4' x 8' (1.2 x 2.4m) garden bed equals 32 ft.^{2} (3m^2). So one bale will easily cover the bed with plenty left over for pathways. If you only have a small space, like a single raised bed or a few large containers, bagged straw is another option. The bags contain far less than a bale, but for small gardens that may be all you need. Plus, they're easier to carry home and less messy.

WHERE TO FIND IT

Straw bales are available at farm supply stores, garden centers, or directly from local farmers. Bagged straw can often be found at hardware stores and garden centers. Make sure to buy straw, not hay—hay contains seeds that can sprout into weeds.

Straw mulch keeps weeds down, moisture in, and soil happy, making it great for beds and pathways.

WOODCHIP MULCH

Woodchips are ideal for pathways, orchards, and other garden beds with trees and shrubs. They emulate the natural mulch found in forests, enriching the soil, retaining moisture, and providing a habitat for beneficial soil organisms.

HOW MUCH DO YOU NEED?

For a 3.5' x 30' (1.1 x 9.1m) orchard bed, calculate the amount needed for a depth of 4" or 0.33' (10.2cm or 0.1m):

- **Area:** 3.5' (1.07m) x 30' (9.14m) = 105 ft.^{2} (9.8m^2)
- **Volume:** 105 ft.^{2} (9.8m^2) x 0.33' (0.1m) = 34.7 ft.^{3} (1m^3)

In this example, you'll need approximately 35 ft.^{3} (1m^3) of woodchips. Most woodchips come in 2 ft.^{3} (0.056m^3) bags, so you'll need approximately 18 bags to cover your bed (35 ÷ 2 = 17.5 bags [1 ÷ 0.056 = 17.9]).

If you have bulk woodchips delivered, they are often sold by the cubic yard (1 yd.^{3} = 27 ft.^{3} [0.76m^3]), so you'll need approximately 1.3 yd.^{3} (1m^3) of woodchips for this example project (35 ÷ 27 = 1.3 [1 ÷ 0.76 = 1.3]).

When planning your garden, don't forget to include woodchips for pathways if you plan to convert them from grass to another ground cover.

WHERE TO FIND IT

Purchase bags of woodchips from garden centers, nurseries, or home improvement stores. Be sure to purchase natural, uncolored mulch that is free of dye to avoid potential toxins.

Use woodchips around trees, shrubs, and paths to enrich soil and retain moisture.

Having woodchip mulch delivered can save money, but be sure you have space, the right tools, and enough energy to move the pile.

For larger gardens or orchards, consider ordering woodchips in bulk from a local tree-service company. Bulk delivery may be more cost-effective when compared to purchasing dozens of bags. Some companies may even provide them for free, but the volume can be unpredictable—typically several cubic yards—so make sure you have enough space for delivery. You'll also need an accessible delivery spot, a wheelbarrow for transportation, a sturdy mulch fork, and a good dose of physical energy. Before accepting bulk woodchips, verify that they are finely ground and free of walnut, as this tree's natural toxins can hinder plant growth.

COMPOST

Compost is gardener's gold, packed with nutrients that improve soil structure and fertility. It's essential for vegetable gardens, raised beds, orchards, and any garden needing a boost of organic matter.

HOW MUCH DO YOU NEED?

For a 3' x 6' (0.9 x 1.8m) in-ground garden with fair soil, calculate the amount needed to top it with 2" or 0.17' (5.1cm or 0.05m):

- **Area:** 3' (0.91m) x 6' (1.83m) = 18 ft.^{2} (1.67m^2)
- **Volume:** 18 ft.^{2} (1.67m^2) x 0.17' (0.05m) = 3 ft.^{3} (0.08m^3)

Most compost comes in 0.75 ft.^{3} (0.02m^3) bags, so you'll need four bags for this garden (3 ÷ 0.75 = 4 [0.08 ÷ 0.02 = 4]).

WHERE TO FIND IT

Purchase it at garden centers, nurseries, or home improvement stores. Look for products labeled "organic" or "OMRI certified" for chemical-free options. Many municipalities offer free or low-cost bulk compost from yard waste programs, but like bulk woodchips, it will take more effort to transport.

SHEET MULCH MATERIALS

Sheet mulching is an affordable, eco-friendly method for suppressing grass and preparing new garden beds. Large sheets of cardboard, newspaper, or contractor's paper effectively block weeds while breaking down into the soil, enhancing its structure. Contractor's paper is especially useful for large spaces, and a few dollars spent on a roll saves time and effort, making application quick and seamless. The thicker the cardboard or paper sheet, the better it smothers vegetation and prevents regrowth.

Compost is pure garden gold, enriching soil health and fueling strong, vibrant plant growth.

Contractor's paper is a convenient alternative to cardboard, especially when covering large areas quickly and easily.

Reusing cardboard as a weed barrier gives it a second life, but covering large areas takes plenty of cardboard and careful overlapping to block weeds.

WEED BARRIER

- **Contractor's Paper:** Affordable and versatile, rolls of this material are ideal for covering both small and large areas. Also known as "builder's paper," it is commonly used as floor protection during home renovations and is readily available at most home improvement stores. Look for it in the paint supplies aisle.
- **Cardboard:** A recycled material that works well for beds no greater than 4' x 8' (1.2 x 2.4m). Remove all tape, plastic labels, and staples. Large sheets can often be sourced for free from bike shops, furniture stores, and appliance retailers.
- **Newspaper:** Suitable for very small gardens but requires many layers and more effort to apply. Look for used newspaper at libraries and coffee shops.

ORGANIC MATERIALS

- **Compost:** Use 2"–8" (5.1–20.3cm), depending on soil quality. More compost is needed for soil that feels sticky, dense, or sandy.
- **Mulch:** Use 2"–6" (5.1–15.2cm).
- **Straw:** Best for vegetable and herb gardens. Do not confuse for hay.
- **Woodchips:** Ideal for orchards and woody plants. No walnut trees if bulk mulch is used.
- **Organic Matter:** Grass clippings, leaves, kitchen scraps, coffee grounds, vegetable garden waste, and other seed- and disease-free organic material.

HOW MUCH DO YOU NEED?

To effectively suppress weeds, apply a single layer of contractor's paper, one layer of cardboard, or 8–12 sheets of newspaper over your entire planting area. For a 4' x 4' (1.2 x 1.2m) garden bed, you'll need approximately 20 ft.^{2} (1.9m^2) of coverage. Contractor's paper is typically sold in rolls measuring 3' (0.9m) in width and various lengths, such as 100' (30.5m)—providing 300 ft.^{2} (27.9m^2) of coverage—or 140' (42.7m)—providing 420 ft.^{2} (39m^2) of coverage. It's advisable to procure more weed barrier than you estimate needing, as it's easy to underestimate the amount required.

FERTILIZER

When compost isn't enough, organic fertilizer gives plants the extra nutrients they need to flourish.

Plants, like people, flourish when provided with the right nutrients. Fertilizer is simply a way to boost your garden's diet, enriching the soil with essential macronutrients—nitrogen, phosphorus, and potassium—as well as vital micronutrients, such as calcium, magnesium, sulfur, iron, and zinc. If your garden beds are generously amended with high-quality compost, you may find little need for additional fertilizer. But often, especially in new gardens or containers, a supplemental organic fertilizer ensures your plants thrive beautifully and produce abundantly.

When selecting fertilizers, you'll notice three numbers prominently displayed on the package; for example, 3-4-4. These numbers represent the percentage of nitrogen, phosphorus, and potassium, respectively. Using the same example, this means there is 3% nitrogen, 4% phosphorus, and 4% potassium in that particular fertilizer.

While you can analyze the chemistry and the makeup of every fertilizer, we suspect you'd rather spend that time in your garden instead. Here's a straightforward guide to simplify your fertilizing approach.

FERTILIZER GUIDANCE BY GARDEN TYPE

- **Vegetable Gardens:** Use a balanced, slow-release organic fertilizer, such as a 3-4-4 formulation, to ensure even growth and robust yields. For a 4' x 4' (1.2 x 1.2m) bed, incorporate 1½ cups (355mL) in early spring, followed by a lighter midseason application of ¾ cup (177mL) if plants seem sluggish.
- **Containers:** Select a slow-release, granular organic fertilizer specifically designed for pots to nourish plants gently and evenly. Look for packages labeled for "containers" or "potted plants." For a 5 gallon (19L) container, mix in 2 tablespoons (30mL) of fertilizer at planting time and then reapply every four to six weeks through the growing season.
- **Orchards:** Fruit trees and berry bushes benefit from fertilizers designed for woody, fruiting plants. Every spring, evenly distribute 2–4 cups (473–946mL) of fertilizer around the outer canopy of each tree. Complement this with regular applications of compost and woodchip mulch.

FERTILIZER GUIDANCE BY NUTRIENT NEED

Plants often communicate their nutrient needs through visual signs.

- **Nitrogen Deficiency:** Pale, yellowish-green leaves and stunted growth. Apply blood meal, feather meal, or cottonseed meal according to the product's recommended rates.
- **Phosphorus Deficiency:** Weak plants with older leaves showing a reddish-purple or bluish-green tint, especially when paired with poor or delayed flowering and fruiting. Incorporate bone meal into the soil, using about 1 cup (237mL) per 4' x 4' (1.2 x 1.2m) bed.
- **Potassium Deficiency:** Leaf edges appear scorched or browned, with increased susceptibility to disease. Apply greensand or kelp meal at a rate of 1–2 cups (237–473mL) per 4' x 4' (1.2 x 1.2m) bed to replenish potassium. If available, ½ cup (118mL) of wood ash from a clean fire pit or fireplace can also be used instead of greensand or kelp meal.
- **Calcium Deficiency:** Manifested by blossom end rot in tomatoes or misshapen fruits. Add crushed eggshells or dolomitic lime, using about ½ cup (118mL) per 4' x 4' (1.2 x 1.2m) bed.
- **Micronutrient Deficiencies:** Symptoms include yellowing leaves (iron deficiency) or distorted growth (zinc deficiency). Incorporate kelp meal at a rate of 1 cup (237mL) per 4' x 4' (1.2 x 1.2m) bed.

SUSTAINABLE FERTILIZING

Ensuring your garden flourishes sustainably involves thoughtful selection of fertilizers. Some fertilizers are derived through processes that can harm the environment. When possible, consider these responsible alternatives.

- **Avoid:** Synthetic nitrogen fertilizers, which contribute to groundwater pollution. **Use Instead:** Blood meal, feather meal, or cottonseed meal.
- **Avoid:** Rock phosphate mined fertilizers, which often harm the environment during extraction. **Use Instead:** Bone meal, a sustainable byproduct of the meat industry.
- **Avoid:** Potash mined from sensitive areas. **Use Instead:** Wood ash from untreated wood, greensand, or kelp meal.

Ultimately, reducing reliance on commercial fertilizers by regularly adding compost and mulch will nurture your garden naturally, sustainably, and abundantly.

WHERE TO FIND THEM

Fertilizers are readily available at garden centers, nurseries, home improvement stores, and online gardening suppliers.

EDGING

Edging around in-ground beds adds beauty, defines your garden's shape, keeps weeds and grass at bay, and can help keep mowers and feet out of your growing space. Good edging creates a polished look while reducing the time you spend on weeding and trimming.

For a quick, budget-friendly option:

- **Trench:** Dig approximately 6" (15.2cm) deep and 6" (15.2cm) wide using a mattock or flat-bladed spade, then fill it with straw or woodchips. This method is simple to install and blends seamlessly with natural garden aesthetics, but it will likely need refreshing every one to two years.

If you're looking for something more permanent, polished, and durable, consider these options:

- **Plastic Edging:** Lightweight and inexpensive, plastic edging is fairly easy to install and works well for straight or gently curved designs. However, it may not withstand heavy mowing and foot traffic.
- **Stone Edging:** Stone provides an elegant look and excellent durability. Bullet-shaped stones—often called "bullet edging"—are ideal for both curves and straight lines, and unlike regular bricks, their interlocking design provides extra stability while making it harder for weeds to infiltrate. They also allow lawn mower wheels to glide over the top for easy, tidy maintenance along the edge. Limestone adds natural beauty but can be costly and challenging to use in curved designs.
- **Metal Edging:** Sleek and minimalist, metal edging (often steel or aluminum) is strong, long-lasting, and great for creating crisp, clean lines. While it's more expensive upfront, metal edging is a worthwhile investment for its durability and ability to withstand weather and wear.

HOW MUCH DO YOU NEED?

Measure the perimeter of your garden to determine how much edging to purchase. For irregularly shaped beds, use a flexible tape measure to follow the contours accurately.

WHERE TO FIND IT

Edging materials are available at garden centers, nurseries, and home improvement stores.

The trench is a simple, budget-friendly garden edge that helps block grass and weeds, but expect to redig it after a couple seasons.

Bullet edging provides a clean, durable border that's easy to install along straight lines or curves.

Metal edging creates crisp lines and withstands weather and wear, making it a long-lasting investment despite a higher upfront cost.

ARBORS AND TRELLISES

Arbors and trellises provide sturdy support for climbing plants like peas, beans, cucumbers, and vining flowers. In addition to maximizing vertical space, they add structure and beauty to your garden.

HOW MANY DO YOU NEED?

The number of trellises or arbors you need depends on your plant selection and garden size. A 4' (1.2m) wide trellis can support six to eight pole bean plants or two to three cucumber vines. For arbors, allow at least 3' (91.4cm) of width for comfortable walking space beneath climbing plants.

WHERE TO FIND THEM

Prebuilt arbors and trellises are available at garden centers, nurseries, home improvement stores, and online. DIY options can be made using cattle panels, salvaged wood, or bamboo. See "Layer to Maximize Growth" (page 60) for creative ways to build trellising systems.

Custom-built cedar arbors offer elegant support for climbing plants, adding vertical beauty while maximizing growing space.

STAKES, STICKS, AND PLANT LABELS

Give your garden the clear guidance it needs with stakes, sticks, and labels—simple materials that help plants thrive and keep your gardening experience organized and stress-free.

Tall steel angle posts provide sturdy, long-lasting support for staking dwarf fruit trees.

STEEL STAKES

Sturdy steel stakes provide essential support for dwarf fruit trees and trellises, ensuring your plants can withstand wind, weather, and abundant yields. To protect the fragile root systems of young dwarf apple and pear trees from strain, position a tall, permanent steel stake next to each tree. Attach the trunk loosely about one-third to one-half of the way up the tree using soft materials that won't cut into the bark, such as wide canvas tree straps, rubber hose spacers (a short length of hose with wire threaded through it), or orchard bands (stretchy commercial tree ties). When installing a trellis, two fence posts at each end works well.

Steel fence posts can be readily found at home improvement or hardware stores. For fruit trees, taller steel angle posts work wonderfully and are available online from retailers.

GARDEN STAKES

Wooden stakes are invaluable tools in marking plant locations and delineating the layout of new garden beds. For a medium-sized garden bed (4' x 8' [1.2 x 2.4m]), 8–12 stakes typically suffice for clearly marking corners, paths, or clusters of plants.

To keep your gardening expenses low, explore local lumber yards or construction sites for scrap wood, which you can often acquire for free or at minimal cost, but you may need to cut them down. Alternatively, hardware stores and garden centers offer precut stakes in wood, bamboo, or metal. For a charming, rustic look, consider pruning straight tree branches in early spring and using these as natural, lightweight garden stakes.

PLANT LABELS

Wooden tongue depressors make ideal plant labels, providing a biodegradable, affordable, and attractive way to identify newly planted seeds and seedlings. One box of 100 tongue depressors will easily last through multiple gardening seasons. Tongue depressors are available at local pharmacies or from various online retailers.

Plant and Seed Sources

Sourcing high-quality plants and seeds is the foundation of a thriving garden. Local nurseries, farmers markets, and community plant sales offer plants that are already adapted to your region, while online retailers provide access to a wider variety of seeds, bare-root plants, and specialty crops. Choosing the right source and knowing what to look for ensures your garden starts strong and remains resilient.

SELECTING THE RIGHT SOURCE

Combining local expertise with online variety will help you create a diverse, resilient, and productive garden tailored to your growing conditions.

POTTED VS. BARE-ROOT PLANTS

- **Potted Plants:** Convenient and can be planted at any time, but they are typically more expensive and may have more transplant shock.
- **Bare-Root Plants:** Typically available online and are more affordable than potted plants, but they must be planted immediately or temporarily "heeled in" until their permanent space is ready.

CHOOSING THE BEST SOURCE FOR YOUR NEEDS

- **For immediate planting and expert advice:** Shop locally at nurseries and farmers markets.
- **For affordable fruit trees, berry bushes, and perennials:** Consider bare-root stock from trusted online retailers.
- **For a wide variety of plants and seeds:** Online companies offer unmatched selection and diversity.
- **For the most affordable approach:** Look for plant swaps, garden clubs, and community plant sales.

LOCAL PURCHASES

Buying plants locally supports your community while increasing the likelihood of success, as these plants have already been grown under similar climate conditions.

While choosing a smaller plant might seem counterintuitive, younger plants experience less transplant shock and adapt more easily. If possible, check the roots to ensure they aren't root-bound before you buy.

CHOOSING HEALTHY PLANTS

When purchasing plants in person, take a few moments to inspect their health before bringing them home.

- **Size:** Smaller, younger plants are often healthier and more adaptable than oversized ones that may suffer from transplant shock. Choose plants that are well-balanced and appropriately sized for their containers. Avoid spindly or overly tall plants.
- **Roots:** Avoid plants with roots growing out of drainage holes, as they may be root-bound and struggle after transplanting.
- **Foliage Health:** Look for vibrant, evenly colored leaves. Steer clear of plants with yellowing, spots, or holes, as these can signal disease or pest issues.
- **Common Pests and Diseases:** Inspect both sides of leaves and stems for signs of insects or disease, such as webs, sticky residue, or unusual spots.
- **Stem and Branch Structure:** Choose plants with sturdy, well-formed stems or branches, avoiding those that are leggy or have weak growth.
- **Weeds:** The presence of weeds in nursery containers can indicate neglect and possible soil contamination.

WHERE TO FIND LOCAL PLANTS AND SEEDS

- **Local Nurseries and Garden Centers:** Offer well-cared-for plants suited to your region's climate along with many seed options. Staff can provide expert guidance.
- **Farmers Markets and Community Plant Sales:** Often feature hard-to-find heirloom vegetable seedlings and locally grown perennials.
- **Plant Exchanges, Seed Swaps, and Garden Clubs:** Great for acquiring well-established perennials and tested local favorites for free or low cost.

Community plant exchanges and sales are a great way to find plants at little to no cost while connecting with fellow gardeners in your neighborhood.

PLANT HARDINESS ZONE MAP

Think of the Plant Hardiness Zone Map as a friendly guide to help you choose perennial plants—fruit trees, berry bushes, and hardy herbs—that will thrive in your garden year after year. It's based on the average coldest temperatures across different regions of the United States, dividing the country into numbered zones. When you see a plant labeled "Hardy to Zone 5," for example, it means that plant can survive the typical winter lows in a Zone 5 garden. Knowing your zone helps you avoid the disappointment of planting a perennial that won't make it through your local winters.

But, like many things in today's world, the weather patterns we've come to rely on are shifting. Climate change is gradually redrawing the map, with warmer winters nudging many areas into higher zones. A place once solidly in Zone 5 may now experience Zone 6 conditions. While this may enable you to try new plants, it also brings unpredictability: early thaws followed by surprise frosts, longer dry spells, or sudden heat waves.

Use the zone map as a starting point, not a strict rulebook. Pair it with your own observations. Notice where snow melts first in spring, which spots stay cooler in summer, or how wind and shade shape your space. Choose resilient plants (many featured in this book) that can handle a bit of variability. And remember, gardening isn't about perfection; it's about adapting, learning, and finding joy along the way.

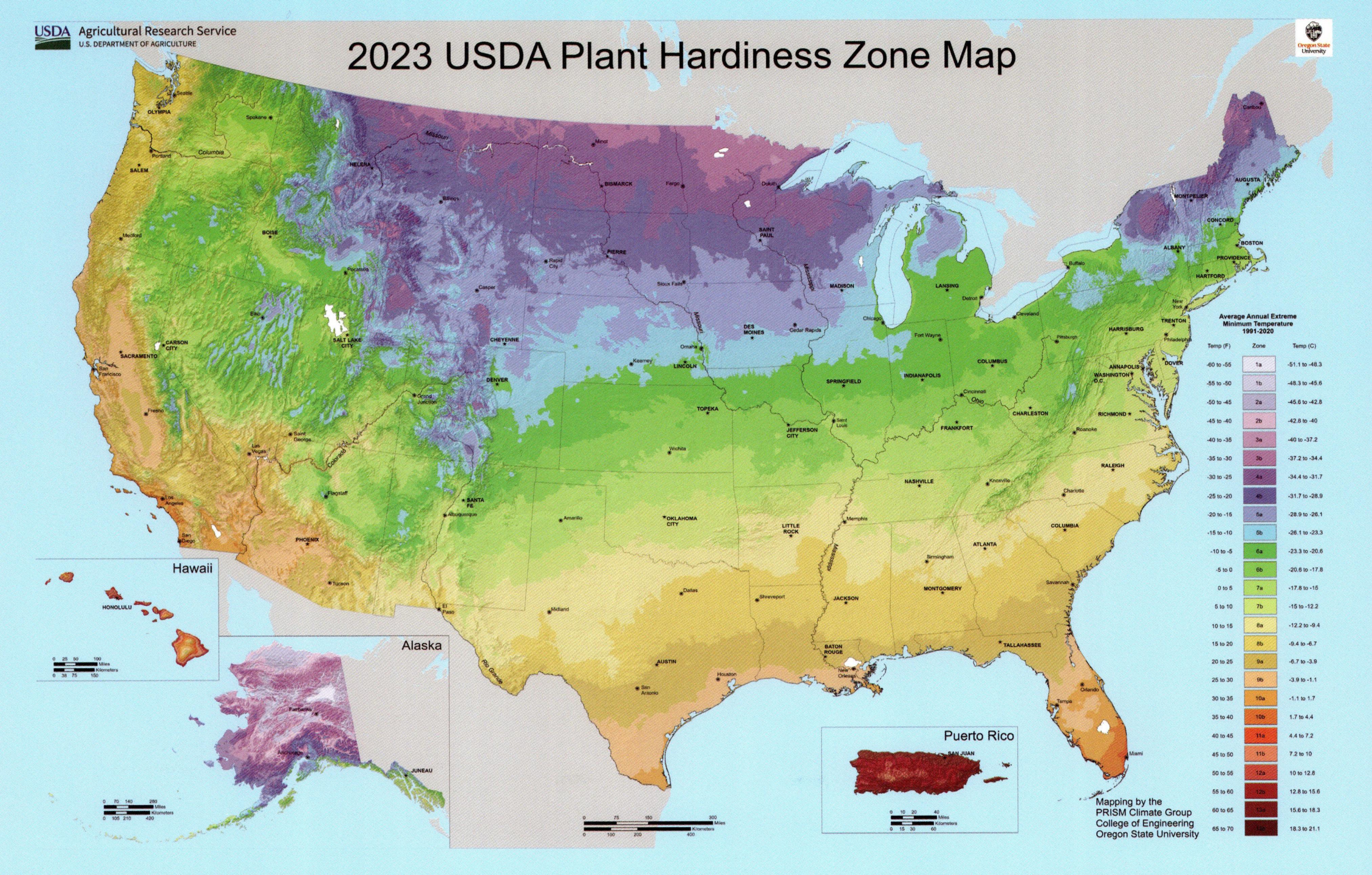

USDA Agricultural Research Service
U.S. DEPARTMENT OF AGRICULTURE
2023 USDA Plant Hardiness Zone Map
Oregon State University
Average Annual Extreme Minimum Temperature 1991-2020
Temp (F) | Zone | Temp (C)
-60 to -55 | 1a | -51.1 to -48.3
-55 to -50 | 1b | -48.3 to -45.6
-50 to -45 | 2a | -45.6 to -42.8
-45 to -40 | 2b | -42.8 to -40
-40 to -35 | 3a | -40 to -37.2
-35 to -30 | 3b | -37.2 to -34.4
-30 to -25 | 4a | -34.4 to -31.7
-25 to -20 | 4b | -31.7 to -28.9
-20 to -15 | 5a | -28.9 to -26.1
-15 to -10 | 5b | -26.1 to -23.3
-10 to -5 | 6a | -23.3 to -20.6
-5 to 0 | 6b | -20.6 to -17.8
0 to 5 | 7a | -17.8 to -15
5 to 10 | 7b | -15 to -12.2
10 to 15 | 8a | -12.2 to -9.4
15 to 20 | 8b | -9.4 to -6.7
20 to 25 | 9a | -6.7 to -3.9
25 to 30 | 9b | -3.9 to -1.1
30 to 35 | 10a | -1.1 to 1.7
35 to 40 | 10b | 1.7 to 4.4
40 to 45 | 11a | 4.4 to 7.2
45 to 50 | 11b | 7.2 to 10
50 to 55 | 12a | 10 to 12.8
55 to 60 | 12b | 12.8 to 15.6
60 to 65 | 13a | 15.6 to 18.3
65 to 70 | 13b | 18.3 to 21.1
Hawaii
Alaska
Puerto Rico
Mapping by the
PRISM Climate Group
College of Engineering
Oregon State University

ABOUT THE AUTHORS

FRED MEYER

Fred Meyer knows that creating a thriving garden isn't about perfection; it's about discovering simple, joyful ways to connect with nature, no matter your space, budget, or experience level. As a certified health and wellness coach (NBC-HWC), master gardener, permaculture designer, and seasoned wilderness guide, Fred has spent years helping everyday people—from students to busy parents to retirees—transform small yards, balconies, and community spaces into beautiful, low-maintenance sanctuaries that nourish both body and soul.

Blending his love for wild landscapes with practical design, Fred is adjunct faculty at the University of Iowa and led hands-on classes through the nonprofit EarthMind Practice. His work spans urban residences, farmsteads, school gardens, mental health centers, spiritual retreats, and businesses, always with the goal of making eco-friendly gardening approachable, affordable, and deeply rewarding.

Fred believes that anyone—regardless of time, space, or skill—can grow food, welcome wildlife, and cultivate a sense of peace right outside their door. His down-to-earth guidance has inspired families, students, and communities to embrace sustainable gardening as a path to greater resilience, beauty, and well-being.

If you've ever felt overwhelmed by traditional gardening advice, Fred's practical, encouraging style will reassure you that nature is ready to do the heavy lifting. You just need to start small and let your garden grow with you.

JEN KARDOS

Jen Kardos understands that in today's fast-paced, uncertain world, we all crave a little patch of peace, and she's passionate about showing people how to find it through simple, nature-connected gardening. As a licensed mental health therapist (LMHC), certified functional medicine health coach (NBC-HWC, FMCHC), and horticultural therapy practitioner, Jen is experienced in helping individuals and families reduce stress, boost well-being, and feel safer while connecting to what really matters.

A lifelong gardener and mother of three, Jen knows firsthand the challenges of balancing family, work, and truly restorative self-care. That's why she fell in love with eco gardening—a flexible, time-saving approach that turns even the smallest spaces into abundant, low-maintenance retreats. Pictures of her garden appear throughout the book.

While she finds growing food and cultivating bird and pollinator habitats immensely rewarding, the garden is also a place to get both lost and reconnected, as well as enjoy meaningful time with family and friends.

Through her private therapy practice and EarthMind coaching work, she has guided people from all backgrounds, whether they're navigating physical or mental health concerns, feeling overwhelmed, or simply seeking a calmer, more meaningful life. While many things are out of our control, nature is always here to ground us—literally and emotionally—and brings us into the present, reminding our hearts and minds that, in this moment, we are supported and safe.

ACKNOWLEDGMENTS

FRED MEYER

This book was grown through the collective wisdom and support of many—human, plant, and otherwise. With a heart full of gratitude, I offer thanks:

- To Elsie Craig, who first placed a trowel in my hand and a love of gardening in my heart. I miss you, Grandma.
- To Toby Hemenway, whose *Gaia's Garden* lit a permaculture fire in me that has never gone out. You are deeply missed.
- To Starhawk and Dave Jacke, who revealed that the real joy of gardening lives in relationships—between plants, people, and place. Your teachings helped me see how much becomes possible when I approach the garden with humility and let nature lead.
- To Stephen Harrod Buhner, whose writing deepened my spiritual connection with plants and the vast intelligence of the living world. Your voice echoes in the leaves.
- To Mary Kirkpatrick and Blair Frank, who consistently show me what generosity and kindness really look like.
- To Jen, whose love, humor, and insatiable curiosity nourish me and my growth. Thank you for always being a patient sounding board when I emerge from my cave with yet another big idea.
- To the many clients and students who asked wise and challenging questions, especially the ones I didn't yet know how to answer. You pushed me to grow in ways I never expected.
- To my new friends at Fox Chapel Publishing. Thank you for your patience, encouragement, and gentle hand-holding as I stepped into the unknown as a first-time author. I couldn't have asked for better guides.
- And most of all, to the plants, insects, birds, and critters who daily remind me how to thrive in community. You are my teachers, companions, and cocreators. May this book honor your quiet wisdom.

JEN KARDOS

I am so grateful to the many teachers and companions I have had on this journey of life. My heartfelt gratitude to:

- Fred, for his endless loving support and belief in me, and our ability to find joy together in the most uncommon and enchanting ways. I am eternally grateful for the endless hours and his persistence at including all the details that brought this book together. And his patience, when I was cantankerous about taking yet another picture for this book.
- My kids—James, Ethan, and Jessica—thanks for putting up with your garden-obsessed, compost-loving, slightly crunchy mom. You've grown into amazing humans, even being subjected to trying all my hippie food and sharing an indoor plant light garden in the drum room.
- My mom and my sister, for their unconditional love and excitement for my book.
- My dad, lovingly missed, who instilled in me a love of geeking out over plants.
- Mary and Blair, for Gaia's Peace Garden, an early physical manifestation of what this book shares and a midwife for all the elements that helped bring this book into being.
- The many beings I have crossed paths and been nourished by: friends, colleagues, and clients whose kindness and curiosity contributed to my growth and knowledge in this book.
- My spiritual teachers—Judy Borich and Laura Tucker—whose presence in my life transformed me in ways that are still unfolding.
- My body and life path, which has been filled with periods of great joy and satisfaction, but also dark nights that served as the greatest teachers. I am grateful for this vessel that has allowed me to experience the awe and pleasures of living on this planet at this time.
- The plants and Mama Mew, who care for me, helped me heal through those dark nights, and brightened my every day.
- The Mystery, the Great Intelligence, with many names that is unseen yet ever-present and source of all love and gifts I offer the world. May my heart and hands humbly be your vessel, and may this book help cultivate whatever we (collectively) need at this time.

PHOTO CREDITS

All photographs by Fred Meyer unless otherwise indicated.

SS = Shutterstock.com, V = Vecteezy.com

Front cover (middle left): Jen Kardos; *front cover (middle right):* Maria skov/SS; *back cover (middle):* Zeb Morris/SS; *page 1:* StockSmartStart/SS; *page 16 (right):* Bob Gassman; *page 17 (top left):* Bob Gassman; *page 17 (bottom left):* Bob Gassman; *page 26 (stem):* eamesBot/SS; *page 26 (soil):* Idalba Granada/V; *page 27:* GoodStudio/SS; *page 30 (right):* Ulza/SS; *page 31:* Alhovik/SS; *page 32 (top):* Jack Hong/SS; *page 33 (bottom left):* Julia Zavalishina/SS; *page 34:* Barillo_Images/SS; *page 35 (right):* Blair Frank and Mary Kirkpatrick; *page 38 (top):* Halfpoint/SS; *page 38 (bottom):* Zeb Morris/SS; *page 40 (bottom):* Dmitri Sorokin/SS; *page 41 (top):* David Rustin/SS; *page 42 (top):* Erika Conrad; *page 42 (bottom):* Jerome.Romme/SS; *page 43 (top):* Karin Jaehne/SS; *page 45:* perfectlab/SS; *page 46 (stem):* eamesBot/SS; *page 46 (soil):* Idalba Granada/V; *page 47:* GoodStudio/SS; *page 48 (bottom left):* GoodStudio/SS; *page 49:* GoodStudio/SS; *page 57 (bottom):* Jen Kardos; *page 58 (top right):* Olga Moreira/SS; *page 60 (center):* Jen Kardos; *page 65 (top):* Jen Kardos; *page 65 (bottom):* Jen Kardos; *page 70 (left):* Jen Kardos; *page 77 (top left):* Mulevich/SS; *page 77 (bottom):* Model Republique/SS; *page 78 (bottom left):* Erika and Rick Conrad; *page 80 (left):* Rose Marinelli/SS; *page 82:* Annie Ventullo; *page 90:* Jen Kardos; *page 95 (center):* Char Farber; *page 96 (left):* Autumn McConeghey; *page 96 (right):* GoodStudio/SS; *page 97 (top):* Svetlana Monyakova/SS; *page 97 (second from top):* iAphasia/SS; *page 100 (bottom):* GoodStudio/SS; *page 106 (bottom right):* Blair Frank; *page 120 (bottom):* GoodStudio/SS; *page 129 (bottom):* Oscar Martinez Troncoso/SS; *page 132 (stem):* eamesBot/SS; *page 132 (soil):* Idalba Granada/V; *page 133:* GoodStudio/SS; *page 135 (center):* Tatevosian Yana/SS; *page 138 (center right):* Jen Kardos; *page 138 (bottom left):* GoodStudio/SS; *page 144 (bottom right):* Budi Sud/SS; *page 145:* Mary Kirkpatrick; *page 148 (bottom):* Jen Kardos; *page 155:* GoodStudio/SS; *page 156:* GoodStudio/SS; *page 163 (bottom right):* GoodStudio/SS; *page 164 (top right):* GoodStudio/SS; *page 165:* Pavlo Burdyak/SS; *page 170:* Bachkova Natalia/SS; *page 171 (top):* Joanne Dale/SS; *page 171 (bottom):* Kit Leong/SS; *page 172 (left):* Tom Korcak/SS; *page 172 (center):* scott conner/SS; *page 172 (right):* Anakumka/SS; *page 173 (left):* Paul Maquire/SS; *page 173 (right):* Joe Kuis/SS; *page 174 (top left):* S.O.E/SS; *page 174 (top right):* Labrynthe/SS; *page 178 (stem):* eamesBot/SS; *page 178 (soil):* Idalba Granada/V; *page 179:* GoodStudio/SS; *pages 188–189:* allakuz/SS; *page 190 (all):* GoodStudio/SS; *page 196 (all):* GoodStudio/SS; *page 198:* GoodStudio/SS; *page 202:* allakuz/SS; *page 206 (bottom):* StockSmartStart/SS; *pages 207–259 (seedling graphic):* Ovidiu Templaru/V; *pages 207–259 (clipboard graphic):* Gatot Supandri/V; *page 207 (top left):* RadulePerisic/SS; *page 207 (bottom right):* Alessio Orru/SS; *page 210 (bottom left):* Favebrush/SS; *page 211 (bottom left):* GoodStudio/SS; *page 214 (bottom right):* GoodStudio/SS; *page 215 (bottom right):* GoodStudio/SS; *page 216 (top left):* Stephan Roeger/SS; *page 216 (bottom right):* weha/SS; *page 217 (top right):* DG77/SS; *page 217 (center right):* MRS.WARAPHON MAKCHANTHUEK/SS; *page 218 (bottom left):* GoodStudio/SS; *page 218 (top right):* Elvan/SS; *page 219 (bottom left):* Leonard Provoid/SS; *page 220 (bottom right):* Oqvector/SS; *page 221 (top right):* KazzyJS/SS; *page 223 (bottom right):* Flash Vector/SS; *page 224 (bottom right):* Favebrush/SS; *page 225 (top left):* Orest Iyzhechka/SS; *page 225 (bottom right):* Andrew Pustiakin/SS; *page 227 (bottom left):* GoodStudio/SS; *page 229 (bottom left):* Melody Mellinger/SS; *page 232 (bottom right):* tanyabosyk/SS; *page 236 (top left):* hanif66/SS; *page 236 (bottom right):* kungfu01/SS; *page 237 (bottom right):* Anton Watman/SS; *page 239 (bottom left):* anmbph/SS; *page 240 (top left):* jessicahyde/SS; *page 241 (bottom right):* Natallia Ploskaya/SS; *page 242 (top right):* giedre vaitekune/SS; *page 246 (bottom right):* weha/SS; *page 247 (bottom right):* Favebrush/SS; *page 248 (center right):* sophiecat/SS; *page 250 (bottom right):* Min C. Chiu/SS; *page 252 (top right):* deenee_dy/SS; *page 253 (bottom left):* Natalia Hanin/SS; *page 259 (top left):* Sunbunny Studio/SS; *page 259 (bottom):* allakuz/SS; *page 260 (stem):* eamesBot/SS; *page 260 (soil):* Idalba Granada/V; *page 261:* GoodStudio/SS; *page 274 (left):* GoodStudio/SS; *page 275 (bottom):* allakuz/SS

FURTHER READING

Interested in diving deeper into the science and strategies behind self-care gardening, permaculture, and sustainable growing?

GARDENING AND PERMACULTURE: GROW WITH NATURE

Discover beginner-friendly guides and nature-based methods that help you grow more with less work. These resources offer practical advice on small-space gardening, organic practices, and simple permaculture techniques—even if you're short on time, money, or land.

Gaia's Garden: A Guide to Home-Scale Permaculture
By Toby Hemenway
If you've ever wondered how to make your garden practically run itself while also helping the planet, *Gaia's Garden* is the place to start. Written in a warm, conversational tone, this book shows you how to grow food, flowers, and beneficial plants together in layered, low-maintenance "guilds" that emulate natural ecosystems.

The Vegetable Gardener's Bible
By Edward C. Smith
This trusted classic is a straightforward, reliable guide to growing vegetables organically and efficiently, even if you've never planted a thing before. Smith's W-O-R-D system (Wide rows, Organic methods, Raised beds, Deep soil) offers a foolproof foundation for high yields and healthy soil without needing fancy equipment or years of experience.

The Vegetable Gardener's Container Bible: How to Grow a Bounty of Food in Pots, Tubs, and Other Containers
By Edward C. Smith
Even if all you have is a sunny balcony, a porch, or a stretch of driveway, you can grow an impressive amount of food—and this book shows you how. With years of experience growing in pots, buckets, and bins, Smith shares his favorite self-watering setups, best-performing plants, and clever layout tricks to turn any space into a beautiful, high-yielding area.

Square Foot Gardening
By Mel Bartholomew
Short on time, space, or confidence? This method makes it incredibly easy to grow fresh food without getting overwhelmed. Bartholomew's system divides beds into simple 1' x 1' (30.5 x 30.5cm) squares, each with a specific plant, so there's no guessing, no wasted space, and almost no weeds. It's a plug-and-play system that delivers reliable results.

University Extension Services
Your state's Extension Service offers free, expert-backed gardening guidance tailored to your local climate. Find planting calendars, soil tips, organic pest control, and plant recommendations specific to your region. They are perfect whether you're growing in beds, buckets, or balconies.

Plants For A Future (PFAF)
www.pfaf.org
A searchable database of thousands of edible and useful plants, especially perennials. Explore cultivation tips; growing conditions; and how to use plants for food, medicine, or habitat. Ideal resource for building a resilient garden with long-term yields.

GARDENING FOR WELLNESS: CULTIVATING CALM, CONFIDENCE, AND CONNECTION

Explore the powerful link between gardening and well-being. These resources delve into how tending plants can reduce stress, restore focus, support mental health, and build emotional resilience right from your balcony, backyard, or windowsill.

The Wellness Garden: Grow, Eat, and Walk Your Way to Better Health
By Shawna Coronado
This guide blends practical gardening with holistic health strategies. You'll learn how to reduce physical strain through accessible design, grow anti-inflammatory foods, and turn your garden into a sanctuary for body and mind. Perfect if you're managing stress, chronic pain, or just want to feel better from the ground up.

The Nature Fix: Why Nature Makes Us Happier, Healthier, and More Creative
By Florence Williams
This engaging exploration of the science behind nature's healing powers shows why even brief outdoor moments can lower anxiety, sharpen focus, and lift your mood. Ideal if you're feeling overwhelmed and want evidence—and encouragement—to spend more intentional time outside, even in the smallest of green spaces.

American Horticultural Therapy Association (AHTA)
www.ahta.org
If you're curious about why gardening feels so healing—or want ideas for using it to support your family, classroom, or community—AHTA offers science-backed insights and real-world examples of how gardens promote emotional and physical well-being. A great place to explore if you're looking to deepen the therapeutic role of your garden.

Attention Restoration Theory (ART)
"The Restorative Benefits of Nature: Toward an Integrative Framework"
By Rachel and Stephen Kaplan
This research helps explain why time in a garden can quiet your mind and help you focus, especially when life feels scattered. ART shows how natural spaces, even small ones, restore your ability to concentrate and recharge. Helpful if you're navigating stress, screen fatigue, or want to bring more calm to your day.

BEYOND THE GARDEN: SKILLS FOR A MORE RESILIENT, JOYFUL LIFE

Gardening is just the beginning. These selections offer tools to help you slow down, restore your health, and live more intentionally. Whether you're healing your body, creating a more mindful daily rhythm, or navigating uncertain times, these books invite you to build a life that feels steady, grounded, and joyful.

The Power of Now: A Guide to Spiritual Enlightenment
By Eckhart Tolle
This gentle guide shows you how to step out of anxiety and into the present moment, right where calm, clarity, and connection live. Through short chapters and simple practices, you'll learn to quiet mental noise, let go of what you can't control, and experience the kind of peace that can turn gardening—or anything—into a restorative act.

The Wahls Protocol: A Radical New Way to Treat All Chronic Autoimmune Conditions Using Paleo Principles
By Terry Wahls, M.D.
Rooted in both science and personal healing, this book lays out a nutrition and lifestyle approach that supports cellular health, reduces inflammation, and builds vitality from the inside out. If you're managing chronic illness, fatigue, or just want to feel better, this protocol connects what you grow to how you heal—through food, sunlight, movement, and care.

INDEX

Note: Page numbers in **bold** indicate plant profiles (with specific descriptive, growing, and harvesting information).

E

F

G

R

S

T

U

V

W

Y